The **Rough Guide** to

Miami &
South Florida

written and researched by

Mark El

D1304619

**ROUGH
GUIDES**

NEW YORK • LONDON • DELHI

www.roughguides.com

Contents

Miami's building booms color section following p.80

Miami's vices color section following p.144

SOUTH BEACH

Color maps section following p.288

◄◄ Ocean Drive, South Beach ◄ Aerial view of South Beach

Introduction to

Miami &
South Florida

For a place built on holidays and hype, Miami lives up to, and revels in, the clichés: the people on the beach are indeed as tan and toned as they are on TV; the weather seldom dips below balmy; the cafés are full of aspiring models; and the nightlife is pumping and hedonistic. A gorgeous, gaudy city, resting on the edge of the Caribbean, Miami abounds with lazy palm trees, and its wide, golden beaches are spacious enough to seem empty even on a sweltering Sunday in high season. The city's

not all beaches and beautiful people, though; what few visitors anticipate is the city's diversity, exhibited in its tropical gardens and excellent modern art museums, as well as its vibrant Cuban and Haitian immigrant communities.

Founded little more than a century ago, Miami has grown up fast from its beginning as a humble trading post, losing its backwater feel with the arrival of Henry Flagler's railroad in 1896. In the 1920s, local businessmen aggressively capitalized on the new vogue for vacations in the sun, and a hotel building boom in Miami Beach ensued, producing some of the greatest Art Deco masterpieces in the US. Aside from a brief period during World War II, Miami remained a prime vacation destination until the early 1960s, when the first wave of Cuban refugees arrived, fleeing a newly installed Fidel Castro and his Communist regime. This set the stage for a further flood of immigrants from Cuba and other Latin American countries; indeed, more than half of Miami-Dade County's current population was born overseas. Because of this, to many further north, Miami is seen as barely part of the US, a place tropically lawless and suspiciously bilingual. Yet at the heart of the city is a glorious

> The city has emerged from its shadowy vice-lined past as a modern jetset playground, something of a cross between Cannes and Manhattan

contradiction: to Venezuelans, Peruvians, Nicaraguans, and other new Latin arrivals, it's a quintessentially American town: ordered, safe, and filled with opportunity.

In some ways, both sides are right. In addition to dealing with its transformation into a multiethnic metropolis over the course of a few furious decades, Miami endured violent, headline-grabbing race riots, an alarming murder rate (at one point the nation's highest), and a reputation as a prominent port-of-entry for the drug trade. However, by the 1990s the situation had reversed course thanks to a stronger local economy and a number of city revitalization projects. Miami's makeover as a hip city was cemented when South Beach was

Bikini cuisine

Miami has developed a homegrown cooking style, ideal for anyone planning to spend hours sunning and posing on the beach. Known variously as **Floribbean**, **Nuevo Cubano**, or **Nuevo Latino**, it first emerged in the mid-1990s via a group of adventurous local chefs who ditched some of the less diet-friendly elements of Latino cuisine – a fondness for deep frying, few (if any) green vegetables – while retaining many of its tasty staples, like avocado and guava. They then added less fatty ingredients, including exotic fruits and fresh fish, and spiced every dish delicately, often using capsicum peppers, citrus marinades, or honey-cinnamon glazes. The mouth-watering results can

be savored in some of Miami's more inventive restaurants; for reviews, see Chapter 12.

Not all South Florida's food is fancy and (virtually) fat free, however. Traditionalists should drive down to the Keys, where almost every restaurant serves a custom version of **Key Lime Pie** and **conch fritters**. Sadly, though, these days it's a misnomer to call either dish a local staple. Thanks to overfishing most of the conch is farmed in the Caribbean and flown in for cooking; and as for so-called Key limes – which actually look like small, hard lemons – they're native to Mexico.

Suggested itineraries

The following are suggested **itineraries** for trips up to a week. They're mainly designed around the key sights and include suggestions for where and when to have lunch. Of course, if any of the days seem too jam-packed for you, skip any of the stops and just wander around.

Two days
- Ocean Drive; Holocaust Memorial; Lincoln Road (lunch); afternoon on the beach in South Beach.
- Design District; Little Havana (lunch); Art galleries of Wynwood; night out at downtown's clubs and bars.

Four days
- Ocean Drive; Holocaust Memorial; Lincoln Road (lunch); afternoon on the beach in South Beach; night out at downtown's clubs and bars.
- Villa Vizcaya; downtown Coconut Grove (lunch); the Kampong.
- Miami Art Museum; Biscayne Corridor (lunch); Design District; evening performance at Arsht Center.
- Venetian Pool; the *Biltmore*; Little Havana (lunch); Art galleries of Wynwood.

One week
The four day plan above plus...
- Deering Estate; Coral Gables' Miracle Mile (lunch); Bill Baggs Cape Florida State Park & Stiltsville.
- Kayaking or biking in Oleta State Recreation Area; North Beach & Normandy Isle's MiMo architecture (lunch); Haulover Park.
- Day in Fort Lauderdale.

"discovered" by fashion photographers, bringing the glitterati, both models and visitors, in their wake. Some of that glamorous sheen has already, perhaps inevitably, worn off, but so have some of the more damaging parts of the city's reputation – making for a constant and welcome defying of expectations for the casual visitor.

Miami's recent history has been defined by a boom in luxury real estate; high-rise condo towers, packed with multimillion-dollar apartments, appear seemingly overnight across the city's skyline. The market for these mansions in the sky has softened, which has given the city a chance to rest, recoup, and survey the radical changes undergone in the last ten years. Even with the odd empty condo, the city has emerged from its shadowy vice-lined past as a modern jetset playground, something of a cross between Cannes and Manhattan. Miami is a city in transformation – and a thrilling place to visit.

▲ Parrot at Jungle Island

What to see

Radiating out from the mouth of the Miami River and stretched along the sandbanks sheltering Biscayne Bay from the ocean, Miami is an enormous city. It's made up of two core areas, which are, technically, separate cities (although most of the amenities are shared): **mainland Miami** and the huge sandbar known as **Miami Beach**. In turn, each of these cities is made up of dozens of small, dense districts. While the central neighborhoods are just minutes' drive from each other, Greater Miami is a large city that's only getting larger: in fact, Metro-Dade County is the size of Rhode Island, and the sprawling suburbs in its western district are some of the fastest-growing in America.

Undeniably, the most famous of the city's dozens of districts is **South Beach**, where its trademark Art Deco buildings were erected in the 1920s and 30s, and whose decadent lifestyle made headlines (and much money) for the city during the 1990s. This is still likely to be the place where you spend the most time: a huge number of the city's hotels are grouped together here, and the strip of Deco edifices along Ocean Drive is iconic Miami. The rest of **Miami Beach** is often ignored. So-called Middle Beach is condemned for its forest of monolithic condo buildings, though the *Fontainebleau Hilton* and adjoining *Edec Roc* hotel are emblematic examples of Miami's other signature style, known as MiMo. There are plenty more mid-century masterpieces in

The Cuban connection

Southern Florida's links to **Cuba** have always been strong – after all, Key West is closer to Havana than to the continental United States. Once Fidel Castro came to power in the early 1960s, Cubans began arriving en masse. Thousands of refugees, mostly middle-class professionals, fled their suddenly Communist homeland and settled in Miami, transforming the old Jewish neighborhood of Riverside into a Spanish-speaking enclave locals nicknamed **Little Havana** (see p.90). They planned to stay until Castro was ousted – over forty years on, despite Fidel's recent retirement and the start of brother Raoul's regime, they're still here.

In fact, expat Cubans have become the most powerful minority in the city: it's almost impossible to win political office in Miami without ground-level support from the Cuban community (the current mayor was elected in the afterglow of his defending refugee Elián González's right to remain in America). Yet for the casual visitor, the refugees' legacy is much less politically charged: rather, there's a Latin flavor to almost every area in Miami, from the dozens of streetside cafés Downtown selling cheap thimblefuls of the sticky espresso known as **cafecito** to the raucous nightclubs in Little Havana and even the **mojitos** that pop up on swanky bar menus across South Beach.

North Beach and Normandy Isle. Bal Harbour's synonymous with luxury shopping, thanks to its legendary mall, while the sandbar's northernmost reaches offer some of the best and widest beaches in the city, especially around Haulover Park and Sunny Isles Beach.

Across Biscayne Bay from Miami Beach lies the city's mainland hub. Thoroughly Latin **Downtown** bustles with Spanish-speaking businesses and small Cuban lunch counters; most major sights can be found along either its central artery, Flagler Street, or on Brickell Avenue, a gleaming canyon of skyscrapers that's home to numerous international banks. Miami's surge of urban

> **After the bustle of Miami, the Everglades' silent, sawgrass plains and vast emptiness are a refreshing surprise**

renewal is most evident in the area just north of Downtown **along the Biscayne Corridor**. After several decades of decay, this district's buzzing, thanks in large part to the new, splashy **Arsht Center** which has drawn Miami's cultural heart to the area. Nearby zones like the Design District and Wynwood are artsy enclaves, filled with showrooms, galleries, and witty modern architecture. The one largely unchanged area here is **Little Haiti**; despite its deep history and lively streetlife, it makes few concessions to outsiders.

Southwest of Downtown, just across the Miami River, lies **Little Havana**, a residential neighborhood of sherbert-colored houses that became the first home of Cuban refugees as they arrived in America. It's still the immigrant heart of the city, though with an increasingly diverse Latin population. Southeast from here, along the soaring Rickenbacker Causeway, lie almost-deserted **Virginia Key** and swanky **Key Biscayne**, the tony island on the bay whose smart central village is sandwiched between Miami's two best parks.

On the city's southern extreme stands **Coconut Grove**, the earliest settlement in the area and an artsier, more bohemian place than much of Miami. Though not the counterculture hotbed it once was, it is home to two of the city's most intriguing sights – the Barnacle and Villa Vizcaya. West from here, the city of **Coral Gables** – which technically isn't Miami at all, but yet another separate city – is a Spanish-inspired confection of Mediterranean Revival mansions and grand civic amenities. The brainchild of one man, George Merrick, it's an eccentric exercise in ego and enthusiasm. To the south, as the suburb of **South Miami** blends with the outskirts of neighboring Homestead, there are several major gardens and animal parks amid the vast stretches of farmland.

▼ Fish off of the Florida Keys

9

▼ Lifeguard hut, South Beach

While Miami and its neighborhoods hold enough to engage a variety of itineraries, the city is also an ideal base for exploring the rest of South Florida. **Everglades National Park** fills up most of the rest of the state's southern tip: after the bustle of Miami, its silent, sawgrass plains and vast emptiness are a refreshing surprise. Come here to birdwatch, hike, or kayak through the backwaters – and expect to see plenty of alligators. Carry on past the Everglades to reach the strip of islands known as the **Florida Keys**, which trail like a broken necklace through the Caribbean. A single road threads through this isolated, rebellious backwater to reach **Key West**, the one-time counterculture hub whose historic buildings have seen rapid gentrification in recent years.

Much like Key West, **Fort Lauderdale**, Miami's northern neighbor, is rapidly upgrading. Just forty minutes' drive from Downtown Miami, it has often been seen as a homely younger sister, the place where retirees lived year-round, their lives punctuated by raucous spring breakers. Today, as new residents have moved into its mid-century homes, it's well on the way to becoming a less attitude-packed answer to South Beach.

When to go

Miami's weather is tropically warm throughout the year: its tender winters have brought snowbirds down from the Northeast for more than a hundred years. **High season** is January through March, when the weather hovers around 80°F (27°C), while rainfall and humidity are low; it's also when crowd-pulling events like the Winter Music Conference and the Miami Film Festival are held.

Low season, June through August, is often unbearably hot, plus stiflingly humid, and hotel rates not surprisingly hit rock-bottom: expect sun most mornings, and tropical downpours come afternoon – you'll need to be an early riser if you want to work on your tan. The **hurricane season** is traditionally May through October, with the occasional flurry in November. Don't fret, though: warning systems are now sophisticated enough that even should a heavy storm roll in while you're there, you'll be alerted in ample time. The best times to visit may well be the **shoulder seasons** – April, May, October, and November; the weather's good, if not flawless, while the hotel bargains are still plentiful.

Miami climate

	Jan	Feb	Mar	Apr	May	Jun	Jul	Aug	Sep	Oct	Nov	Dec
Average daily temperature												
max (°F)	75	76	79	82	85	88	89	89	88	84	80	77
max (°C)	24	24	26	28	30	31	32	32	31	30	27	24
min (°F)	59	60	64	68	72	75	76	77	76	72	67	61
min (°C)	15	15	18	19	23	24	25	25	24	23	17	15
Average rainfall												
inches	2.0	2.1	2.4	2.8	6.2	9.3	5.7	7.6	7.6	5.6	2.7	1.8
mm	51	53	61	72	158	237	145	192	194	143	67	46

▼ Seven Mile Bridge

20

things not to miss

It's not possible to see everything that Miami and South Florida have to offer in one trip – and we don't suggest you try. What follows is a selective and subjective taste of the area's highlights, from its remarkable beaches and playful architecture to inventive food and vibrant nightlife. They're arranged in five color-coded categories to help you find the very best things to see, do, and experience. All entries have a page reference to take you straight into the text, where you can find out more.

01 **Seven AM on South Beach** Page **53** • One of the few times you'll be able to enjoy the world-renowned beach in relative solitude is during the early-morning crystal-white light.

02 **The beaches of Fort Lauderdale** Page **208** • The sands here are just as wide, clean, and golden as their Miami counterparts, and the casual, laid-back vibe's a welcome relief to the catwalk-conscious scene further south.

03 **Casa Casuarina** Page **54** • Better known as the Versace mansion, this macabre landmark is now a high end, four figures-a-night boutique hotel.

04 **Lincoln Road** Page **59** • Whether you're posing, blading, or window-shopping, the best place to spend an afternoon is this pedestrianized outdoor mall in South Beach. Grab a coffee or a cocktail at one of the dozens of sidewalk cafés.

05 **Miami Art Museum** Page **41** • Visit this outstanding Downtown modern collection, which showcases top-tier conceptual art that's intelligently but accessibly curated.

13

06 Stiltsville Page **119** • This village of seven ramshackle huts standing in the mudflats off Key Biscayne is charged with precious modern Miami history.

08 Villa Vizcaya Page **114** • Opulent, excessive, and unmissable, Vizcaya is Coconut Grove's early wealth made manifest in one crazy, Baroque palace.

07 Michy's Page **152** • Famed local chef Michelle Bernstein runs this homey neighborhood restaurant with her husband; it's the best place to taste her spectacular, simple modern American cooking – and unlike many brand-name chefs, she's still often found working in the kitchen.

09 MiMo architecture Page **73** • Swooping, whimsical and full of movement, the architectural style which followed Deco is slowly gaining similar respect – and preservation, as some of its fiercest examples are now protected from the wrecking ball.

10 The Anhinga Trail Page **219** • Even the least naturally inclined can tackle this short trek through the swathes of Everglades sawgrass – often rewarded by up-close encounters with several of the local alligators.

11 **Fort Jefferson** Page **244** • Stand at the edge of the world in the thrillingly isolated Dry Tortuga islands, the last of the Florida Keys.

12 **Key Lime Pie and conch fritters** Page **245** • Two local staples of the Florida Keys that every visitor should try: a slice of the lemon-meringue-like Key Lime Pie and a handful of those chewy, deep-fried nuggets.

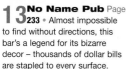

13 **No Name Pub** Page **233** • Almost impossible to find without directions, this bar's a legend for its bizarre decor – thousands of dollar bills are stapled to every surface.

14 **Mainland Miami's Nightlife** Page **163** • The clutch of new clubs and bars – like *Studio A*, *Pawn Shop Lounge* and *Nocturnal* – on Miami's mainland more than matches the appeal of South Beach's fabled nightlife spots. Indeed, generous licensing laws also mean later opening hours for many mainland clubs.

15 **The Deering Estate** Page **122** • For some rare peace and nature only a short drive from the city, this is a serene counterpoint to the flashy opulence of its sibling estate at Vizcaya.

16 The Rubell Collection Page 83

• Art mavens, hoteliers, and real estate developers, the Rubells have enough money and taste to buy the best contemporary art around; their enormous collection is ably displayed in this huge space in Wynwood.

17 The Arsht Center Page 80 • Cesar

Pelli's soaring masterpiece is a major addition to the downtown skyline, best viewed at night when it twinkles like a twin-bodied spaceship.

18 The Holocaust Memorial Page 60 •

This masterful, sobering memorial is located in South Beach, home to one of the heaviest concentrations of Holocaust survivors in the US.

20 The Venetian Pool Page

103 • Coral Gables' civic amenities don't come better than this – a quarry turned lagoon that's both lounge-worthy and historic.

19 Cafecito at David's Café

Page 141 • Savor the thimblefuls of Cuban coffee that keep Miami going – there's nowhere better for a quick shot than at *David's* on the beach.

Basics

Basics

Getting there

Unless you are coming from close by in Florida, the quickest and easiest way of getting to Miami is to fly.

Airfares to Miami and South Florida invariably depend on the season: international rates are often highest June through August – ironically, when Miami's weather is often at its most unpredictable – while domestic fares peak during the warm winter months when the weather's at its best. Both domestic and international travelers will find that prices drop during the "shoulder" seasons – March–May, September–October – which makes it an appealing time to visit. Remember, too, that fares during the Christmas and New Year's period will always be at a premium, and that flying on weekends ordinarily adds $40–50 to the fare for each leg; price ranges quoted below assume midweek travel.

Flights from the US and Canada

Most domestic flights touch down at **Miami International Airport** (MIA): carriers offering frequent services include American (Miami is its hub for frequent flights to the Caribbean), Delta, and Continental. Increasingly, more travelers are opting to fly to **Fort Lauderdale International Airport** (FLL), 40 minutes north of Miami: if you join them, expect bargain fares – most of the budget carriers like JetBlue and Spirit touch down here.

The usual off-season price range for flights **from the Northeast and Mid-Atlantic** (New York, Boston, and Washington, DC) is $200, although New York can be much cheaper as the NY–Miami route is highly competitive. As budget carriers jostle for a share in this lucrative market, rates can drop to astonishingly low levels – even $50 each way. **From the West Coast**, expect non-stop fares to start at $300 while you'll pay from $200 or so to fly in from Chicago and the rest of the **Midwest**.

If you're traveling **from Canada**, Air Canada has direct flights to Miami from Toronto and Montréal (around Can$350 round-trip).

Flights from the UK and Ireland

There are daily **nonstop flights** to Miami **from London Heathrow** with British Airways and Virgin Atlantic, plus regular service by Continental and American airlines. These flights take about 9 1/2 hours, though following winds ensure return flights are always an hour or so shorter than outward journeys. Flights out usually leave Britain mid-morning, while flights back from the US tend to arrive in Britain early in the morning. Most other airlines serving Miami, like Air France and KLM, fly from London via their respective European or American hubs. These flights take an extra two to five hours each way, depending on how long you have to wait for the connection.

Return **fares** to Miami run around £700 between June and August and at Christmas, though £500 is the more usual range. Prices in winter often fall to around £350. More flexible tickets to Miami, requiring less advance booking time or allowing changes or refunds, cost from £100 more whenever and from whomever you buy.

Aer Lingus offers direct service **from Dublin** to New York and Boston (around €400 off-peak round-trip), with connecting service on to Florida.

Flights from Australia and New Zealand

Because of the enormous distance, there are no direct flights to Miami **from Australia and New Zealand**. Travelers should fly to Los Angeles or San Francisco – the main points of entry to the US – and make their way from there. Of the airlines, United Airlines, Air New Zealand, and Qantas are the best at arranging trouble-free connecting service to Miami.

A basic round-trip economy class ticket on these airlines out of Sydney or Mel-

Fly less – stay longer! Travel and climate change

Climate change is the single biggest issue facing our planet. It is caused by a build-up in the atmosphere of carbon dioxide and other greenhouse gases, which are emitted by many sources – including planes. Already, flights account for around 3–4 percent of human-induced global warming: that figure may sound small, but it is rising year after year and threatens to counteract the progress made by reducing greenhouse emissions in other areas.

Rough Guides regard travel, overall, as a global benefit, and feel strongly that the advantages to developing economies are important, as are the opportunities for greater contact and awareness among peoples. But we all have a responsibility to limit our personal "carbon footprint." That means giving thought to how often we fly and what we can do to redress the harm that our trips create.

Flying and climate change

Pretty much every form of motorized travel generates CO_2, but planes are particularly bad offenders, releasing large volumes of greenhouse gases at altitudes where their impact is far more harmful. Flying also allows us to travel much further than we would contemplate doing by road or rail, so the emissions attributable to each passenger become truly shocking. For example, one person taking a return flight between Europe and California produces the equivalent impact of 2.5 tons of CO_2 – similar to the yearly output of the average UK car.

Less harmful planes may evolve but it will be decades before they replace the current fleet – which could be too late for avoiding climate chaos. In the meantime, there are limited options for concerned travelers: to reduce the amount we travel by air (take fewer trips, stay longer!), to avoid night flights (when plane contrails trap heat from Earth but can't reflect sunlight back to space), and to make the trips we do take "climate neutral" via a carbon-offset scheme.

Carbon-offset schemes

Offset schemes run by **climatecare.org**, **carbonneutral.com** and others allow you to "neutralize" the greenhouse gases that you are responsible for releasing. Their websites have simple calculators that let you work out the impact of any flight. Once that's done, you can pay to fund projects that will reduce future carbon emissions by an equivalent amount (such as the distribution of low-energy light bulbs and cooking stoves in developing countries). Please take the time to visit our website and make your trip climate neutral.

ⓦ**www.roughguides.com/climatechange**

---

bourne will cost around Aus$1700 during low season and Aus$2800 high season, while from Auckland (to Los Angeles) budget NZ$2300/3000, with an additional NZ$100 for departures from Christchurch or Wellington. Once in the US, it will cost you around US$350 to connect to Miami – ask about various coupon deals that are often available with your main ticket.

If you intend to visit Miami as part of a world trip, a **round-the-world** (RTW) ticket offers the greatest flexibility. In recent years, many of the major international airlines have allied themselves with one of two globe-spanning networks: the "Star Alliance" includes Air New Zealand, United, Lufthansa,

Thai, SAS, Varig, and Air Canada, while "One World" combines British Airways, Qantas, American Airlines, AerLingus, Cathay Pacific, Iberia, and LANChile. Both networks offer RTW deals with three stopovers in each continental sector you visit, with the option of adding additional sectors relatively cheaply. Fares depend on the number of sectors required, but start at around Aus$2200 (low season) for a US-Europe-Asia-and-home itinerary. If this is more flexibility than you need, you can save Aus$200–300 by going with an individual airline (in concert with code-sharing partners) and accepting fewer stops.

Airlines, agents, and operators

If you book your tickets **online**, keep in mind that you'll need to be flexible about your departure and return dates to get the best prices from these sites. Make sure you read the small print before buying, too, as it can be difficult, if not impossible, to claim refunds or change your ticket, especially on last-minute deals.

Online booking

ⓦ www.expedia.co.uk (in UK), ⓦ www.expedia.com (in US),
ⓦ www.expedia.ca (in Canada)
ⓦ www.lastminute.com (in UK)
ⓦ www.opodo.co.uk (in UK)
ⓦ www.orbitz.com (in US)
ⓦ www.travelocity.co.uk (in UK), ⓦ www.travelocity.com (in US), ⓦ www.travelocity.ca (in Canada) ⓦ www.zuji.com.au (in Australia), ⓦ www.zuji.co.nz (in New Zealand)

Airlines

Air Canada ☎ 1-888/247-2262, UK ☎ 0871/220 1111, Republic of Ireland ☎ 01/679 3958, Australia ☎ 1300/655 767, New Zealand ☎ 0508/747 767, ⓦ www.aircanada.com.
Air France US ☎ 1-800/237-2747, Canada ☎ 1-800/667-2747, UK ☎ 0870/142 4343, Australia ☎ 1300/390 190, SA ☎ 0861/340 340, ⓦ www.airfrance.com.
Air New Zealand Australia ☎ 13 24 76, New Zealand ☎ 0800/737 000, UK ☎ 0800/028 4149, USA ☎ 1800-262/1234, Canada ☎ 1800-663/5494, ⓦ www.airnz.co.nz.
American Airlines ☎ 1-800/433-7300, UK ☎ 0845/7789 789, Republic of Ireland ☎ 01/602 0550, Australia ☎ 1800/673 486, New Zealand ☎ 0800/445 442, ⓦ www.aa.com.
ATA (American TransAir) US ☎ 1-800/435-9282, ⓦ www.ata.com.
bmi US ☎ 1-800/788-0555, UK ☎ 0870/607 0555 or ☎ 0870/607 0222, Ireland ☎ 01/407 3036, ⓦ www.flybmi.com.
British Airways US and Canada ☎ 1-800/AIRWAYS, UK ☎ 0870/850 9850, Republic of Ireland ☎ 1890/626 747, Australia ☎ 1300/767 177, New Zealand ☎ 09/966 9777, South Africa ☎ 114/418 600, ⓦ www.ba.com.
Continental Airlines US and Canada ☎ 1-800/523-3273, UK ☎ 0845/607 6760, Republic of Ireland ☎ 1890/925 252, Australia ☎ 02/9244 2242, New Zealand ☎ 09/308 3350, International ☎ 1800/231 0856, ⓦ www.continental.com.
Delta US and Canada ☎ 1-800/221-1212, UK ☎ 0845/600 0950, Republic of Ireland ☎ 1850/882 031 or 01/407 3165, Australia ☎ 1300/302 849, New Zealand ☎ 09/977 2232, ⓦ www.delta.com.
JetBlue US and Canada ☎ 1-800/JET-BLUE, ⓦ www.jetblue.com.
Northwest/KLM US ☎ 1-800/225-2525, UK ☎ 0870/507 4074, Australia ☎ 1-300/767-310, ⓦ www.nwa.com
Spirit Airlines US and Canada ☎ 1-800/772-7117, ⓦ www.spiritair.com.
United Airlines US ☎ 1-800/UNITED-1, UK ☎ 0845/844 4777, Australia ☎ 13 17 77, ⓦ www.united.com.
US Airways US and Canada ☎ 1-800/428-4322, UK ☎ 0845/600 3300, Ireland ☎ 1890/925 065, ⓦ www.usair.com
USA 3000 Airlines US ☎ 1-877/USA-3000, ⓦ www.usa3000airlines.com.
Virgin Atlantic US ☎ 1-800/821-5438, UK ☎ 0870/380 2007, Australia ☎ 1300/727 340, SA ☎ 11/340 3400, ⓦ www.virgin-atlantic.com.

Agents and operators

ebookers UK ☎ 0800/082 3000, Republic of Ireland ☎ 01/488 3507, ⓦ www.ebookers.com. ⓦ www.ebookers.ie. Low fares on an extensive selection of scheduled flights and package deals.
Holiday Shoppe New Zealand ☎ 0800/808 480, ⓦ www.holidayshoppe.co.nz. Great deals on flights, hotels, and holidays.
North South Travel UK ☎ 01245/608 291, ⓦ www.northsouthtravel.co.uk. Friendly, competitive travel agency, offering discounted fares worldwide. Profits are used to support projects in the developing world, especially the promotion of sustainable tourism.
Trailfinders UK ☎ 0845/058 5858, Republic of Ireland ☎ 01/677 7888, Australia ☎ 1300/780 212, ⓦ www.trailfinders.com. One of the best-informed and most efficient agents for independent travellers.
STA Travel US ☎ 1-800/781-4040, UK ☎ 0871/230 0040, Australia ☎ 134 STA, New Zealand ☎ 0800/474 400, SA ☎ 0861/781 781, ⓦ www.statravel.com. Worldwide specialists in independent travel; also student IDs, travel insurance, car rental, rail passes, and more. Good discounts for students and under-26s.
travel.com.au Australia ☎ 1300/130 482 or 02/9249 5444, ⓦ www.travel.com.au, New Zealand ☎ 0800/468 332. Comprehensive online travel company, with discounted fares and packages to Miami.

Trains

The **Amtrak** (☏1-800/USA-RAIL, ☺www.
amtrak.com) **trains** along the Eastern corridor (of which Miami is the southern hub) are
arguably the best in the country – but that's
not saying much. Even with recent service
improvements, traveling by train's a more
picturesque than punctual option, and is
best for those with flying phobias or anyone
looking for a leisurely alternative.

From New York, the **Silver Meteor** and
Silver Star reach Miami via Orlando (daily
service); the other option is the less-direct
Palmetto, which zigzags across Florida, taking in Jacksonville and Tampa before finally
hitting Miami. Expect to pay between $150
and $400 for a round-trip and for the journey
to take anything between 26 and 29 hours,
depending on highly likely delays. Check for
offers on the Amtrak website – which also
provides a booking service – or by phone. If
Miami is part of a longer journey, Amtrak and
VIA TK offer a **North America Rail Pass**. It
allows thirty days unlimited travel for $999 or
Can$1149 high season (June–mid-Oct) and
$709/Can$675 low season (mid-Oct–May);

there's a ten percent discount for seniors
and students.

Buses

A bus is usually the cheapest transportation
option, but it takes forever and you'll have to
try and sleep in those seats – think of it as an
endurance test. **Greyhound** (☏1-800/231-
2222, ☺www.greyhound.com) prices for
a 7-day advance purchase on round-trip
tickets should hover around $125 from New
York (27 hours), $140 from Boston (1 1/2
days), $140 from Chicago (1 1/2 days), $150
from Los Angeles (2 1/2 days).

Greyhound Discovery Passes buy unlimited travel on the entire Greyhound network,
but are only really worthwhile for travelers
including Miami as part of a longer itinerary,
or for those coming from the West Coast.
This pass is valid across the entire country
for periods of between seven days ($283)
and sixty days ($645). Passes like these for
overseas visitors must be bought before
leaving home: most travel agents can oblige,
as can specialist agents like STA and Trailfinders.

Arrival

Most visitors arrive in Miami via one of the two major regional airports, though the
city is equally well connected by Greyhound buses and Amtrak trains. Major US
interstates shuttle drivers directly into Downtown Miami – and a great view of the
Miami skyline can be seen from the approaching elevated highways.

By air

Most flights at **Miami International Airport**
(☏305/876-7000, ☺www.miami-airport.com),
only six miles west of Downtown. While the
airport's well connected to the rest of the city,
be aware that there's limited signage at the
airport itself. Its hub-and-spoke design makes
the airport tricky to navigate, so allow plenty of
extra time for check-in upon departing.

Once on the ground, most people opt to
take a **taxi**. The rates have been simplified

and standardized into seven flat-fare zones,
so there's no risk of overcharging: a one-
way trip to South Beach costs $32, and Key
Biscayne $40 (for full fare information, see
the airport's website). An alternative for solo
travelers is the **SuperShuttle** minivan, which
will deliver you to any address in Miami for
$10–16 (☏305/871-2000 or 1-800/622-
2089, ☺www.supershuttle.com) – if you
want to book a trip back to the airport, call
24 hours in advance.

Road names and numbers

Numerous major thoroughfares in the city have nicknames alongside their official designations; the following should provide some quick reference if you're listening for traffic information on the radio or asking for directions.

Collins Avenue is Hwy-A1A
Dolphin Expressway is Route 839
Don Shula Expressway is Route 874
Florida's Turnpike (Homestead Extension) is Route 821
John F. Kennedy Causeway is Route 934
Julia Tuttle Causeway is I-195
LeJeune Road in Coral Gables is also SW 42nd Avenue
MacArthur Causeway is I-395
Palmetto Expressway is Route 826 (which is known as 163rd Street on its way to the beach)
South Dixie Highway is Hwy-1, south of the city
Tamiami Trail is Hwy-41 (and becomes **SW 8th Street** also known as Calle Ocho)

For the patient or budget conscious, there are also **public bus** connections from the airport to the main transit hubs: #7 goes Downtown, a trip of 30 minutes or so ($1.50, exact fare required; every 15–30min Mon–Fri 5.20am–8.50pm, every 20–40min Sat & Sun 6.20am–7.30pm), or the "J" Metrobus that trundles out to the beaches ($1.50 plus a 50¢ surcharge to South Beach; daily 24 hours; every 20min during peak hours, less frequently at night). For additional schedule information, call ☎305/770-3131 (Mon–Fri 6am–10pm, Sat & Sun 9am–5pm) or check ⓦwww.miamidade.gov/transit

Several domestic budget airlines, including JetBlue and Spirit, use **Fort Lauderdale Hollywood International Airport** (☎954/359-1200, ⓦwww.broward.org/airport) as their South Florida hub. It's a perfectly viable alternative to the mess that is Miami airport, but make sure to factor into the cost any car rental – driving is effectively the only efficient way to shuttle from Fort Lauderdale down to Miami or Miami Beach, unless you're prepared to trundle to the Tri-Rail and shuttle down to Miami that way (see p.26).

By bus or train

Of the several **Greyhound** stations in Miami, the Miami West station at 4111 NW 27th St (☎1-800/872-7245, ⓦwww.greyhound.com) is the busiest and just a short cab ride from the airport. If you're planning to connect to the beaches or coming to and from Key West, you're better aiming for the Downtown

hub at 100 W 6th St (☎305/374-6160). The latter station is in Overtown, a less than salubrious part of the city, especially by night, so take care when in transit here. Greyhound connects Miami directly with Key West, West Palm Beach, and Fort Myers, with ongoing service across the country.

Miami is on the **Amtrak** Silver Service route, linking South Florida with New York City via Washington, DC, and the Carolinas. The main station, at 8303 NW 37th Ave, is seven miles northwest of Downtown (☎305/835-1222 or 1-800/USA-RAIL, ⓦwww.amtrak.com). The best way to connect with the rest of the city is to hop on Metrobus #L, which terminates in South Beach; en route, it connects with the Metrorail station (see p.25) eight blocks away, where you can hop a local commuter train to Downtown, Coconut Grove, or Coral Gables.

By car

Driving **from the north**, you're likely to approach Miami on I-95, the freeway that runs down the entire length of Florida's east coast and deposits you in Downtown Miami. From here, the MacArthur and Julia Tuttle causeways both lead to the beaches.

If you're coming up **from the Keys**, Hwy-1 leads north through Coconut Grove and Coral Gables to Downtown and beyond. However, it's a slower suburban route, with plenty of stoplights – you'd do better turning off onto the Palmetto Expressway, which skirts the western edge of Miami before turning east through its northern portion, or taking Florida's Turnpike from Hwy-1 and then the Don Shula Expressway (which connects to the Palmetto Expressway).

Coming into the city **from the west**, you're likely to be driving Hwy-41, or the Tamiami Trail – follow this until it becomes SW 8th Street, which slices its way into the center of the city

Getting around

Getting around Miami is a cinch, mostly because the compact layout of the tourist hub of South Beach means that the easiest option is to walk. If you plan to linger exclusively in this area, there's no need for a car: hop in a taxi if your feet need a rest, or you could even rent some rollerblades (for rental info, see p.189). Elsewhere in the city, Coconut Grove is also compact enough to handle on foot while many people staying in Key Biscayne rely on biking; otherwise, in Coral Gables, along the Biscayne Corridor or in Little Havana, a car will make sightseeing much quicker and more convenient.

If you do stick to **public transport**, you'll be surprised at how easy it is to use, despite locals' constant grumbling. The buses and trains are all cheap, clean, and run on regular schedules; the one caveat is that bus and train networks are not well coordinated, so connecting between them can involve 5- or 10-minute hikes on foot.

Buses

Both buses and local trains are run by **Metro-Dade Transit** (Mon–Fri 6am–10pm, Sat & Sun 9am–5pm; ☎305/770-3131, ⓦ www.miamidade.gov/transit). Maps for all Metro-Dade services can be picked up at

Government Center Station, 101 NW 1st St, which is the main bus terminal; alternatively, there are route maps inside each bus. Bus travel is not a speedy option, so allow plenty of time; it's a good choice if you're staying Downtown or at the beaches, but connecting from Coconut Grove or Key Biscayne to anywhere else by bus is a painfully long process – you'll normally need to take one route to Government Center and then change onto a second bus to reach your destination.

Even so, **buses** in Miami are surprisingly pleasant; they're clean and chillingly air-conditioned, and the network criss-crosses the city 24 hours a day. **Fares** require

---

Useful bus routes

Unfortunately, there's little logic to the lettering and numbering of **bus routes**: as a guide, most, but not all, lettered buses include some part of the beaches in their track. Useful routes from Downtown's Government Center hub are as follows:

South Beach – #C, #K (along Washington Ave), #S (along Alton Road)
Miami Beach – #K, #S
Coral Gables – #24
Miami International Airport – #7
Key Biscayne – #B
Little Havana – #8
Coconut Grove – #48
Biscayne Corridor – #3 (along Biscayne Blvd)

Miami Tours

Given that Miami is one of the prime tourist destinations in North America, there are surprisingly few walking or bus **tours** on offer: we've listed the scant few below, and you can find exact itineraries and detailed information on each by checking the appropriate website.

Astonishingly, there are no regular walking tours of history-packed Coral Gables, though occasionally the city does run one – call City Hall at ☎305/446-8800 for information.

Tour operators

GoCar Tours ☎1-888/462-2755, ⑭www.gocartours.com. Scooter rental and tour combined; these two-seater yellow buggies offer a pre-recorded, GPS-guided self-tour at high speed. $50 for first hour, daily rate $150.

Historical Museum of South Florida ☎305/375-1621, ⑭www.hmsf.org. Tours by boat, bus, bike and foot, masterminded by encyclopaedically knowledgeable local academic Dr Paul George. Each lasts 2–3 hours. $25–42 per person.

Miami Cultural Tours ☎305/416-6868, ⑭www.miamiculturaltours.com. Nicknamed the Urban Tour Host, David Brown and his team specialize in the city's ethnic neighborhoods like Liberty City, Little Haiti and Little Havana. From $50 per person, including a meal.

Miami Design Preservation League ☎305/672-2014, ⑭www.mdpl.org. Offers both docent-led guided tours (Tues, Weds, Fri, Sat & Sun at 10.30am, Thurs at 6.30pm; $20 per person) and self-guided audio tours ($15).

$1.50 in exact change, including dollar bills; there's a 50¢ surcharge for a **transfer slip** that can be used to connect with another bus or service in the Metro-Dade network, like Metrorail. These transfer slips are valid for two hours from the moment you board the first bus.

If you're planning on staying in town for a while, consider buying a monthly **Metropass**. Available from any store displaying the Metro-Dade Transit sign, it costs $75 and is on sale from the 20th of each month. It provides unlimited rides on both Metrobus and Metrorail services.

There's a dedicated shuttle service, run by the county and known as the **South Beach Local**, that takes visitors around the Art Deco historic district on a loop from South Pointe Drive, along Washington Avenue, behind Lincoln Road mall and down West Avenue (25¢; every 10–15 mins, Mon–Sat 7.45am–1am, Sun 10am–1am; ☎305/770-3131). **Coral Gables** also has its own free shuttle service, making the city drastically more convenient for anyone without a car (route maps and info at ⑭www.coralgables.com/CGWeb/trolley.aspx). It runs north-south along Ponce de Leon Boulevard from the Metrorail stop to Calle Ocho (Mon–Thurs 6.30am–8pm, Fri

6.30am–10pm; ☎305/460-5070). There are stops on almost every block.

By train

Metrorail trains, also run by Metro-Dade Transit (see opposite), amble along a single line connecting the northern and southern suburbs, hugging Hwy-1 through Coconut Grove and Coral Gables (daily 5am–midnight, with reduced service after 6pm). Useful stops are Government Center (for Downtown and the main bus depot), Vizcaya (2-minute walk to the mansion, see p.114), and Coconut Grove. Douglas Road and University are the designated Coral Gables stops; best to use the former during daylight hours, as you can connect with the trolley service. Frankly, though, the most direct way to Coral Gables is to hop on a bus from Government Center that deposits you at the heart of the Miracle Mile. Single-journey **fares** on the Metrorail are $1.50 (exact change only) – buy a token from one of the machines and drop it into the turnstile at the foot of the stairs.

The **Metromover** system is a **free** automated monorail that ribbons around the Downtown central business district. The inner loop cinches the main sights including Government Center and Bayfront Park; the outer loop extends service to the Omni Mall north and the Brickell business district south of the river (inner loop runs daily 24 hrs, outer loop runs daily 5.30am–midnight, later during events at the American Airlines arena; ☏305/770-3131). The Metromover is reliable, fast, and clean, if a little limited – take it for a good view of the city and to get your bearings when you arrive.

The **Tri-Rail** system is a local commuter train service that was introduced in 1989 in an attempt to cut congestion along the coastal corridor between Miami and West Palm Beach (☏1-800/874-7245, ⒲www. tri-rail.com). Service is heaviest during rush hours and only 7 trains run (each way) daily at weekends (weekdays 4am–8.40pm, weekends 6am–8.30pm). If you want to use it for day-trips out of town – there are 18 stops, including Hollywood, Fort Lauderdale, and Fort Lauderdale airport – take the Metrorail to the station at 1149 E 21st St and hop onto the Tri-Rail there; **fares** vary according to distance: round-trip $3.50–9.25, weekend all-day pass $4.

By car

Driving in Miami is practical and reasonably easy: the city's crisscrossed by a network of **expressways** that will shuttle you quickly from district to district – we've listed the key roads (and their various names) in the box on p.23. As in any city, expect these freeways to be heavily congested during rush hour so allow extra time, for example, if you're trying to make a flight in Fort Lauderdale.

Most of the **bridges and causeways** that connect the islands to the mainland are free – two exceptions are the Rickenbacker Causeway from Key Biscayne ($1.25) and the Venetian Causeway (10¢).

Parking

Parking is no problem in most areas – Coral Gables has plenty of spaces, as does Downtown. The two shopping centers in Coconut Grove have ample facilities, and everywhere there's streetside parking (25¢ for 15 minutes) for the nimble and patient: just keep plenty of quarters in the car.

The beaches are a somewhat different story, though don't be put off by doomsayers who liken finding parking on South Beach to winning the lottery. Avoid the jams on Ocean Drive whatever the time; if you're looking for roadside metered parking, your best shot is away from the beach around Alton Road, or along the lower edges of Washington Avenue. There are three municipal lots in South Beach which normally have ample space, costing $1/hour: their overnight parking rates vary – 7th Street and Collins Avenue is $14/night, while the lots at both 13th Street/Collins Avenue and 17th Street/Washington Avenue will set you back $8/night. Few of the old Art Deco hotels have their own lots, so they offer pricey valet parking – though this often entails paying someone else to drive your car to one of the municipal lots; you'll save plenty by doing it yourself.

Car rental agencies

Alamo US ☏1-800/462-5266, ⒲www.alamo.com.
Avis US and Canada ☏1-800/331-1212, UK ☏0870/606 0100, Republic of Ireland ☏021/428 1111, Australia ☏13 63 33 or 02/9353 9000, New

---

The streets of Miami

Driving in Miami Beach is relatively easy, since the grid system of streets is logical and consistent; but back on the mainland, the city's **street-ordering system** can at first seem rather confusing. To make it more manageable follow this simple system: The city's grid is centered on the junction of Flagler Street and Miami Avenue: from that point, the four quarters tagged NE, NW, SW, and SE fan out. To find a street once you know its quarter, use the **PARC mnemonic**: Places, Avenues, Roads, and Courts run north–south, while everything else runs east–west.

In a maddeningly typical display of autonomy, **Coral Gables** ignored this system. Instead, the area was artistically streetscaped as per the City Beautiful tradition, its spaghetti-loop suburban roads and dead ends perhaps its most European feature. To find your way around here, keep the map at the back of this book at hand.

Zealand ☎09/526 2847 or 0800/655 111, ⓦwww.avis.com.
Budget US ☎1-800/527-0700, Canada ☎1-800/268-8900, UK ☎0870/156 5656, Australia ☎1300/362 848, New Zealand ☎0800/283 438, ⓦwww.budget.com.
Dollar US ☎1-800/800-3665, Canada ☎1-800/229 0984, UK ☎0808/234 7524, Republic of Ireland ☎1800/575 800, ⓦwww.dollar.com.
Enterprise US ☎1-800/261-7331, ⓦwww.enterprise.com.
Fox Rent-a-Car US ☎1-800/225-4369 ext 1, outside US 310/641-3838 ext 1, ⓦwww.foxrentacar.com
Hertz US & Canada ☎1-800/654-3131, UK ☎020/7026 0077, Republic of Ireland ☎01/870 5777, New Zealand ☎0800/654 321, ⓦwww.hertz.com.
National US ☎1-800/CAR-RENT, UK ☎0870/400 4581, Australia ☎0870/600 6666, New Zealand

☎03/366 5574, ⓦwww.nationalcar.com.
Thrifty US and Canada ☎1-800/847-4389, UK ☎01494/751 500, Republic of Ireland ☎01/844 1950, Australia ☎1300/367 227, New Zealand ☎09/256 1405, ⓦwww.thrifty.com.

Taxis

Taxis are abundant on the streets, and drivers will stop when they see you waving. Alternatively, you can call to book a taxi – try Central Cab (☎305/532-5555) or Metro Taxi (☎305/888-8888). Aside from the flat-rate services from the airport, fares aren't especially cheap – $1.70 for the first eleventh of a mile, and 20¢ for each additional eleventh of a mile. In case of complaints, call ☎305/375-2460.

The media

The news media in Miami are obsessed with three things: tourism, real estate, and Cuba. For international and national news, you're best picking up a copy of the locally printed New York Times or tuning into a cable network. Where Miami does shine, though, is in its magazines – as befits as glossy a city as this, the home-grown lifestyle magazine, Ocean Drive, is a superb, if frothy, read.

Newspapers and magazines

There's only one local **newspaper** in Miami, the 100-year old *Miami Herald* (35¢ weekdays, $1 Sunday), which also publishes a daily Spanish-language edition, *El Nuevo Herald*. The best day to buy is Friday, when the *Herald's* comprehensive weeklong entertainment supplement is included. It's a rather toothless publication, though Pulitzer Prize–winning columnist Leonard Pitts Jr is a high point. An alternative is the Fort Lauderdale–based *South Florida Sun-Sentinel*, which is gaining ground on the complacent *Herald*. For exhaustive detail on the area in which you're staying, pick up one of the weekly local rags like Key Biscayne's *Islander News* and the *Coral Gables Gazette*. For a snarkier take on what's happening in the city, the anti-establishment

freesheet *New Times* (ⓦwww.newtimesmiami.com) is a must-read – it's also terrific for listings. Published weekly, the *New Times* is available from drop boxes across the city.

Miami has plenty of local **magazines** – after all, you need something to browse on the beach. The elder statesman is South Beach-centric *Ocean Drive*, jammed with ads for the latest clubs and photographs of local celebrities; you can buy it on newsstands, but it's usually available free at hotels. Competitors come and go frequently, unable to replicate *OD's* gushy-but-glam riff on South Beach life – at time of writing, freebie glossies include *944* and *Nikki Beach*.

Spanish-speakers are in for a treat – aside from *El Nuevo Herald*, most newsstands in the city carry Spanish-language editions of big-name magazines like *Glamour* and *Harper's Bazaar*.

Radio

Unsurprisingly, you'll find many of South Florida's **local radio stations** either specialize in Latin music or keep Latin megastars like Shakira or Marc Anthony in heavy rotation. On FM, try mainstream pop-loving Y-100 (100.7 FM), the nonstop club mix of Party (93.1 FM), or the easy-listening Lite FM (100.5 FM). A safe harbor if you're struggling to find satisfying local news is National Public Radio **(NPR)**, the listener-funded talk station with a refreshingly honest take on news and chat (in Miami, 91.3FM, though frequencies vary in the Keys and Fort Lauderdale). To check for local frequencies for the World Service log on to the **BBC** (Ⓦ www.bbc.co.uk/worldservice), **Radio Canada** (Ⓦ www.rcinet.ca), or the **Voice of America** (Ⓦ www.voa.gov).

Travel essentials

Costs

While the high cost of accommodation, food, and drink is compensated somewhat by a wealth of inexpensive activities, there's no getting around the fact that the former are going to eat up a lot of your budget. Most of your major purchases, whether hotel or car rental, will require a credit card deposit, even if you wind up paying the total in cash.

Accommodation prices vary – for beachside hostels, a bed will cost $30 or so but an upscale boutique hotel could run $700. A rule of thumb is to allow $120 including tax for a reasonable private room.

Prices for good **food** don't automatically take a bite out of your wallet, and you can indulge anywhere from the lowliest (but still scrumptious) burger shack to the chicest restaurant helmed by a celebrity chef. You can get by on as little as $30 a day, but realistically you should aim for around $60; if you're sampling South Beach's swanky spots, though, add a hundred dollars or more to that.

Public transit options are usually affordable, with the best deals being the multi-day or weeklong transit passes for riding on buses, light rail, and subways. But given the cheap car rental rates Florida's known for – usually around $150–200 per week – it's a much more efficient way to explore the city as a whole and gives you the chance to venture to its less touristed corners more easily.

Keep in mind, though, that for those under 25 years of age, there are often supplements of $20 a day tacked onto car rental fees.

Also take into account that added to the cost of most items you purchase is a state and city – but not federal – **sales tax**: at the moment, Miami-Dade county's surcharge is 7 percent on anything you buy. Note, too, that there's a hotel tax of 12.5 percent of the rack rate, charged by the hotel and paid to the county.

Crime and personal safety

In the 1980s, Miami had the worst reputation for crime of any major metropolitan area in the US, but these days, tourist carjackings and random shootings are long gone. In fact, the city's now largely a safe and easy place for visitors to wander round, whatever the time of day or night – the streets of South Beach, for example, are still packed with people at 1am so you shouldn't feel isolated walking home alone from a bar. Downtown may be deserted outside business hours, but is largely crime-free. The only areas where it's still important to be vigilant are Overtown and Liberty City, which can be nasty come nightfall; the Biscayne Corridor's rapidly gentrifying, but the Boulevard's a better place to drive than stroll down.

As far as your personal responsibility goes, always **carry ID at all times**. Two

Australia Moonah Place, Yarralumba, Canberra, ACT 2600 ℡02/6214 5600, ⓦwww.usembassy-australia.state.gov/embassy
Canada 490 Sussex Drive, Ottawa, ON K1P 5T1 ℡613/238-5335, ⓦwww.usembassycanada.gov
Ireland 42 Elgin Road, Ballsbridge, Dublin 4 ℡01/668-7122, ⓦwww.usembassy.ie
New Zealand 29 Fitzherbert Terrace, Thorndon, Wellington ℡04/462 6000, ⓦwww.usembassy.org.nz
UK 24 Grosvenor Square, London W1A 1AE ℡020/7499 9000, 24hr visa hotline ℡09068/200 290, ⓦwww.usembassy.org.uk

pieces should suffice, one of which should have a photo: a passport or driver's license and credit card(s) are best. Overseas visitors (often surprised to learn that **the legal drinking age is 21**) might want to carry their passport, unless they have a photo-style driving license.

Miami was renowned for a spate of violent **carjackings** in the early 1990s, but it's an almost non-existent problem now. Still, there are simple precautions you can take to keep yourself safe. Any car you do rent should have nothing on it – such as a particular license plate – that makes it easy to identify as a rental car. When driving, under no circumstances stop in any unlit or seemingly deserted urban area – and especially not if someone is waving you down and suggesting that there is something wrong with your car.

Similarly, if you are "accidentally" rammed by the driver behind, do not stop but drive on to the nearest well-lit, busy area and phone the police at ℡**911**. Keep your doors locked and windows never more than slightly open. Hide any valuable out of sight, preferably locked in the trunk or in the glove compartment (any valuable you don't need for your journey should be left in your hotel safe).

Electricity

Like elsewhere in the Continental US, Miami's electricity supply is 110V AC.

Entry requirements

Keeping up with the changes to US entry requirements since 9/11 can feel like a hopeless task. Nonetheless, there are several basic rules as detailed on the US State Department website ⓦ**travel.state.gov**.

Under the **Visa Waiver Program**, if you're a citizen of the UK, Ireland, Australia, New Zealand, most Western European states, or other selected countries like Singapore, Japan, and Brunei (27 in all), and visiting the United States for less than ninety days, at a minimum you'll need an onward or return ticket, a visa waiver form (typically supplied on the plane), and a **Machine Readable Passport** (MRP). MRPs issued before October 2005 are acceptable to use on their own; those issued from October 2005 to October 2006 must include a digital photograph of the passport holder; and those issued after October 2006 require a high-tech security chip built into the passport. It is up to the various countries covered by the Visa Waiver Program to provide such passports to their citizens; for more information, inquire at American embassies or consulates.

If you're in the Visa Waiver Program and intend to work, study, or stay in the country for more than ninety days, you must apply for a regular visa through your local US embassy or consulate. You will not be admitted under the VWP if you've ever been arrested (not just convicted), have a criminal record, or been previously deported from or refused entry to the US. Visitors admitted under the Visa Waiver Program cannot extend their stays beyond ninety days. Doing so will bar you from future use of the program.

Canadian citizens, who have not always needed a passport to get into the US, should now have passports on them when entering the country. If you cross the US border by car, be prepared for US Customs officials to search your vehicle. Remember, too, that without the proper paperwork, Canadians are barred from working in the US.

29

Foreign consulates in Miami

Australia, 2525 SW Third Avenue Suite 208, Downtown Miami ☎305/858-7633
Canada, 200 S Biscayne Blvd, Suite 1600, Downtown Miami ☎305/579-1600
Denmark, PH 1D, 2655 Le Jeune Rd, Coral Gables ☎305/446-4284
France, 1395 Brickell Ave, Suite 1050, Downtown Miami ☎305/403-4150
Germany, 100 N Biscayne Blvd, Suite 2200, Downtown Miami ☎305/358-0290
Netherlands, 701 Brickell Ave, 5th floor, Downtown Miami ☎786/866-0480
UK, 1001 Brickell Bay Drive, Suite 2800, Downtown Miami ☎305/374-1522

Health

Foreign travelers should be comforted that if you have a serious accident while you're in Miami, emergency services will get to you sooner and charge you later. For emergencies, dial toll-free ☎911 from any phone. If you have medical or dental problems that don't require an ambulance, most hospitals have a walk-in emergency room: for the nearest hospital, check with your hotel or dial information at ☎411. The same applies for dental work.

Should you need to see a doctor, lists can be found in the *Yellow Pages* under "Clinics" or "Physicians and Surgeons." Be aware that even consultations are costly, usually around $75–100 each visit, payable in advance. Keep receipts for any part of your medical treatment, including prescriptions, so that you can claim against your insurance once you're home.

For minor ailments, stop by a local **pharmacy**, many of which are open 24 hours (including the Walgreens at 1845 Alton Rd, South Beach ☎305/531-8868). Foreign visitors should note that many medicines available over the counter at home – codeine-based painkillers, for one – are prescription-only in the US. Bring additional supplies if you're particularly brand loyal.

By far the most common tourist illness in Miami is sunburn: year-round the summer sun can be fierce, so plenty of protective **sunscreen** (SPF 15 and above) is a must. Surfers and swimmers should also watch for **strong currents and undertows** at some beaches: we've noted in the text where the water can be especially treacherous. Note that despite the media's frenzied circling around the story of man-eating sharks, it's still a blip on beach safety compared with sunburn and swimming difficulties.

Health and wellness resources

Counseling Lines Crisis Counseling Hotline ☎305/358-4357; HIV Care Resource ☎305/576-1234 or ⒲www.careresource.org; Rape crisis ☎305/585-7273.
Emergency Rooms Jackson Memorial Medical Center, 1611 NW 12th Ave ☎305/585-1111; Mercy Hospital, 3663 S Miami Ave ☎305/854-4400. In Miami Beach: Mt Sinai Medical Center, 4300 Alton Rd ☎305/674-2121.
Women's Health & Contraception Miami Women's Healthcenter, North Shore Medical Center, 1100 NW 95th St (☎305/835-6105), offers physician referrals and mammograms among other things. Planned Parenthood of Greater Miami, 681 NE 125th St, North Miami (☎305/895-7756, ⒲www.ppgm.org) can provide STD and pregnancy testing and counseling.

Insurance

In view of the high cost of medical care in the US, all travelers visiting the US from overseas should be sure to buy some form of **travel insurance**. American and Canadian citizens should check that you're not already covered – some homeowners' or renters' policies are valid on vacation, and credit cards such as American Express often include some medical or other insurance, while most Canadians are covered for medical mishaps overseas by their provincial health plans. If you only need trip cancellation/interruption coverage (to supplement your existing plan), this is generally available at about $6 per $100.

Rough Guides has teamed up with Columbus Direct to offer you travel insurance that can be tailored to suit your needs. Products include a low-cost **backpacker** option for long stays; a **short break** option for city getaways; a typical **holiday package** option;

and others. There are also annual **multi-trip** policies for those who travel regularly. Different sports and activities (trekking, diving, etc) can be usually be covered if required.

See our website (Ⓦwww.roughguidesin-surance.com) for eligibility and purchasing options. Alternatively, UK residents should call ☎0870/033 9988; Australians should call ☎1300/669 999 and New Zealanders should call ☎0800/55 9911. All other nationalities should call ☎+44 870/890 2843.

Internet access

Internet access is available all over Miami and South Beach in particular. Prices are generally $7–9 per hour, or $1 for five minutes. The best places to surf are at the public library (see below), which offers 45 minutes free, or the no-charge access at the Museum of Science (see p.115). Otherwise try the *Cybr Caffe*, 1574 Washington Ave (daily 9am–1am; ☎305/534-0057).

Laundry

Many hotels will have some kind of laundry service, albeit a pricey one. You can also try the Wash Club of South Beach, 510 Washington Ave (8am–midnight; ☎305/534-4298), or Clean Machine, 226 12th St (open 24hr; ☎305/534-9429). If you fancy a drink while you wash, try the *Laundry Bar* (see "Gay Miami," p.174).

Library

The biggest is Miami-Dade County Public Library, located Downtown at 101 W Flagler St (Mon–Sat 9am–6pm, Thurs until 9pm; Oct–May also Sun 1–5pm; ☎305/375-2665, Ⓦwww.mdpls.org).

Mail

Mail between the US and Europe generally takes about a week. Postage stamps are available at any local post office; some bank ATMs also sell them, at a premium. Postcards and letters overseas are now charged at the same flat rate of 90¢. When sending, note that letters to US addresses that don't carry the **zip code** are liable to get lost or at least delayed; if unsure, check the correct 5+4 number combination with the zip-code finder at Ⓦwww.usps.com.

Letters sent to you c/o **General Delivery** (known elsewhere as **Poste Restante**) must include the post office zip code and will only be held for thirty days before being returned to sender, so make sure there's a return address on the envelope. You can also usually ask to have mail held at a hotel or, if you're a cardholder, at an American Express office.

Post offices

Most post offices are open Mon–Fri 8am–5pm, Sat 8.30am–1.30pm, or longer hours – these are the larger branches but there are many around town: check Ⓦwww.usps.com for additional locations.

1300 Washington Ave, South Beach ☎305/538-2708
500 NW 2nd Ave, Downtown ☎305/373-7562
251 Valencia Ave, Coral Gables ☎305/443-2532
3191 Grand Ave, Coconut Grove ☎305/529-6700
739 Washington Ave, Homestead ☎305/247-1556

Maps

The **maps** in this book, along with the free city plans you can pick up from the Miami CVB in its *Visitors Planning Guide*, will be sufficient to help you find your way around. If you want something more comprehensive, the Rough Guide *Map to Miami and the Keys* is unbeatable ($8.95, Can$13.50, or £4.99) – the waterproof paper will last through even a torrential summer afternoon shower, and attractions, restaurants, and hotels are clearly marked. Otherwise, the *Streetwise Miami* map at $5.95 is dependable (Ⓦwww. streetwisemaps.com).

If you're planning on traveling to the Everglades and down to the Keys, Rand McNally produces good commercial state maps for around $4. The American Automobile Association (☎1-800/222-4357, Ⓦwww.aaa. com) provides free maps and assistance to its members, and to British members of the AA and RAC.

Money

Most visitors find that there's no reason to carry large amounts of cash or traveler's checks to Miami. Automatic teller machines (**ATMs**), which accept most cards issued by domestic and foreign banks, can be found almost everywhere; call your own bank if you're in any doubt. Try to limit your ATM visits by pulling out larger amounts of cash as you'll be charged $1–4 per transaction for using a different bank's network.

Bank hours are generally from 9am to 5pm Monday to Thursday, and until 6pm on Friday; the big bank names are Wells Fargo, US Bank, and Bank of America.

Credit and **debit cards** are the most widely accepted form of payment at major hotels, restaurants, and retailers. You'll be asked to show some plastic when renting a car, bike, or other such item, or to start a "tab" at hotels for incidental charges; in any case, you can always pay the bill in cash when you return the item or check out of your room.

US **traveler's checks** are a safes way for overseas visitors to carry money, and the better-known checks, such as those issued by American Express and Visa, are treated as cash in most shops.

Youth and student discounts

Once obtained, various official and quasi-official **youth/student ID cards** soon pay for themselves in savings. Full-time students are eligible for the **International Student ID Card** (ISIC, ⓦ www.isiccard.com or www. isic.org), which entitles the bearer to special air, rail, and bus fares and discounts at museums, theaters, and other attractions. You only have to be 26 or younger to qualify for the **International Youth Travel Card**, which carries the same benefits. Prices on these cards range from $22 in the United States to A$37 in Australia and £9 in the UK; they are readily available online through STA Travel and other outlets.

Opening hours and public holidays

The opening hours of specific attractions are given in the relevant accounts throughout the guide. As a general rule, Miami isn't a morning city – all that late-night partying can take its toll. Most offices will be fully staffed by 9.30am, but often stores won't open until late morning around 11am or so, especially in Miami Beach. The counterpoint to this is that most amenities will be open later than in many other cities: expect stores in places

like Lincoln Road to stay open until 10pm most nights, bars until 4 or 5am, and restaurants to continue serving until 1am. The one major exception is in Coral Gables, where local licensing laws mean bars must shutter by 2am.

Tourist attractions are more forgiving: most museums will be open 10am–6pm and a few art galleries stay open until 9pm or so once a month. Smaller, private museums close for one day a week, usually Monday or Tuesday.

On the national **public holidays** listed in below, stores, banks, and public and federal offices are liable to be closed all day.

Jan 1 New Year's Day
Third Mon in Jan Martin Luther King Jr's Birthday
Third Mon in Feb Presidents' Day
Last Mon in May Memorial Day
July 4 Independence Day
First Mon in Sept Labor Day
Second Mon in Oct Columbus Day
Nov 11 Veterans' Day
Fourth Thurs in Nov Thanksgiving
Dec 25 Christmas Day

Phones

Miami has two **area codes** – the original prefix (☏305), and a newer one to accommodate additional lines (☏786). Note that although numbers in the Keys share the same prefix as Miami, the call is charged as long distance, not local. The cheapest way to make long-distance and international calls is by purchasing a prepaid **phone card**, commonly found in $5 and $10 denominations in newsagents or mini-markets. The rate using such cards from the USA to most European and other western countries is only 2/3¢ per minute; they also provide the lowest rates to developing countries. Such cards can be used from any touchpad phone but there is usually a surcharge for using them from a payphone.

If overseas travelers wish to use their **mobile phones** (always referred to as cell phones in the US), check with your service provider that your phone will work in the US and what the roaming charges will be, or if you can use a local SIM card in it (though that will change your number to an American one). If you find out your phone won't work in the States, you might consider renting one.

Calling home from abroad

Note that the initial zero is omitted from the area code when dialing the UK, Ireland, Australia and New Zealand from abroad.
Australia international access code + 61 + city code.
New Zealand international access code + 64 + city code.
UK international access code + 44 + city code.
Republic of Ireland international access code + 353 + city code.
South Africa international access code + 27 + city code.
For codes not listed here, dial 0 for the operator, consult any phone directory or log onto ⓦ www.countrycallingcodes.com.

Senior travelers

South Florida's popularity with so-called "snowbirds" from the Northeast means that there are often senior-specific discounts and packages offered by hotels here. Amtrak, Greyhound, and many US airlines offer discounts to anyone who can produce ID that proves they're over 62: don't expect hefty price breaks, but it's always worth checking. Museums and art galleries are better, and most will charge a reduced student/seniors rate, often to those 55 or older.

Any US citizen or permanent resident aged 62 or over is entitled to free admission for life to all national parks, monuments, and historic sites, using a **Golden Age Passport**, for which a once-only $10 fee is charged; it can be issued at any such site.

Useful senior contacts

AARP ☎ 1-800/304-4222, ⓦ www.aarp.org. Can provide discounts on accommodation and vehicle rental. Membership open to US and Canadian residents aged 50 or over for an annual fee of US $12.50
Elderhostel ☎ 1/877-426-8056, ⓦ www. elderhostel.org. Runs extensive educational and activity programs, including art appreciation, glassblowing, and historic sightseeing. Programs generally last 3–5 nights and costs are in line with those of commercial tours.
Saga Holidays ☎ 0800/096 0078 or +44 1303/771 190, ⓦ www.saga.co.uk. The UK's biggest and most established specialist in tours and holidays aimed at older people.

Time

Miami is on **Eastern Standard Time**, five hours behind Greenwich Mean Time and three hours ahead of Pacific Standard Time.

Daylight savings takes place between the first Sunday in April and the last Sunday in October.

Tipping

Wait staff in restaurants and bar expect **tips** of at least fifteen percent. A hotel porter should get $1–2 per bag; if he's lugged your suitcases up several flights of stairs, make it $3–5. Chambermaids get $1–2 per guest for each day; valet attendants get $2.

Tourist information

Miami's CVB produces a comprehensive free visitors guide every year and you can contact them to have information and brochures mailed to your home. Once in Miami, you can stop by its offices Downtown – though its out-of-the-way location means that you'll often be better relying on the Miami Beach Chamber of Commerce instead or on the Miami Design Preservation League's Welcome Center at 1001 Ocean Drive.

We've listed all the local chambers of commerce and tourist offices below. For transportation information head to the **Metro-Dade Center**, adjoining the Cultural Center Downtown. This high-rise (also called the **Government Center**) chiefly comprises county government offices, but useful bus and train timetables can be gathered from the **Transit Service Center** (daily 7am–6pm; ☎ 305/770-3131) by the Metrorail entrance at the eastern side of the building.

Tourist offices and information centers

Coconut Grove Chamber of Commerce Mon–Fri 9am–5pm, 2820 McFarlane Rd, Coconut Grove ☎ 305/444-7270, ⓦ www.coconutgrove.com.

Coral Gables Chamber of Commerce Mon–Fri 9am–5pm, 360 Greco Ave, Suite 100, Coral Gables ☎305/446-1657, ⊛www.coralgableschamber.org.

Greater Miami Convention & Visitors Bureau Mon–Fri 8.30am–6pm, 701 Brickell Ave, Downtown #2700 ☎305/539-3000 or 1-800/933-8448, ⊛www.miamiandbeaches.com. There's a satellite information center at the Miami airport on level 2, Concourse E, open daily 5am–10pm.

Key Biscayne Chamber of Commerce Mon–Fri 9am–5pm, 88 W McIntyre St, Suite 100, Key Biscayne ☎305/361-5207, ⊛www. keybiscaynechamber.org.

Miami Beach Visitor Center Mon–Fri 9am–6pm, Sat & Sun 10am–4pm, 1920 Meridian Ave, Room 831, South Beach ☎305/672-1270, ⊛www. miamibeachchamber.com.

North Beach Development Corporation Mon–Fri 9.30am–5.30pm, 210 71st St, North Beach ☎305/865-4147, ⊛www.gonorthbeach.com.

Sunny Isles Beach Resort Association Mon–Fri 9am–2pm, 17070 Collins Ave, Sunny Isles Beach ☎305/947-5826, ⊛www.sunnyislesfla.com.

Travelers with disabilities

Florida law requires that all public buildings must be **wheelchair accessible** and have appropriate bathrooms, and Miami's city buses have handgrips for wheelchair users and are all able to 'kneel' to make access easier; the Tri-Rail and Metromover systems are also adapted for full disabled access. The one frustration for disabled travelers to Miami is likely to come in South Beach: the rooms and elevators in the old hotels there are tiny and so can often feel cramped for wheelchair users. In fact, disabled travelers might be better staying at a newer resort elsewhere in the city and commuting to sightsee and sunbathe on South Beach – there's a disabled access point to the beach at 10th Street close to the MDPL headquarters.

SATH, the Society for Accessible Travel and Hospitality, in New York (☎212/447-7284, ⊛www.sath.org), is a not-for-profit travel-industry group of travel agents, tour operators, hotel and airline management, and people with disabilities. They pass on any inquiry to the appropriate member, though you should allow plenty of time for a response.

The City

The City

Downtown Miami

W
ith its gleaming office buildings towering over smaller Cuban-owned businesses, **Downtown Miami**, also known as the Central Business District (or CBD), simultaneously shows the city at its most Anglo and its most Latin. From a distance, the sparkling high-rises make Miami look much like any other modern American metropolis; it's only when you're standing below those skyscrapers, surrounded by jostling crowds and noisy traffic, that the feel of a Latin American capital takes over. If the place feels a bit overwhelming, don't be discouraged – Downtown is actually one of Miami's most compact districts, and holds two of the area's best museums, while offering the clearest sense of the everyday influence Cuba has on the city, from office workers lighting at tiny streetside cafés for a midmorning *cafecito*, or Cuban coffee, to the bilingual signage in almost every store. The Cuban music spilling from almost every store onto the sidewalk is likely these days to be accompanied by the banging and crashing of construction; Downtown's the target for much of the new high-rise condo development mushrooming around the city. Despite the real estate slowdown that's swept through Florida in recent times, the construction of new Downtown apartments continues; estimates are that, by 2010, there will be 30,000 extra homes on the market, which will transform not just the skyline but also the atmosphere here. The impact of those new residents has been stronger south of the river, where there's now a bona fide nightlife scene; the CBD, though, is empty as ever by 8pm.

Geographically, the Miami River divides Downtown: on the south bank, big business and big buildings line **Brickell Avenue**, known as "Millionaires Row" in the early twentieth century. The surrounding area, bounded by I-95 to the west, Coconut Grove to the south, and Biscayne Bay to the east, is known as **Brickell**; boasting one of the densest concentrations of new high-rise homes, it is becoming the district of choice for Miami's young professionals.

North of the river, things are less modern but more interesting. **Flagler Street** functions as the city's central artery, joining **Bayfront Park** with the **Metro–Dade Cultural Center** to the west. It's a commercial bazaar that hums with jewelers, fabric stores, and cheap electronics outlets. There are few name-brand shops here: this is a place of diners and discounters, with stores in low-slung buildings playing loud music and spilling their wares out onto the sidewalk. At the same time, Flagler Street also offers up a successful showcase of the architecture on which modern Miami was built, beginning with the **Alfred I. DuPont Building**.

Further north, past the iconic, if derivative, **Freedom Tower**, are **Overtown** and **Liberty City**, two of Miami's historically black neighborhoods. Though they've yet to benefit from the economic upsurge elsewhere in the city, they exude a fierce sense of history, and it's worth visiting one or both during the day or on an organized tour.

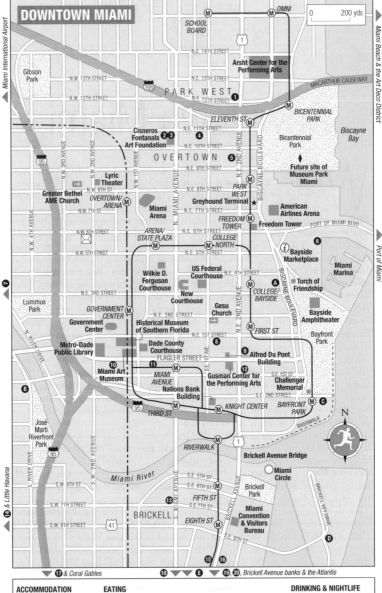

DOWNTOWN MIAMI

Little Haiti, the Design District & Miami City Cemetery ▲

0   200 yds

Miami Beach & the Art Deco District

Miami International Airport

SCHOOL BOARD

Ⓜ OMNI

Ⓜ

Arsht Center for the Performing Arts

N.E. 14TH STREET

N.E. 13TH STREET

MACARTHUR CAUSEWAY

Gibson Park

N.W. 13TH STREET

N.W. 12TH STREET

P A R K   W E S T

N.E. 12TH STREET ❶

BICENTENNIAL PARK

Biscayne Bay

ELEVENTH ST

Ⓜ

Bicentennial Park

N.E. 11TH STREET

Cisneros Fontanals Art Foundation ❷❸

❹

N.E. 10TH STREET

O V E R T O W N

❺

Ⓜ

Future site of Museum Park Miami

N.E. 9TH STREET

N.W. 1ST AVENUE

N. MIAMI AVENUE

N.E. 1ST AVENUE

N.E. 2ND AVENUE

BISCAYNE BOULEVARD

Lyric Theater

N.W. 8TH ST

OVERTOWN/ ARENA Ⓜ

N.E. 8TH STREET

PARK WEST

Ⓜ

Greater Bethel AME Church

Miami Arena

Greyhound Terminal

N.E. 7TH STREET

American Airlines Arena

N.W. 7TH ST

ARENA/ STATE PLAZA Ⓜ

FREEDOM TOWER Ⓜ

Freedom Tower

PORT OF MIAMI BLVD

N.W. 6TH STREET

COLLEGE NORTH Ⓜ

N.E. 6TH STREET

N.W. 5TH STREET

N.E. 5TH STREET

ⓘ Bayside Marketplace

❻

Miami Marina

Wilkie D. Ferguson Courthouse

US Federal Courthouse

N.E. 4TH STREET

Ⓜ

Ⓐ COLLEGE/ BAYSIDE

Torch of Friendship

N.E. 3RD STREET

New Courthouse

BISCAYNE BOULEVARD

Bayside Amphitheater

Lummus Park

GOVERNMENT CENTER Ⓜ

Gesu Church

Historical Museum of Southern Florida

N.E. 2ND STREET

Ⓜ

N.E. 2ND AVENUE

Ⓜ FIRST ST

Government Center

Dade County Courthouse

N.E. 1ST STREET

❽

Bayfront Park

N. RIVER DRIVE

Metro-Dade Public Library

FLAGLER STREET

S.E. 1ST AVE.

❾ Alfred Du Pont Building

❿ Miami Art Museum

⓫

MIAMI AVENUE

Ⓜ

S.E. 1ST ST ⓬

Challenger Memorial

Gusman Center for the Performing Arts

Nations Bank Building

S.E. 2ND STREET

Ⓜ KNIGHT CENTER

BAYFRONT PARK

Ⓜ Ⓒ

José Martí Riverfront Park

Ⓜ THIRD ST

N

S. 2ND AVENUE

S. 3RD AVENUE

S. MIAMI AVE.

Ⓜ

Miami River

RIVERWALK

Ⓜ

RIVERWALK

Brickell Avenue Bridge

S.E. 5TH ST

Ⓜ

◯ Miami Circle

S.E. 6TH ST

Brickell Park

S.W. 6TH ST

FIFTH ST

SE MIAMI AVENUE

BRICKELL AVENUE

BRICKELL KEY DRIVE

& Little Havana ⓯

S.W. 7TH STREET

⓭

S.E. 7TH ST

Miami Convention & Visitors Bureau

BRICKELL

EIGHTH ST

Ⓜ

Ⓓ

41

S.W. 8TH ST

S.E. 8TH ST

⓯ ⓰

▼ ⓱ & Coral Gables

▼ ⓲ ▼ Ⓔ ▼ ⓳, ⓴, Brickell Avenue banks & the Atlantis

95

395

1

N.W. 3RD AVENUE

N.W. 2ND AVENUE

N.W. 4TH AVENUE

N.W. 11TH STREET

N.W. 10TH STREET

N.W. 9TH STREET

⓮

⓱

ACCOMMODATION

The Four Seasons Miami	E
Holiday Inn Marina Park – Port of Miami	A
Intercontinental	C
Mandarin Oriental	D
Miami River Inn B&B	B

EATING

Big Fish Mayami	12
Garcia's Seafood Grille	7
Grimpa Steakhouse	15
Karlo Bakery	14
La Loggia	11
La Paris	13
Las Palmas	12
Los Ranchos	6
Morton's Steakhouse	19
Perricone's Marketplace	18
Raja's	9
Rosa Mexicano	16
Rosinella	20
Soya & Pomodoro	8
Tobacco Road	13
Top Hat Deli	10
Tutto Pasta	17

DRINKING & NIGHTLIFE

M-Bar	D
Metropolis	5
Nocturnal	2
Pawn Shop Lounge	1
Space	3
Studio A	4
Tobacco Road	13

The CBD is definitely a place to visit during the day – at weekends and in the evening, restaurants usually shut down since few of the would-be tenants have yet moved into their new Downtown homes. However, public transportation is thorough and an elevated monorail, the free **Metromover** (see p.25), circles Downtown's main loop, making it a handy way to orient yourself.

Flagler Street and around

The heart of Downtown Miami is **Flagler Street**, named after railroad magnate Henry Flagler (see box on p.254), the financial godfather who helped found the city but refused its first residents' polite request to name their home after him; he compromised, and they dubbed the main drag in his honor. The street is choked with cheap fabric stores, electronics shops, and, for some reason, dozens of discount shoe outlets. The other notable industry downtown is gemstones: the **Seybold Building**, which sprawls for a block between Miami and NE 1st avenues, is a hotbed hub of diamond trading – expect fair prices, but also be informed and prepared to haggle (it's not for amateurs).

Along the street are a few architectural highlights, as well as the mother lode of Miami's cultural elite (at least for now): the **Metro–Dade Cultural Center**. This ochre-colored, low-slung building stands out amid the gleaming metal and glass that dominates the rest of Downtown; it's full of grand intentions as a public space, but falls a little flat. Architectural pioneer Philip Johnson designed the complex to ape an old fort, echoing the Mediterranean Revival style found elsewhere in the city: the result is a series of anodyne ranch buildings around a communal piazza that remains eternally empty thanks to the punishing Miami sun, though local bums tend to hang out here during the day. Still, at the moment, the Center boasts two of Downtown's top attractions, the **Historical Museum of South Florida** and the **Miami Art Museum**.

The Alfred I. DuPont Building and the Gusman Center for the Performing Arts

Two notable buildings stand along the eastern portion of Flagler Street. Near SE 2nd Avenue, the **Alfred I. DuPont Building**, at no. 169, is one of the best examples of Depression Moderne design in the city, with its simple but imposing black facade. Now home to the Florida National Bank, the first floor is open to the public, so feel free to wander through during office hours and catch its spectacular and ornate interior. Note especially the fanciful wrought-iron screens, frescoes of Florida scenes, and bronze bas-relief elevator doors with egrets and herons.

Opposite the DuPont Building, at no. 174, the Olympia Theater at the Gusman Center for Performing Arts (℗305/374-2444, ⓦwww.gusmancenter.org) was built in 1926 as a vaudeville house. Much like the Mathesons and their mustard-gas millions (see p.116), the theater's benefactors, the Gusmans, profited through government contracts in World War I; theirs was to provide condoms for departing American soldiers. The building's hodgepodge of architectural styles best approximates a Spanish-Moorish theme, with turrets, towers, and intricately detailed columns, and recent renovations have brought out the stunning moldings in its lobby ceiling; it's also noteworthy as the first air-conditioned building in Miami. However, the only way you'll be able to see inside the whole building (and not just the lobby) is by catching a performance (see p.169 for ticket information) – if you do, note the kitschy ceiling in the auditorium, twinkling with fake stars and the illusion of slowly moving clouds.

Burdine's and the Coppertone sign

Further west along Flagler, on the corner with Miami Avenue, stands the first in the **Burdine's** department store chain at no. 22; this site, along with the rest of the chain including its South Beach outpost is now owned by, and rebranded as, Macy's. The structure's notable for its Streamline Moderne design, all hard edges rounded off and corners curved to convey gentle movement; the extension across Miami Avenue was put up immediately after World War II. This first outpost of "Florida's department store" was founded as a dry goods shop in 1898, a mere two years after the city was incorporated, by William Burdine, who traded refined sugar, cloth, and nails for Native American pelts.

Crossing over Miami Avenue onto West Flagler Street, look for the giant relief of the famous **Coppertone sign** – a young girl whose pet dog is tugging down her bikini bottom – that was based on a seaside snapshot (it's not, as urban legend sometimes has it, Jodie Foster). Though it's in a poor state now – the result of hurricane damage a few years ago – the sign's a downtown icon; it was originally located along Biscayne Boulevard, but moved here when the building to which it was attached was demolished. It's showcased simply because the office block was owned by a preservation-minded member of the Dade Heritage Trust, which spearheaded the campaign to save the sign.

The Miami-Dade County Courthouse

Continue west along the street and you'll hit the four forbidding Doric columns that mark the entrance to the **Dade County Courthouse**, 73 W Flagler St (☎305/275-1155). Built in 1926 around a still-extant courthouse – where public hangings used to take place – this was Miami's tallest building for fifty years until it was superseded by the 55-story First Union Financial Center on South Biscayne Boulevard. Its night-lights used to show off a distinctive stepped pyramid peak intended to serve as a constant reminder to would-be wrongdoers of where they'd end up. It was no idle boast, as originally this peak was the location of the courthouse's onsite jail. Prisoners were known to throw dampened toilet paper down onto passing pedestrians, so the holding cells were moved in 1961.

The Historical Museum of Southern Florida

Looming above the piazza's western flank, the **Historical Museum of Southern Florida** (Mon–Sat 10am–5pm, third Thurs of each month 10am–9pm, Sun noon–5pm; $8, $10 combined ticket with Miami Art Museum; ☎305/375-1492, ⓦwww.hmsf.org) is home to detailed, interactive displays covering Florida from the prehistoric up until the present. Some of the exhibits are a little worn around the edges, but there's plenty to entertain kids including dress-up boxes with period clothes and pioneer toys, while for adults, there's a small but instructive map collection detailing the gradual European charting of the area.

Where perhaps the museum is strongest, though, is its post-1950s display: a pair of tiny boats used by Cuban and Haitian refugees to reach Miami in the late 1970s sits next to TVs running archive news footage showing local hostility to the Mariel Boatlift in 1980. Also well chronicled are the fluctuating fortunes of Miami Beach, from its early days as a celebrity vacation spot – with amusing photos of 1920s Hollywood greats – through to the renovation of the Art Deco district. In its first-floor **research facility**, the Historical Museum houses the archives of the now-defunct *Miami News*, the city's first daily newspaper, and walk-in visitors are welcome to scan the decades of news and photography on site.

The Miami Art Museum and Main Public Library

Across from the Historical Museum, the **Miami Art Museum**, 101 W Flagler St (Tues–Fri 10am–5pm, third Thurs of each month 10am–9pm, Sat & Sun noon–5pm; $8, $10 combined ticket with Historical Museum, free admission second Sat of each month and every Sun; ☎305/375-3000, ⊛www.miamiartmuseum.org), holds a remarkable collection of postwar art, setting modern masterpieces alongside quirky, newer works. The first floor of the building offers a rotating selection, refreshed four times yearly, from the museum's own collection. Accessible and intelligently curated, notable works include sketches by Robert Rauschenberg and art stuntman Christo, a huge open cube work by Sol Lewitt, and surrealist pioneer Marcel Duchamp's *Boîte en Valise*, which consists of witty *maquettes* of his previous masterworks, all in a handy carrying case. Yet it's the museum's conceptual art collection that is most stunning, especially the bevy of works by the late Cuban-American artist Felix Gonzalez-Torres. His remarkable pieces are designed to change through viewing – such as a stark ream of embossed paper that visitors are intended to sample sheet by sheet, or a help-yourself pile of candy stacked in a stark white corner that dwindles with every hungry passerby. The upstairs area is usually dedicated to shows staged as part of the MAC@MAM program – Miami Art Central, or MAC, founded and funded by Venezuelan art collector and Coca-Cola bottling heiress Ella Fontanals-Cisneros (see p.46), left its South Miami standalone home and moved here last year; she now uses her cash and connections to bring impressive temporary works to the site.

The biggest news here, though, is the building itself. The museum is set to move in 2012 to a new site at Museum Park (see p.45), one reason the institution lured Terence Riley, architect and onetime curator of design at New York's MoMa, to be its new director in 2006. Riley's team has already started referring to the new home with subtle digs ribboned through the displays. On one wall, look for the photo of the 20-foot tall Niki de St Phalle sculpture, *Red Nana* – too large for the current site, it remains in storage in Paris until it can be installed in the museum's new home.

Opposite the museum looms the **Main Public Library** (Mon–Sat 9am–6pm, Thurs 9am–9pm, Sun 1–5pm; closed Sun in summer), which, besides the usual lending sections, has temporary painting and photography exhibits showcasing local literary and artistic talents – the narrow focus of which typically makes them worth checking out – as well as a massive collection of Florida-related magazines and books.

The Gesú Church

Just north of the Alfred I. DuPont Building stands the **Gesú Church**, 118 NE 2nd St (frequent English, Spanish or bilingual masses throughout the week; ☎305/379-1424), home to Miami's oldest Catholic parish. The original wooden building, called the Church of the Holy Name, was completed in 1898 on land that Henry Flagler donated to the city for use as a church and school. This large Mediterranean Revival replacement was built in 1925 and sticks out amid the cramped storefronts of Downtown, painted peach sherbet and lemon meringue colors. The church's foamy, baroque appliqué exterior is more noteworthy than its stout inner sanctum; designed without pillars so that the Jesuits would have unobstructed sightlines for their fiery sermons, the interior's framed by modern stained glass from Munich.

The US Federal Courthouse and around

Two blocks northwest from the Gesú Church, the unremarkable 1931 Neoclassical structure at 300 NE 1st St was originally the city's post office, but was commandeered a year later to serve as the **US Federal Courthouse** (Mon–Fri 8.30am–5pm; ℡305/523-5100). Most voluntary visitors stop by for a glimpse of Denman Fink's 25-foot painting, *Law Guides Florida's Progress* – depicting Florida's evolution from swampy backwoods to modern state – in the small courtroom on the second floor (for more of his work, head over to Coral Gables; see p.103). The work, funded by a parallel government body to the WPA, is more impressive for its size rather than skill, but look for Fink's portrait of his young nephew, George Merrick, the founder of Coral Gables, delivering produce. The mural's usually accessible to visitors, provided there's no closed-door court case in session – call in advance to check and make sure to **bring photo ID**. Merrick's isn't the only notable public artwork in the building: In 1985, fresco artist David Novros was commissioned to decorate the building's medieval-style inner **courtyard**, to which his bold, colorful daubs make a lively addition.

The soon to be outdated **New Courthou**se next door replaced this older structure as the city's main legal facility in the late 1960s, when Miami's soaring crime rate outstripped its capabilities (main entrance on N Miami Ave; Mon–Fri 8.30am–5pm). It's a gruesome creation of concrete and glass, and was poorly designed – it's difficult, for instance, for lawyers to present evidence clearly to the audience in the courtroom. At time of writing, it was ready to be superseded by a soaring new structure a block away at 400 N Miami Ave. Named after a recently deceased federal judge, the **Wilkie D. Ferguson Courthouse** was designed by local firm Arquitectonica. A shiny blue and white undulating ship of a place, the design is meant to have symbolic significance: it's made up of two towers, representing the opposing sides of a court argument, linked by a clear glass shard standing for truth and justice. With its distinctly 1980s-SciFi aesthetic, the whole thing looks more like an overgrown model of an evil ruler's house from *Star Wars*.

Bayfront Park

At the east end of East Flagler Street is **Bayfront Park**, 301 N Biscayne Blvd (℡305/358-7550, ⓦwww.bayfrontparkmiami.com). It's a pleasant enough urban greenspace, dotted with sculpture and large, leafy trees, though the lack of significant shade around its wide benches makes them a less than comfortable spot to dawdle for most of the year. There's no specific local connection to Isamu Noguchi's white geometric *Challenger Memorial* at the park's southwest corner – it's simply here because the park's current design was completed in 1986, around the same time as the space shuttle exploded mid-flight, and the designer included the monument as a late addition. Before that, Bayfront Park – laid out on reclaimed land dredged from the bottom of the bay in the 1920s – was best known as the site of the attempted assassination of President-elect Franklin D. Roosevelt by a disaffected Italian bricklayer, Giuseppe Zangarra (Roosevelt survived, but the mayor of Chicago Anton Cermak, who was standing close by, died of his wounds; Zangarra went to the electric chair just over a month later).

At the opposite end of the park stands the highly charged **Torch of Friendship**, which commemorates a burning local issue and another, more controversial president. Built in 1960, then rededicated in JFK's memory four years later, it centers on a lighted torch that was once surrounded by crests of every Latin American country save one. Cuba's emblem was purposefully omitted, with backers intending to add the crest only when Cuba was free of communism. The site's now rather forlorn and the city takes little interest in it; it's also missing many of the original crests, meaning Cuba's omission no longer stands out.

At its northern tip, the park leads into the **Bayside Marketplace**, 401 Biscayne Boulevard (usual hours Mon–Thurs 10am–10pm, Fri–Sat 10am–11pm, Sun 11am–9pm; ℡305/577-3344, ⓦwww.baysidemarketplace.com), which features

▲ The Brickell skyline

upscale chain stores and restaurants in an open-air complex by the water, and is usually packed with tourists. There's also a small, unofficial tourist information booth at its entrance that's good for maps.

South of Miami River

To reach the southern portion of Downtown, head south across the bridge – crowned by a moody, modern statue of a crossbow-toting Tequesta warrior and his wife; in doing so, you'll pass from the soul of the city to its wallet. This area, known as **Brickell** (rhymes with "pickle"), is Miami's financial center. Metaphorically speaking, old money was the foundation of this area; and early developers Mary and William Brickell, who ran a trading post nearby, planned a wide tree-lined avenue that could be built up with mansions for their friends. In doing so, they created the city's most desirable neighborhood – it was *the* address in 1910s Miami – and Brickell Avenue soon earned the nickname **Millionaires Row**.

From the late 1970s, Miami emerged as a corporate banking center, cashing in on political instability in South and Central America by offering a secure home for Latin American money, some of which needed laundering. Since then, Miami has maneuvred to become second only to New York in serving as the headquarters of international **banks**; and the forest of mirrored buildings that cluster along Brickell Avenue sprouts new offshoots every year. After a nondescript few decades, recent years have seen the Brickell area returning to that gleaming heyday, as the intensive construction of luxury residential condos and high-end condo-hotels like the *Four Seasons* have drawn wealthy young professionals to live close to their offices. In fact, it's here that you'll find the bulk of downtown's new restaurants, bars, and nightlife.

The Miami Circle

Local developer Michael Baumann purchased the triangle of land east of Brickell Avenue and wedged against the Miami River – once the site of a 1950s apartment complex – for $8 million in the mid-1990s and planned to throw up a premium-priced high-rise. As per local ordinance, archeologists were hired to clear the area for construction and, surprisingly, they made a great discovery – a coral rock circle, 38 feet in diameter and carved four feet deep into the bedrock, carbon-dated to be at least ten thousand years old. It's now known as the **Miami Circle** (Ⓦwww.flheritage.com/archaeology/projects/miamicircle).

Its age is the only indisputable thing: experts argue over the Stonehenge-esque circle's original purpose, whether it was a religious, community, or commercial center, or even who might have built it. While they debate, others are considering how best to display the find. Years of wrangling have left the Circle's future uncertain – in 2003, it was covered with weather-protecting bags of sand and gravel. Past plans had suggested covering the carvings with a thatched roof or clear plastic shell, but funding has fallen short. The bizarre solution at the visitors' center – which local preservationists promise will open by early 2010 – will be to display a scale replica only eight feet wide. For updates on the surreal situation, check with the Dade Heritage Trust (☎305/358-9572, Ⓦwww.dadeheritagetrust.org).

The one winner has turned out to be developer Baumann, who was able to strongarm the city into paying $27 million to purchase the land back from him, turning a tidy profit without laying a single brick. But development on the promontory here didn't halt with this historical glitch. The onetime *Sheraton* hotel next door was leveled to make way for a new Philippe Starck-designed luxury condo tower, ICON, which also contains a branch of the *Viceroy* boutique hotel; neither, however, offers a public view of the Circle.

The Atlantis

At 2025 Brickell Ave, **The Atlantis** apartment is the project that turned the Arquitectonica design team, husband and wife architects Laurinda Spear and Bernardo Fort-Brescia, from wannabes to A-listers. The complex was built on the site of one of the grandest mansions on Millionaires Row, the Mitchell-Bingham residence, home to Mary Tiffany Bingham, sister of glass guru Louis. Like a cored apple, The Atlantis has a square hole through the middle, filled with a single palm tree, a Jacuzzi, and a fire-engine-red spiral staircase. Completed in 1982, its playful design is even more eye-catching now amid the earnest bombast of nearby skyscrapers; it clearly owes much to the stylish mischief of mid-century pioneers like Morris Lapidus. You won't be allowed inside unless you know someone who lives there, which might be just as well: even its designers admit the interior doesn't live up to the exuberance of the exterior, and claim the building to be "architecture for 55mph" – in other words, seen to best effect from a passing car.

North of Downtown

North of the Downtown loop, sights thin out considerably and neighborhoods grow rougher: patches like **Bicentennial Park** are closer to the crime-hobbled Miami of the 1980s than the glossy city of today However, the city's announced ambitious plans to gussy up this unloved strip with the arrival of a new museum complex, among other things. The **Port of Miami** here is also one of the busiest cruise-ship docks in the world, and on any given day you can drive down MacArthur Causeway to the beach to see half a dozen mammoth ships queuing patiently at the dock.

One of the most arresting additions to the local skyline is the **American Airlines Arena** on the old Port of Miami site. A high-profile project for local design celebrities Arquitectonica, the AA Arena looks like a giant origami sculpture floating by the bay, its stark, rounded walls tucked in like stowed wings. It's the site of many big-name concerts as well as home to the Miami Heat basketball team (see p.188). Directly opposite the arena is the **Freedom Tower**, now part of Miami Dade College.

Beyond the Freedom Tower, you're on the western fringe of some of the city's most impoverished neighborhoods. The sketchiness here, though, is slowly changing thanks to the emergence of trendy nightclubs in the warehouse neighborhood of Park West (see p.80), the visual art explosion of Wynwood (see p.81), and the new Arsht Center (see p.80).

Freedom Tower

Often called "Miami's Ellis Island," the ornate **Freedom Tower**, 600 N Biscayne Blvd, served not only as an immigration processing post but also as a community center for the more than 360,000 Cuban refugees who arrived between 1961 and 1974. It was one of three replicas of Seville's Giralda bell tower built in Miami by the same architects, Schutze and Weaver, who designed New York's Grand Central Station: the others were the *Roney Plaza* hotel in Miami Beach (since demolished), and Coral Gables' *Biltmore* hotel (see p.104).

Since its 1925 construction as the headquarters of the *Miami Times* newspaper, this Mediterranean Revival structure has lain more often empty than occupied thanks in part to its impractical and eccentric shape, with a high, narrow turret, and little versatile office space. Its recent history has been turbulent, to say the least: in 1997, telecoms billionaire Jorge Mas Canosa bought the place for his **Cuban-American National Foundation** which announced splashy plans to open a museum. When he died soon after, those schemes foundered and the historic pile was sold again, this time to Pedro Martin's Terra Developers; he promised to restore the old building while using the acreage around it to build glaringly ugly new high-rise condos. As the real estate boom in Miami busted, though, Martin's plans looked reassuringly less profitable. Martin took a tax write-off instead and deeded the hulk to nearby Miami Dade College, which says it will rehab the tower into a public museum with classroom spaces.

Bicentennial Park

Bicentennial Park, 1075 N Biscayne Blvd, has been troubled from the day it opened in 1977 (the men running the food stands on opening night were mugged for the day's takings). For over 25 years, its 35 acres – originally an oily storage lot for shipping containers from the nearby Port of Miami – have served mainly as a refuge for the area's homeless. The park's iffy profile, though, is set to radically change as the city turns its attention to overhauling the space at an estimated cost of $600 million.

For starters, the name will be changed to **Museum Park** – a nod to its role as fresh home for a re-imagined Museum of Science, currently in Coconut Grove (see p.115), and Downtown's Miami Art Museum (see p.41). The latter museum has already unveiled the design for its new digs, dreamed up by Herzog & deMeuron, the Swiss firm responsible for San Francisco's copper-clad DeYoung Museum and London's iconic Tate Modern conversion. MAM's new home, which in sketches looks like sheets of paper and cardboard boxes suspended and strung together by spindly straws, should be ready for the public by 2012. The new Science Museum may or may not add an aquarium, and plans don't call for it to decamp until a year after MAM. The remaining nineteen acres of the park will be upgraded into a leafier, vagrant-free public greenspace, with a central tear-shaped lawn for picnicking. Check both ⓦwww.museumparkmiami.com and ⓦwww.miamiartmuseum.org for updates.

CIFO/Cisneros-Fontanals Art Foundation

Billionaire art patron Ella Fontanals-Cisneros' second contemporary space in town – the first, Miami Art Central, is part of the Miami Art Museum (see p.000) – is **CIFO**, 1018 North Miami Avenue (Thurs–Sun 10am–4pm; free; ☎305/455-3380, ⓦwww.cifo.org). It's housed in a former boxing gym that was gloriously made over by architect Rene Gonzalez. For its shimmering exterior, Gonzalez manipulated images of bamboo forests then reproduced the pixelated results as millions of individual tiles – it's worth a detour if only to gawp at this beautiful feat. The interior hosts edgy, contemporary rotating shows taken from Cisneros' vast holdings, as well as site-specific grants to artists.

Overtown

Northwest of Downtown lies **Overtown**, originally known as Coloredtown, one of the oldest neighborhoods in Miami. Local zoning laws forbade the sale of land to blacks except in this area after Miami was founded in 1896, and it was soon securely cordoned off from the rest of Downtown by the railroad. Even so, a settlement developed that was larger even than the existing black neighborhood in Coconut Grove. By the 1930s, Coloredtown was a vibrant entertainment district: NW 2nd Avenue between 6th and 10th streets was variously known as "Little Broadway," "The Strip," and even "The Great Black Way."

One of the driving forces behind Little Broadway was the black promoter **Clyde Killens**, who started out as a drum accompanist for silent movies. From there, the outlandish Killens achieved pre-eminence managing hotels and nightclubs, not to mention being one of the first black Miamians to register to vote. He succeeded in part thanks to the segregationist policy that ensured that while black entertainers like Dorothy Dandridge were wowing white crowds at sellout shows on Miami Beach, they would have to stay at hotels in the Overtown ghetto.

Although the postwar years proved tough for the local economy, Overtown's decline accelerated rapidly in the 1960s, as the construction of the I-95 Expressway devastated the area. It was nothing less than an act of urban social vandalism, with twenty thousand people forcibly displaced and disconnected from all social amenities. The neighborhood never recovered, and it became a poster child for Miami's crime problem in the late 1980s. Now, although it's slowly clawing its way back to economic health, the district's still a dangerous place for visitors even in the daytime, and the best way to see it is on an organized tour (see p.48).

The Overtown Historic District

If Coloredtown was Miami's Harlem, then its counterpart to the Apollo Theater is the **Lyric Theater**, 819 NW 2nd Ave. It's at the center of a rather desolate two-block area now known as the **Overtown Historic District**, and is owned and promoted by the Black Archives (see p.48). Black entrepreneur Geder Walker, who dreamt of rivaling Europe's grand opera houses, built the theater in 1913, but by the late 1940s it had been converted into a church. Now restored to its original opulence, it is the only standing reminder of the district's funky heyday, when the likes of Nat King Cole and Lena Horne were regular visitors. Despite redevelopment, it has yet to reopen fully for public use, mired in planning rows – the Black Archives wants to add a four-story addition to the rear while Miami is trying to build a gaudy new condo complex on the three city-owned acres next door, to enormous local opposition.

Nearby stands the Black Archives' other attraction in the area, the 1915 **D.A. Dorsey House** at 250 NW 9th St; the interior's not open to the public, as it houses some of the charity's administrative offices. It's famous as the home of the city's first black millionaire: Dana Albert Dorsey started out as a carpenter and shrewdly racked up his money by buying land, building houses, and renting them to blacks. Astonishingly, his real-estate portfolio included the land that's today hyper-exclusive Fisher Island (see p.64); he'd intended to build an upscale black resort there in 1918 before changing his mind and selling his holdings a few years later. Built as a wedding gift to his new wife, the house had high-tech touches like electricity in every room; sadly, the structure that currently stands is actually a replica, albeit an authentic one. The other major sight of interest is the **Greater Bethel A.M.E. Church**, 245 NW 8th St, notable mainly as the oldest black congregation in Miami (dating back to the year of the city's incorporation, 1896) and for its large Mediterranean Revival structure.

The Miami City Cemetery

Just north of Overtown, at 1800 NE 2nd Ave, lies Miami's original cemetery, founded in 1897. With its separate black section to the west plus white and walled Jewish sections to the east, the **Miami City Cemetery** (☎305/579-6938) is the final resting place for early pioneers, including Julia Tuttle (see p.252). The cemetery's now in a rundown part of town and so can be rather dangerous – many of the graves are littered with used syringes, anything valuable has been stolen, and the family vaults of early Miami bigwigs have had their doors torn off by the homeless seeking shelter – so it's best seen on an organized tour (☎305/375-1621, ⓦwww.hmsf.org), though the Woodlawn Cemetery (see p.95) has richer pickings for grave hunters.

The Liberty City riots

May 1980 was a grueling month for race relations in Miami. First, thousands of Cuban refugees poured into the city as part of the **Mariel Boatlift** (see p.92), causing widespread resentment. Then, the tinder of tensions waiting for a spark in Miami's black community finally ignited. There had been sporadic protests before: notably, what officials called a **"civil disturbance,"** which claimed the lives of four people in Liberty City in 1968, at the same time Richard Nixon was accepting the Republican presidential nomination at the Convention Center on the beach. The disturbance grew out of a protest against perceived bias in the criminal justice system as well as high local levels of unemployment, and it's ironic to note that one reason the Republicans picked Miami was the county's promise that urban unrest so common in other cities at the time, notably Chicago, could never happen here.

But the O.J. Simpson trial of its day was the **Arthur McDuffie murder case**, which set Miami's black neighborhoods ablaze. McDuffie was a black former Marine turned insurance salesman with no criminal record, who was stopped by four white police officers in December 1979 and beaten to death. They later claimed that he had provoked them by making an obscene gesture as he rode past on a borrowed motorbike. Tried in Tampa to avoid inflaming local passions, the four police officers were found not guilty (by an all-white jury) on **May 17, 1980**, six months to the day after McDuffie's death; the news came at 2.42pm and within hours the riots had started. The citywide curfew that followed lasted nearly a week: by then, disturbances had reached as far south as Homestead. Whereas previous riots had been primarily aimed at property, in protest at slum conditions, this was racial violence: shocking stories, notably that of a young white motorist dragged from his car and mutilated by the mob, made headlines across America. When it was over, eighteen people had died, both white and black, with more than four hundred injured – plus property damages valued at more than $200 million.

Liberty City

Much further northwest, **Liberty City** has wider streets and more parkland than Overtown, but can be just as dangerous and again is best visited during the day by car or with a tour.

The district centers on **Liberty Square**, at NW 12th Avenue between 62nd and 67th streets. This sprawling low-rise development, nicknamed "Pork'n'Beans" by locals on account of its pinkish-orange color, was the first public housing project in the state, opening in February 1937; thanks to its modern amenities, like indoor plumbing, it quickly began drawing blacks from Coloredtown. Today, the identical row houses, separated by threadbare lawns and barely affording residents any privacy, are much less appealing – note the remnants between 63rd and 64th streets of the six-foot-high segregation wall erected to keep the black and white communities separate. Look, too, for tributes to the late civil rights leader Martin Luther King: there's a particularly moving mural at NW 62nd Street and 7th Avenue, the hub of the local economy and home to a few interesting stores and restaurants.

On the southwestern fringes of Liberty City, the **Black Archives History and Research Foundation of South Florida**, 5400 NW 22nd Ave (Mon–Fri 9am–5pm; ☎305/636-2390), houses historical documents gathered from the local community; it was founded by a dynamic local librarian, Dorothy Jenkins Fields, in 1974 when she tried to research elements of local black history and discovered there was no dedicated facility. The archives, though, are not designed for drop-in visitors; call ahead if you want to use the facilities or go on a **tour** of Overtown and Liberty City (groups of ten or more necessary). The only other local attraction is the **African Heritage Cultural Arts Center**, 6161 NW 62nd St (☎305/638-6771, ⓦwww.miamidade.gov/parks/parks/african_heritage.asp), which offers Afrocentric classes in performing and fine arts along with a small gallery and theater.

South Beach

For most Miami visitors, the charms of the rest of the city are eclipsed by seductive, chic **South Beach**, a colloquial designation for the area that stretches from the southernmost tip of Miami Beach north to 23rd Street (for the rest of Miami Beach, see "Central Miami Beach and north," Chapter 3). This is the place most people visualize when Miami is mentioned, and the partying and palm trees along the streets perpetuate the image. Here, row upon row of Art Deco gems – especially along the much-photographed **Ocean Drive** – look exactly as they do on film: sleek, classic, and ultra cool. For all its world fame, it's astonishing to realize that this neighborhood is so compact – the bulk of the Miami sandbar is home to just ninety thousand residents.

Reaching north from 5th Street to Lincoln Road, bounded by the ocean to the east and Meridian Avenue to the west, the **Art Deco Historic District** holds almost every building that has made modern Miami famous. Walk around the area along the two main commercial drags, **Washington and Collins avenues**, or through the artsy **Española Way**, and you'll see dozens of architectural masterpieces, although don't forget to look up – some of the best signage and ornamentation is on the upper stories or the roofs of these buildings. While the tip of the island, **South Pointe**, is still gentrifying and a little edgy, there are parts of the District, notably along Ocean Drive between 5th and 10th streets, which have been worryingly Disneyfied despite the stringent preservation orders. This is where you'll find sidewalk cafés showcasing congealed samples of menu items and ferocious carnival-barker staff hailing passersby to take a table. Further north it's as fun and stylish as ever: there are funky restaurants and hotels in the area around the junction of Collins Avenue and Lincoln Road, and **Lincoln Road Mall** is a great place to stroll even if you don't plan to spend. Floating just off the coast of the South Beach sandbar, a smattering of mostly man-made **islands** is notable largely for their celebrity residents.

Some history

Although the pioneer **John Collins** had lamely tried to launch fruit farming in the early 1900s further up the beach near what's now 41st Street, it wasn't until he joined forces with the money and determination of entrepreneur **Carl Fisher** that South Beach germinated. When Fisher drew up his original plan, he wanted to create a winter playland, to be called "Fairyland" – a story that many gay locals recount with ironic relish. His dream of a resort came true, if not his plans for its name: by the 1920s and 1930s, what we now know as South Beach had become the heart of wealthy America's winter season. (For more on Collins, see Lake Pancoast, p.69.) But after World War II, when soldiers (including Clark Gable) billeted here for training left, the smart set moved north to newer hotels in Central Miami Beach, and the district began to crumble.

▲ Central Miami Beach

A ❶ & ❷ ▲

Sunset Island No. 4

W. 21ST ST

Bayshore Municipal Golf Course

Bass Museum of Art

22ND ST

Collins Park

20TH ST

20TH ST

19TH ST

Holocaust Memorial

Miami Beach Chamber of Commerce

18TH ST

19TH ST

Miami Beach Convention Center

18TH ST

Temple Emanu-El

The Fillmore Miami Beach

17TH ST

21ST ST

B

C **D**

4
5
E
F

6 **G**

10

Delano Hotel

H
K
L

3

7

9

J

Belle Isle

11 **13** **12**

Lincoln Theater

LINCOLN ROAD MALL

14

LINCOLN ROAD

15

Colony Theater

20 **16**

21

Art Center of South Florida

17

18

23

25

I

19

22

24

M

N

O

Collins Avenue

See map opposite for details

26

ESPANOLA WAY

Flamingo Park

14TH ST

13TH ST

12TH ST

13TH ST

12TH ST

Miami Beach Police

11TH ST

P

Q

10TH ST

9TH ST

8TH ST

Art Deco Welcome Center

Lummus Park

R

South Shore Hospital

7TH ST

6TH ST

S

Parking Garage

T Park Central Hotel

27

28

5TH ST

MACARTHUR CAUSEWAY

Electrowave Park N Ride

30

29

31

4TH ST

Sanford L. Ziff Jewish Museum of Florida

3RD ST

SOUTH POINTE

U
V

ATLANTIC OCEAN

Causeway Island

2ND ST

Miami Beach Marina

34

32 **33**

35

37

38

1ST ST

COMMERCE ST

39

First Street Beach

Terminal Island

Biscayne Bay

BISCAYNE BOULEVARD

40

South Pointe Tower

South Beach Pier

South Pointe Park

Government Cut

N

South Pointe Park

▼ Fisher Island

Electrowave Shuttle route

Art Deco Historic District

0   100 yds

SOUTH BEACH

(side labels)
Downtown Miami, Airport & Venetian Islands

Flagler Memorial Island

Star, Palm & Hibiscus Islands

Downtown Miami, Airport, Jungle Island, Island Gardens & Miami Children's Museum

(street names)
SUNSET DRIVE
NORTH BAL RD
ALTON ROAD
N MERIDIAN AVE
CONVENTION CENTER DR
JACKIE GLEASON DRIVE
PARK AVENUE
LIBERTY AVE
COLLINS AVE
JAMES AVE
WASHINGTON AVE
VENETIAN CWY
BAY ROAD
PURDY AVE
WEST AVE
BAY ROAD
WEST AVENUE
ALTON ROAD
LENOX AVENUE
MICHIGAN AVENUE
JEFFERSON AVENUE
MERIDIAN AVENUE
EUCLID AVENUE
PENNSYLVANIA AVE
DREXEL AVE
COLLINS AVENUE
OCEAN DRIVE
EUCLID AVENUE

ACCOMMODATION				EATING			
Albion	I	The Raleigh	F	A La Folie Café	45	Macaluso	9
Anglers Resort	S	The Ritz-Carlton		Afterglo	55	Madiba	7
Aqua	M	South Beach		Ago	D	Maison d'Azur	S
Best Western		Royal Hotel	nn	Balans Lincoln		Miss Yip Chinese	
South Beach	ee	Royal Palm	N	Road	16	Café	11
Catalina	ii	Sagamore	K	Barton G	26	News Café	64
Clay Hotel		The Setai	B	Big Pink	35	Nobu	D
and Hostel	W	The Shelborne	E	Bond St	C	OLA	6
Delano	H	Hotel Shelley	jj	Books & Books		Pizza Rustica	15 & 62
Doubletree		The Shore Club	D	Café	14	Prime 112	36
Surfcomber	G	SoBe You		Casa Tua	10	Puerto Sagua	67
Essex House	ff	South Beach	Q	David's Café	59	Quattro Gastronomie	
European Guesthouse	R	Plaza Villas	Z	De Vito South Beach	33	Italiane	20
Gansevoort South	A	The Standard		Eleventh St. Diner	58	Social Miami	K
The Hotel	mm	Miami	J	Fratelli La Bufala	29	Sushi Samba Dromo	18
Hotel Ocean	bb	The Tides	cc	Front Porch Café	49	Table 8	41
Island House	Y	Townhouse	C	Gino's	65	Talula	1
Jazz on South		The Tropics Hotel		Icebox Café	23	Tantra	48
Beach Hostel	V	& Hostel	O	Jerry's Famous Deli	42	Tap Tap	28
The Loft Hotel	gg	Hotel Victor	dd	Joe's Stone Crab	40	Taverna Opa	38
Mondrian	P	Villa Paradiso	X	Kobe Club	30	Taystee Bakery	47
Ocean Hotel		The Wave	U	Kung Fu Chu	8	Toni's Sushi	56
and Hostel	hh	Whitelaw Hotel	ll	La Marea	cc	Van Dyke Café	17
The Park Central	T	The Winterhaven	aa	La Sandwicherie	51	Wish	mm
Pelican Hotel	kk			Le Provence	22		

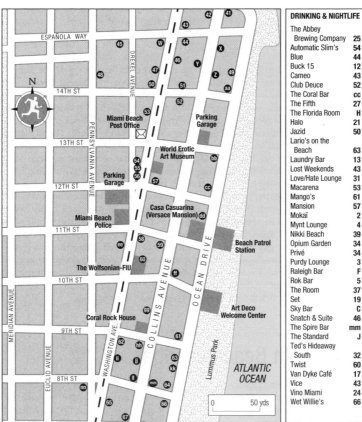

DRINKING & NIGHTLIFE

The Abbey	
Brewing Company	25
Automatic Slim's	54
Blue	44
Buck 15	12
Cameo	43
Club Deuce	52
The Coral Bar	cc
The Fifth	27
The Florida Room	H
Halo	21
Jazid	50
Lario's on the	
Beach	63
Laundry Bar	13
Lost Weekends	43
Love/Hate Lounge	31
Macarena	53
Mango's	61
Mansion	57
Mokaï	2
Mynt Lounge	4
Nikki Beach	39
Opium Garden	34
Privé	34
Purdy Lounge	3
Raleigh Bar	F
Rok Bar	5
The Room	37
Set	19
Sky Bar	C
Snatch & Suite	46
The Spire Bar	mm
The Standard	J
Ted's Hideaway	
South	32
Twist	60
Van Dyke Café	17
Vice	43
Vino Miami	24
Wet Willie's	66

SOUTH BEACH

51

The Jews of South Beach

The British and the Spanish were all too happy in the eighteenth century to encourage settlement of their new colony by anyone who was willing – even Jews, who can be found in the earliest records of the Sunshine State.

Jews were among Miami Beach's first settlers in the early twentieth century, too – founding **Joe's Stone Crab** restaurant in 1913, for one thing (see p.149 for review) – though they were ghettoised by an edict (supported by the staunchly anti-Semitic **Carl Fisher**) that prevented them buying land north of 5th Street. It wasn't until such laws were loosened after World War II that the local Jewish population exploded, though no local historian can offer a definitive explanation as to why. The most commonly accepted thesis cites the large portion of **soldiers** billeted here in converted hotels for training during the war; many, it's noted, were from New York or elsewhere in the Northeast and a large chunk of them were Jewish. After the war was over, suffering from the condition nicknamed "sand in their shoes," they returned to live in the sunny resort of which they had such fond memories. They were joined by another group made rootless by the same war: **Holocaust survivors**, whose community here was, at one point, the second largest in America.

By the 1970s, the Jewish community reached its peak: it's estimated that ninety percent of South Beach's population was Jewish, largely retirees from the Northeast who'd long spent winters here. Since then, the number has tailed off under pressure from gay gentrification and the increasingly mass appeal of the area, though experts still say that fifteen percent of South Florida's current population is Jewish, making it one of the highest concentrations of Jews in the country.

By the 1980s, South Beach had become a no-go area, shared by geriatric retirees and criminals, many of them undesirables left over from the Mariel Boatlift (see p.92). But the origins of its hip rebirth can be found in a single advertisement from that same era: the first-ever shill in 1982 for Calvin Klein's now iconic underwear. The shot starred the spectacular abs of Olympic pole-vaulter Tom Hintnaus, who posed in nothing but briefs and a tan against a stark white deco roof. The ad piqued his fellow fashionistas' curiosity about the location, and by the end of the decade the eye-popping image had lured German catalog photographers; in turn, they discovered South Beach's unique combination of spectacular early-morning light, rock-bottom prices, and lack of expensive shooting permits.

Those shutterbugs, their models and hangers-on soon started spending extended periods in South Beach (Klein was already a regular and still has a house here). Developers noticed its advantages, too – not to mention the beautiful people who had begun to enjoy them. One of the first groups to decamp to the area in the late 1980s was Miami's **gay community**, which was soon rehabbing the area piecemeal much as the developers were on a larger scale, recreating the resort and its funky, fabulous scene. Even if many in the local gay community have now moved on (especially further up the coast, either to Normandy Isle, p.72, or Fort Lauderdale, p.203), South Beach retains its glossy, glamorous reputation.

The South Beach sandbar

South Beach itself isn't exactly packed with sights and museums, but even the most culture-hungry visitor to Miami should set aside at least an afternoon to make the most of its main draw: the wide golden spit of sand that rims the tip and Atlantic

▲ Pools and palm trees, South Beach

edge of the island. The **beach** is dotted with concessionaires, some linked to nearby hotels and others independently run, but all of which will rent deckchairs and umbrellas for a few bucks; but you don't need to shell out to sunbathe – the strip of sand nearest the sea is public property, so you can throw down a towel anywhere by the ocean's edge, no matter how intimidating the set-up behind it. If driving to the beach, there's ample parking (bring plenty of quarters) though the streetside spaces can fill up quickly, especially at weekends. Handy municipal lots include the multi-story car park on 7th Street at Washington Avenue, though the smaller garage on 13th Street at Collins Avenue is cheaper for longer stays (just $8 maximum for 24 hours).

Along Ocean Drive

You may not see many photo shoots taking place along Ocean Drive at 7am any more, but the early-morning light is still spectacular; it's easy to understand why South Beach became the fashion location of choice in the early 1990s and it's well worth getting up early one morning to enjoy. One of the first hotels to cater to the fashion crowd was the **Park Central** at no. 640, with its signature octagonal porthole windows. It's all too fitting given that the *Park Central* was ground central for glamour when it debuted in 1937 – the Henry Hohauser-designed hulk was a favorite of Clark Gable, Carole Lombard, and Rita Hayworth. Today, the area hotels here are being joined by increasing numbers of condo conversions, as the final few Art Deco shells remaining derelict are spiffed up and sold as luxury lofts – even Italian jeans-maker Diesel, which owns and runs the *Pelican Hotel* here (see p.134 for review) and had planned to turn the onetime *Carlyle Hotel* into its worldwide head-quarters, saw its financial value and instead chose to sell the shell for millions.

The place to strut that well-toned, well-tanned, well-waxed body – man or woman – is **Lummus Park**, bordering Ocean Drive between 5th and 15th streets.

53

It was named after pioneer brothers, J.E. and J.N. Lummus, who ran competing banks in Miami's early days (J.N. was also elected the first mayor of Miami Beach); the Lummus family were also real estate speculators, and sold the waterfront land to the city with the proviso that it always be a public beach – in the process, securing the value of the hotels they owned overlooking it. Although the gleaming beach seems quintessentially Miami, the fine white sand was actually imported from the Bahamas to replace the too-coarse local variety. You can rent deckchairs and umbrellas from one of many concessions on the waterfront, and there are bathrooms and showers on the grassy boardwalk that separates the beach from Ocean Drive. Open-air concerts are often staged here and it's also the site of the throbbing Winter Party each March (see p.173, "Gay Miami"). Notice too the quirky, ornamental lifeguard towers painted in neon colors and designed by local artists including Kenny Scharf – they're a fun addition to the seafront, if rather bedraggled now.

Casa Casuarina

One of the most popular tourist sights on the beach, **Casa Casuarina** (☎305/672-6604, ⓦwww.casacasuarina.com), the former home of murdered designer Gianni Versace, at 1114 Ocean Drive, is not open to the public. The original structure was built in 1930 as a spare-no-expense private home by Alden Freeman; like Florida-loving Henry Flagler (see p.154), his wealth came from Rockefeller's Standard Oil company, though Freeman inherited his millions from family investments in the firm (the free-spending Freeman vowed to die poor, and almost managed it, despite his staggering wealth). Freeman's pad was intended as a replica of the Alcázar de Colón in Santo Domingo, the home built by Christopher Columbus's son in 1510, which is claimed to be the oldest house in the Western Hemisphere. A friend of Freeman's called it Casa Casuarina, or House of the Pine, after a lone casuarina or Australian pine tree that survived 1926's devastating hurricane. Upon Alden's death seven years later, it was sold to one of his friends who chopped it up into apartments; the complex became known as the Amsterdam Palace and limped along until 1992, by which time it was little more than a hovel. Versace, however, saw potential in the place, and snapped up the whole complex; he then transformed it into his dream home, shipping in mosaic artists from Italy and frescoing ceilings with abandon, like a modern counterpart to Hearst Castle in California. Naturally, locals nicknamed it the **Versace Mansion**.

What Versace is most remembered for by history-minded locals, though, was one brazen act of architectural vandalism. Just before a preservation order could be enacted, he also purchased the adjoining *Revere Hotel*, a masterpiece of Miami Modernism, and promptly knocked it down to build a swimming pool and guesthouse (see p.264, "Contexts: Architecture"). That aside, Versace was a popular, easygoing member of the South Beach community, often spotted in local bars and clubs, and his murder on the steps here by serial killer **Andrew Cunanan** in 1997 shattered the safe illusion of South Beach's hedonistic abandon. After his death, the mansion was snapped up by developer Peter Loftin, who's believed to have paid $19 million for the place. In 2004, after years of dithering as to whether he'd open a hotel, a fashion museum, or a club, Loftin finally committed to transforming the place into a jet-set members-only pad: with initiation fees around $20,000, the club failed to catch the jetset's attention. Loftin abandoned the club concept and has resorted to running the place as a boutique hotel, opening up Versace's onetime quarters to anyone willing to shell out $1000 or more a night.

▲ The Albion Hotel

The Art Deco Welcome Center

Headquarters of the Miami Design Preservation League, the **Art Deco Welcome Center** (daily 9.30am–6.30pm; ℡305/672-2014, ⓦwww.mdpl.org) sits at 1001 Ocean Drive on Lummus Park. Located in a jaunty Nautical Deco building, complete with faux smokestack and portholes on its lower decks, it's also the headquarters for the local Beach Patrol. The informative, self-guided audio tours produced by the League are unmissable, plus there's a small free museum that makes a smart starting point for a comprehensive Art Deco tutorial. The League also arranges the Art Deco Weekend each January in the Historic District (see p.196, "Festivals and events").

Washington and Collins avenues

Named in honor of one of Miami Beach's pioneers, **Collins Avenue** (also known as Hwy-A1A) is the main traffic artery running the length of the island and, eventually, north to Fort Lauderdale's beachfront. At its southernmost end, one block west of Ocean Drive, it's crammed with hotels in all price ranges, as well as South Beach's swankiest shopping strip between 5th and 8th streets. Look, too, for the squat, flat-roofed bungalow cobbled together from irregular blocks of the porous local stone on the corner of 9th and Collins: known as the **Coral Rock House**, it is one of the oldest single-family homes on Miami Beach. Built in 1918 by Avery Smith, who operated the first ferry service from the mainland to the beach and is considered by many to be the great grandfather of the city's tourism industry, it was eventually converted to commercial use. The last tenant, a restaurant, decamped in the early 2000s. There was then a monumental tussle between preservationists and developers gimlet-eyed at the value of the land. It's hard to say who won, as the new owner, developer Michael Stern, was granted a permit to lop off the rear portion and level an historic 1920s Mediterranean Revival addition behind the main building. In response, he guaranteed to restore

Decoding Art Deco

Miami became a haven for Art Deco in large part owing to the wrecking power of South Florida's **hurricanes**. In 1926, the city was leveled by a devastating storm, and architects taken with Art Deco rebuilt whole blocks in the newly modish style. Sleek and cheap (a few gallons of poured concrete was all it took), Deco was ideal for developers anxious to throw up fresh hotels as quickly as possible, although shoddy construction methods doomed some treasured buildings to demolition less than fifty years later.

In the mid-1970s, many Art Deco buildings, sound or unsound, were seen as old-fashioned and scheduled to be razed for condo construction – at least they were until one woman, **Barbara Baer Capitman**, began a relentless campaign for their preservation. Thankfully, she succeeded, and in 1979 the 1200-building **Art Deco Historic District** was formally declared in South Beach, which simultaneously gave the once unloved Deco piles cultural status and safety from the wrecking ball.

Art Deco style in general is far from uniform, and one of its core features is a ready absorption of local influences. It's worth nothing, though, that the pastel colors usually associated so strongly with it aren't original; instead the paint schemes were a marketing gimmick Capitman and her chums devised in the 1980s. Originally most buildings were whitewashed, their features picked out in dark brown or navy blue. For more on Miami's architecture and the full story of Capitman's crusade, see Contexts: Architecture (p.261) at the end of this book.

Miami styles

Tropical or **Miami Deco**: Most popular in the 1920s–1930, this is the base style from which all the other local Deco types derive. Look for ornamental **eyebrows** above the windows, the signature mark of Miami Deco, which proved more than decorative as they cast shade to help keep rooms cool in the days before air conditioning (as a rule, the wider the eyebrow, the later the building). Observe, too, **repetitions of three** – windows or columns, for example – as well as **decorative reliefs and murals**, whose frequent palm tree, fountain, and flamingo subject matter localized the style. Even when first constructed, rooms in Deco hotels tended to be sparse and stark,

---

the remainder by early 2010, putting up a $400,000 bond should he miss the deadline.

Whatever the fate of this old coral rock construction, there is at least one other example of Miami Beach pioneer architecture nearby that's in no danger of demolition: the **Coral House**, at 1030 Washington Ave, a further block west from the beach, that's now part of the *Best Western South Beach* complex. It was built in 1922 by French immigrant Henri Levy, who went on to found Normandy Isle (see p.72); the hotel has long said it plans to reopen it as a restaurant but has always declined to confirm a date. Otherwise, Washington Avenue is South Beach's commercial heart, where supermarkets and schools stand alongside nightclubs and cheap cafés. Although the low-rise buildings seem architecturally unappealing, most have simply had their Art Deco features hidden behind false frontage, and are gradually being restored as the strip gentrifies. Even so, Washington Avenue is still as gritty as the Deco district gets, and having a stroll here is a welcome antidote to the vacation atmosphere of the other main drags. It also holds two star attractions: the **Wolfsonian-FIU** and the rotunda-topped local **Post Office**, as well as the unappealing **World Erotic Art Museum**.

Wolfsonian-FIU

Built around a single private collection, **The Wolfsonian**, at 1001 Washington Ave (Sat–Tues noon–6pm, Thurs & Fri noon–9pm; $7, free every Fri 6–9pm;

and expense was focused on common areas. Some of the most typical examples of these reliefs can be found on the Lincoln Theater on Lincoln Road (see p.59), while most of the earlier hotels along Ocean Drive and Collins Avenue display the obsession with three so characteristic of Tropical Deco.

Depression Moderne: This style appeared with the onset of the Great Depression in the 1930s, and was **less ostentatious and ornamental** than its predecessor. Instead of splashing out on the exterior, money was spent more subtly on interior creations like murals and ironwork. The US Post Office (see p.58) is the best example of this style in South Beach; Downtown's Alfred I. Du Pont Building is another outstanding local example (see p.39).

Streamline Deco: Popular 1930s–1940s, Streamline Deco bridges the simplicity of early Deco and the goofy playfulness of Miami Modern (MiMo), the space-age architectural style of the 1950s so obsessed with speed (for more on MiMo, see box on p.73). As in many MiMo designs, the elements of Streamline buildings are designed to give a **feeling of movement**, and the hard edges are **rounded off** – see the adjoining *Cardozo* and *Carlyle* hotels on Ocean Drive (see p.53). A more extreme version of fluid movement is **Nautical Deco**, which uses fake smokestacks, porthole windows, and railings to mimic grand oceangoing liners – see the *Albion Hotel* (see p.132) and the Miami Design Preservation League headquarters at 1001 Ocean Drive.

Mediterranean Revival: Not all local buildings are part of the Deco family, though. In the 1920s–1930s, **Mediterranean Revival** was a contemporary alternative for those who disliked the sleek modernity of Art Deco: about a third of the district's buildings are classified as Mediterranean Revival. Many at the time sniffed that this was how gangsters and movie stars – those with more money than taste – liked to commission houses. Structures in this style are **asymmetrical** to give the impression of organic extension over time, and often have **ornate ironwork** and **tile roofs.** Two strong examples of this style are Casa Casuarina on Ocean Drive (see p.54) and the whole of Española Way (see p.58).

ⓣ305/531-1001, ⓦwww.wolfsonian.org), showcases the vast acquisitions of Mickey Wolfson, heir to a local TV and movie fortune and scion of the Wolfson family. He was one of the pioneers of South Beach's renaissance, and his museum is dedicated to decorative and propaganda arts from 1885 to 1945 – fitting for a resort, like South Beach, that was built half on publicity and half on pretty buildings. Wolfson's trinkets are housed in a solid Mediterranean Revival building that originally served as the headquarters of Washington Storage. This was one of the companies that catered to the wealthier residents of South Beach in the 1920s, stashing the contents of their holiday homes for safekeeping during hurricane season – there are several contemporary photographs in the museum's lobby.

The best sections focus on the dozen or so World's Fairs held in the early twentieth century: the anachronistic propaganda that companies used in such showy pavilions is superbly jarring today. Take, for example, Heinz and its tribal Deco statuary, representing happy natives from the different countries that joyfully contributed ingredients to Heinz's 57 varieties. Another standout is the large collection of political propaganda, including bombastic, highly stylized posters promoting the Fascist cause between the wars. Despite some outstanding individual pieces (look for work by British Arts and Crafts pioneers like William Morris as well as Art Nouveau icon Charles Rennie Mackintosh), the museum's confusingly laid out, with different exhibits muddled together; overall, it is frustrating in its lack of focus. The temporary exhibitions are often high profile and more satisfying; check the website for up-to-date schedules.

Note the 1939 **Bridge Tender's House**, a funky steel hut on the sidewalk in front of the building that was shipped in from the 27th Street Bridge to save it from demolition in the 1980s. It's been used for some time as a home for temporary modern art exhibitions overseen by the museum.

The World Erotic Art Museum

Hidden upstairs on the second floor of a gritty commercial block is **The World Erotic Museum**, 1205 Washington Avenue (daily 11am–midnight; $15; ☎305/532-9336). The cobbled-together set-up is home to the collection of erotic ephemera amassed by a filthy-minded rich widow – Miami's philanthropic answer to Dr Ruth – who's put on show everything from cheeky, bottom-baring Victorian figurines to an example of a pillow book, Japan's calligraphic version of the Kama Sutra. It's such a shame that the impressive holdings are so poorly shown – the WEAM is witless, unsexy and eminently skippable.

United States Post Office

The main branch of Miami Beach's **Post Office** (Mon–Fri 8am–5pm, Sat 8.30am–2pm; ☎305/672-2447, ⓦwww.usps.com), 1300 Washington Ave, is an architectural gem built in 1937 during the Great Depression and funded by the federally funded WPA. Its sweepingly curved Depression Moderne exterior stands out like a smooth, squat turret against the rows of boxy Deco buildings nearby; note the classically inspired touches like the loggia and cupola. During business hours, it's worth stepping inside to see the ornately bombastic metalwork that fills the rotunda, the decoration of the roof with the dome of heaven as well as the geometric murals by realist Charles Hardman, which were added in 1940. The three panels depict the conquest of Florida's Indians, and were only cooked up after Hardman's original plan to showcase the pleasures of the state – boating and beaches, mostly – was dismissed as not dignified enough. Look, too, at the post office boxes in the smaller room behind the loggia: they're original and still feature the fascias of the original alphabetical combination locks.

Española Way

Continue north along Washington Avenue past 14th Place to reach the six-block Mediterranean Revival development known as **Española Way**, or the "Spanish Village Historic District." The popular story is that the street was masterminded by entrepreneur Carl Fisher as an antidote to growing enthusiasm for Art Deco, a concrete statement in favor of the Mediterranean Revival style that he preferred. In fact, the pedestrian strip, a mustard and ochre explosion of narrow alleys and deliberately uneven buildings, was conceived in 1925 as an artists' colony by hotelier Newton Roney, who devised it as Miami's answer to New York's Greenwich Village and Paris's Montmartre. Thanks to the collapse in real estate the next year, Española Way limped along until the arrival of Cuban bandleader Desi Arnaz (later to find fame as the real- and TV-life husband of *I Love Lucy*'s Lucille Ball). Arnaz is the hero of the frequently repeated and self-promoting (if dubious) story that the rumba dance craze of the 1930s kicked off here on Española Way before taking the US by storm. Arnaz is said to have written *The Miami Beach Rhumba* while playing at his home venue here, the *Village Tavern*, located inside the then swanky hotel that is now the *Clay Hostel* (see "Accommodation," p.139).

The strip's at its most aggressively faux-dilapidated between Washington and Drexel avenues, where you'll also want to avoid the cluster of mediocre sidewalk cafés. There's a patchy artisans' **market** here Friday through Sunday (Fri 7pm–midnight, Sat 10am–midnight, Sun 11am–9pm) with rather too many home-made candles for sale, as well as small craft stores and a few artists' studios.

Lincoln Road Mall

Along the northern edge of the Art Deco Historic District stands **Lincoln Road Mall**. Originally laid out in 1912 by pioneer Carl Fisher, it was always intended as Miami Beach's commercial hub. By the 1940s, Lincoln Road was home to upscale department stores like Bonwit Teller and Saks, as well as swanky car showrooms for Fleetwood and LaSalle. But the boom further north on the beach, powered by mega-hotels like the *Fontainebleau* (see p.70), drew upscale shops away; it was only natural for the local council to tap store-designer-turned-architect Morris Lapidus, the man behind the *Fontainebleau*'s opulent design, to revive and rethink the strip here in 1959. Lapidus claimed that he "designed Lincoln Road for people – a car never bought anything," and to do this he pedestrianized six blocks and installed whimsical space-age structures to provide intermittent shade for strolling shoppers. The pricey stores and restaurants trickled back, and for a while it again was "The Fifth Avenue of the South." As South Beach declined in the 1970s, those chi-chi shops dribbled away yet again (they're now mostly in Bal Harbour to the north). Lincoln Road's current renaissance began in the mid-1990s, and the strip is now crammed with trendy restaurants, sidewalk cafés, and boutiques. This is where South Beach struts its stuff every Sunday afternoon – rollerblading, dog-walking, or window-shopping – and the place has arguably replaced Ocean Drive as the local heart of the area.

The mall itself is bookended by two Art Deco theaters: the sleek, low-rise **Colony Theater**, no. 1040, and the pristine **Lincoln Theater**, no. 541, home of the always reliable New World Symphony (see p.168, "Performing arts and film"). The Lincoln, especially, has some remarkable Tropical Deco reliefs, featuring far-out, triffid-like palm trees painted in deep shades of green; the interior, sadly, retains few of its original features.

One of the quirkier attractions on Lincoln Road, the **Art Center of South Florida** at nos. 800, 810, and 924 (studios daily 11am–10pm; ℡305/674-8278, ⓌWwww.artcentersf.org), was founded in 1984 when real estate prices had hit rock bottom. This collective spreads across three buildings and provides 52 studios for artists and sculptors: alongside traditional painters, you'll find plenty of edgier works in mixed media, photography, and even textiles. Each artist works and exhibits on site, so feel free to wander around the studios or stop by the official gallery space at no. 800 – the work's better than its now highly commercial location might suggest.

North of Lincoln Road

Stepping **north of Lincoln Road** and beyond the Art Deco Historic District, you'll find that the sights thin out as the buildings become larger, more eclectic and ramshackle. The Deco-esque hotels along upper Collins Avenue, like the swirly *Shelborne* at no. 1801 and Ian Schrager's *Delano* at no. 1685, with its Aztec headdress-like turret, were constructed later – and are therefore larger and more space age – than their counterparts further south. Some of their playful architectural flourishes are precursors of the style known as Miami Modern (MiMo) that would explode after World War II. Nowadays, this upper end of Collins Avenue in South Beach is home to many of the best bars in town, and has usurped Ocean Drive's position as the place to party.

A block inland, at 1700 Washington Ave, just above 17th Street, stands **The Fillmore Miami Beach at the Jackie Gleason Theater of Performing Arts** (T305/673-7300, W www.livenation.com). Originally the Miami Beach Auditorium, it was renamed in honor of the star of the classic TV show *The Honeymooners* after his death in 1987. Comedian Gleason was lured down to Miami by Hank Meyer, who was in charge of Miami's publicity in the 1960s. Meyer knew Gleason was tired of New York's long winters and had a passion for golfing, so he worked with the CBS network to bring Gleason and his entourage down to the city in a blaze of publicity. It worked and from 1964, *The Jackie Gleason Show* was filmed here, acting as little more than a weekly primetime advert for the joys of life in South Florida. Gleason's show was canceled after five seasons, so in the 1970s, Morris Lapidus was tasked with transforming his auditorium into a performing arts theatre. For decades, the Gleason was home to Broadway touring shows and tryouts, before the new mainland Arsht Center (see p.169) siphoned away its commercial lifeblood. In 2007, the 2600-seater space was reinvented as a rock venue, and renamed the Fillmore, a nod to the iconic San Francisco spot new owners Live Nation are intending to clone across the country. One thing remains from its Lapidus-era renovation: the sexy, abstract sculpture *Mermaid* in front of the main entrance with its blonde ponytail, the work of pop art pioneer Roy Lichtenstein.

Opposite the Fillmore is the grand **Temple Emanu–El** synagogue, 1701 Washington Avenue (T305/538-2503, W www.tesaboe.org), whose savvy rabbi snatched headlines in 2007 when he tried auctioning off the lifetime rights to front row seats at the 1400 capacity space online (starting bid, $1.8m). It was a smart way to juice attendance for a congregation that had been dwindling since its thousands-strong peak in the 1940s. Rabbi Kliel Rose not only offered seats 1 and 2 in row 1, but bundled the package with free parking, custom-made prayer shawls and yarmulkes, and, of course, the tax write-off. Rabbi Rose managed to nab headlines but, despite eleven thousand hits, not a buyer for the two VIP seats.

A couple of blocks north, at 1901 Convention Center Drive, are the massive white walls of the **Miami Beach Convention Center** (T305/673-7311). This was once a premier venue for prestige exhibitions, although it's now long been bypassed by newer, warehouse-like convention centers elsewhere. It was here that Richard Nixon received the Republican Presidential nomination in August 1968, just as Miami's racial tensions finally flared into violence with the Liberty City riots (see p.47).

Further north, the cramped offices of the **Miami Beach Chamber of Commerce** (Mon–Fri 9am–6pm, Sat & Sun 10am–4pm; T305/672-1270, W www.miamibeachguestservices.com), 1920 Meridian Ave, offers maps and details on tours of the area, although it's often easier to stop by the Miami Design Preservation League's Art Deco Welcome Center on Ocean Drive (see p.55).

The Holocaust Memorial

A visit to the **Holocaust Memorial** just blocks from the sidewalk cafés and jostling crowds of Lincoln Road, at 1933–1945 Meridian Ave (daily 9am–9pm; free; T305/538-1663, W www.holocaustmmb.org), is a contemplative, sobering experience. Its presence here is a reflection of the large number of Holocaust survivors who chose to make Miami Beach their home.

Graphic and unflinching, the memorial centers on a sculpture by Tony Lopez; it's a massive, cast bronze hand stretched in desperate supplication to the sky, reaching up through a cluster of dozens of agonized human figures that tumble from, and cling to, the arm like spindly insects. The attention to detail here is astonishing, from the memorial's address noting the years of European persecution of the Jews last century to the Auschwitz ID number tattooed to the sculpture – Lopez was careful to choose a fictitious one.

To reach his central sculpture, visitors pass through curved black granite colonnades, etched with archive photographs that pull no punches in their depiction of concentration camp horrors, then down a darkened tunnel that echoes with the voices of modern Israeli children singing songs from the Holocaust era. The dark walls around the hand are filled with the names of those who died in the death camps. The memorial is bracketed by two eloquent sculptures: it begins with a depiction of a mother protecting her two fearful children, punctuated by a quote from *The Diary of Anne Frank*: "… that in spite of everything I still believe that people are really good at heart." As you exit, there lie the original mother and children, now dead, accompanied again by Anne's words: "… ideals, dreams and cherished hopes rise within us only to meet the horrible truths and be shattered."

The Bass Museum of Art

The only fine art museum on Miami Beach, the **Bass Museum of Art** (Tues–Sat 10am–5pm, Sun 11am–5pm; $8; ☎305/673-7350, ⓦwww.bassmuseum.org), 2121 Park Ave, began as the local public library when a bunch of local socialites donated a few hundred books to the city. It later became a museum to house the private collection of European art accumulated by local bigwigs John and Johanna Bass, who donated the place to the city in 1963. The Bass has long been housed in a stark, temple-like 1930 Art Deco building designed by Russell Pancoast, the architect grandson of beach pioneer John Collins, whose family also gave their name to nearby Lake Pancoast (see p.69). When further exhibition space was needed for the Basses' 3000-strong holdings, Pancoast himself was recruited for the extension, ensuring a harmonious design; he built the south and north wings in 1937 and 1950 respectively. Japanese architect Arata Isozaki was brought in for an expansion project in the 1990s intended to triple the display space while uniting the museum with the Miami City Ballet (see p.169, "Performing arts and film") and the local library to form the **Miami Beach Cultural Park**. Isozaki's swooping white box with its wide central ramp was grafted unobtrusively onto the Park Avenue side of the plot, and is an ideal exhibition venue.

It's a shame the holdings themselves are so hit and miss. At first glance, the collection seems studded with star names like Jordaens and Van Dyck; but most are represented by minor or studio works – even Rubens' much admired *Holy Family* is disappointing, as much the work of his assistants as the master himself. Standouts include the sixteenth-century Flemish tapestry *The Tournament*; a notable drawing collection with gems by Daumier and Toulouse-Lautrec; and a sunny altarpiece jointly painted by Ghirlandaio and Botticelli. The temporary exhibitions are far more impressive, ranging from a recent review of the architects who shaped Miami Beach's skyline to paintings, sculpture, and furniture from the Art Deco period in Paris.

South Pointe

Towards the tip of the island, **South Pointe** is pimpled with high-rises you won't see elsewhere in South Beach, owing to sluggish preservation orders that allowed developers to bulldoze buildings at will: the first of these high-rises, South Pointe Towers, has been joined by several more, approved before new zoning laws came into effect.

South of Fifth (or "SoFi" as local real estate agents have taken to calling it) was originally the city's Jewish ghetto since Fifth Street marked the northernmost point where Jews could buy housing. By the late 1980s, though, it had been taken over by crack houses and criminals, spurred by the arrival of undesirables in the wake of the Mariel Boatlift. For this reason, gentrification has proceeded more slowly than elsewhere in South Beach, and it's a still a little rawer than the manicured streets further north. There are many unpleasant examples of late 1980s Neo-Deco garishness – angular concrete buildings in turquoise, ochre, and raspberry, conjuring an image of Art Deco with shoulder pads. Even so, it's worth checking out one notable old building, the former **Brown's Hotel** at 112 Ocean Drive, now home to hip steakhouse *Prime 112* (see p.150, "Restaurants"). This small, boxy 1915 structure was the first hotel built on Miami Beach. When it was restored in 2001, the new owners moved it a few feet west of the original site and, in the process, helped dispel a long-held local legend that *Brown's* was built on top of a shipwreck; no relics of any kind were found.

At the end of Washington Avenue, there's a pleasant waterfront greenspace, **South Pointe Park** (daily 8am–sunset), with wide lawns and good facilities that's a sleepy place to pass the afternoon; it's worth stopping by on Friday evenings when its open-air stage is the venue for enjoyable free **music events** (details are posted up around South Beach). **Surfers** should note that the waves here are widely regarded as the best in the area.

The park looks out over **Government Cut**, a waterway first dredged by Henry Flagler in the nineteenth century to create easy access to the growing Port of Miami. In so doing, he amputated the southernmost tip of South Beach to create exclusive **Fisher Island** (see p.64). The waterway has been substantially deepened since then, and is now the main route by which Miami's endless parade of cruise ships on the Caribbean circuit reach the main harbor. Even these days, you might also witness an impounded drug-running vessel being towed along by the authorities. Don't be surprised, either, to hear the neighing of horses: Miami Beach's police horses are stabled on the eastern side of the park.

The Sanford L. Ziff Jewish Museum of Florida

Housed in a deconsecrated Art Deco synagogue at 301 Washington Ave, the **Sanford L. Ziff Jewish Museum of Florida** (Tues–Sun 10am–5pm; $6, free on Saturdays; ☎305/672-5044, ⓦwww.jewishmuseum.com) commemorates the history of Jews in Florida from the late 1600s until today. Finished in 1936, the building is one of architect Henry Hohauser's earliest local projects, and has been lovingly restored, including the eye-catching Moorish-style copper dome.

In addition to temporary shows, the building houses a permanent exhibition that's compact, but so crammed with information that it's overwhelming in its thoroughness; make sure to ask one of the many docents bobbing around the building to take you on an informal tour – they're extremely knowledgeable and friendly. Though the early documents and photographs are interesting enough, the museum's at its strongest when exposing how recently anti-Semitism continued unchecked in South Beach, with hotel signs from the 1950s that guaranteed guests "Always a view, never a Jew" (prejudice that is even more astonishing given that Mitchell Wolfson, father of Wolfsonian museum-founder Mickey, had been elected mayor of the city in 1941). One of the most awkwardly poignant documents is a brief letter written in 1929 by the mayor of St Louis to Carl Fisher: in it, he asks Fisher if he would get "his best friend of Earth, Mr. William Lewin," courtesy in his golf club. The mayor goes on to write that he would be "everlastingly grateful," as he knows that, "on account of [Lewin's] nationality," it could be a problem. For more on the history of the Jews in South Beach, see the box on p.52.

The Islands

Miami Beach is surrounded by dozens of small islands, most of them man-made and residential like **Fisher Island** and unlikely to detain a casual visitor; the exception is recently redeveloped **Watson Island**, site of both the Miami Children's Museum and Jungle Island (formerly known as Parrot Jungle) and soon home to the swishy condo-marina combo known as Island Gardens. And though there are no specific sights on islands like **Star** and **Palm**, it is there that wealthy South Beachers live undisturbed, and a drive through these or the chain of **Venetian Islands** shows what everyday life is like, far from the boutiques and hotels of Ocean Drive.

Many expected this isolation to change with the arrival of hotelier Andre Balazs' spa-meets-celebrity retreat, *The Standard Miami*, although that hotel's proved less of a hipster magnet than anticipated, and the Venetian Islands remain largely overlooked by visitors. In fact, the last time the islands here made major headlines was over twenty-five years ago, when art stuntmaster **Christo** wrapped eleven of them in 200-foot-wide bright pink plastic skirts for two weeks in 1983 – a project he called *Surrounded Islands*.

It's tough to reach any but Watson Island by **public transport** and there are no official tours; instead, you'll need a car or moped to cruise along the Venetian or MacArthur causeways and to explore the hushed, mansion-lined streets.

The Venetian Islands and the Flagler Memorial Monument

This necklace of six islands is threaded together by the Venetian Causeway toll road; what's now the Causeway was originally the site of the Collins Bridge, the first permanent connection between the beach and the mainland, built in 1913. The Causeway now runs between five neat artificial islands – **Rivo Alto**, **DiLido**, **San Marino**, **San Marco**, and **Biscayne** – as well as the raggedy but natural **Belle Isle** (picturesquely renamed from the original Bull Isle). There's little to see on any of them other than the exteriors of upscale private residences, but a casual drive along the Causeway is a pleasant detour (plus it's a great place for jogging) – while their names serve as yet another example of Miami's glaring obsession with Venice.

Just south of the Venetian cluster, the **Flagler Memorial Monument** sits on its own specially constructed island, a byproduct of the extensive dredging nearby during the late 1910s. The sculpture was commissioned in 1920 by Carl Fisher in memory of the father of Miami, railroad magnate Henry Flagler; with this gesture, Fisher hoped to align himself with Flagler's hallowed memory. The monument consists of four giant statues representing Industry, Prosperity, Education, and Pioneering, who stand looking out over the water, their backs to an enormous obelisk. While money has been set aside for restoration, the statues remain in bad shape, missing chunks of their faces or hands, and riven with deep cracks thanks to pollution, neglect, and vandalism; its profile hasn't been helped by the fact that it's impossible to visit without a private boat.

Palm, Hibiscus, Star, and Fisher islands

While **Palm** and **Hibiscus** islands were dredged expressly for luxury housing in the early twentieth century, **Star Island** was initially designed to house the Miami Beach Yacht Club and was only converted to residential use in the 1920s. Certainly prime real estate now, they are crammed with swanky private homes. Residents of the aptly named Star Island include loud-mouthed Rosie O'Donnell; renaissance man-cum-vodka spokesperson Diddy; and expat Cuba's answer to Prince Charles and Lady Di, Emilio and Gloria Estefan.

As for Palm Island, its most infamous ex-resident is Al Capone, who snagged a lavish house here by using a local lawyer as his frontman for the purchase; Capone finally succumbed to syphilis here in 1947. All three islands are public and accessible from MacArthur Causeway – just tell the gatekeeper that you're sightseeing and he should let you through, although the high fences and thick hedges around most of the homes means there's little to see.

Fisher Island, just across Government Cut, has always been the poshest of all the islands. In the 1920s, Carl Fisher sold it to William Vanderbilt and his wife Rosamund, who built a spectacular winter estate here. It's passed through several hands since then, and is now an exclusive resort, virtually inaccessible to anyone other than hotel guests or full-time residents of the condo developments and then only by boat (℡305/535-6000, ⓦwww.fisherisland.com).

Watson Island

Eighty-six-acre **Watson Island** has been transformed with the arrival of two high-profile attractions, **Jungle Island** and the **Miami Children's Museum**. Before then, it was an embarrassing eyesore for the city, known mostly as a landing area for seaplanes and haven for local vagrants. The current city plan to scrap the seaplane terminal and replace it with a luxury development known as **Island Gardens**, complete with hotel and mooring space for mega-yachts, faced fierce opposition from locals, who claimed what was left should remain open parkland. They failed, and the $600 million project, including two hotels and a public park (a sop to those opponents), should be completed by late 2009. Note that there's plentiful, if pricey parking, on the island if you're coming by car. Otherwise, you can catch **bus** #S, #K, or #C from either Downtown or South Beach.

Jungle Island

Jungle Island (daily 10am–6pm; $28, ages 3–10 $23, parking $7; ℡305/258-6453, ⓦwww.jungelisland.com) started life as a bird park known as Parrot Jungle. It was opened in 1936 by Franz Scherr, a parrot-loving Austrian immigrant, who – inspired by Monkey Jungle (see p.124) – rented some land in South Miami and bought two dozen squawky macaws for display. Seventy years later, Scherr's brainchild moved to this spot and was rechristened Jungle Island, befitting its expanded site and attractions (the old location, filled with lush vegetation, has been converted into a public park, see p.122). This aviary-cum-gardens is now a sprawling, zoo-like attraction, home not only to three thousand parrots but also to five hundred or so other creatures, including monkeys and reptiles. Although the

▲ Flamingos at Jungle Island

smooth walkways and antiseptic foliage of the new site lack some of the original's haphazard charm, it's still a must-see, thanks largely to the moody, gaudy birds who always seem to be staring straight at you while they sit, in cages or open feed cones, waiting for you to hand them morsels (25 cents from dispensers around the park) – the tingly sensation of their eager, leathery tongues grasping for treats is a memorable, if bizarre, part of the package.

The Manu Encounter is supposed to replicate a wild Peruvian mountainside, said to have the highest bio-diversity on earth, though the scratchy windows on the enclosure somewhat dampens its rugged effects. Better is the replica of the Everglades habitat, with plants floating in the water like a sea of grass and local fauna hanging about; look for the rare albino alligator that looks like it was molded from white chocolate. There are warm water African penguins, too, as well as a private beach with play area if younger ones' attention wanders. The hokey shows at the onsite arenas are worth a stop, not for creaky tricks like a bicycling parrot, but to see some of the larger birds, including a vulture and a deadly cassowary from Australia. Sporting a dayglo blue head, red wattle and black body, one jugular-aimed swipe of the bird's razor sharp claws can fell any human. Jungle Island's

65

most enduring sight is a little more peaceful – its vast flock of tame, candy-colored flamingos that stand motionless in a specially built pond.

Ichimura Miami-Japan Garden

East of Jungle Island's multi-story car park sits the rebuilt **Ichimura Miami-Japan Garden**, best known for its fat laughing statue of the god Hotei. Managed by Jungle Island, but separate from it and free to enter, the garden itself – all stone lanterns and boulders – is wrapped in a cocoon of concrete for tranquility's sake. The Hotei sculpture sits outside the wall, facing the Causeway, chuckling at the passing cars. Note that the flora here, aside from a few bonsai and some black bamboo, isn't indigenous to Japan; rather it's a next-best recreation amid Miami's tropical climate though it's a frustrating experience for anyone but expert botanists, since there isn't a single placard or label indicating which plant is which. Even so, the gurgling water noise tinkling around the greenspace makes this a soothing place to linger away from the roaring freeway next door.

Miami Children's Museum

Housed in a building designed by local firm Arquitectonica, the new **Miami Children's Museum** (daily 10am–6pm; $10; $1/hour parking; ☏305/373-5437, ⊛www.miamichildrensmuseum.org), 980 MacArthur Causeway, sits like a row of jagged white teeth studded with cavity-like portholes on the southern edge of Watson Island. It's an ideal place to distract younger children for an afternoon, with exhibits aimed firmly at the pre-school crowd. The displays themselves are impressive, including a bank where you can design your own currency and a farm-cum-supermarket, where youngsters harvest produce and then follow its path to the store. The dress-up box for would-be showgirls and boys is a delight, as is the world music studio, which encourages kids to discover musicians and instruments from other countries. While kids may not notice, their guardians may be put off by the fact that everything in sight blares with corporate sponsorship – even the Emergency Room is branded by a local hospital. To burn off any excess energy, head for the central atrium's Castle of Dreams, a mosaic-encrusted house bursting with slides and tunnels.

Central Miami Beach

and north

A rt Deco and all-night parties give way to Modernism and massive tower blocks as South Beach settles out into **Miami Beach** proper. Although many visitors rarely stray up Collins Avenue past 23rd Street, there's plenty to see here – notably some fine mid-century, so-called MiMo architecture – even if the sights are more scattered than in South Beach. One sure-fire reason to brave the trek, though, is for the beaches: the strips of sand here are uniformly wider, cleaner, and better maintained than the scraps packed with people at the southern tip.

This chapter covers a necklace of confusingly named neighborhoods, strung one after the other along the artery of **Collins Avenue**, which runs the entire length of the Miami Beach sandbar. The forty blocks from 23rd to 63rd streets form what's known as **Central Miami Beach** (also sometimes known as Middle Beach): this area is home to a mix of mid-century hotels and monolithic condo complexes. Between 63rd Street and 87th Terrace, **North Beach** is increasingly recognized for its collection of fine Miami Modernist buildings, including the cluster on the old world–obsessed **Normandy Isle**. An unfussy but unremarkable ten-block middle-class settlement of shops and bungalows, **Surfside** collides with the toniest local spot **Bal Harbour**, home to the namesake luxury mall, housed in a decidedly un-chic concrete center. Beyond the shops lie the nude beaches at **Haulover Park**, plus the most sumptuous sands on the island, unfortunately located in the onetime package-holiday destination of **Sunny Isles Beach**, which has aggressively remade itself as a luxury-by-numbers hideaway. Continuing on, Collins Avenue passes through **Golden Beach**, the northernmost community on the sandbar, before eventually reaching Fort Lauderdale (see Chapter 21).

Central Miami Beach

Though it wouldn't develop to its extent until after South Beach, **Central Miami Beach** was in fact settled first. In the 1920s and 1930s, the oceanfront here, especially north of what's now 44th Street, boasted multimillion-dollar mansions owned by rich families like the Firestone Tire clan. But these sprawling estates were demolished in the 1950s to make way for condos and grand hotels. Those hotels presented Rat Pack celebrities like Frank Sinatra and Sammy Davis Jr an A-list hangout in what was then a true seafront Vegas, whether they were performing

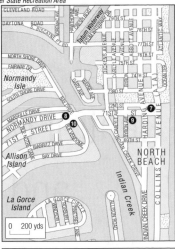

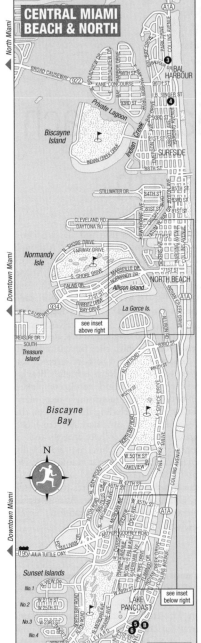

CENTRAL MIAMI BEACH & NORTH

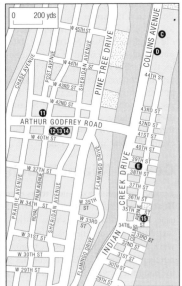

EATING		ACCOMMODATION	
Arnie & Richie's Deli	11	Circa 39	E
Buenos Aires Bakery	7	Days Hotel	
Café Prima Pasta	9	Thunderbird Resort	A
The Food Gang	4	Eden Roc	C
The Forge	14	The Fontainebleau	D
Lemon Twist	10	Gansevoort South	B
Miami Juice	1		
Mr Chopstik	12		
Rascal House	2	**DRINKING & NIGHTLIFE**	
Santa Fe News		Café Nostalgia	15
& Coffee	3	Glass at The Forge	13
Talula	6	Mokaï	5
Tamarind Thai	8		

or vacationing. When the smart set moved on, housing here split between two groups: Latin expats looking for *pied-à-terres* and seniors wanting to spend their last years soaking up the sun. Inevitably, this diminished the area's vibrancy, and it's only now that Central Miami Beach is starting to warm up again as a holiday destination.

This underappreciated area is where the **Miami Modern**, or MiMo (MY-moe), style first flourished; it's at its fiercely whimsical best in places like the *Fontainebleau Hilton* and *Eden Roc* hotels (for more on MiMo, see box, p.73). The value of these and other buildings has been recognized with the creation of the **John S. Collins Oceanfront Historic District** between 22nd and 44th streets, bestowing the same protection (if not prestige) on landmarks here as in South Beach's Art Deco Historic District. North from here, above 44th Street, Collins Avenue continues on through what's known as **Condo Canyon**, an endless row of residential skyscrapers, brightly colored but architecturally bland, eventually crossing 63rd Street, the northern boundary of Central Miami Beach.

Lake Pancoast

Miami Beach's next trendy drag is the formerly dormant **23rd Street**; it's now home to clubs like *Mokaï* (see p.163), and abuts the beach's newest clutch of hotels like the *Gansevoort South* (see p.134) and a soon-to-open *W*. Just north is the easily overlooked **Lake Pancoast**, a puddle of water between 24th and 26th streets that was crucial for pioneer settler John S. Collins. He faced a problem when growing avocados and mangoes on his plantation here: shipping. So he took what was marshy land and burrowed through it from Indian Creek across the sandbar. He called the new waterway Lake Pancoast after his son-in-law, Thomas; later, the Collins-Pancoast families built their mansions here, overlooking the lake – those buildings are sadly long gone. Lake Pancoast's waters flow into the Collins Canal and from there, out into Biscayne Bay.

Pine Tree Drive and North Bay Road

West of Collins Avenue, across the intracoastal waterway of Indian Creek from Lake Pancoast, sit the mansions of Miami Beach's old-money families, on and around **Pine Tree Drive**. This was one of the first areas to be tamed when Europeans settled on the beach and is named for the windbreak of Australian pines that one of those settlers, John S. Collins, planted here upon his arrival.

Though Pine Tree is the main drag through this residential area, visitors will be far more interested in **North Bay Road**, a few blocks west. This is where many of the boldface names who call Miami home – at least part-time – have bought mansions, and though there are no publicly organized tours here, there's also nothing to stop a casual visitor cruising up and down the streets here to check out the manses. North Bay Road between 40th and 60th streets is known as **Millionaires Music Row**, as there's barely a house that isn't owned by a major pop star – at least on the west side. It's a must-live option for two reasons: the spectacular sunset-facing views and the fact that the eastern mansions are overlooked by that crowd of towers in Condo Canyon, where apartments can easily be rented by pesky paparazzi.

Past Bay Road residents here have included Jennifer Lopez, who offloaded her house at No. 5800 for $13.9 million nine months after marrying Marc Anthony; Michael Jackson spent chunks of time holed up at no. 5930, known as "Whitehall" in his post-Neverland era; while Calvin Klein's pad, a surprisingly modest ochre-and-brown house on the 4400 block, was once owned by singer Ricky Martin. Two other remaining residents: the surviving Bee Gees, who still live in homes either side of Lopez's old manse. Close by, the four artificial

Sunset Islands are also popular with celebrities like Lenny Kravitz and Anna Kournikova.

Forty-first Street

It was on the site of what's now **41st Street** that Collins established his first plantation, growing potatoes, avocados, and bananas, though there's no evidence of his early farm today. Instead, the strip is the heart of Miami Beach's Jewish community – tagged, ironically enough, Arthur Godfrey Road in honor of the 1940s radio personality, a notorious anti-Semite (a hotel he co-owned in Bal Harbour, the now-demolished *Kenilworth*, had a sign informing guests: "No dogs or Jews allowed"). Today, 41st Street is dotted with kosher restaurants and neighborhood stores, busiest on a Saturday when the local orthodox community gathers for temple. Stop by **Arnie & Richie's Deli** for a true taste of the local flavor (see review, p.142): open for more than fifty years in the same spot, it's one of the few survivors of the many New York–style kosher cafés that once littered Miami Beach and catered to its huge Jewish population.

The Fontainebleau and the Eden Roc Hotel

One of the masterpieces of Miami Modernism, **the Fontainebleau** (T305/538-2000, Wwww.fontainebleau.com), 4441 Collins Ave, resembles a giant white space-station perched on the beach. Designed by store-dresser-turned-architect **Morris Lapidus** (who called his style "the architecture of joy") and opened in 1954 on the site of the former Harvey Firestone mansion, the central chateau building was loathed by critics at the time for its swooping, curved wings and outlandish decoration.

Despite the architectural drubbing, the hotel quickly became ground zero for glamour: it snagged big-name stars as guests – including Judy Garland and Elvis Presley – as well as making cameos in the hottest movies (the James Bond classic *Goldfinger*, for one). Frank Sinatra, a regular visitor, had a suite permanently set aside for his use. Besides reliably brattish movie-star behavior – starting a scrambled-egg fight in the coffee shop and hurling deckchairs off his balcony – he also shot many scenes here as the private-eye hero of the Sixties classic *Tony Rome*.

Though its gleaming white facade is still much as Lapidus intended, the building's interior suffered greatly over the years from aggressive modernization. A recent renovation – estimates put the amount anywhere between $500 million and $1 billion – has restored much of the interior's tarnished glory, albeit with more than a dash of Vegas glitz. The 22-acre site has been completely overhauled, with owner Jeffrey Soffer joking that only the concrete remained from its previous incarnation. Soffer's makeover has included closing long-time cabaret spot *Club Tropigala* to replace it with a thumping nightclub run by the same team as *Pure* in Las Vegas; tweaking the pools to make them more adult-friendly (gone is the massive fibreglass octopus known as Cookie who'd loomed over the kids' play area); and renovating common areas to emphasize Lapidus's original touches. The brutal 1970s escalators that once dominated the entranceway have been torn out, and its focal point is once again the *terrazzo* floor, patterned with Lapidus's trademark bow ties, as well as the immense, Belgian glass chandeliers.

The original hotel is the comma-shaped structure now known as the Chateau building. Two condo towers to the south, approved by Lapidus just before his death in 2001, have joined the Chateau; he called them the exclamation points to his original design. The so-called Spite Wall to the north was also set to be demolished in favor of a third addition, but it received a last-minute reprieve (see box opposite). Little wonder Lapidus loved those showy towers – his aesthetic was

Towering ego

Morris Lapidus's half-moon-shaped main hotel was actually built on the instructions of original **Fontainebleau** owner **Ben Novack**, but Lapidus – never a shrinking violet – was all too happy to take credit for its innovation. The two new condo towers that were added to that structure aren't, in fact, the first additions – that distinction goes to the 17-story northern wing tacked on in the 1960s. And the reasons behind its construction – as much emotional as financial – offer a clear glimpse of the larger-than-life characters of Lapidus and Novack.

Ben Novack was, by all accounts, a tricky boss, and few lasted long in his employ. An exception was his right-hand man, **Harry Mufson**, who secretly bought the patch of land immediately to the north of the hotel and tapped then-rising star Lapidus to design a hot new rival to the *Fontainebleau*, an ocean-liner-inspired design intended to trump his past masterpiece. Mufson's mischievous plan worked perfectly: after opening in 1956, his **Eden Roc** was the venue for Elizabeth Taylor's birthday bash, and Jayne Mansfield honeymooned in one of its suites.

Incensed, the ornery Novack had an ingenious and equally vengeful response. He put up the monstrous **tower** on the *Fontainebleau*'s northern edge, instructing his new architect – Lapidus refused to be involved – that every guestroom should face south. That way, he reasoned, there would be nothing but a massive concrete wall abutting the *Eden Roc*; and even better, Novack's tower would block the sun from reaching the newer hotel's lavish new pool. Mufson sued and lost; there was (and, in fact, still is) no law protecting access to sunlight in Florida. Instead, the city allowed him special permission to build a second pool closer to the beach out of shadow's reach.

Ironically, standing near to the *Eden Roc*'s so-called sundeck pool is the best way to see the nastiest touch in Novack's so-called "Spite Wall": five tiny windows cut into the beachfront corner of the top two floors. They mark the site of his own apartment and allowed him alone to look down on the cheeky upstart hotel. Novack's petty hulk was almost pulled down by the hotel's new owner, developer Jeffrey Soffer, as part of his mega-makeover: he wanted to replace it with a soaring glass tower and was granted permission to level the building. Thankfully, though for history-minded locals, economics intervened: Soffer underestimated the construction costs of his new tower by $150 million and to save the extra dollars, decided to let the original building stand.

driven not just by excess but also by a sense of theater. A trademark touch was the way he incorporated unnecessary staircases into his buildings to enable "grand entrances" – look for one example leading from the left of the lobby to the mezzanine balcony that was often used by ballgown-clad debutantes in the hotel's heyday (their escorts simply took the elevator directly to the main floor).

The nearby **Eden Roc** hotel, 4525 Collins Ave (☎305/531-0000 or 1-800/327-8337, ⓦwww.edenrocresort.com), is another curvy Lapidus confection, crowned with a giant green sign intended to ape the smokestack of an ocean liner. The *Eden Roc*, too, is finally receiving some architectural TLC, a $110 million makeover focusing largely on the rooms; its lobby has been snappily restored to its original design, and its sunken sofas are a slinky throwback to the times of the Rat Pack. There are also plans to add a contemporary tower that will enlarge the hotel by three hundred or so rooms; for reviews of these hotels, see p.137, "Accommodation."

Indian Creek

In Central Miami Beach, Collins Avenue skirts along the edge of the wide, peaceful intracoastal waterway known as **Indian Creek**. The boats grow larger as you travel further north, like ocean-bound answers to the luxury condos that overlook them.

It was on one of these moored houseboats that **Andrew Cunanan**, the serial killer who murdered Gianni Versace in 1997 (see p.54), was found dead from a self-inflicted gunshot wound. To avoid ghoulish profiteering, the boat itself was seized by the city for demolition – although not before the owner's onsite manager was able to offer impromptu crime-scene souvenirs for sale to passers-by.

Despite this bloody incident, the canal is a soothingly calm place; the shady benches dotted regularly along the grassy path make for a glorious, lazy stroll by the water. It's also the site of one of Miami's most exciting and unusual residential developments: **Aqua** (Ⓦwww.aqua.net), on lozenge-shaped Allison Island on the creek's northern tip. Taste-making real estate magnate Craig Robins – who first promoted South Beach and then revived the Design District (see p.83) – built this urban utopia a couple of years ago, handily gated to keep out the riff-raff (though visitors shouldn't have a problem sneaking a look around). To design this brand-new village, Robins tapped boldfaced architectural names like Hariri & Hariri, Walter Chatham, and Alison Spear; there are low-rise condo clusters as well as individually designed single-family homes plus the public art for which he's become known. The showstopper is Richard Tuttle's massive mural *Splash* along the side of Chatham's building, a massive Jackson Pollock–style painting: it looks as if a giant object landed in a pool of multicolored paint and left giant spatters all up the side of the gleaming white building nearby.

North Beach and Normandy Isle

By the end of the 1980s, the area between 63rd Street and 87th Terrace, or **North Beach**, began absorbing those who'd been economically or socially expelled from the newly cool South Beach. They brought with them social problems of their own as crime rates rose and the infrastructure of this working class community frayed. Now North Beach is at last picking up, thanks to aggressive investment in businesses and buildings. There are also some good restaurants around the area's heart at **71st Street**, as well as a huge oceanfront park and a new beachfront boardwalk.

Another reason for renewed interest is that the area offers the densest concentration of **MiMo architecture** anywhere in the city, from hotels to apartment complexes and even single-family homes. Preservationists recently scored a triumph when eight blocks of the eastern side of Collins Avenue from 63rd to 71st streets were designated the North Beach Resort Historic District. This area includes masterpieces like the **Sherry Frontenac** hotel at 65th and Collins, with its jazzy neon signs, and the stone-grill-fronted **Golden Sands** at 69th and Collins. Sadly, such conservation efforts came too late to protect the **Carillon**, a MiMo gem at 69th and Collins – it has been hollowed out and turned into upscale condos; at least the Carillon's original sign was preserved, as were the weird holes in the overhang of its rooftop in the main building. In fact, the architect's original plan for the place called for bells to hang in those holes, but the developer's money ran out and the bells were never cast. Just outside the district stands **Ocean Terrace**, a two-block slice of low-rise MiMo buildings between 73rd and 75th streets.

Head west across the 71st Street Bridge to find the buzziest spot around here, **Normandy Isle**. It's home to a swelling number of gentrification-minded gays, many refugees from increasingly mainstream South Beach drawn here by its fine **MiMo buildings** like the salmon-colored Bayside Apartments, 910 Bay Drive, or the complex at 125–135 North Shore Drive, its angular entrance looking like two snaggle-toothed incisors. Normandy Isle was developed by a Frenchman, Henri

Woggles. Cheeseholes. Delta fins. Pylons. Not the names of future NFL teams, these are the most prominent design touches that distinguish **Miami Modernism**, or MiMo. This umbrella term for local mid-century buildings was only coined in 1999 by preservationists hoping to call attention to the clusters of long-overlooked buildings they were then fighting to save, much as Barbara Baer Capitman had crusaded on behalf of Art Deco three decades earlier (see p.56).

These particular 1950s and early 1960s structures have the same clean lines and graphic shapes of their contemporaries across the country. But what sets Miami Modernism apart are the heat- and beach-specific touches: **bright, poppy colors** (contrast this with Art Deco's original all-white schemes) and **maritime imagery**. Landmarks in a city where vacations were a way of life, these buildings were intended to divert and amuse, hence the proliferation of playful, non-functioning touches like **woggles** (a term Morris Lapidus coined for floating amoeba-like shapes) and **cheeseholes** (where holes are bored through concrete like bubbles in Swiss cheese). In fact, Lapidus had **eight guiding principles** whose impact can be seen on almost every building he oversaw: get rid of corners; use sweeping lines; manipulate light to create unusual effects; introduce drama whenever possible; keep changing the floor levels; keep people moving; use plenty of color; and take advantage of what he called the Moth Complex – the fact that people are attracted to light.

For more on MiMo's place in Miami's architectural timeline, see Contexts: Architecture (p.261) or check ⓦwww.mimo.us. The latest crop of MiMo buildings to seize historians' imaginations are the motels that rim Biscayne Boulevard, and preservationists have launched a "MiMo on BiBo" movement to snare the same kind of protection slowly being afforded the beachside buildings (see p.80). Back on the beach, the North Beach Development Corporation runs sporadic **tours** of the neighborhood's architectural haul; call or check the website for upcoming schedules (ⓣ305/865-4147, ⓦwww.gonorthbeach.com).

MiMo styles

While Deco's prevailing style shifted over time, MiMo manifested itself in different ways simultaneously – the explosion of construction in the 1950s, buoyed by America's postwar optimism and the birth of mass consumer culture, allowed architects plenty of wiggle room with their woggles. Still, there are three main styles:

Resort MiMo: The best-known style, used mostly in Miami Beach's hotels, twinned clean-lined towers with jazzy entranceways, usually a car-friendly *porte cochère*. It was the interiors, though, which really stood out. Always movie-set glamorous, they were intended to turn holidays into Hollywood: staircases for grand entrances (a signature Lapidus touch), lashings of marble, and gold-plated aluminum. Sadly, few examples of such impressive interiors remain – the restorations of the *Fontainebleau* and *Eden Roc* are the best approximation – but two other hotels on Collins, the *Sherry Frontenac* at no. 6565 and the *Dezerland Hotel* at no. 8701, have exemplary exteriors.

Iconic Modernism: This style can be best thought of as appliqué architecture. Most of these buildings are simple, often square boxes, but are spiffed up with goofy, eye-catching details: boomerang and delta shapes, pylons, or parabolic arches. Two strong examples are the shopping center entranceway at 6616 Collins Ave and the stunning, bright yellow synagogue, Temple Menorah, designed jointly by Gilbert Fein and Morris Lapidus at 620 75th St.

Vernacular MiMo: The most restrained and practical of the styles, Vernacular MiMo still has plenty of playfulness – vertical fins and stucco reliefs as decoration or snazzy balcony rails – but the buildings themselves are much more in keeping with the austere International Style prevalent in that era. This was the cheapest way to erect a MiMo building, and was often used on apartment blocks rather than public spaces like hotels. An exception is the *Golden Sands* at 6901 Collins Ave, with its radiator-grille facade; as for apartments, a fine example is the bubblegum-pink complex at 6890–6896 Abbot Ave.

▲ The Normandy Isle Fountain

Levy, who immigrated in 1900 and quickly made his fortune running moviehouses in Cincinnati; after moving to Miami, Levy snapped up two large but uninhabited mangrove islands on the bay side of Miami Beach (his own home, the Coral House on Washington Avenue in South Beach, still stands; see p.56). Levy then parceled off the land and sold it ready for construction; to evoke the exoticism of his homeland he named the roads after French towns and provinces – hence Normandy and Biarritz drives. Urban planners have recently noted that the area's civic amenities and layout owe a large debt to the resort town of Granville in northern France.

Surfside and Bal Harbour

Moving north along Collins Avenue, **Surfside**, the next major settlement, is a self-contained, unremarkable beachside community that spans from 88th to 96th streets. The blocks here are full of one- and two-story single-family homes, as well as neighborhood amenities along Harding Avenue including a post office, drugstore, and banks.

Unless you need to make a pit-stop, skip Surfside in favor of tony **Bal Harbour**, which begins at 96th Street. Bal Harbour's most telling feature is its name, anglicized to underscore pretensions to culture, history, and wealth; it's somewhat ironic, then, that Miami Beach's most self-consciously ritzy area should have such humble beginnings. It was originally nothing more than a soldiers' training camp in World War II; and the town only incorporated in 1946 when many of those soldiers – who fondly remembered Miami – came back from the war and settled here permanently. Bal Harbour's sleepiness has been somewhat disturbed by the imminent arrival of two deluxe hotel-condo complexes: *St Regis Hotel & Residences*, set to rise on the former site of the Sheraton by the end of 2009; and a smaller but equally pricey *Regent Hotel* that should receive its first visitors around the same time.

Those hotels are likely to draw overnighters exhausted after a day trawling through the area's best-known landmark, the **Bal Harbour Shops**, 9700 Collins Ave (T305/886-0311, Wwww.balharbourshops.com). This bi-level, open-air mall positively drips with designer names: Fendi, Prada, and Gucci all have their Miami outposts here. The mall may be a fun place to window-shop, but don't expect any bargains – even the cafés are premium-priced. Clearly, though, someone's spending: Bal Harbour usually ties with the Caesars Mall in Las Vegas as the most lucrative mall per square foot in the whole country.

Haulover Park and north

Moving on north from Bal Harbour brings you to the nude beaches at **Haulover Park** – in fact far more salubrious than their racy reputation might suggest. The golden coastline here stretches for several sand-packed miles before delivering you to the mouth of package-holiday hell – though, admittedly, it's a golden-sand-capped hellmouth – in **Sunny Isles Beach**.

Haulover Park

Famous for being Miami's one nude beach, **Haulover Park** (daily sunrise–sunset; free, parking $4; T305/947-3525 Wwww.miamidade.gov/parks/parks/haulover_park.asp), 10800 Collins Ave, is far more than that: the glorious, wide sands make a visit here worth the trip, wherever you're staying, not to mention the excellent facilities – showers, picnic tables, and bathrooms – along the boardwalk that runs parallel to the oceanfront.

The barefoot mailmen

Visitors to the Haulover Beach boardwalk will notice a plaque commemorating a forgotten piece of Florida history – the barefoot mailmen.

Florida was the last state east of the Mississippi to join the US, gaining full statehood in 1845, and its civic amenities were often primitive until a widespread railway network was established in the 1920s. The postal service was especially underdeveloped: mail traveled between settlements in South Florida on a circuitous route that sometimes took a letter to New York and back again before delivering it.

This frustrating and impractical service ended in 1885 when **the Barefoot Mailman service** was established. For seven years, mail traveled between scattered coastal settlements the only way it could – on foot. Eleven mailmen used the beach as their road for the trek **from Palm Beach to Miami**. The 136-mile journey was a six-day round-trip, and included 56 miles in a small boat and eighty by land. Overnights were spent at houses of refuge run for shipwrecked sailors in Orange Grove and Fort Lauderdale, and individual travelers wanting to walk with the postmen for their own safety could pay $5 to join the trip. The barefoot mail route ended when a new country road was built connecting Palm Beach with Lemon City, then the largest settlement in the Miami area, and a stagecoach service began.

The "clothing optional" section to the north is clearly marked by warning signs on the footpath, although you don't have to strip off to sunbathe even there: either way, there's a volleyball court for sporty nudists, and an unofficial gay section at the northernmost end between sections 27 and 29. For several years, a contingent of prudish local residents has been sneakily campaigning to nix the nudists, petitioning the city for a new school to be built nearby; standard zoning laws would apply and so forbid nude bathing. Their nefarious plan has been hampered by the fact that Bal Harbour's population is largely retirees with grown children, but the campaign continues, albeit with less vim – however, if you're determined to bathe in the buff call the number listed to double check it's still permitted.

Sunny Isles Beach

Poor **Sunny Isles**. This blatant Las Vegas rip-off was founded in 1952 expressly as a holiday resort and dozens of natty motels quickly sprung up along the ample beach; two were even named *Sahara* and *Suez* in Vegas's honor. However, the resort soon lost its luster and spent much of the rest of the century languishing as an undesirable package-holiday destination. In the last decade, it's aggressively tried to shake off that image by levelling the funky mid-Century motels and replacing them with could-be-anywhere condo-hotel towers. Now, the beachfront is rimmed with a row of ritzy, soulless skyscraper hotels from the likes of Donald Trump; they sit crammed together like giant bowling pins. What's more, since there were no preservation laws enforced to preserve some of the district's outstanding vernacular architecture, those classic Vegas-inspired motels that once hugged the sand are gone – no more concrete sheikhs in front of the *Sahara*, no more white and gold sphinxes in front of the *Suez*. The lone survivor, at least at time of writing, was the nondescript *Ocean Palm Motel* at Collins and 157th Street, which peeks out apologetically from behind adjoining high rises. Essentially, the area's a shameful example of development gone wild in South Florida and a healthy reminder of how well South Beach has juggled the needs of preservation and commerce.

The sumptuous **beaches** do provide some saving grace, however. While elsewhere in southern Florida, resorts have been bedeviled by coastal erosion, Sunny Isles' heavy investment in renourishment – where dredged sand is dumped onto thinning shoreline – has paid off. The downside to this ocean floor harvesting is that shifting the sands has altered the tide-flow and created dangerous new riptides that can catch swimmers off guard. Come spend the day baking on the beach then head back to a funky hotel elsewhere instead of risking the sky-high rates at the five star hulks here. The biggest draw now is likely the *Rascal House* diner (see p.151)

Golden Beach

Golden Beach holds little of interest for the visitor. As A1A threads through this subdivision, drivers are thrown back into the Miami of the early 1980s when there were so many seniors in Miami Beach that it earned the nickname "God's Waiting Room." The aligning houses and condos are still stocked with old ladies enjoying the warm weather and tanning through retirement, yet the number of blue hairs has certainly dwindled in the last twenty years. If you stay on A1A, it will eventually, via the nondescript resort town of Hollywood, bring you to Fort Lauderdale, although it's a roundabout route and you're better off using faster, interior roads like I-95; however, if you turn off at 163rd Street, you'll find one of Miami Beach's overlooked gems, the Oleta River State Recreation Area.

Oleta River State Recreation Area

The **Oleta River State Recreation Area**, 3400 NE 163rd Street (daily 8am–sunset, $3 for single visitor, $5 for up to eight people in one vehicle; ☎305/919-1846, ⓦwww.floridastateparks.org), is a terrific hideaway – though it can fiendish to find. Drive through the spaghetti junction at 163rd Street in Sunny Isles Beach, then cross the bridge towards the mainland neighborhood of North Miami Beach; the park's easily missed entrance is on the south side of the road, opposite the shopping mall.

The 1000-acres here feels like a slice of the Everglades spliced onto the tip of the Miami Beach sandbar; when exploring, it's hard to believe that you're only ten minutes' drive from downtown. Forests of mangroves and sea grape trees cluster along the waterways and rivers that crisscross this promontory, jutting out into Biscayne Bay, and the best way to explore is by kayak or canoe. There's a **rental concession** by the main car park, which also hires bikes if you want to hit the network of mountain biking trails (pick up a map of them from the ranger at the park entrance). Otherwise, lazier types can bring a packed lunch and chill out at one of the waterfront picnic pagodas. There are even fourteen cabins here, each sleeping up to four and with air conditioning and electricity but no linens (☎1-800/326-3521, ⓦwww.reserveamerica.com; $45 per night).

North along the Biscayne Corridor

Nowhere is Miami's twenty-first century transformation more evident than in the chunk of formerly unloved land that sits just north of downtown known as the **Biscayne Corridor**. The main drag here, **Biscayne Boulevard**, was once the central artery flowing between Miami and Fort Lauderdale, bringing traffic, motels, and diners to the area in equal measure. But when the connection was severed by the construction of the I-95 freeway in the 1960s, everything changed. In the heady days of the cocaine cowboys, Biscayne Boulevard became the OK Corral. The playful, poppy MiMo motels that once catered to commuters soon started renting rooms by the hour, while the classic mid-century mansions nearby became crack dens. But when the economic high from cocaine deals dwindled, more law-abiding locals slowly started reclaiming the stunning buildings and in the past several years, that renaissance has rapidly accelerated. Now, it's by far the buzziest chunk of Miami and well worth the $25 cab ride from South Beach.

It's almost impossible to keep pace with the radical changes here. At its southernmost end, the area known as **OMNI** has been transformed by music. Classical and Broadway tunes are on show at the skyline-changing Arsht Center, while thumping dance music spun by brand-name DJs pours out from the warehouse clubs of **Park West** every weekend. Just north of here sits **Wynwood**, which has quickly gone from a working-class, Puerto Rican neighborhood to a gallery-crammed visual arts hub – the private collections on show to the public here, notably that of the Rubells, are some of Miami's most impressive and detour-worthy museums. Continue on to the **Design District**, and you'll hit a funky, if somewhat artificial retail hub; now full of high-priced homeware stores and cutting edge boutiques, it'll soon be home to high style residential high-rises, too.

Gentrification hasn't yet reached Little Haiti, the next neighborhood north along Biscayne Boulevard. A robust neighborhood, it evolved in the last twenty years thanks to the arrival of thousands of Haitian refugees, and though it has few sights it is refreshingly authentic and a great place to try cheap, tasty Caribbean food. Biscayne Boulevard snakes up into the lower-middle-class suburbs, starting with **North Miami**, incongruously home to the snazzy Museum of Contemporary Art-North Miami, and then hitting the confusingly named mainland settlement **North Miami Beach**, where you'll bizarrely find a reconstructed medieval monastery from Spain.

Museum of Contemporary Art

BISCAYNE CORRIDOR

N

Museum of Contemporary Art

Belle
Meade
Island

Vagabond Motel

Back
No 9

LITTLE
HAITI

Legion
Park

Legion Park
Picnic Islands

DuPuis
Building

Morningside Park
Picnic Islands

Caribbean
Marketplace

MORNINGSIDE

Morningside
Park

LAKE ROAD

DRINKING & NIGHTLIFE

Boteco	2
Churchill's Hideaway	8
Circa 28	19
Magnum Lounge	3
Mike's at Venetia	23
One Ninety	9
The Pawn Shop Lounge	25
PS14	24
Soho Lounge	16
Stop Miami	17

DESIGN DISTRICT

Living Room
Building

Design & Architecture
Senior High School

AIRPORT EXPRESSWAY

Moore
Park

JULIA TUTTLE CAUSEWAY

EATING

55th Street Station	6
A Café	11
Adelita's Cafe	20
Bin #18	22
Dogma	4
Domo Japones	12
Enriqueta's	18
Lakay Tropical Ice Cream	10
Laurenzo's	1
Lost and Found Saloon	15
Michael's Genuine Food & Drink	14
Michy's	5
Out of the Blue	21
The Secret Sandwich	13
Soyka	7
Sushi Siam	7

MIDTOWN
MIAMI

Rubell
Collection

Margulies
Collection

MoCA
at Goldman
Warehouse

WYNWOOD

World
Class Boxing
The Scholl
Collection

Bacardi Building

Margaret
Pace Park

Biscayne
Island

SCHOOL
BOARD

Arsht Center for the
Performing Arts

BICENTENNIAL
PARK

Watson
Island

0   500 yds

South Beach

Central Miami Beach

The OMNI Mall and north

Builtin the 1980s to revitalize the area, the **OMNI Mall** at 14th Street and Biscayne Boulevard failed miserably. Now, however, the OMNI area looks set to thrive thanks to the construction of Cesar Pelli's showstopping Arsht Center next to the mall. There have even been mumblings about repurposing the unloved hulk of a shopping center as a school or similar civic amenity, though those haven't progressed beyond the discussion stages.

North of here, the street's lined with motels, which mushroomed when Biscayne Boulevard was the throughway to Fort Lauderdale: most remain crack dens but their names – the *Gold Dust*, *Shalimar*, *Sinbad* – and jaunty signs hearken back to the Swinging Sixties. The most notable, **The Vagabond Motel** at 7301 Biscayne Blvd, was sold to new owners who've turned it into a funky mall; built by Robert Swartzburg, the same architect behind the Aztec-inspired *Delano* (see p.133), it's a MiMo masterpiece, complete with jagged streetside neon sign. Preservationists are pressing for the city to declare the area a historic district like South Beach or Mid-Beach – it's been tagged "MiMo on BiBo" – to encourage other new owners to buy out those mid-Century beauties. For updates, check the local MiMo association's website, ⓦwww.mimoboulevard.org, which also occasionally lists architectural tours.

Close to the Arsht Center lies **Park West**, a warehouse district the city has cannily designated a nightlife zone, granting 24-hour liquor licenses to a cluster of clubs along 11th Street with the idea that it will draw traffic and congestion away from South Beach's choked nightlife. It's working, albeit slowly – the crowd here may be smaller, but it's much hipper than at most of the venues across the Causeway. For information on Park West's clubs, see p.162, "Nightlife."

The Arsht Center

Masterminded by architect Cesar Pelli, the enormous **Arsht Center** (ⓣ305/949-6722, ⓦwww.carnivalcenter.org) between 13th and 14th streets links three performance spaces in two huge buildings straddling Biscayne Boulevard. The Carnival Symphony Hall is a 2200-seat shoebox-design space intended to maximize acoustics; the slightly larger Ziff Ballet House is devoted to opera, dance, and Broadway-style shows; and the tiny Studio Theater, with a flexible 200-seat auditorium, is available to local arts groups. The one old landmark sits in the courtyard between the two structures, an octagonal, whitewashed Art Deco tower. It was the showy crenellated entrance to a huge Sears store, built in 1929, that once sat on the site; in fact, the corporation donated the land to the city expressly for this center.

Arguably the best time to appreciate Pelli's building is by night, speeding past on the I-95 freeway, which makes the twinkling, space-age building look like a delicate alien craft that's idling quietly in the center of Miami. The technology within Pelli's structure is similarly state-of-the-art, with the auditoriums boasting superb soundproofing to prevent ambient noise from polluting the performance. Sadly, the onsite art – much touted as the building was planned – falls rather flat. It's uninspired stuff, including a glass tiled mural by Cundo Bermudez and strangely retro terrazzo floor art from José Bedia, that's only worth checking out if you're onsite for a performance.

Seeing the building glowing contentedly is misleading, as this has been a troubled project from the outset. Construction began in 2001 and the center was scheduled to debut by 2004 – problems pushed back the opening two years and swelled the budget by a staggering $134 million. The center's first chief, Michael Hardy, resigned in 2007 amid claims of all-round ineptitude; the splashy center

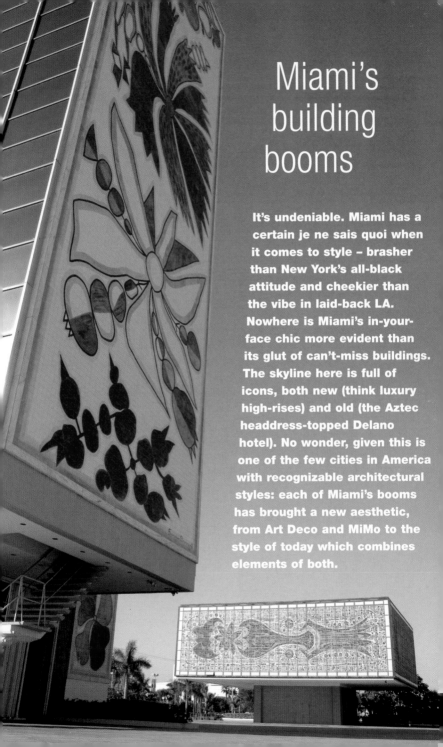

Miami's building booms

It's undeniable. Miami has a certain je ne sais quoi when it comes to style – brasher than New York's all-black attitude and cheekier than the vibe in laid-back LA. Nowhere is Miami's in-your-face chic more evident than its glut of can't-miss buildings. The skyline here is full of icons, both new (think luxury high-rises) and old (the Aztec headdress-topped Delano hotel). No wonder, given this is one of the few cities in America with recognizable architectural styles: each of Miami's booms has brought a new aesthetic, from Art Deco and MiMo to the style of today which combines elements of both.

From Deco to Modernism

Miami Beach has the weather to thank for its signature **Art Deco** look – not the sun, but the destructive power of Florida's hurricanes. Just as the resort's popularity was peaking in the 1920s, a devastating storm leveled most of its hotels. The owners turned to the quickest and cheapest contemporary style to replace them: Art Deco.

Made from poured concrete, the boxy buildings were a smart and stylish solution: architects added touches like reliefs of flamingos or tropical palms as a nod to Miami's climate. However, after World War II, both South Beach and its buildings fell out of fashion; the old hotels became low-rent rooming houses, while paint on the apartment blocks blistered in the sun. By the 1970s, in an attempt to revive the area, plans were made to start demolishing these outmoded buildings, until conservationists protested to have the entire area declared a **landmark**. Such was their success that today, renovating a Deco hotel is a complex process – it took so long to approve Diesel Jeans' plan to rehab the oceanfront *Carlyle Hotel* into its world headquarters that founder Renzo Rossi decided it was cheaper to sell the shell as-is (it's now morphed into high-end condos).

Miami's second building boom came in the postwar era, a time of optimism, consumerism, and TV dinners. As those Deco piles to the south started to rot, elsewhere in the city – notably along the mainland's Biscayne Boulevard and in North Beach on the oceanfront sandbar – a new style of poppy architecture was flourishing. Championed by the master of excess, **Morris Lapidus**, the style is now known as **Miami Modernism**, or MiMo; outlandish poured concrete ornaments subbed for Deco's sleek simplicity –

The Delano Hotel ▲
Ocean Terrace ▼

City Hall ▼

tail fins and spires dotted seemingly at random on the swirling new buildings. And no hotel or apartment was complete without a huge *porte cochère*, ideal for that hulking new Cadillac to idle under. Soon enough, the MiMo buildings fell out of favor and into disrepair just as Deco had a decade earlier. And, like Art Deco, it took conservationists to agitate for the movement's recognition and preservation, starting in the late 1990s.

Modern Miami

Miami is firmly in the midst of its third architectural act – one largely confined to the mainland. A new aesthetic is emerging combining the sleek lines of deco with MiMo's playful poppishness. Of course, some of the skyscrapers peppering the skyline now are bland-looking deluxe condos, but many developers have recognized the value of high-style high-rises. Purchasers gladly paid premium prices to live in designer **Philippe Starck**'s first building, humbly dubbed Icon, on South Beach in the early 2000s; the same has been true in his just-completed project, a downtown condo complex perched in a prime by the Miami River. Not all of the architects reshaping Miami are imported, either: one homegrown star is **Chad Oppenheim**, the mastermind behind most of the soon-to-rise towers in the Design District. He jostles for prominence with **Arquitectonica**: the firm, run by husband-wife team Bernardo Fort-Brescia and Laurinda Spear, first came to prominence by designing the Pop Art-influenced Atlantis Building in Brickell. The splashiest skyline addition is courtesy of star architect **Cesar Pelli**: his stunning Arsht Center for the Performing Arts lolls like a glittering beast over Biscayne Boulevard downtown.

▲ Vagabond Motel
▼ The Fontainebleau Hotel

▼ Arsht Center

The Atlantis apartments ▲

Albion Hotel ▼

Ocean Terrace bandshell ▼

Ten must-see buildings

The following are Miami's best examples of Deco, MiMo and contemporary architecture.

▶▶ **The Albion Hotel** There's no better illustration of the sleek, steamship-inspired Streamline Deco movement than this hotel. See p.132.

▶▶ **The Arsht Center for the Performing Arts** Cesar Pelli's showpiece is accented by a Deco tower in its center – a remnant of the Sears department store once on the site. See p.80.

▶▶ **The Atlantis apartments** Arquitectonica's first experimental building is cored like an apple, with a palm tree and staircase set halfway up its facade. See p.44.

▶▶ **The Bacardi Building** Pull off the road to best appreciate the detailed mosaic-like facade, designed by Brazilian architect Francisco Brennand. See p.81.

▶▶ **City Hall** A Deco gem that's preserved the original white-and-navy color scheme displaced in the 1970s in favor of the now-famed pastel yellows and pinks. See p.113.

▶▶ **The Delano Hotel** MiMo guru Robert Swartzburg has two signature buildings still standing: this hotel, crowned with an Aztec-style headdress, and the slinky *Vagabond Motel* on Biscayne Boulevard. See p.133.

▶▶ **The Fontainebleau Hotel** The masterpiece of the master of MiMo, Morris Lapidus, is a fiesta of cheeseholes, woggles and other fun-but-pointless details. See p.70.

▶▶ **Miami Beach Post Office** The simple exterior/ornate interior of this squat column-like structure is an outstanding example of the Depression Moderne style. See p.58.

▶▶ **The Ocean Terrace bandshell** Recently restored to its swooping, sherbert-colored best, it now hosts free concerts. See p.72.

▶▶ **Temple Menorah** A collaboration between Lapidus and Gilbert Fein, this bright yellow, boxy synagogue is covered with architectural appliqué details. See p.73.

lost $2.4 million in its first year, yet Hardy was still awarded a forty percent pay raise. A new team, led by the popular and populist-minded Lawrence Wilker, has taken over, but whether they can lure the masses to the place is still debatable. The nervy atmosphere was further exacerbated in early 2008 when the complex underwent a name change less than two years into a decade-long pact with the local Carnival cruise line. The pile's now known officially as the Adrienne Arsht Center for the Performing Arts of Miami-Dade County – everyone calls it the Arsht Center for short – in honor of the art-minded donor who pumped $30 million of her own money into the place.

The Arsht Center is home to four resident companies – Concert Association of Florida, Florida Grand Opera, Miami City Ballet and New World Symphony – plus a Best of Broadway season of shows. For more information, see p.169, "Performing arts and film."

The Bacardi Building

Looming above Biscayne Boulevard like a gleaming robot, the **Bacardi Building** (T305/573-8511), at no. 2100, is a masterpiece of Modernist architecture, best known for the white and blue floral murals that sprawl across its northern and southern facades. Designed and installed by Brazilian artist Francisco Brennand in 1963, they're made from individually fired ceramic tiles. There's a small **museum** of uninteresting Bacardi rum memorabilia on the main floor – a satellite of the original in Cuba – but it's only sporadically open to the public: call the main number a couple of days in advance, requesting a specific access time and the custodians will usually be happy to allow brief visits. The squat, square building next door was an addition to the complex ten years later; its interior walls are made almost entirely of stained glass.

Wynwood

North and east of the Omni performing arts hub sits **Wynwood,** Miami's emerging visual arts HQ, hemmed in by major roads on each side – I-95, I-195, I-395, and Biscayne Boulevard. Long a predominantly working-class, Puerto Rican neighborhood, its low rents were discovered by artists several years ago, who've swarmed here to commandeer its spaces as workshops-cum-homes. There are plenty of vibrant new **galleries** speckled throughout, especially along N Miami Avenue, and it's become a bona-fide hub of first-rate contemporary art (for gallery picks, see p.184 "Shopping"). Most exhibition spaces have some form of map or guide available gratis – look also for the glossy *Wynwood: The Art Magazine* (T786/274-3236, Wwww.wam-magazine.com), or the handier, pocket-sized *MAG/Miami Art Guide* (T305/573-9530, Wwww.miamiartguide.com).

The galleries tend to be spread out, so it's best to tour by car. The liveliest time to stop by is the second Saturday of each month, when the galleries are open 7–10pm, with drinks available and artists on site. Wynwood's also become the go-to space for local collectors keen to share their acquisitions and tastes with the public. Real estate moguls the Rubells have long showcased the **Rubell Collection** here; developer Marty has his **Margulies Collection at the Warehouse**; South Beach landlord Tony Goldman donated a temporary space for **MoCA at the Goldman**; a former gym's now home to **World Class Warehouse Boxing – The Scholl Collection**; and Coca-Cola bottling heiress Ella Fontanals-Cisneros has her **CIFO Foundation** set-up just south of here (see p.46). The only local art collecting icon missing is Key Biscayne-based philanthropist Rosa de la Cruz, though she too has just announced plans for a huge showcase of her holdings that should open by 2009.

Art Basel Miami Beach

Despite the name, it's the Wynwood district which is most transformed during the annual fair known as **Art Basel Miami Beach**. The high point of the local art world's calendar, it's a four-day extravaganza held during the first week of December. This satellite fair of the snooty original (held each June in Switzerland) has transfixed the city since it started in 2002: it not only lures thousands of big spenders to town – hotel rates are the highest of the year, matching New Year's Eve – but it also has helped validate the emerging local art scene.

Of course, since this is Miami, Art Basel here is as much about parties as paintings. Compared to the Swiss original, where there's a single bar where collectors gather each night, the Miami version has dozens of glittering, champagne-drenched parties thrown by Cartier, Pucci et al every night. It's great value for rubbernecking, especially as the celebrity quota increases each year. But for true art fiends, aside from the pricey main show at the Convention Center (intended to sell six-figure artworks to multimillionaires) there are now almost two-dozen cheaper, satellite fairs held simultaneously, all of them in and around Wynwood. PULSE (Ⓦwww.pulse-art.com/miami/) has the edgiest and highest quality art – expect most works to cost $2–10,000 – while SCOPE (Ⓦwww.scope-art.com) and NADA (Ⓦwww.newartdealers.org) are cheap places to pick up work by undiscovered talent, often for just a few hundred bucks.

The other major change to the area is utterly unrelated to its art-heavy revival. Mammoth retail and residential development **Midtown Miami**, a sprawling 56-acre development on the eastern side of N Miami Avenue (Ⓦwww.midtownmiami.com), arrived a couple of years ago; the old buildings of the Buena Vista Railyards were razed to make way for new townhomes and condos, as well as a massive mall. There's little retail-wise to lure a casual visitor, but the arrival of big box mainstays like Target and Circuit City has been a major boost for the nascent gentrification of the homes around here.

MoCA at Goldman Warehouse

One of Wynwood's newer sights is **MoCA at Goldman Warehouse**, 404 NW 26th St S (Weds–Sat noon–5pm; donation; Ⓣ305/573-5441, Ⓦwww.mocanomi.org/warehouse.htm). Real estate maven and South Beach pioneer Tony Goldman – who owns both *The Hotel* and *Park Central* hotels – leased a hulking old building here to the North Miami-based museum (for the nominal rent of $1 per year) so that it could operate a satellite space. Opened in 2005, the vast space will remain active until early 2010, when the mothership's on-going extension should be completed. Shows here are curated by artworld rockstar Bonnie Clearwater, and recent exhibitions have included the lyrical, multi-layered architectural paintings of Puerto Rican Enoc Perez and the subversive work of mixed media artist Christian Holstad.

World Class Boxing – The Scholl Collection

There's a trend in contemporary art towards megalithic installations, and collectors Dennis and Debra Scholl's **World Class Boxing** space, 170 NW 23rd St (by appointment; free; Ⓣ305/438-9908, Ⓦwww.worldclassboxing.net), is geared specifically towards such enormous creations. This onetime gym is used by the couple to showcase works that are too enormous for them to enjoy at home, or site-specific commissions that capitalize on the shell-like set-up. Past shows have included Dutch video artist Aernout Mik and LA-based Mark Bradford, who repurposes discarded signage into vast collage-like sculptures.

The Rubell Collection

Housed in a cavernous warehouse once used by the DEA to store evidence, the **Rubell Collection**, 95 NW 29th St (Weds–Sat 10am–6pm; $5; ☎305/573-6090, ⓦwww.rubellfamilycollection.com), is hands down the most important, impressive and fun of Wynwood's private showcases. Pioneers of the neighborhood, genial couple Mera and Don Rubell converted this building into a home for their passionate hobby in 1996, just three years after arriving in Miami from New York City. In 2004, the Rubells pumped even more money into the collection, doubling its available exhibition space, adding a sculpture garden and café. It's a good thing, too – the more of the family's astonishing pieces on view at any one time, the better. Each of the four family members who collect have a strong individual viewpoint; but instead of hobbling the collection, the quartet's impeccable but eclectic taste has turned the holdings into one of the most comprehensive art surveys of the past thirty years. Exhibits rotate frequently, but look for works by Cindy Sherman, including one of her earliest photographs, plus punk modernist Jeff Koons, Jean-Michel Basquiat, and graffiti master Keith Haring, whom the Rubells championed early on in his career.

The Margulies Collection at the Warehouse

The **Margulies Collection** is a stark showcase for the collection of a local developer with a passion for modern art (Sept–April Weds–Sat 11am–4pm, closed May–Aug; free; ☎305/576-1051, ⓦwww.marguliewarehouse.com). Opened in 1999, it's housed a user-friendly space filled with nooks and crannies where individual works can be effectively spotlit. Note that Margulies is known for his **photography**, whether WPA-era classics by Walker Evans and Eudora Welty or modern installations by the likes of Vanessa Beecroft, though any show is likely to include a variety of media. A recent exception was an all-sculpture set-up, a 65-piece retrospective that included Isamu Noguchi's seductively phallic stone *Man* and Andy Warhol's stack of faux-branded cardboard *Brillo Boxes*. Margulies also owns fine examples of on-the-rise artist Ernesto Neto's dripping, sensual sculptures made from nylon stockings, plus Do-Ho Suh's bizarre recreation of his New York apartment corridor in pink netting, light switches and door handles included; another standout is the creepy work by Gilles Barbier, which shows a half-dozen wax figures representing arthritic heroes in a super-powered old-age home.

The Design District

Heading north from Wynwood, you'll reach the **Design District**, bounded by 36th Street and 41st Street between Miami Avenue and Biscayne Boulevard. This tract of land was originally a pineapple plantation owned by Theodore Moore, known as the "Pineapple King of Florida." On a whim, Moore opened a furniture showroom in 1921 on NE 40th Street and created what became known as Decorators' Row. During Miami's Art Deco building boom of the 1920s and 1930s, this was the center of the city's design scene, filled with wholesale interiors stores selling furniture and flooring. By the early 1990s, though, the district was derelict, crime-ridden, and filled with factories, with only a handful of interiors shops still holding out – most had been lured to move north to Fort Lauderdale's new Design Center of the Americas building. That's when developer **Craig Robins**, one of the masterminds behind the gentrification of South Beach, moved in and began buying buildings, spearheading the regeneration process with aggressive plans, including an emphasis on public art and sculpture.

He's succeeding – little wonder, given that the city's recent building boom rivaled that of the 1920s; after all, those thousands of new apartments needed fixtures and furniture, even if they're now struggling to find buyers. Almost overnight, the Design District's main drag along **40th Street** has been reborn as a temple to the *Dwell* lifestyle of conspicuous but elegant consumption, and the district is now dotted with high-priced houseware boutiques alongside marquee names like Knoll and Holly Hunt, as well as restaurants like *Michael's Genuine* (see p.152) and clothing stores such as Y-3. The two blocks between 2nd and Miami avenues along 40th are also the site of the **Decorators' Walk of Fame** – a tenuous claim at best – where stars embedded into the sidewalk honor long-forgotten interiors designers from the area's first heyday, like Aaron T. Euster.

This whole neighborhood is set to transform even further during phase two of Robins' plans – the much-delayed arrival of fifteen new buildings, mostly high-rise condo towers, set to sprout among the low-slung streets while a new square, Oak Plaza, will be constructed between 39th and 40th streets around an existing cluster of trees. The aim is to remedy the Design District's lack of energy: the showrooms and stores are gleaming, but the sidewalks often seem deserted, so Robins plans to lure residents to join his business tenants to live in those high-rise condo towers.

For now, the district is liveliest during business hours Monday through Saturday, or on **Gallery Walk** night – dates vary, so check Ⓦwww.gallerywalk.wordpress. com for schedules.

The Living Room Building

A neighborhood mascot of sorts for the district, **The Living Room Building** can be found at 4000 Miami Ave, at the junction with 40th Street. A whimsical landmark, with a sense of the district's campy fun, the low-rise office building's signature feature was designed by local husband-and-wife architects Rosario Marquart and Roberto Behar. It's an entranceway that has been turned inside-out and decorated with 40-foot walls, a giant concrete couch, and oversized lamps, all painted in fruity pinks and oranges. Topping it off, there's even a "painting" on the wall – or, rather, a gloriously simple hole through which the sky and shifting clouds can be seen. After lying empty and unkempt for several years, the building has finally found a fitting tenant at time of writing: the Living Room Theater (see p.170), a movie house from Portland, Oregon. The new tenants plan to transform the structure, retaining its signature entranceway but building an entirely new rear that will be home to eight screens of arthouse and indie flicks.

Design and Architecture Senior High

Design and Architecture Senior High (Ⓣ305/573-7135, Ⓦwww.dashschool. org) or DASH, is what's known as a magnet school – publicly funded, but selective in its students. Fittingly given the neighborhood, this high school at 4001 NE 2nd Ave specializes in the arts, and is housed in a former mall for design showrooms that was converted by Arquitectonica in the late 1980s. Only five hundred teenagers study here, each of whom tests in via a portfolio and onsite art exam in the eighth grade. A year later, each must choose a major among architecture, film technology, graphic design, and fashion to complement the regular school curriculum. It's an unusual school in other ways, too: there's no mandatory physical education, for instance, and no football team, either – instead, students can play golf, soccer, bowling, and basketball or take rhythmic dance classes. Of course, there's no public access to the school's interior but look for the twin column sculp-

▲ DASH Arquitectonica Sculpture

tures in the playground, again by Marquart and Behar, and yet another example of Robins' commitment to public art. *Kids!* is a pair of polychrome life-sized statues of a boy and girl; their animated gestures are based on the two central figures in Raphael's *School of Athens* fresco in Rome. Another recent addition: the wavy fence out front, designed by industrial icon Marc Newson and installed during the Art Basel/Design Miami fair in 2007 (see box p.82.)

Little Haiti

Bounded on the east and west by Biscayne Boulevard and I-95, and running from 54th to 85th streets, **Little Haiti** is a residential neighborhood seldom visited by tourists. In contrast with Little Havana, this is an economically struggling district, and, unlike Miami's Cubans, the city's Haitian community has yet to make significant inroads in politics or business (though the city of North Miami Beach did recently elect the first Haitian-American mayor in the country).

Originally known as **Lemon City**, it was, along with Coconut Grove, one of the area's earliest European settlements. Haitians first started arriving here en masse in the late 1970s, fleeing the corrupt Duvalier regime, and Miami became the second most popular destination after New York City; almost sixty thousand Haitians had arrived here by 1981. Today, Little Haiti is an undiluted immigrant neighborhood, with residents who live, shop, and work within its confines (one of them is well regarded novelist Edwidge Danticat). Street signage is in both English and Kreyol, and you'll hear French spoken in some stores.

To get some of the local flavor it's best to wander along the central drag of NE 2nd Avenue, and simply enjoy the Caribbean colors, music, and smells. Do be mindful, though: the area is relatively safe, but it's still a good idea to stick to both the main streets and the daytime.

NE 2nd Avenue

With buildings painted in ripe colors of raspberry and lime, and daubed with handwritten signs, not to mention music blaring out of the odd record store, **NE 2nd Avenue** has a distinctly Caribbean feel to it. Adding to the effect is the brightly colored ironwork of the **Caribbean Marketplace** at no. 5927, modeled after a similar bazaar in Haiti's capital, Port-au-Prince. It was designed by local architect Charles Harrison Pawley as an urban renewal project to showcase Haitian crafts while drawing tourist dollars to the area. Unfortunately, the bank foreclosed on the venture owing to bad management, and the Marketplace has been shuttered several years.

Don't be surprised to see chickens wandering round among the pigeons at the unnamed park three blocks north at 62nd Street and NE 2nd Avenue, which marks one of the hubs of the neighborhood. Next to the park stands the simple, Modernist **Notre Dame** church, which acted as a processing center for the stream of Haitian immigrants who arrived in Miami in the late 1970s. The church is still the heart of the neighborhood, attached to the Pierre Toussaint Center, which provides everything from medical care to job listings for local residents.

On the corner of 62nd Street and NE 2nd Avenue, one of the oldest houses in Miami, the **DuPuis Building**, sits in what was once the heart of Lemon City. This white porticoed structure, built in 1902, first housed Lemon City's doctor, John DuPuis, and his pharmacy; at the time, it was the only concrete building north of Downtown. Later it was turned into the local post office before finally being abandoned several decades ago. Now derelict, it's still a rare remaining sign of how early European settlement took place here. Plans have been long mooted to transform the building into a tourist office, though they've yet to move beyond the conceptual stage.

Fifty-fourth Street

The heart of Miami's *voudou* and *Santería*culture (see box, oppposite) is **54th Street**, especially along the blocks immediately west of NE 2nd Avenue, where it's lined with several *botanicas*. Here, believers can purchase ritual potions, candles, and statuettes. Almost all will permit a casual visitor to browse their merchandise, although the (mostly female) owners are notoriously tight-lipped with strangers. It goes without saying that photographing the racks of gaudy statuary and glass jars packed with herbs is both rude and foolish.

Back No. 9

A new and highly recommended attraction in the area is the quirky **Back No. 9** mini-golf course, located north of the Design District at 7244 Biscayne Boulevard (Thurs & Fri 5–10pm, Sat & Sun noon–6pm; $5 adults, $3 kids; ☎305/984-3231, Ⓦwww.uppereastsidegarden.com). Refreshingly tongue-in-cheek (the adult entry

A secretive Caribbean religion with an oral tradition, **Santería** was one of the many spiritual hybrids created by colonial rule. Despite their forcible baptizing, the conversion of slaves brought from their homes in Africa to the New World proved to be largely cosmetic. To preserve their own religions, the gods, or **orishas**, in the African pantheon were "translated" into Christian saints, so that they could be worshiped without fear of reprisal. (Thus, the popular male *orisha* Shangó, who's quick-witted and –tempered, ruling drums and dance, bizarrely became St Barbara.) Even the name *Santería* began as slang, when colonial Spaniards noticed how greatly their African slaves venerated the saints rather than Christ.

Much like the gods of Ancient Greece, *orishas* have flaws and favorites: each is identified with a given color, food, and number, and all require **animal sacrifices** and human praise for nourishment. Altars in *Santería* temples will often be covered with offerings of cigarettes or designer perfume – the *orishas* are apparently all-too-human in their vulnerability to flattery and expensive gifts. Religious services, conducted in secret by a priest or priestess, involve channeling the gods through dances and hypnotic trance.

In Africa, each priest was associated with a single god and channeled that one alone, but as the religion came under threat in slave times, many priests began communing with the entire pantheon to preserve the worship of all the gods. This had two effects: firstly, that some *orishas* holy in the Caribbean are no longer venerated in Africa, since the city-states that held them dear were wiped out by the slave trade. Secondly, that the gods in American *Santería* became more closely linked in myth and practice than was traditionally the case.

Santería's certainly a flexible religion, and there are many different incarnations – the Mexican version, for instance, is known for extensively incorporating local icons like the Virgin of Guadeloupe. The Cuban strain, though, is very African, and is strongest in the poor, sugarcane-farming Oriente province; it's closely related to, although distinct from, Haiti's **voudou** tradition.

Estimated numbers of those practicing *Santería* worldwide vary wildly, from sixty thousand up to five million; regardless, it has a hidden but powerful role in local Miami society, as many people are at least part-time believers. Wandering round the city, you'll see signs of *Santería* activity if you look hard enough – **streetside offerings**, usually nailed to holy kapok trees, are common in Little Havana and Little Haiti. There's also much sensationalist reporting when *Santería* offerings are discovered near local courthouses, supposed attempts by family members to invoke the *orishas'* help during trials.

fee includes a rum-spiked piña colada), the course started as lark on the roof of the *Albion Hotel* in South Beach during Art Basel Miami Beach in 2006. Owner/creator Peter Rozek tapped local art world pals like Hernan Bas, Cristina Lei Rodriguez, and Daniel Arsham to custom-design holes; it was such a hit that he found the project a permanent home here inside a garden center. Amusingly, none of the holes are named so it's up to individual players to prove their art-world savvy by spotting different artists' work. Rozek rotates out a different work each month – stop by on the last Saturday for the hole's retirement party complete with DJ. There are also outdoor movie screenings most Thursday nights ($7).

North Miami

Continuing along Biscayne Boulevard, the ten square miles or so from 103rd to 163rd streets comprise the suburban sprawl of **North Miami**, one of the many nondescript but pleasant enough subdivisions stretching north of the city proper.

It's noteworthy solely for the avant-garde **Museum of Contemporary Art-North Miami**.

Museum of Contemporary Art-North Miami

At 770 NE 125th St (Tues–Sat 11am–5pm, Sun noon–5pm, last Fri of each month open 7–10pm; $5, Tues donation suggested; ⊤305/893-6211, ⓦwww.mocanomi .org) sits the large, Charles Gwathmey-designed **Museum of Contemporary Art-North Miami**, set back from the shopping strip on an open plaza. While it only opened in 1996, the museum is set to undergo a $17m expansion – also helmed by Gwathmey – that will triple the amount of exhibition space by 2010.

MoCA presents at least eight different displays each year, focusing on contemporary art – whether solo retrospectives on Keith Haring, Frank Stella or Helen Frankenthaler, or surveys of the latest video installation techniques. Whatever the topic, expect a first-rate show, thanks largely to the connections and charisma of powerhouse chief curator Bonnie Clearwater; almost single-handedly she has made this out-of-the-way site a must-see stop on the new South Florida art circuit. Clearwater also oversees a smallish permanent collection that's on rotating display. It includes painting by Julian Schnabel, sculpture by Mariko Mori, oversized installations by Teresita Fernandez – including a room-sized space that looks like an emptied pool – and Thomas Hirshhorn's *Diorama*, a consumer waste-filled version of a Natural History Museum case. Don't miss the sweet pop-art installation fixed on the wall of the museum's interior courtyard, either. Jack Pierson's spelled-out 'PARADISE' was the first piece the museum acquired after opening, and it's made using his much-copied signature of mismatched, multicolored neon letters – these ones were actually discarded signage from several Las Vegas hotels. The onsite gift shop is impressive for its unusual selection of art books and funky kids' toys.

North Miami Beach

Cross 163rd Street and you'll arrive in the confusingly named and somewhat deprived suburb called **North Miami Beach** – not the safest neighborhood, so keep your wits about you if you plan to wander. Like so many subdivisions in the city, its founders wanted to leverage an association with the glamour of Miami Beach when first selling land plots, and decided that the small matter of being on the mainland rather than the sandbar proper was no reason not to call the place North Miami Beach. Here you'll find one of the city's oddest sights, William Randolph Hearst's **Ancient Spanish Monastery**.

The Ancient Spanish Monastery

Oddly anachronistic among the gas stations and strip malls, the **Ancient Spanish Monastery**, 16711 West Dixie Hwy (Mon–Sat 9am-4.30pm, Sun 1–4.30pm; free; ⊤305/945-1461, ⓦwww.spanishmonastery.com), is an unremarkable medieval building, the 1133 Monastery of St Bernard de Clairvaux from Segovia, Spain. But its complicated history is far more interesting than the surprisingly diminutive structure itself.

Early in the twentieth century, media magnate **William Randolph Hearst** scoured Europe for beautiful architectural souvenirs, snapping up whatever took his fancy; he then dismantled everything and shipped it to America, where most items were stitched together as part of Hearst Castle in California. The monastery, though, didn't make it as the ruins were quarantined by customs on arrival in New York, thanks to an outbreak of foot-and-mouth disease in Spain. The boxes never reached the West Coast – problems with Hearst's finances obliged him to auction them off, and the rubble gathered dust in a Brooklyn warehouse for almost thirty years. It wasn't until the early 1950s that the forlorn chunks were purchased as a tourist attraction by Allen Carswell, who also rebuilt the Cloisters Museum in northern Manhattan.

Unfortunately, though, the eleven thousand crates were opened during the quarantine so that hay within could be burned; at the time, no one had noted which block belonged in which box – with the result that there were dozens of spare stones left after the eventual reconstruction. (Those stones were recycled, and now form part of another church building, the Parish Hall, on the same site.) The Monastery is a working Episcopal church with a tiny chapel that was formerly the monks' refectory; the cloisters themselves are small and rather frayed around the edges.

The site's difficult to reach without a car – **bus** #3 from Downtown and #H, #E, and #V from the beaches drop you off at the corner of 163rd and West Dixie Highway; if you're determined to make the trip, call ahead to check whether it's open, especially at weekends, as hours can be erratic since the space is regularly rented out for events on Fridays, Saturdays and Sundays. Frankly, for a glimpse of old-world architectural glamour, a jaunt to Vizcaya (see p.114) is not only far easier but also much more rewarding.

Little Havana

A quiet district of sherbet-colored, low-rise buildings and dilapidated houses, **Little Havana,** southwest across the river from Downtown, is where the vibrant Cuban streak that colors Miami is most vividly seen. Wandering the streets, it's not unusual to see statues of Cuba's patron saint, the Virgin Mary, in residential gardens, and rare to find a newspaper box on the street that sells the English-language *Miami Herald* rather than *El Nuevo Herald*. Along **Calle Ocho** (aka SW 8th Street), the neighborhood's main drag, tiny stores and restaurants with hand-painted signs stand elbow to elbow; the other main thoroughfare, the **Cuban Memorial Boulevard,** is a quiet residential street rimmed with modest bungalows with a collection of monuments to the motherland clustered along its median. If the weather's co-operating, it's easy to forget you're not in Latin America: salesmen will come into restaurants to peddle videos or CDs while you eat, and the neighborhood *McDonald's* even serves *café cubano* alongside its Big Macs and apple pies.

What is now Little Havana only became largely Latin after Fidel Castro took power in 1959, and Cuban refugees – drawn here by the proximity and low rents – soon set about creating a replica of their homeland in America. They were unofficially fettered by the Miami city council, which attempted to deny business licenses anywhere north of 8th Street to those who didn't speak English, thereby confining newcomers to southwest Miami. Soon, though, upwardly mobile refugees gained an economic foothold in their adopted city – so much so, in fact, that Little Havana is increasingly a misnomer, as the successful Cuban community, especially the YUCAs (Young, Upwardly-Mobile Cuban Americans), decamps to wealthier neighborhoods, especially Coral Gables.

That said, this is still a heavily Latin residential area, and proper sights are few and far between: most visitors come to eat authentic Cuban food like *vaca frita* (fried beef), buy a hand-rolled cigar made from tobacco grown from Cuban seeds, or just browse the shops. Take time, though, to walk around the back streets – at least in daylight hours – for this is where you'll see the real signs of a transplanted ethnic community: there may be a man selling fruit from his van on a quiet corner or crude posters haranguing passers-by about the latest political injustice in local government. The city council is also trying to energize the area through a program called **Cultural Fridays** (℡786/314-5922, 🌐www.viernesculturales.com): on the last Friday of each month, Calle Ocho between 10th and 16th avenues is transformed into a venue for music and street stalls, in an attempt to turn the neighborhood into more of a destination.

Along the Cuban Memorial Boulevard

The Cuban Memorial Boulevard, SW 13th Avenue between Calle Ocho and SW 12th Street – close to the houses of many former political prisoners and Brigade 2506 members – is home to several monuments, often draped in Cuban flags. The

LITTLE HAVANA

0   400 yds

LATIN QUARTER

Riverside Park

José Marti Riverfront Park

Máximo Gómez Park

Bay of Pigs Museum

Tower Theater

Brigade 2506 Memorial

Cuban Memorial Boulevard

VIZCAYA Ⓜ

Museum of Science and Space Transit Planetarium

Villa Vizcaya

▼ Coconut Grove

Downtown ▶

◀ Unidos en Casa Elián

◀ Woodlawn Cemetery

◀ & Coral Gables

ACCOMMODATION

Miami River Inn B&B	A

EATING

Ayestaran	4
Casa Juancho	5
Casa Panza	13
El Cristo	8
El Fogon	17
El Rey de las Fritas	12
Guayacan	7
Habana Vieja	15
Hy Vong	6
Karlo Bakery	18
La Bodeguita Martinez	10
Los Pinarenos	14
Nuevo Siglo	9
Sergio's Cafeteria	16
Versailles	3
Yambo	2

DRINKING & NIGHTLIFE

Casa Panza	13
Club Típico Dominicano	1
Hoy Como Ayer	11

hexagonal **Eternal Torch in Honor of Brigade 2506**, at the corner of SW 13th Avenue and Calle Ocho, is topped with a metal lamp that memorializes one of the fiercest incidents in Cuban exile politics. Named after the ID number of one of the brigade's fallen members, it features the brigade's crest, commemorating the incident that put JFK below only Castro in many Cuban-Americans' esteem. In April 1961, a ragtag band of US-trained Cuban exiles landed at the Bay of Pigs in an abortive attempt to overthrow Fidel Castro's regime. They were all either captured or killed

– 117 men died fighting or drowned when their ship sank, while 1180 were taken prisoner. Depending on personal political affiliations, locals will tell you that the reason the invasion failed was either the soldiers' lack of preparation or JFK's lack of interest in Cuba – he withheld air support that may have changed the battle's outcome. Each year on April 17, a dwindling number of veterans gather here in their fatigues to reaffirm pledges of patriotism in exile to their Cuban homeland.

A block or so south stands a cluster of other monuments: there's a simple stone column commemorating **José Martí** and a moody bronze bust of **Antonio Maceo**, both heroes of Cuba's War of Independence with Spain. Notice the doleful statue of the Virgin Mary – she cradles a decapitated baby Jesus, whose state of disrepair underscores the brooding isolation of the monuments – as well as the stark **Island of Cuba Memorial** featuring a large bronze map. Looming over the loose group of monuments on the Cuban Memorial Boulevard is a massive kapok tree, holy to the Afro-Cuban religion of *Santería*(see box, p.87): you'll frequently see offerings left at its base.

Cubans in Miami

Proximity to the Caribbean island has long made Florida a place of refuge for Cuban dissidents and economic migrants. A raft ride from Cuba's northern shore, propelled by prevailing currents, can take only four days to arrive in South Florida. From **José Martí** in the 1890s to **Fidel Castro** in the early 1950s, the country's radicals have come here to campaign and raise funds, and numerous deposed Cuban politicians have whiled away their exile in Florida. However, until Fidel's time, New York, not Miami, was the center of Cuban émigré life in the US.

It was during the mid-1950s, when opposition to the Batista dictatorship – and Cuba's subservient role to the US – began to assert itself, that a trickle of Cubans started arriving in the predominantly Jewish section of Miami called Riverside, moving into low-rent properties vacated as the extant community grew wealthier and moved out. In fact, when **Fidel Castro** took power in 1959, he was enthusiastically welcomed here as part of his eleven-day tour of the USA (it was only later, after he broke off diplomatic relations, that the world found out how bloody and widescale his oppression of political dissidents had been). Back home, though, the affluent Cuban middle classes who stood to lose the most under Castro's increasingly hardline communism were soon packing their bags en masse and moving to Miami. These doctors, lawyers, and entrepreneurs helped transform the small existing Cuban community into what's now known as **Little Havana**.

Many regarded themselves as the entrepreneurial sophisticates of the Caribbean. Stories abound of formerly high-flying Cuban capitalists who arrived penniless in Little Havana, took menial jobs, and, over the course of two decades (and aided by a formidable network of old expats) toiled, wheeled, and dealed their way to positions of power. Their influence stretched further than South Florida; leading Miami Cubans also exerted considerable influence over the US government's policy toward Cuba with their 800,000 votes and hefty campaign contributions.

The second great Cuban influx into Miami was of a quite different social nature and racial composition: the **Mariel Boatlift** in May 1980 brought 125,000 predominantly Black islanders from the Cuban port of Mariel to Miami. Unlike their more worldly predecessors, these arrivals were largely poor and uneducated, and a fifth of them were fresh from Cuban jails – incarcerated for criminal rather than political crimes. Bluntly put, Castro had dumped his criminals and misfits on Miami. Only a few of them wound up in Little Havana: most *marielitos* settled in South Beach, where they proceeded to terrorize the local community, becoming a source of embarrassment to Miami's longer-established and determinedly respectable (and white) Cubans.

Calle Ocho and around

Southwest 8th Street runs through the whole of Miami, morphing into the Tamiami Trail as it skirts Coral Gables' northern boundary and shoots out into the Everglades. It's between SW 8th and 27th avenues, though, where it earns the moniker of **Calle Ocho**, as a staunchly Spanish-speaking commercial drag, lined with stores and restaurants plus local landmarks like **Máximo Gómez Park** and the **Tower Theater**.

Máximo Gómez Park

West along Calle Ocho from the Brigade 2506 memorial, **Máximo Gómez Park**, at the corner of SW 14th Avenue (daily 8am–6pm), is officially named after a hero of the Cuban War of Independence (even if he was Dominican-born). This gated concrete hideaway is nicknamed "Domino Park" – despite the clichéd image, old Cuban men really do gather here to play dominoes and spend the day argu-

Yet local division gives way to fervent agreement when the subject turns to Fidel Castro: he's still universally detested. Cubans even suspected of advocating dialogue with Castro have been killed; one man had his legs blown off in the 1980s for suggesting that violence on the streets was counterproductive, and the Cuban Museum of the Americas was firebombed for displaying the work of Castro-approved artists and closed down because of it.

The energy and money expended against Castro is phenomenal. The late telecoms billionaire **Jorge Mas Canosa**, who acted as unofficial king of Miami's Cuban community, earmarked much of his fortune for massive lobbying attempts in Washington to keep Castro economically isolated and politically vilified. He helped nurture **the Helms-Burton Bill**, passed in the early 1990s under sponsorship of the right-wing senator Jesse Helms. Broadly speaking, this act prevented any president from changing America's hardline approach to Cuba. Bill Clinton initially baulked at these political handcuffs and only signed the bill after a long delay in response to Cuba's downing a US military helicopter. Even so, Cuban lobbyists' reach in DC has been dwindling since then: George W. Bush's eight-year regime showed an indifference to Cuba that would have been unthinkable in the Reaganite Republican 1980s. In fact, Bush's only major move was to further restrict family or compassionate visits by expats to once every three years, which did little but generate resentment among Miami's Cubans who often missed funerals or weddings unless willing to break the law and travel home via a third country.

Of course, the biggest headline-grabber was the case of **Elián González**, the little boy returned to his father in Cuba after his mother died during an abortive raft trek as a refugee. Mention of the case still rouses loathing for Clinton in Miami's Cuban community – by supporting the legality of the boy's repatriation he made himself the least popular president since JFK among locals. This sad mess, which has seemed to blight everyone involved, did produce a winner: **Manny Diaz**, the lawyer who defended Elián's right to stay in America, is now a very successful mayor of Miami.

But no doubt the biggest test for Miami's Cuban community lies ahead. At time of writing, Fidel had finally announced his retirement; firebrand brother **Raoul Castro** was named his successor. Despite the predictions of Capitalist revolution after Fidel's departure that have long been spouted by vocal armchair politicians, the transition was smooth. What happens when Raoul, too, ages out of ruling and needs another ideologue to replace him, no one can guarantee. What is certain, however, is that should Miami's Cuban expats ever return to their beloved mother country, they will face a daunting task, trying to govern a very different island from the one they left behind.

▲ A kapok tree and statue on Cuban Memorial Boulevard

ing about politics. In fact, access to the park's open-air tables is (quite illegally) restricted to men over 55. Bear in mind that these old-timers are camera-fierce rather than camera-shy, and don't take kindly to the attentions of enthusiastic visitors. The fence and key cards that guard its entrance aren't geared to prevent tourist intrusion, though – they were installed after a spate of shootings in the 1980s. You shouldn't have any problem stopping by during the day, though, as the gates will normally be open.

The Tower Theater

The two blocks west of the domino players have been gussied up into a pedestrianized park and renamed Domino Plaza, but it's an unappealing and artificial place to dawdle. Instead, stop and admire the astonishing exterior of the **Tower Theater** at 1508 SW 8th St, a 1930 Art Deco masterpiece, with its shiny, rounded steel signage, and sleek blue and white spire. Notable as the first theater in Miami to add Spanish subtitles in 1960, it's now owned by the City of Miami and operated by Miami Dade College, which runs sporadic film programs – for details, see p.170, "Performing arts and film."

The Bay of Pigs Museum

The small **Bay of Pigs Museum**, 1821 SW 9th St (Mon–Fri 10am–9pm, Sat 10am–2pm; free; ⊺305/649-4719, ⓦwww.bayofpigsmuseum.org), is crammed with ephemera associated with the invasion, also commemorated on the Cuban Memorial Boulevard. There are maps, uniforms, guns, military plans, and of course, a full roll-call of Brigade 2506 plus extensive photographs. The snapshot of Cuban history it offers is intriguing, but it's mostly of interest to specialists and partisans – it was set up, of course, as little more than a myth-sustaining exercise and yet another bastion of anti-Castro propaganda. There's also an onsite library, largely in Spanish, with documents on Cuban history and the Bay of Pigs invasion itself. The museum recently launched a fundraising campaign to custom-build a new three story, cutting-edge site for its holdings, though at time of writing there's no confirmation of when or if this will go ahead – check the web site for updates.

Woodlawn Cemetery

Even further west, at 3260 SW 8th St, lies the enormous, serene **Woodlawn Cemetery** (daily sunrise–dusk; ⊺305/445-5425), crowded with mausolea and statuary and filled with the manicured graves of many prominent local figures. The father of Coral Gables, **George Merrick**, is buried here, but not in the Merrick plot: his wife Eunice Peacock – whose parents had been pioneers in Coconut Grove (see p.110) – had him moved into her own family's area two decades after he died. It's also the final home for several expat Cuban bigwigs, including two deposed presidents: **General Gerardo Machado**, unseated in 1933, and **Carlos Prío Socarras**, one of the prime movers behind Machado's downfall, who was himself driven from office (and the country) in 1952. Also interred in the mausoleum (and marked only by his initials) is **Anastasio Somoza**, dictator of Nicaragua until overthrown by the Sandinistas in 1979, and later killed in Paraguay; look, too, for the black marble wall, a tribute to the **Unknown Cuban Freedom Fighter**, one of the many killed during the abortive Bay of Pigs invasion.

Northern Little Havana: Unidos en Casa Elián and the Orange Bowl

On the northwestern reaches of Little Havana, at 2319 NW 2nd Street, is the **Unidos en Casa Elián** museum. This is the house where the seven-year-old headline-maker Elián González stayed during his stormy time in Miami. Elián was a flashpoint in Miami politics: after his mother was killed trying to reach America with her son on a raft in November 1999, he was forcibly returned to his father who'd remained in Cuba by the federal government, despite enormous local pro-

▲ The Versailles restaurant

test. This house has been turned into an oddly discomforting museum in his honor by great-uncle Delfin González: display cases house Elián's playthings, alongside dozens of photo-collages and mawkish poems written in tribute by local residents. Frankly, the only reason to come here is in an attempt to understand how raw and vivid a wound the Elián controversy carved into Miami's Cuban community – as this house shows, it's far deeper than an outsider might suspect. Its opening hours are erratic and unpredictable (nominally Sun 10am–6pm), and there's no public phone to check in advance.

This area was also once home to the historic **Orange Bowl**, due north from Máximo Gómez Park at 1501 NW 3rd St. It was known locally as the place where JFK accepted the Brigade 2506 flag after the Bay of Pigs debacle and promised to return it in "free Havana." (Older Cuban exiles grimly joked that he was referring to a well-known bar in Miami, rather than the city). In early 2008, though, the stadium was abandoned by its highest profile tenant – the University of Miami's football team, who decamped with a 25-year contract to play at Dolphin Stadium on the Broward County border – and the site flagged for demolition and redevelopment. Plans for the area are unclear, though it may be used as space for a new home for the Florida Marlins baseball team.

Coral Gables

A curate's egg of urban planning, **Coral Gables** is separated from Miami proper by more than just politics. It has a distinct local council and residential regulations, and seems to regard itself as an upper-class cousin to Miami, sandwiched as it is between gritty Little Havana and oddball Coconut Grove. Its twelve square miles of broad boulevards and leafy streets are lined with elaborate Spanish- and Italian-style architecture, along with civic amenities like fountains and even a swimming pool. Intended by founder George Merrick to inspire civic pride in its residents, some say the plan for this European-style city has worked a little too well: this is the snootiest part of Miami, and its architectural beauty is somewhat blighted by a suburban smugness you won't find elsewhere.

Still, it's a fascinating place to visit, largely because almost all the landmarks that sprouted during its development still stand. The **Merrick House**, George Merrick's charming family home, remains, as do projects like the majestic **City Hall** and the **Miracle Mile** downtown. The grandiose **Biltmore Hotel** has reopened for business, while the delightful **Venetian Pool** is an unmissable Miami sight. The **International Villages** and **the Entrances** are spectacular follies, born jointly of Merrick's grand vision and sales savvy, adding further variety to the city's European-style architecture. Indeed, even the street layout is European, with winding roads that amble through a haphazard grid of residential streets and tiny, ground-level white rocks that act as street signs – remember to bring a map to navigate.

Some history

Whereas Miami's other early property developers built cheap and fast in search of a quick buck, the creator of Coral Gables, **George Merrick**, fired by the **City Beautiful Movement** (see Contexts: Architecture, p.262), was equal parts entrepreneur and aesthete. Merrick was inspired by the Shaker Heights suburb in Ohio, a City Beautiful project planned by a pair of wealthy brothers that boasted wide greenspaces and fancy buildings. Merrick's pedigree was impeccable – his preacher grandfather had made millions with a questionable cure-all called "Fink's Magic Oil" – and he himself would become a fleeting millionaire through a combination of idealism, ego, and sheer salesmanship. Merrick appointed his uncle, artist **Denman Fink**, as Coral Gables' creative director; recruited **Phineas Paist**, one of the architectural masterminds behind Villa Vizcaya (see p.114), to plan the plazas, fountains, and artfully-aged stucco-fronted buildings; and employed **Frank Button**, a landscape gardener who'd worked on Chicago's Lincoln Park enlargement, to oversee all the greenspaces.

Merrick envisioned a **Floridian Venice**, a city floating on, and by, the water. He further declared that no two houses could be the same, and that all designs had to be approved by the official city architect. The layout and buildings of Merrick's

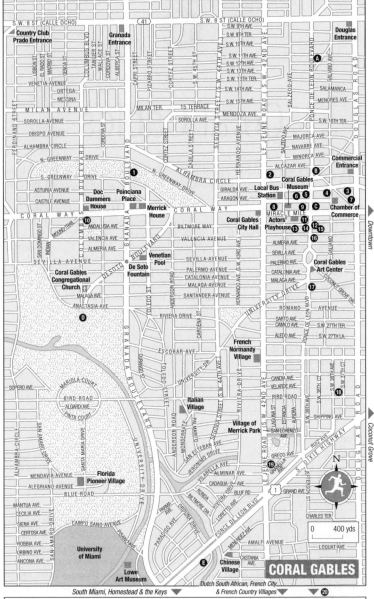

South Miami, Homestead & the Keys ▼   Dutch South African, French City & French Country Villages ▼   20

CORAL GABLES

ACCOMMODATION	EATING				Sacha's Café	15
Best Western Chateau	Books & Books Café	6	Chocolate	House of India	7	Titanic Brewery	20
Bleau	A	Bugatti's	14	Fashion	13	Les Halles	12	**DRINKING**
Biltmore	D	Burger Bob's	1	Miss Saigon Bistro	4	**& NIGHTLIFE**
Gables Inn	E	Caffè Abbracci	8	Christy's	17	Mykonos	10	The Globe	2
Hotel Place St Michel	B	Canton	16	Gables Diner	5	Nena's	3	John Martin's	9
Westin Colonnade Hotel	C	Chef Innocent at		Giardino		Ortanique on the	Titanic Brewery	20
	Restaurant St Michel	A	Havana Harry's	19	Mile	11	
			The Globe	2		

own suburb quickly took shape, often in ingenious ways. He transformed an abandoned quarry (used to supply the porous **coral rock** that gave his own homestead and later the whole city its name) into the Venetian Pool, and disguised the construction ditches that ringed the infant Coral Gables into a network of canals.

As the city took shape, Merrick focused on his own flair for selling, combining snappy sloganeering ("Where Your Castles in Spain are Made Real") with publicity stunts like a Spanish-themed land auction in 1921, or the ninety coral pink buses he bought to ferry in prospective residents from across Florida. Merrick spent a then mind-boggling $3m on marketing in less than four years; in that same time, the city brought in more than $150 million.

Coral Gables' heyday was short-lived. Soon after the **Biltmore Hotel** first opened, Miami was devastated by a major hurricane in 1926, and its tourism lifeblood was cut off. Ironically, the carefully built, ornamental city of Coral Gables was the district least damaged by the winds – even the towering *Biltmore* held firm. But the Great Depression set in before the local economy could recover, and Merrick's money soon disappeared. His company, the Coral Gables Land Corporation, had directly guaranteed all the personal mortgages of his Shangri-La-seeking settlers, and couldn't survive the economic collapse of 1929. Merrick retreated to Lower Matecumbe Key in the Florida Keys to run a resort that his wife Eunice's parents had bequeathed her until it, too, was wrecked by a hurricane in 1936. Merrick finally returned to the area to serve as postmaster of the City of Miami until his death in 1942; he's buried next to Eunice in Woodlawn Cemetery (see p.95).

Merrick's dream lives on, however, as local residents have collectively embraced his grand design, enacting stringent ordinances on everything from appropriate color schemes to the size of "For Sale" signs in yards (5"x8") and even the times during which unsightly trucks may be parked outside a private house (in fact, the city even publishes a handy booklet, *Frequent Code Violations*, so that locals will know what they can and can't do). As affluent, second-generation **Cuban-Americans** have begun to move into the area, some say that Coral Gables, not Little Havana, is the new center of Miami's Cuban community. Still, there's little commercial evidence of Cuban presence here – this is one place in Miami where it's hard to find a quick *cafecito*.

The Entrances

Merrick was an entrepreneurial showman, and his plan to ring Coral Gables with eight impressive **entrance gates** was but one of his theatrical flourishes; he reasoned that these entranceways would evoke a sense of place before there were even houses here. He had originally planned on eight entrances to frame the main access roads, but only four were completed before funds ran out. Three of these, all along a two-and-a-half-mile stretch of SW 8th Street, are well worth seeking out.

At the junction with Douglas Road, the million-dollar **Douglas Entrance**, also known as the Puerta del Sol, was the most ambitious, consisting of a gateway and tower with two expansive wings of shops, offices, and artists' studios. During the 1960s, it was almost bulldozed to make room for a supermarket, but survived to become a well-scrubbed business area, still upholding Merrick's Mediterranean themes. Further west, at the junction with Granada Boulevard, the sixty-foot-high, vine-covered **Granada Entrance** is based on the entrance to the city of Granada in Spain – a massive Renaissance gateway erected by Carlos V in the sixteenth century. The **Country Club Prado Entrance**, at the junction with Country Club Prado is an elaborate recreated Italian garden, bordered by freestanding stucco and brick pillars topped by ornamental urns and gaslamps. The fourth entrance, **Commercial** (also known as the Alhambra), is at the corner of the Alhambra Circle and Douglas Road but doesn't come close to matching the others in flair or style.

▲ The Miracle Mile

If you don't particularly wish to see the Entrances, the best way into Coral Gables from points east is along SW 24th Street – also called Coral Way – which turns into the Miracle Mile between Douglas Road (SW 37th Avenue) and LeJeune Road (SW 42nd Avenue).

The Miracle Mile and around

The so-called **Miracle Mile** wasn't the main commercial drag in Merrick's plan (that was Ponce de Leon Boulevard); rather, this strip of stores was cooked up in the 1940s by George and Rebyl Zain, married entrepreneurs who moved to Coral Gables from New York. Until recently, the strip was rather forlorn, filled with cobwebby ladies' boutiques and bridal emporia, yet it's now recharging its retail batteries with an aggressive redevelopment plan that's lured casual cafés and shops back to the main street. Another major incentive to pedestrians is the free **trolley service** (T305/460-5070) shuttling north-south through downtown: it runs along Ponce de Leon Boulevard from the Metrorail stop to Calle Ocho (Mon–Thurs 6.30am–8pm, Fri 6.30am–10pm), with stops on almost every block.

As for nightlife, the local government loosened area liquor laws, allowing bars to remain open until 2am (rather than midnight) in the hope of re-energizing this segment of Downtown. The council's efforts worked, generating a buzzier scene on weekday evenings when staff from many of the big-name businesses that have offices locally stop by for drinks or dinner after work and often remain out late. Architecturally, the Miracle Mile strip is filled with Mediterranean Revival buildings of only passing interest, save for the occasional standout.

The Westin Colonnade Hotel

Halfway west along the Miracle Mile, the **Westin Colonnade Hotel** (T305/441-2600) can be found at 180 Aragon Ave (just north of the Mile), at the corner of Ponce de Leon Boulevard. The building was meant to house Merrick's local real-estate sales office, but was completed only months before the 1926 hurricane that wiped him out. It served as a sometime movie soundstage in the 1930s and 1940s until Los Angeles decisively eclipsed Miami as the home of America's infant film industry; during the war, it became an army training facility and parachute factory. Today, it's an upscale yet unremarkable hotel and one of the more architecturally impressive buildings on the Miracle Mile – be sure to take note of its ornate center fountain, as well as the stylistic spiral and peak flourishes on the structure itself. For a review of the hotel's amenities, see p.138, "Accommodation."

The Actors' Playhouse at the Miracle Theater

Originally built in the 1940s as Coral Gables' main cinema, the **Actors' Playhouse**, 280 Miracle Mile (℡305/444-9293, Ⓦwww.actorsplayhouse.org), was converted to a theater in the mid-1990s to provide a home for an acting company displaced by Hurricane Andrew. The classic theater has been sensitively restored, and stylish accents like the intricately etched glass in the lobby and a gleaming, metallic ticket booth embellish the otherwise rather plain Art Deco building, a standout among Coral Gables' usual Old World building style. In addition to hosting traveling productions, the Playhouse's two small auditoria feature readings by local writers and performances by the resident children's theater company. For ticket information, see p.168, "Performing arts and film."

The Coral Gables Museum

The Coral Gables Museum (Ⓦwww.coralgables.com), 285 Aragon Ave, was meant to open in 2007, but delays have pushed the opening back three years at least. When it finally debuts, its five thousand square feet of exhibition space will showcase decades' worth of memorabilia that have been stashed in boxes in the Coral Gables Merrick House (see p.102). The collection, ranging from line drawings and plans for the *Biltmore* to old letters, will be housed in this former police and fire station, designed by Phineas Paist in 1939 – look for the muscular busts of firemen sculpted as reliefs above the garage doors.

Coral Gables City Hall

At the western end of the Miracle Mile, **Coral Gables City Hall**, 405 Biltmore Way (Mon–Fri 8am–5pm; ℡305/460-5217, Ⓦwww.coralgables.com), was planned as the heart of the city. This coral rock building, designed by the prolific Paist, is set at the busiest intersection in downtown Coral Gables – a pity, since the noise and traffic diminish its impressive façade. Fronted with twelve stately columns as well as a replica of the city's seal, it's topped off by a multi-tiered, Spanish-inspired clock tower and plenty of ornamental moldings. Paist drew direct inspiration from the City Hall of Philadelphia, but tweaked the design by incorporating local elements like marine animals frolicking on the column's capitals. Inside, sales posters from Coral Gables' heyday are on display, as well as newspaper clippings that illustrate how frenzied the Florida land boom of the 1920s truly was. There's also a blandly decorative **mural** of the *Four Seasons*, painted by the ubiquitous Denman Fink, in the belltower cupola; it was recently spiffed up after years of neglect – note that while three of the seasons are represented by young women, winter's the old man.

Coral Gables Art Center

Merrick was careful to keep his sales and artistic staff separate: he built what's now the Colonnade Hotel for the former, while Denman Fink, Phineas Paist, and their staffs were housed at the **Coral Gables Art Center** at 2901 Ponce de Leon Blvd. Each person had an office that overlooked the magnificent spiral staircase in the main turret, a view enjoyed today by developers of the nearby Old Spanish Village complex, who have taken over the rickety building to use it as a suitably retro sales center for their own Merrick-inspired mixed use development. One distinct advantage of its current use: visitors can easily duck inside to see its interiors, though sadly the lyrical blue and white cloud painting on the ceiling above the staircase – Merrick's nod to the building's artistic purpose – has been covered with a cream topcoat, albeit temporarily.

Coral Way and DeSoto Boulevard

The forced rebirth of downtown Coral Gables is most glaring as the Miracle Mile turns back into **Coral Way** immediately west of LeJeune Road (or SW 42nd Street). Here, Mediterranean Revival high-rises proliferate, nurtured by a canny scheme that rewards those who construct in a locally appropriate style: called a Mediterranean Bonus, the reward allows any such new structure to be twenty percent larger than a modernist counterpart, say sixteen stories rather than thirteen. Even so, Coral Way is an oddly soulless strip, and there's little to detain the casual visitor. The most pleasant detour is a wander round the residential streets south of Coral Way, canopied with enormous banyan trees. Stop by Fink's **DeSoto Fountain** near the Venetian Pool: it's an imposing centerpiece at the junction of Granada and DeSoto boulevards and another example of Merrick's determination to provide aesthetic as well as civic amenities. Most streets here are named for Spanish provinces and towns, usually pilfered by Eunice Merrick from Washington Irving's book, *The Alhambra*. The few that aren't (Bird Road and Douglas Road, for example) were chosen by officials of Dade County and honor notable early locals.

Move west along Coral Way and you'll come across three interesting houses after crossing Toledo Street. **Merrick House**, the first, was George's family home and is now a museum. Further west stands **Poinciana Place** at no. 937, one of the earliest structures in the city, built close to Merrick's home when he married Eunice Peacock in 1916: its Mediterranean Revival style would serve as a template for later constructions. **Doc Dammers House**, at no. 1141, is unfortunately hard to see, stashed behind lush greenery on a large corner plot at Columbus Boulevard. This elaborate two-story home (now a private residence) belonged to New Yorker Dammers, a smooth-talking auctioneer who'd come to the area on the bidding of Carl Fisher to sell land in Downtown Miami. He was then employed by Merrick to bring his magic to Coral Gables: his tricks included gifts like boxes of grapefruit and trinkets given to the audience in between each lot, which guaranteed him a healthy crowd. Once a plot had been sold, the building plans and coral rock needed to construct a house were provided free of charge. When the city was incorporated, his fame among locals was high enough to secure him the post of first mayor of Coral Gables.

The Coral Gables Merrick House

Designed by George's eccentric and artistic mother Althea, the **Coral Gables Merrick House**, 907 Coral Way (Wed & Sun, 45-minute tours begin at 1pm,

2pm & 3pm; $5; ⓣ305/460-5361), recently reopened after years of renovation, designed to shore up the building and make it more visitor-ready. The only part not yet refreshed at the time of writing was the kitchen, which preservationists were still squabbling over. The question at hand was should it be remade in a facsimile of the 1920s original or modernized to be fully functional for the house's new part-time gig as a for-rent corporate event space.

Otherwise, the place is a compact showpiece of Floridian shotgun design, its central ventilating hallway and wraparound veranda ideal for muggy South Florida summers. The simple wooden structure at the rear of the building was home to the Merricks when they arrived in 1889 from New England to run a 160-acre fruit and vegetable farm. The venture was such a success that the shack was later augmented by a grander house of coral rock and termite-resistant local pine: it was christened Coral Gables, passing its name on to the city that later grew up around the family farm. The dual blows of the property crash and a citrus blight led to the gradual deterioration of the house, until restoration began in the 1970s. The house now showcases artwork by Denman Fink, as well as Merrick memorabilia and an informative video that gives an overview of Coral Gables history. Upstairs, look for the chest Merrick received from King Alonso XIII of Spain, who decorated him in 1927 for creating a Spanish-inspired city in North America. There's a pleasant rustic grotto decorating the entrance to the small servant's house at the rear: the grotto was once much larger, until Merrick's practical mother sold some land to pay for her grandsons' dental work.

By the entrance to the car park, don't miss one oddball remnant of Coral Gables' past that demonstrates how aesthetic considerations always overruled practical ones in Merrick's vision. His traffic STOP signs were originally at ankle level to avoid interrupting vistas – until, of course, they proved rather unsafe; there's an example of one in the undergrowth here.

Venetian Pool

South of the Coral Gables Merrick House, at 2001 DeSoto Boulevard, is the magical **Venetian Pool** (daily 11am–4.30pm, though closed Mon outside of summer and longer hours in warmer weather; April–Oct $10, children under 13 $6.75, Nov–March $6.77/$5.50; ⓣ305/460-5356, ⓦwww.venetianpool.com), originally known as the Venetian Casino. As local coral rock was plundered to build the original homes in Coral Gables, an unsightly quarry developed in the heart of the area, which Merrick, along with uncle and artist Denman Fink, ingeniously transformed into one of Miami's most appealing attractions. Merrick knew from the outset it was one of Coral Gables' most appealing features, and he used it as a makeshift sales center in the earliest days of the city. Officially intended as another civic project for the benefit of local residents, it's a delightful place to spend an afternoon.

Despite its ornamentation, the pool was never designed with the social elite in mind; admission was cheap and open to all, and even today, local residents get a special discount. Surrounded by shaded porticos, wrought-iron railings, palm-studded paths, and Venetian-style bridges, the deep-blue water winds its way through coral rock caves and spills over two waterfalls – there's even a landlocked beach for sunbathers and a junk food-heavy concession stand with delicious curly fries. Locker rooms are spotless, as are the tiled colonnades that display photographs of the pool in its heyday, when watersport celebrities like Johnny Weismuller (famous as the first onscreen Tarzan) and Esther Williams performed here. Until recent changes in labor laws, one of the perks of employment as the head lifeguard was to live onsite, in the ornate turret above the ticket hall; the old apartment, now an office, still has a small kitchen and bathroom attached.

Coral Gables Congregational Church

Southwest from the Venetian Pool, the **Coral Gables Congregational Church**, 3010 DeSoto Blvd (℡305/448-7421, ⓦwww.coralgablescongregational.org), is another of Merrick's lofty civic projects, designed as a replica of a church in Mexico – he donated the land and dedicated the building to his late father, a Congregational minister. The church itself is a bright, ornate Spanish Revival flurry whose belfry echoes the imposing tower of the *Biltmore* across the street. The interior is dark, more Spanish Inquisition than Spanish Revival, with plenty of elaborately-wrought ironwork and fine acoustics, especially notable during the regular jazz and classical concerts held here (see p.168, "Performing arts and film"). Sunday services are held at 9.15am and 11am.

The Biltmore Hotel

Merrick's crowning achievement – aesthetically if not financially – was no doubt the **Biltmore Hotel**, 1200 Anastasia Ave (℡305/445-1926 or 1-800/727-1926, ⓦwww.biltmorehotel.com), which wraps its broad wings around the southern end of DeSoto Boulevard. The third in a trio of Miami towers inspired by the Giralda belltower in Seville, Spain (the others were the now-demolished *Roney Plaza* hotel in South Beach and Downtown's Freedom Tower, see p.45), the *Biltmore* looms majestically over Coral Gables. Its architecture is Mediterranean Revival with a strong Moorish influence shown in its ornate surface decorations: the hotel looks most like a movie set, with 25-foot-high frescoed walls, vaulted ceilings, and immense fireplaces. It was the last word in elegance when completed, especially notable for an enormous chevron-shaped pool, and it attracted celebrity guests like Judy Garland and Bing Crosby. One of the seamier celebs who frequented the place was Miami staple Al Capone, who hosted splashy parties on the 13th floor in what's still unofficially known as the "Capone Suite"; it's said that the ghost of his bodyguard, Fats Walsh, killed while his boss was supping at the Prohibition-era speakeasy stashed on the same floor, still wanders the hotel's hallways late at night.

Surprisingly, given its grand scale, the hotel took less than a year to construct: from March 1925, workers lived in a tent city nearby and worked 24 hours a day to meet the opening date of January 15, 1926. One thousand VIPs were brought down from New York on a luxury train and genuine Venetian gondoliers punted guests through the Coral Gables waterways to the nearby beach. Since then, the *Biltmore* has weathered rough seas: the hotel was sold to new owners during the Depression, became a military hospital for burn victims after World War II – the pool was fenced in and the giant ochre building was whitewashed. Then, following the hospital's closure, it was an illicit hangout for local teenagers. Eventually, it was renovated at a cost of $55 million, a project that included partially filling in the pool, as it was too deep for modern safety regulations. The *Biltmore* reopened as a hotel in 1993 but the new owners promptly went bust and it closed again for two years before current management took over.

Merrick's hotels

Before the *Biltmore* was constructed as his showpiece, Merrick had put up six smaller hotels where he could host prospective residents when they came down for site inspections of their real-estate deals. One, the *Hotel Seville*, became today's 27-room *Hotel Place St Michel* (see p.137); the best preserved, though, is the *Cla Reina* – now the *La Palma* restaurant (116 Alhambra Circle). The exterior, with its enclosed courtyard and decorative ironwork, looks much as it did during Merrick's heyday.

If you can't afford to stay here (for a review, see p.137), at least step in to marvel at the space. It's easy enough to wander round without a guide: otherwise, there are **free tours** every Sunday at 1.30, 2.30, and 3.30pm – though these are rather rote and disappointing.

The neighboring annex, the west wing of the Biltmore Hotel officially known by the absurdly po-faced tag Conference Center of the Americas, is also open to the public. It is as stately as it sounds and is worth dipping inside for a closer look at its painstakingly renovated Beaux Arts features. Most people turn up to knock a ball along the lush fairways of the **Biltmore Golf Course**, which in the hotel's glory days hosted the highest-paying golf tournament in the world; for golfers, it's a par 71 course designed by Donald Ross.

South Coral Gables

The southern reaches of Coral Gables are primarily residential, aside from the campus of the **University of Miami**, built in the 1920s on land donated by Merrick (with the theory that a world-class city would need a world-class university). The school almost went bankrupt in its early years, but is now a thriving institution, known especially for its sports teams; though the football team's last decade has been less successful than its storied past, local devotion to the 'Canes remains undimmed (see p.190, "Sports, fitness, and ocean activities").

Merrick's late additions to the city plan, architectural stunts known as the **International Villages**, are mostly in this area (see box, p.106), and it's here you'll find the **canals** that sparked Coral Gables' claim to be the Venice of America. In fact, much like the Venetian Pool, they're simply dolled-up byproducts of construction: having hewn chunks of coral rock from the ground to build houses, Merrick simply filled the holes with water and called them canals, employing gondoliers every night to authenticate his claim.

Even before the great hurricane of 1926, the market for housing in Merrick's new city had begun to soften. To revive interest, he worked with Myers Y. Cooper, a banker and former governor of Ohio, to cook up a gimmick that's now one of the area's signature features: the **International Villages**. Fourteen were planned, each representing a different style and each overseen by different architects. Unfortunately, constraints of time and money dictated only seven were built: the hoped-for remainder had showy themes like Japanese, African Bazaar, Persian Canal, and Tangier, as well as the more restrained Neapolitan Baroque and Mexican Hacienda. Today, the seven standing are among the priciest real estate in the city.

The eight buildings of the **Chinese Village** (bounded by Sansavino Ave, Castania Ave, Menendez Ave, Maggiore St, and Riviera Drive) were designed by Henry Killam-Murphy, who'd lived in the Far East and just completed buildings for Yale University in China. They're arguably the most dazzling, notable for their brightly colored roofs and ornately carved balconies; ironically, though, they fetch the lowest real-estate prices because the over-the-top design is an acquired taste. Another photogenic cluster, the **French Normandy Village** (the 400 block of Viscaya Ave at LeJeune Rd), looks thoroughly Elizabethan, thanks to thick, chocolate-brown-beam-studded stucco facades and red-tile roofs. It has weathered surprisingly well, too, given that it was once owned by the University of Miami and housed five fraternities, then was turned over to soldiers' barracks in World War II.

Close by, the **Dutch South African Village** is less eye-catching (the 6600–6700 block of LeJeune Rd). Look for the gabled and dormered roofs inspired by homes built by wealthy Boer settlers in South Africa, as well as connecting windows that make the two-storied houses look like bungalows. In contrast, check out the grand colonial-style mansions of the **Florida Pioneer Village** (the 4300–4600 block of Santa Maria St); in the Greek Revival style, they feature pillars and verandas as well as incongruous white-picket fences.

Eighteenth-century-style townhouses make up the **French City Village** (the 1000 block of Hardee Rd); you'll know them by the four-foot-high walls that surround the buildings, enclosing courtyards and kitchen gardens. Its rural companion, the **French Country Village** (the 500 block of Hardee Rd and around) includes buildings designed to echo French farmhouses, with steeply pitched, crossed-gabled roofs, wrought-iron balconies, and, best of all, huge back yards.

Finally, the **Italian Village** (bounded by San Antonio Ave, San Esteban Ave, Monserrate St, and Segovia St) is a larger, looser collection of homes in Italian country and Venetian styles, and as a result stand out less from their Mediterranean Revival neighbors; to identify them, look for exterior stairways and walled gardens.

For some time, six of the seven quirky clusters were designated as National Historic Landmarks – with all the prestige and red tape that brings to the owners. Residents of the French City Village held out against this bothersome honor until 2002, when one owner's garish exterior paintjob – a deep mustard that had been approved by the city but offended the neighbors – led them to reconsider

The Lowe Art Museum

From its beginnings in 1950 as Miami's first professional exhibition space in a few rooms on the University of Miami campus, the **Lowe Art Museum**, 1301 Stanford Drive (Tues, Wed, Fri & Sat 10am–5pm, Thurs noon–7pm, Sun noon–5pm; $7; ⊤305/284-3535, ⊛www.lowemuseum.org), has grown through acquisitions and renovations to be one of the largest museums in Florida. Its collection is large and diverse, featuring nineteenth-century, contemporary, Native American, and Renaissance art. There's even a sizeable amount of Cuban ephemera, thanks to a donation from the controversial Cuban Museum of the Americas in Little Havana, which closed its doors in 1999. Unfortunately, though, that diversity is its downfall: the Renaissance collection is sprawling and nondescript, while the Impressionist works are primarily small, early canvases by Sisley and Monet. Works that do stand out include the eerily lifelike *Football Player* by local sculptor Duane Hanson, and some paintings by pop innovator Roy Lichtenstein. Overall, it's pleasant enough, but not a patch on better collections at the Miami Art Museum Downtown (see p.41) or at the Margulies, Rubell or MOCA collections in Wynwood (see pp.81–83).

Coconut Grove

The latent pioneer spirit of South Florida surfaces in **Coconut Grove**, an area known for being both tolerant and, at times, ornery. It's always seemed uneasy about being a part of Miami, which annexed it in the late nineteenth century. Eccentrics and artists have made their homes here for more than a century (the local Hare Krishna temple is just off Virginia Street), and older locals will usually treat outsiders with politeness plus a little suspicion. In recent years, the area has gentrified somewhat, blighted by bland shopping centers and towering bay-view apartments, but it has somehow managed to remain a refreshingly off-kilter, resoundingly real place.

From its beginning, the Coconut Grove community has been diverse: having sprung up after the Civil War around the tropical plantation of a Confederate doctor, the area was originally home to migrant Bahamian laborers and liberal-minded Anglo settlers, as well as characters like wacky philosopher-environmentalist Ralph Middleton Munroe (who built the house at the Barnacle State Historical Site – see p.110). Facilities in the town were highly developed by 1896, with a library, churches, a yacht club, and the first school in Dade County. Up until then, a chunk of dense hardwood hammock had kept the new city of Miami at bay, but city growth and Henry Flagler's railroad merged the two, and Coconut Grove was soon annexed. The populace – galvanized by their early independence, as well as the many liberal-minded artists and leftists who migrated here thanks to tolerant attitudes – has tried to secede several times since then; there are still activists pushing the cause today.

Separatist attitude aside, Coconut Grove is still part of Miami proper – in fact, the **Miami City Hall** moved here to the Dinner Key Marina on Biscayne Bay in the 1950s. Geographically, the southwestern portion of the area is leafy and residential, with chunks of thick hammock and enormous canopies of greenery on most streets, while pedestrian-friendly **central Coconut Grove** holds two well-known shopping centers. East from here, there's the once countercultural, now well-tended **Peacock Park**, as well as the sublime **Barnacle** building and the superb **Kampong** botanical garden. Moving north up Bayshore Drive past City Hall, Biscayne Bay is lined with greenspace before arriving at **Villa Vizcaya**, the spectacularly overwrought mansion built by millionaire James Deering.

Central Coconut Grove and around

The **Grove's central district** is compact and walkable, with shops and restaurants fanning out northwest from the intersection of Main Highway and Grand Avenue. **CocoWalk**, a hacienda-inspired outdoor mall, was a revitalizing force for the neighborhood when it was built in the early 1990s, and is still a social hub. By comparison, the older and more monolithic **Shoppes at Mayfair in the Grove**

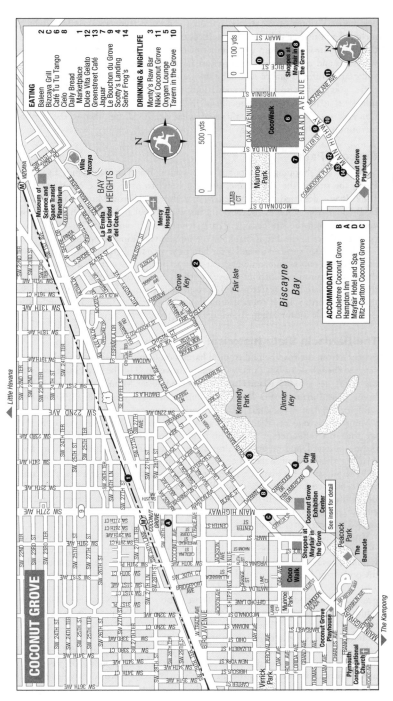

COCONUT GROVE

EATING

Baleen	2
Bizcaya Grill	C
Café Tu Tango	6
Cielo	8
Daily Bread Marketplace	1
Dolce Vita Gelato	12
Greenstreet Café	13
Jaguar	7
Le Bouchon du Grove	9
Scotty's Landing	4
Señor Frog's	14

DRINKING & NIGHTLIFE

Monty's Raw Bar	3
Nikki Coconut Grove	11
Oxygen Lounge	5
Tavern in the Grove	10

ACCOMMODATION

Doubletree Coconut Grove	B
Hampton Inn	A
Mayfair Hotel and Spa	D
Ritz-Carlton Coconut Grove	C

just across Virginia Street is less appealing – despite regeneration efforts which included a hotel (see p.138) and the offices of ad agency Crispin Porter Bogusky, the public areas are home to nondescript chain stores and the odd, zigzagging walkways and ugly copper sculptures are far from inviting. Better to head south, and grab a coffee at one of the many sidewalk cafés lining Main Highway. While there, you might also want to take a look around the neighborhood's southern side – or, as it's known colloquially (if unfortunately) "Black Coconut Grove." Centered on Charles Avenue, this somewhat depressed area throws the wealth surrounding it into sharp relief.

Peacock Park

South of the shopping centers and overlooking Biscayne Bay stands **Peacock Park**, the site of the *Peacock Inn*, the first hotel to open in the Miami area in 1882. It was designed by Barnacle owner Ralph Middleton Munroe and owned by British settler Charles Peacock and his wife, Isabella. After the building was demolished and the site became a park, it was the epicenter of Coconut Grove counterculture in the 1960s thanks to the hippies who camped out here.

Today it's been spruced up and is the best of several local greenspaces, with a few public tennis courts and some peculiar abstract sculptures sprinkled throughout; this is where most of Coconut Grove's festivals take place like the foodie Taste of the Grove in late January (see p.196). It's especially pleasant for the superb views of the bay it affords – and if rollerblading along the catwalk of Ocean Drive in South Beach is a little intimidating, come here and practice first.

The Barnacle State Historical Site

Set back from the road behind tropical hardwood hammock (the foliage that once covered the whole of what's now Coconut Grove), one of the city's most intriguing sights lies at 3485 Main Hwy: Ralph Middleton Munroe's pagoda-pioneer house, **The Barnacle** (Fri–Mon 9am–4pm; tours depart at 10 & 11.30am, 1 & 2.30pm; $1; ℡305/442-6866, ⓦwww.floridastateparks.org/thebarnacle).

Munroe was one of Miami's first snowbirds, drawn from New York by the weather in a vain attempt to cure his dying wife's TB in the 1870s. Despite her death, he stayed, and became wealthy through the salvage business, rescuing and reselling the cargo of wrecked commercial ships. Munroe built the Barnacle in 1891 to showcase his own eco-friendly engineering theories. He quickly became an eccentric curiosity to locals, mostly thanks to his devotion to Transcendentalism (which advocated self-reliance, a love of nature, and a simple lifestyle) and his close friendship with Bahamians and Seminoles. By the 1920s, when tourists first started scoping out his home, he was a confirmed oddity.

Munroe used local materials plus tricks he learned from nautical design to make the house as durable as possible. For one, he built the house completely above ground to prevent flooding and improve airflow – helping to alleviate some of the discomfort of living year-round in Miami's humidity – and, after remarrying in 1908, raised the building further, adding a floor under the original one when his growing family needed extra room. There's also a recessed veranda that enables windows to be open during rainstorms and skylights that allow air to be drawn through the structure. The wide overhang on each story, designed to give shade from the sun, exudes a vaguely oriental vibe.

The only way to see inside the house is on a guided tour; inside, you'll see many original furnishings alongside some of Munroe's intriguing photos of pre-settlement Coconut Grove. The grounds are also a pleasant place to dawdle: once a

▲ The Barnacle State Historic Site

month major fundraisers are held here, featuring live classical music played from the veranda while the audience lolls on the waterfront lawn. There's also a weekly sunset yoga class overlooking the bay on Wednesday nights – check the website or call for details of both.

Coconut Grove Playhouse

Opposite the Barnacle on the main road is a rather forlorn blue-and-white Mediterranean Revival building at 3500 Main Hwy that until 2006 housed the **Coconut Grove Playhouse**. Financial problems have shuttered the theater and it shows no signs of reopening soon. The playhouse started as a movie theater in 1926, switching over to live performances in the mid-1950s when an entrepreneur bought the abandoned building hoping to bring Broadway to Coconut Grove. He certainly invested heavily in its refurbishment – there were lavish onsite apartments for the stars with gold plumbing fixtures in some bathrooms – and, at least initially, he succeeded, luring performers like Tallulah Bankhead and Chico Marx. The theater's greatest claim to fame, though, is that Samuel Beckett's *Waiting for Godot* (starring Bert Lahr, of *Wizard of Oz* fame) had its US premiere here in 1956. For updates on any potential future productions, check the website at Ⓦwww. cgplayhouse.com.

Charles Avenue

In the nineteenth century, there was a small Bahamian village called Kebo on the site that Coconut Grove now occupies, and many black immigrants settled here during Miami's construction boom, notably along what's become **Charles Avenue**. It's remained a largely black, working-class neighborhood and is noticeably less chichi than surrounding areas. There aren't many specific sights, other than a few so-called "shotgun" houses on the 3200 block of Grand Avenue, built in the 1920s and 1930s around long, narrow hallways: cheaply made at the time from local hardwoods, they're now cherished for the same reason. Notice how the cemetery, at no. 3650, is tiled with gravestones: owing to the combination of hard coral rock and a close-to-the-surface water table, coffins here could not be sunk deep into the ground, and so the dead were buried in unusually shallow graves.

Plymouth Congregational Church

On the southern edge of the district stands the small neighborhood church of **Plymouth Congregational**, 3400 Devon Rd at Main Highway (Mon–Fri 8.30am–4.30pm; ℡305/444-6521, ⓦwww.plymouthmiami.com). It has a striking, vine-covered coral-rock facade – and remarkably, this finely crafted exterior was the work of just one man. The 375-year-old main door, hand-carved in walnut, looks none the worse for its journey from an early seventeenth-century monastery in the Basque region of Spain. The dark interior of the church sadly doesn't live up to its spectacular exterior, but if you're determined to poke around inside, call ahead to the church office and make an appointment.

The Kampong

The 11-acre **Kampong** garden (Mon–Fri 9am–2pm, $10; ℡305/442-7169, ⓦwww.ntbg.org/gardens/kampong.php) at 4013 Douglas Rd is a hard-to-find gem – look for the semicircular entrance and tiny street-number sign along a stretch of residential mansions. The nearby Fruit and Spice Park (see p.000) may be better known, but the Kampong (a Malaysian word meaning "cluster of houses" or "extended family") is far more impressive, home to an extraordinary range of more than five thousand tropical flowering and fruit trees or plants.

The collection was cultivated by the late lumber heiress Kay Sweeney, who bought both house and plot from the family of botanist David Fairchild in the 1960s. Like Fairchild, Sweeney was not just a plant fiend but confirmed globetrotter, and she picked up interesting specimens on her travels then sent them back to be planted here alongside Fairchild's existing species. The result is an eclectic, far-reaching display with an emphasis on Asia: highlights include wide-leafed philodendra, used as impromptu umbrellas, and ylang ylang plants, whose pungent fragrance is the basis for Chanel No. 5. There are also more than fifty species of mango, as well as offbeat fruits like the round, dark-skinned *bael* from India, a hard-shelled citrus that Fairchild himself used to eat daily as a natural laxative.

The Asian-inspired (and less intriguing) house is crammed with native artifacts and most significant locally as the site of the meeting where Fairchild and activist Marjorie Stoneman Douglas conceived the Everglades charter designed to protect that drying-up wilderness from development.

Bayshore Drive and around

From Peacock Park, **Bayshore Drive** heads northeast, skirting Biscayne Bay and running by most of the sights in the area. Southwest off of Bayshore Drive, along Pan American Drive, you'll find the **Miami City Hall**, as well as the Marina, a mooring for lines of ultra-pricey yachts.

Continuing north, the **Silver Bluff** stretches between the 1600–2100 blocks. This limestone ridge is where the earliest Coconut Grove settlers made their homes, on one of the highest and safest points in the flat and flood-prone city. These settlers were later joined by the well-heeled notables of 1910s Miami, and today the area remains a preserve of the tasteful and wealthy, with the early mansions replaced by equally expensive modern counterparts.

Finally, further up the drive you'll come to the last sights of Cococut Grove, just below Little Havana: magical **Villa Vizcaya**, kids' mecca the **Museum of Science and Space Transit Planetarium**, and the Modernist church **La Ermita de la Caridad del Cobre** – a shrine to Our Lady of Charity.

Miami City Hall and around

The cheerful **Miami City Hall**, 3400 Pan American Drive (☎305/250-5300), provides a rare dash of Deco in Coconut Grove. A flared white building flecked with blue reliefs, the structure was built on the bay in 1934 as a terminal for Pan American Airlines' seaplane service to Latin America – the reliefs of winged globes and rising suns are Pan Am's insignia. The company began flying from here in 1930, and its first passenger terminal was a houseboat dragged to this spot from Cuba and anchored to pilings. That temporary structure was replaced by this swooping building, which was then commandeered to serve as naval base during World War II; Pan Am's last flight here was in 1945.

The building subsequently became an unlikely site for Miami's City Hall, mostly thanks to the age-old animosity between the city proper and its annexed, formerly independent subdivision; it didn't help matters when it was announced that Miami paid a then-astonishing $1 million in the 1950s to take it over, with much local grumbling about wasting public money. The grand globe that once graced its lobby is now in the Museum of Science, albeit in a sorry state (see p.115), and there's no public access to the building's interior – a pity, given the murals near

The Lizard King takes off in Miami

Coconut Grove's famed eccentricity and tolerance of countercultures made it a natural refuge for hippies in the 1960s – although their mass arrival stirred up the area's other signature emotion, ornery crankiness, in equal measure. While the hippies slept in Peacock Park or lounged in the churchyards, locals grumbled about the dozens of stoned teenagers wandering the streets asking for money.

The crackdown on counter culture came in March 1969, during the infamous Doors concert at the **Dinner Key Auditorium** at which **Jim Morrison** was said to have dropped his leather trousers and exposed himself to the crowd. It's impossible now to know the truth of what happened. Certainly, the concert's greedy promoter had oversold the venue by more than eight thousand tickets, packing 13,000 people into a small building without air conditioning on a hot spring night. Unquestionably, Morrison was blind drunk when he took the stage, having missed his flight to Miami and filled the time until the next plane knocking back booze. When he appeared, very late and incoherent, the overcapacity crowd charged the stage. Although some who attended the concert still insist that he merely taunted the crowd and exposed nothing, a warrant (signed by a junior in the local attorney's office who'd attended the concert) was issued five days later. It claimed that Morrison had asked "Do you wanna see my cock?" before baring his crotch, an act that constituted, in the attorney's words, an "attempt to precipitate a riot."

Eighteen months later at his **trial**, he pleaded not guilty and was cleared of the felony charge of lewd and lascivious behavior. However, Morrison received hard-labor sentences totaling 240 days for exposure and profanity, which were still under appeal when he died in Paris in July 1971. Either way, reaction to this incident across the country was surprisingly vocal: many radio stations dropped Doors tracks from their airplay schedules, *Rolling Stone* printed a scathing article on the band, and many venues in The Doors' upcoming tour canceled their bookings. More than thirty years later, incensed and devoted fans are still campaigning for the Lizard King's pardon.

the ceiling which record the history of flight, running from da Vinci to, naturally, Pan Am. However, you can get close to a small plaque in front that reminds visitors this is where the veterans of the Bay of Pigs stepped ashore after their release from Cuba in 1962.

Just south of here, near the end of Bayshore Drive, **Dinner Key** can be found, named after a popular early twentieth-century picnic spot; it was a small island in Biscayne Bay until joined to the mainland for defensive reasons during World War I. Nearby is the former Dinner Key Auditorium, where Jim Morrison was charged with indecent exposure after allegedly dropping his leather trousers onstage in 1969 (see box on p.113) – it's now called the Coconut Grove Exhibition Center.

⑦ Villa Vizcaya

In 1914, farm-machinery mogul **James Deering** followed his brother Charles (of Charles Deering Estate fame; see p.122) to Florida and blew $22 million re-creating a sixteenth-century Italian villa within the belt of vegetation between Miami proper and Coconut Grove. It took two years and one thousand workers – ten percent of Miami's then population – to build his monumental folly, **Villa Vizcaya** (daily 9.30am–4.30pm; $12, free tours every 40min; ☎305/250-9133, ⓦwww.vizcayamuseum.com) at 3251 S Miami Ave. A temporary spur was even constructed from the nearby railroad simply to bring materials into the courtyard during the building phase, and like an early twentieth-century Elton John, every day Deering filled each room of his villa with fresh flowers, and never let good taste get in the way of acquisition; in a grandiose PR stunt, he arrived by yacht on Christmas Day 1916 to move in. He and his decorator-in-chief Paul Chalfin spent several summers in Europe cherry-picking dozens of classical, Renaissance, and Rococo antiques, all geared to convincing Vizcaya's visitors that the structure was at least four hundred years old. Taken individually, the rooms are appealing, but in a single house this orgy of styles is an architectural sugar rush.

Still, Vizcaya is an unmissable sight. Inside, don't miss the spectacular ceiling in the East Hall, the earliest of all in the house, and the master clock in the Butler's Pantry, to which all other clocks at Vizcaya were linked to keep in sync. The villa was high-tech as well as old world, outfitted with elevators, fire sprinklers, and a telephone switchboard; every bedroom had an en-suite bathroom, and there were thirty servants living on site to minister to Deering and his guests' every need. Of course Deering was only in residence for four months of the year, through the winter – the rest of the time he spent back home in Chicago.

Notwithstanding its Spanish name, the house is another example of Miami's obsession with the watery old-world glamour of Venice, notably the waterfront *terrazzo* and stone barge; the sculptures of mermaids and mermen on the barge are by Sterling Calder, father of mobile designer Alexander. One exciting recent innovation is the commissioning of local contemporary artists to create **site-specific installations**, inspired by the house and its contents. These temporary shows pop up around the property throughout the year: past participants have included Cristina Lei Rodriguez, who produced one of her signature oozing plastic topiaries, and a choppy, avant-garde movie by video artist Catherine Sullivan. Call or check the website for upcoming artists.

The rest of the **grounds** are undeniably beautiful – the orange jasmine maze garden and the mythological statues lining the walkways are stunning – though much reduced from their 180-acre, seven-island heyday; look for the map inside the house that shows a rendering of their initial opulence before the land was sold to developers building what's now Mercy Hospital. Making the place even more surreal, the walkways are often clogged with teenage girls, enveloped in gloriously over-the-top meringue dresses; they're being officially photographed for their *quince*, the Cuban version of a Sweet Sixteen.

The Museum of Science and Space Transit Planetarium

Dedicated to making science simple, the **Museum of Science** (daily 10am–6pm; $20; ☎305/646-4200, ⓦwww.miamisci.org), 3280 S Miami Ave, is great for kids – but less so for adults – with interactive exhibits and a rolling program of live demonstrations from in-house educators. In its main hall sits the Pan Am Globe, which was once the centerpiece of the airline's terminal in Coconut Grove: the museum acquired it in 1960, and, in a fit of political correctness ten years later, repainted it to show geographical features rather than political boundaries.

Off the left of the main lobby in the same building, the **Space Transit Planetarium** features the standard domed auditorium, but its presentations are better than average, with shows on the hour. There's a wildlife refuge attached, which houses the usual injured birds and snakes, although the Miami Seaquarium's a better choice if you want to learn about animal rescue (see p.117).

The museum's been in stasis for some time while lawmakers argue over its proposed move to Museum Park Miami, a specially constructed cultural hub to be shared with the Miami Art Museum. In 2004, local voters approved a $275m budget for the project and an architect has been chosen – modernist Brit Sir Nicholas Grimshaw, best known for the Eurostar terminal at Waterloo station – though at time of writing, firm plans were impossible to pin down. Conservative estimates put the unveiling of the new digs no earlier than 2012.

The Church of La Ermita de la Caridad del Cobre

Looking rather like an angular meringue half-dipped in dark chocolate, the modernist church **La Ermita de la Caridad del Cobre** perches on the waterfront near Mercy Hospital at 3609 S Miami Ave (daily 8am–9pm; ☎305/854-2404, ⓦwww. ermitadelacaridad.org), close to the southeastern border of Little Havana. Named for Cuba's patron saint, the Virgin of Charity, and known affectionately as "La Ermita," the church is the spiritual center of Cuba-in-exile. Built on 10¢ donations from newly arrived immigrants, it was consecrated in 1973 and significantly renovated (this time through $1 donations) twenty-five years later. Iconic and symbolic, every element of the building resonates with the island country: the six concrete columns forming the mantel represent the six traditional provinces that existed before Castro, while beneath the altar, there's Cuban soil, sand, and rock, salvaged from a wrecked refugee boat. Finally, an emotive, if patchy, sepia mural behind the altar traces the history of Cuban immigration, and the conical-shaped church is angled to allow worshipers to look out across the bay in the direction of Cuba.

Key Biscayne and Virginia Key

T
he island of **Key Biscayne**, with its luxury apartments and enormous mansions, has long been one of the most desirable addresses in Miami. It's not unusual to see old-fashioned, white-uniformed nannies wheeling their baby-buggy-bound charges between condo complexes, and the overall impression is of a secluded and wealthy community that's hardly ruffled by its proximity to the city. Most people, though, are drawn here by the **beaches** and **parks**, which are some of the lushest around the city.

So named because the island was thought to be part of the Florida Keys (it isn't), Key Biscayne is what South Beach would have become without the Deco and the decadence. It was settled at the same time during the 1910s, though as a farming community rather than as a resort. However, when wide-scale agricultural development quickly proved impractical – rabbits nibbled on the tasty coconut-palm shoots – the island fell largely into the hands of the Matheson family, who had made millions from the chemical industry, providing blue jean dye to Levi's and mustard gas to the US government during World War I. Once this first wealthy family made the island their secluded home, Key Biscayne became known as a privacy-cherishing place where the wealthy could live undisturbed; even President Nixon spent his winters here. Recently, its reputation for seclusion and safety has also attracted rich expats from Latin America, and it's estimated that two-thirds of the island's population is now Hispanic.

Unless you have access to a boat, **getting to Key Biscayne** will require taking the soaring Rickenbacker Causeway from Downtown ($1.25 toll for vehicles), which stops off at **Virginia Key** along the way. Since Key Biscayne was never intended as a resort, services for visitors are still patchy: public transport is almost nonexistent – you can take bus #B from Downtown (service ends at 7pm), or better still, rent a bike (see p.189, "Sports, fitness, and ocean activities").

Virginia Key

Nonresidential **Virginia Key** is an unavoidable, if scenic, obstacle on the way to Key Biscayne. The quiet island houses several marine research facilities, as well as the **Miami Seaquarium**. Besides this attraction, there's not much more to do here other than stretch out on fine **Virginia Key Beach** at 4000 Virginia Beach Drive (daily 8am–sunset; cars $2; ☏305/960-4600, ⓦwww.virginiakeybeachpark.net), reached by a two-mile lane that winds through a cluster of woodland. Opened in

1945, during the years of segregation, this huge swathe of land was set aside for Miami's black community (chosen, cynics might say, for its proximity to a large sewage works); it's still largely and unofficially a facility for the local African-American community. It's recently undergone a million-dollar renovation to upgrade its tatty facilities; future plans include adding a black history museum in one of the still-standing historic buildings as well as a children's carousel and mini-train ride around the grounds. Otherwise, the beach is best known as the location of local institution *Jimbo's* (see review p.160), a place that's part-bar, part-junkyard – if you want to dodge the nominal entrance fee to the beach, tell the guard you're going to *Jimbo's* and it will be waived.

The Miami Seaquarium

The theme-park-style **Miami Seaquarium**, 4400 Rickenbacker Causeway (daily 9.30am–6pm, box office closes 4.30pm; $32, children 3–9 $25; ☎305/361-5705, Ⓦwww.miamiseaquarium.com), is one of the city's major family attractions. It offers the usual performing spectacles, such as those starring Lolita the 8000-pound acrobatic killer whale, who leaps and jumps through one show daily at noon; and a trio of dolphins performs tricks to a thumping track

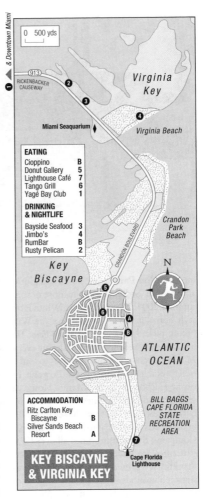

EATING
Cioppino   B
Donut Gallery   5
Lighthouse Café   7
Tango Grill   6
Yagé Bay Club   1

DRINKING & NIGHTLIFE
Bayside Seafood   3
Jimbo's   4
RumBar   B
Rusty Pelican   2

ACCOMMODATION
Ritz Carlton Key Biscayne   B
Silver Sands Beach Resort   A

KEY BISCAYNE & VIRGINIA KEY

of cheesy dance music. Feeding sessions throughout the day are ring-mastered by one of the park's rangers, who'll provide detailed background on the animal species in question. The crocodile sessions are especially fun; to see the reptiles at their hungriest and most ferocious, be sure to visit on a hot day, as the sun stimulates their appetites.

The Seaquarium's also one of the foremost marine-life rehab centers in the area: especially interesting are the turtles, often rescued from Biscayne Bay after eating plastic bags they've mistaken for jellyfish, and the some half-dozen manatees, a docile yet fiercely intelligent species now under constant threat of injury (and eventual extinction) by modern speedboats.

Key Biscayne

Key Biscayne is split roughly into three sections on the axis of Crandon Boulevard, the island's main drag: the small **Village of Key Biscayne** is bookended by sprawl-

▲ Jimbo's Bar

ing **Crandon Park** to the north and glorious **Bill Baggs Cape Florida State Park** at the south. Sadly, one of the more notorious sights in the Village was torn down in summer 2004: Nixon's Winter White House at 500 Bay Lane. A nondescript ranch-style home, it was where plans for the Watergate burglary were discussed and where Nixon picked up a copy of the *Miami Herald* one morning in 1972 to read of the break-in; the seemingly insignificant event (only featured by the paper because two Miami Cubans were involved) was to lead to Nixon's resignation two years later. The other notable residence here is also gone. Located at what's now the entrance to Hurricane Harbor, the grand Mashta House (an Egyptian name meaning "home by the sea") was originally owned by chemical magnates the Mathesons; it was allowed to fall into disrepair and then the sea in 1950. It was a jarring presence, as the dominant housing across the island then was cheap, prefab places churned out by the Mackle Company; they mushroomed all over Key Biscayne. Today, those cheap but historic structures are under threat as they're demolished to make way for McMansions; thankfully, a preservation movement is swelling and you can still see some Mackles scattered around – look for the single-story homes in between the new buildings, squeezed awkwardly into smaller plots.

To find out more about these and other mostly vanished historical sites around the island, stop by the **Chamber of Commerce** at 87 W McIntyre, Suite 100 (Mon–Fri 9am–5pm; ℡305/361-5207, Ⓦwww.keybiscaynechamber.org), which can provide an informative map. Other than that, there's little to do in the center of town and most visitors head straight for one of the nearby beaches.

Crandon Park Beach

As part of living in one of the best natural settings in Miami, the people of Key Biscayne have access to one of the finest landscaped beaches in the city – **Crandon Park Beach** (daily 8am–sunset; $5 per car; ℡305/361-5421, Ⓦwww.miamidade. gov/parks/parks/crandon_beach.asp), located a mile past Virgini Key along the main drag, Crandon Boulevard. The three-mile stretch is popular with families, and it's easy to understand why: the golden beach is wide and glorious, and the ocean sandbar reduces waves and eliminates riptide, making swimming safe and easy. However, be advised that on weekends the park is filled by the sounds of boisterous kids and hisses of sizzling barbecues – if it's peace and quiet you're after, you'd do better to head down to the less popular southern coast of the island.

Bill Baggs Cape Florida State Park

The verdant **Bill Baggs Cape Florida State Park** (daily 8am–sunset; $5 per car, $3 per car for solo drivers, $1 for pedestrians and bike riders; ☎305/361-5811, ⓦwww.floridastateparks.org/capeflorida/default.cfm) is named after the late Florida newspaper editor who campaigned for its creation. Hurricane Andrew leveled the park in 1992; the many exotic plants here, such as the shallow-rooted Australian pine, had little chance against the 220mph winds. The park is slowly returning to normal through a rigid replanting program, which aims to reintroduce tougher, indigenous species, using as its guide a historical list of vegetation that could be found here in the nineteenth century.

Stretching the park's length, a wide **boardwalk** divides the picnic shelters from the soft, sandy beach. Along the boardwalk, the concession next to the *Lighthouse Café* has rentals for bikes, rollerblades, ocean kayaks, and windsurf boards, as well as deck chairs and umbrellas; you can also bring your tackle and try your luck on one of the eight fishing platforms. The **beach** itself is dotted by natural "umbrellas" of young palm trees.

At the southernmost tip lies the restored **Cape Florida Lighthouse**, an 1845 replica of the one built twenty years previously which was destroyed in the first Seminole War. The lighthouse only remained in use until 1878, and now serves as a navigation beacon. The only way to climb the 118 steps up the 95-foot-high structure is on a ranger-led **tour** (Thurs–Mon 10am & 1pm; free; limited to the first ten people to arrive); you'll see the lighthouse keeper's original quarters, as well as stunning **views** of Key Biscayne and South Beach to the north, and the last few huts of **Stiltsville** (see box below) to the south.

⑧

Stiltsville

A few hundred yards off the southern tip of Key Biscayne, **Stiltsville** is an undeniable oddity. At the settlement's height, it comprised 27 houses standing on stilts above the ocean mudflats: now, only seven remain, their number winnowed down by successive hurricanes. Six of the buildings are nondescript; the seventh is the only photo-worthy exception, as it looks like a row of arrows shooting from the sea to the sky.

Stiltsville's origins are murky: some claim that shacks first appeared in the bay as early as the 1920s for Prohibition-era parties, while others maintain that the settlement was erected by local fishermen as a tax dodge in the 1940s. Eventually, it became a regular party venue – one notable institution was the short-lived *Bikini Club*, a bar that opened in the early 1960s where any girl in a bikini got a free drink. Either way, it's now technically part of Biscayne National Park, and was for a while caught up in byzantine federal government regulations: owners couldn't carry out repairs, but the seven houses were also denied official historic status as none of the original buildings remain, and those that still stand are less than fifty years old. Local preservationists responded with a fierce campaign, Save Our Stiltsville (ⓦwww.stiltsville .org), which managed to persuade government politicos to establish a board that would not only oversee what public use the remaining buildings would serve, but also raise funds for their repair and restoration; to date, sadly, they're still not yet open for public visits or tours. And whether the rickety structures can survive many more of Florida's hurricane seasons remains to be seen.

South to Homestead

ew visitors venture into the polished suburbs that sprawl out to the **south of Miami**, but it's here you'll sense a distinctly Floridian feel to life, a slower pace that's dominated by the land, as opposed to the breathless, cosmopolitan vibe of urban Miami. Parks and gardens abound, as well as some of the city's most idiosyncratic attractions, scattered nearby meandering Old Cutler Road and **Highway 1** – or the South Dixie Highway, as it's also known – as it carves its way down to agricultural **Homestead** and, finally, Florida City and the Keys (see Chapter 23).

Touring this area is impractical without a car, for while there is fragmented local bus service in each town, little public transport joins the centers. It's better to **rent a car** (for rental companies, see "Basics," p.26) and shuttle between the attractions – you can easily take in most of what the region has to offer in two days or so – and then, if you're so inclined, head down to the Keys. Unless where we've suggested otherwise, along Hwy-1 it's best to **stick to the main route:** attractions are rather scattered and despite reasonable signage, it's all too easy to get lost in the latticework of side roads that quilts the surrounding area.

South to Homestead

Moving south from Coral Gables and Coconut Grove, you arrive at the suburb now known as **South Miami**, originally dubbed Larkins in honor of the pioneer dairy farmer who first settled the area. These days, it's not milk but money that's abundant: this is one of the wealthiest suburbs in the city, filled with expansive and expensive new mansions occasionally interrupted by a golf course or two. Just past Coral Gables, Hwy-1 is mostly lined with gas stations and porn stores, and often choked with traffic, and it's far better to head down **Old Cutler Road**, a pleasant drive from Coconut Grove through a thick belt of woodland, where you'll find a series of worthy sights, beginning with the **Fairchild Tropical Garden**, with its showy collection of exotic plants; nearby, the **Charles Deering Estate** offers a dignified taste of pioneer wealth.

Further west, just a short detour over the Florida's Turnpike, the **Miami Metrozoo** is an enormous, sophisticated facility that's home to hundreds of animals. If you're a keen gardener, detour along **186th Street** south from here, off either the Turnpike or Hwy-1. It's lined with garden centers and greenhouses selling pricey tropical plants (heavily featured in the book *The Orchid Thief* and the movie it begat, *Adaptation*) – many of which are open to the public; just don't expect any bargains. If you want to browse rather than buy plants, better to stay on Hwy-1 until you reach the vast **Fruit and Spice Park**. After passing through the rundown and rather depressing town of Naranja – its name ("orange" in Spanish) a clue to

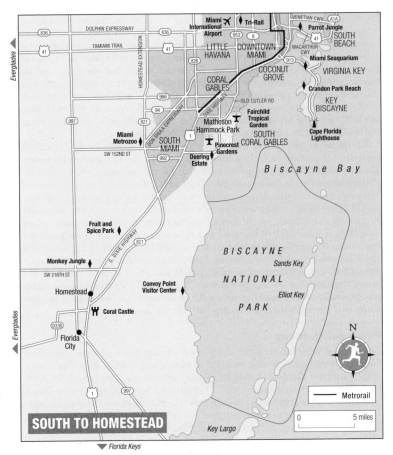

both the dominant local industry and language – the last sight before you hit no-nonsense Homestead is **Monkey Jungle**, where the visitors are in cages and the monkeys roam free.

Matheson Hammock Park

On the weekends, thousands flock to **Matheson Hammock Park** (daily 6am–sunset; $4 per car; ☎305/665-5475, ⓦwww.miamidade.gov/parks/parks /matheson_beach.asp), at 9601 Old Cutler Rd, to picnic, use the marina, or take a dip in the artificial lagoon. This greenspace was a coconut plantation before becoming a public park in 1930, and today it's great for small children but has little to offer adults. The rest of the sizeable park is much less crowded, and you can easily while away a few hours strolling around the wading pond – popular with people catching crabs – or along the winding trails above the mangrove swamps.

Fairchild Tropical Garden

South from Matheson Hammock Park, at 10901 Old Cutler Rd, lies **Fairchild Tropical Garden** (daily 9.30am–4.30pm, tram tours every hour until 3pm; $20;

☎305/667-1651, ⊛www.fairchildgarden.org). Founded on the site of a former mango plantation by botanist David Fairchild and his palm-crazy friend Robert Montgomery in 1938, the garden was built to be a living encyclopedia of exotic plants for locals, and resident scientists still scour the world for unusual or endangered species to add to the collection. The garden's collection was devastated by Hurricane Andrew, turning two-thirds of the plants into little more than tropical coleslaw, but fifteen years later the scars are healing well, and there's little evidence to the casual eye of any damage. That said, given the garden's wallet-busting admission fees, the less well-known, cheaper and equally enchanting Kampong (see p.112) might be a better choice for green-thumb tourists.

The easiest way to take in the 83-acre garden – the largest tropical botanical garden in the continental United States – is on one of the 45-minute **tram tours**. The tour winds through the garden's different habitats, including a fine collection of rare plants from the Bahamas and the Tropical Rainforest area, specially watered by an ingenious tree-irrigation system that supplements South Florida's insufficient rainfall. As a research institution, Fairchild works with scientists all over the world to preserve the diversity of the tropical environment; many of the plant species here, such as Cape Sable Whiteweed and Alvaradoa, are extinct in their original environments, and efforts have been made to re-establish them in their places of origin. That said, it's the Windows to the Tropics hothouse that's perhaps the biggest draw, filled with beautiful bromeliads, orchids, and other sensitive plants. It also houses the garden's most famous resident, "Mr Stinky," a six-foot-high Sumatran *Amorphophallus titanum* that's famous for the exceedingly rare blooming of its giant flower that's been described as smelling like "rotting elephant corpse."

Pinecrest Gardens

Ten minutes' drive further south along Hwy-1 brings you to the tony suburb of Pinecrest, a residential pitstop en route to Homestead and the Keys that's home to the **Pinecrest Gardens**, 11000 Red Road (daily 9am–sunset; free; ☎305/669-6942, ⊛www.pinecrestgardens.com). The original home of what's now Jungle Island (see p.64) operates as a delightful park; the place is Marie Celeste-like, since – aside from a new sign in retro lettering on the Flintstones-esque *porte cochère* – it looks almost the same as it did when it was filled with the noisy squawk of parrots. There are deserted cages scattered around, succulents shade the walkways, skittish lizards race across the paths, and turtles laze in the streams threading around the paths – though geese are now swimming on the lake instead of flamingos. Another plus: it's usually empty and silent, which gives the entire set-up a soothing quality, as does the lack of maps that allows visitors to get pleasantly lost. There's an onsite kids' playground, as well as plenty of picnic tables for lunch alfresco.

The Deering Estate

Although Charles Deering's younger half-brother James was the millionaire mastermind behind Villa Vizcaya (see p.114), his own rustic **Deering Estate** (daily 10am–5pm, last admission 4pm; estate tours daily 10.30am, 3pm; $7; ☎305/235-1668, ⊛www.deeringestate.org) at 16701 SW 72nd Ave could not be more different from Vizcaya and its opulent excess.

Both brothers, originally from the Midwest, had retired to Florida; but while James wanted fountains and formal gardens, Charles – a wealthy industrialist turned amateur botanist – set about creating an estate that would preserve the area's natural vegetation. He bought the moribund town of **Cutler** and tore it down, sparing only one building, Richmond Cottage, an inn on the route from Coconut Grove to Key West. After he modernized and electrified the cottage,

Deering built an adjoining stone house to hold his multi-million-dollar art collection (which included works by Toulouse-Lautrec, Gauguin, and Whistler). Both houses were tricked out in the Mediterranean Revival style, with a strong Moorish influence. The facade was built from oolitic limestone – a stone considered useful for the Revival style, since it erodes delicately in the rain and sea air, affording an artful illusion of age. The mansion's interior seems equally old: all echoing halls, dusty chandeliers, and checkerboard-tile floors, it carries a Gothic spookiness.

Deering lived here for a short time before his death in 1927, but under the terms of his will the estate remained in the family until the 1990s, when it was sold to the City of Miami and opened as a park. Unfortunately, there's little to see inside either structure, as he donated his art collection to the Art Institute of Chicago after the hurricane of 1926, while his daughters sold off much of the furniture once their mother died. Nevertheless, the estate is a tranquil respite from the ritziness of the rest of Miami, ideal for an afternoon spent reading a book by the ocean on its sweeping front lawns.

Free **ranger-guided trips** into the woodland hammock on four-wheel-drive golf carts are fascinating, taking in Charles Deering's own avocado groves, local plants, and a 1500-year-old Tequesta burial mound where the remains of two dozen human beings, dating back ten thousand years, have been found. **Chicken Key**, just offshore from the Deering Estate, is so named because it was used as a poultry pen by Native Americans; the Deering Estate runs canoe tours out to the unspoilt landscape of the now chicken-free isle for $25, including estate admission (usually Sat & Sun 8.30am, as well as occasional moonlit excursions; reservations essential – call for upcoming schedule).

The Miami Metrozoo

One mile west of the Florida Turnpike and three miles west of US-1, the **Miami Metrozoo**, 12400 SW 152nd St (daily 9.30am–5.30pm, last admission 4pm; $14, children 3–12 $10, children 2 and under free; tram tour $5, all day onsite monorail pass $2.80; ☎305/251-0400, ⓦwww.miamimetrozoo.com), is a vast compound where hundreds of species are grouped according to their native continent: there are familiar animals, like giraffes and ostriches, alongside less commonplace creatures such as the llama-like *guanaco* and the *anoa*, which resembles a small buffalo. The whole place, though, is dominated by the screeching, constant howling of the different monkeys onsite; it isn't hard to track their cages, just follow the noise ricocheting around the park. The zoo is well designed, with humane, open enclosures – more moat-and-hill than fence-and-cage – and the frequent plaques employed to detail each species' survival status is a great educational opportunity for kids. At time of writing, the zoo was prepping a brand new $90 million habitat, Amazon & Beyond, which should open (if it sticks to schedule) by early 2009.

It's best to arrive early, as most of the animals are liveliest before the baking midday sun takes hold; visitors, though, can hop onto the air-conditioned monorail that runs through the park if the heat becomes unbearable. Whatever time you arrive, there should be a **feeding demonstration** – they're on a rolling schedule, to allow visitors a chance to talk with the animals' knowledgeable keepers; the zoo's famous group of white Bengal tigers (only one of which is actually white) is fed at 11am while the keepers' meerkat chat is at 12.30pm.

The zoo was one of the attractions worst hit by Hurricane Andrew – though the damage was mostly structural, and only twenty out of one thousand animals were killed. The birdhouse sustained the worst harm and was rebuilt as a showy aviary called the **Wings of Asia**. Designed like ancient ruins, it's an impressive display, leading visitors through the evolution of Asian birds from dinosaurs; the trip's set to a squawky soundtrack from today's endangered avian species. Walk slowly, as the undergrowth is full of shy, flightless birds that dart out and scamper across the path but are otherwise easily overlooked. Look for the Silk Floss Tree, the sole tree left standing after the hurricane; and pause to see the golden-billed toucans who sit, roped off from the rest, calmly staring back at visitors.

The Fruit and Spice Park

As the name suggests, the 30-acre **Fruit and Spice Park**, a few miles south from the Metrozoo at 24801 SW 187th St (daily 10am–5pm; free tours at 11am, 1.30pm, 3pm; $6; ℡305/247-5727, ⓦmiamifruitandspicepark.com), houses exotic fruit and spice plants. The different fruits and plants are grouped together by species or theme – for example, an oddball banana plantation showcases fifty different varieties, as well as a poisonous plant patch, carefully screened off from visitors. There's even a citrus quarantine to keep their specimens safe in response to the devastation wrought locally by blight.

Disappointingly, though, there are no maps available for those who'd rather walk through the grounds unaccompanied and the labeling of plants is also spotty. Unless you happen to arrive when a tour's departing, this minimally informative set-up makes the park a must-see only for avid gardeners and plant fanciers – the best part for the less interested will be the wide range of free fruit ready to eat in the gift shop (only the fallen produce is available for sampling). For the casually curious, it's far better to hit the Kampong in Coconut Grove (see p.112).

Monkey Jungle

An amateur primate behaviorist first set up this park at 14805 SW 216th St to observe monkeys in the wild; when funding got tight, he began charging admission, and **Monkey Jungle** was born (daily 9.30–5pm, last admission 4pm; $26, children 3–9 $20, children under 3 free; ℡305/235-1611, ⓦwww.monkeyjungle.com). Now there are thirty species living here including a roaring pack of howler monkeys and some wide-eyed red ruffed lemurs – supposedly with the twist that the monkeys roam free, while humans visit in caged walkways. It's a diverting, if not especially informative, biopark, though plenty of the monkeys *are* in cages, and signage on species and habitat is frustratingly infrequent. Bring quarters to feed the animals: in a clever touch, dishes dangle from chains over the walkways, which the monkeys have learned to reel in like fishermen once a passing human has stocked a platter with seeds.

Homestead and around

Decimated when the nearby airforce base closed down, **Homestead** has now been hit hard by citrus blight, and the area's definitely seen better times (see box on opposite). One positive by-product of its agricultural economy, though, is a thriving **"pick your own"** business, where for a nominal cost per pound you can pick produce to take home – look out for the roadside signs. It's a great option if you're heading into the Everglades, where few supplies are available. In addition, the town is filled with itinerant fruitpickers, lending it a sort of bordertown transience. The palm trees that suddenly appear in the median of Highway 1 as you hit town only add to its rural feel, and to take a look around – though there's not much to see – follow Krome Avenue south to reach the center of town.

The last two places of interest before Hwy-1 curves down to the Keys are the twin delights of the eerie, magical **Coral Castle** and the mostly-underwater **Biscayne National Park**, a must-visit for any snorkel or dive enthusiast.

If you're headed south to the Keys after visiting sights in the area rather than returning to Miami, a better place to stop overnight than Homestead is in **Florida City**, just further south along Hwy-1. Things are much perkier here: in a smart move, the town's refashioned itself into a sort of **gateway to the Keys** for holidaymakers, thereby lessening its reliance on fruit farming, and bolstering the local economy, though there's little noteworthy to see in Florida City itself – in fact, it's most notable as the first town on the route to feel completely free of Miami's energetic, Latin influence. One valuable amenity in Florida City is the terrific **Tropical Everglades Visitor Information Center** (Mon–Sat 8am–4.45pm, Sun varies; ℡305/245-9180 or 1-800/388-9669, Ⓦwww.tropicaleverglades.com), at 160 Hwy-1, close to the junction with Hwy-9336 (344th Street). It offers a wealth of information on attractions around Homestead and in the Keys, but is particularly strong (of course) on the Everglades.

The Coral Castle

The **Coral Castle**, a memorable – if tacky – stop-off at 28655 Hwy-1 (daily 7am–9pm; $9.75, children 7–12 $5, children under 6 free; ℡305/248-6345, Ⓦwww. coralcastle.com), is as unique and odd as the story behind it. Ed Leedskalnin, a 5-foot-tall, 100-pound immigrant, allegedly built it as a tribute to the 16-year-old fiancée, Agnes Scuffs, who jilted him in his native Latvia. Heartbroken, he traveled the world, working as a stonemason, logger, and rancher, and eventually found himself in Florida in 1918 thanks to a nasty bout of TB. Buying land near Homestead a few years later, he quarried coral rock from his land and, singlehandedly, used this rock to build a simple house as well as an ornamental garden decorated with crescent moons and heart-shaped tables.

No one knows how this tiny man moved such massive blocks of stone: he worked at night, and never revealed his methodology to anyone before dying in 1951. Engineers have consistently scoffed at his feats, until trying and failing to replicate them – scientists are still baffled by the nine-ton gate, for example, which can be moved with a hefty push from a single finger.

The esoteric iconography of the Coral Castle is pegged to Leedskalnin's fascination with astronomy, astrology, and ancient Egypt. He used divining rods to check the area's alignment with ley lines, or supposed linear configurations of ancient sites, and, surprisingly, electromagnetic testing has confirmed their presence

Hurricane Andrew vs. Homestead

Homestead hit the headlines on August 24, 1992, for all the wrong reasons: it was here that **Hurricane Andrew** hit with full force. Although a comparatively compact storm, its winds reached speeds of more than 200mph – at least, that's the estimated force, as the official windspeed gauge broke at 164mph.

The three towns of Homestead, Florida City, and Naranja were puréed, and Homestead Air Force Base was also wrecked – it later closed, with a devastating effect on the local community. Once the storm passed on, heading toward Louisiana, it had left sixty thousand houses destroyed, 200,000 people homeless, and damage that would cost an estimated $20 billion to repair – one of the greatest natural disasters in modern American history.

Since then, the physical scars have healed – buildings have been reconstructed in the towns and farmland has been replanted. However, the economic wound is still with Homestead and the surrounding area continues struggling to thrive, providing a gritty glimpse of Florida life. For more on hurricanes in Florida, see p.256.

▲ The Coral Castle

– there's a cluster of ley lines especially thick around the Moon Pond. This has made the Coral Castle an important site for local New Agers, and there have even been several Wiccan "baptisms" on the site. Whatever the explanation behind its construction, the Coral Castle is a kitschy and surreal stop-off.

Biscayne National Park

Unique among national parks as 95 percent of it is under water, **Biscayne National Park**, 9700 SW 328th St (daily except Christmas 7am–5.30pm, sea accessible 24 hours a day; free; ℡305/230-7275, Ⓦwww.nps.gov/bisc), is well worth the 9-mile, 20-minute detour. The excellent **visitor center** (9am–5pm) at

Convoy Point lies at the end of a featureless road, Canal Drive or 328th Street, nine miles from Hwy-1. Technically, the Florida Keys begin here with the tiny Boca Chita Key (which special forces used to commandeer as an isolated training ground); and the **reef** in this park is the same **coral formation** that draws enthusiastic snorkelers and divers to the John Pennekamp State Park (see p. 226), off Key Largo.

The reef is much better preserved and more spectacular here than at the better known dive sites further down the coast, and if you're planning only one reef trip in the area, make it this one or Looe Key in the Lower Keys (see p.232). There are several ways to visit it, with its living coral sheltering shoals of brightly colored fish; all are run by the same concessioneer, operating out of Convoy Point. The lazy way is on a ranger-guided, three-hour glass-bottomed boat trip (daily at 10am; $24.45; reservations essential on ☏305/230-1100), but it's worth the effort taking the afternoon jaunt, when you can actually snorkel around the coral for the same amount of time (daily 1.30pm; $26 including all equipment; reservations essential). Call to check on schedules as they can vary, and trips may also be canceled due to bad weather.

The other way to enjoy Biscayne National Park is by visiting one of the barrier islands, Elliott Key and Boca Chita Key, located seven miles out to sea. Overnight **camping** is permitted – there are restrooms on both islands, but Elliott Key also has showers and drinking water, as well as a ranger station. Once there, there's little to do other than sunbathe or hike an easy six-mile trail round the island's forested spine. The overnight camping fee at both keys is $25. If you don't have your own boat, the concessioneer also runs daily trips, weather permitting: Boca Chita leaves at 10am on the glass-bottomed boat ($25 round-trip, reservations essential) and Elliott Key at 1.30pm with the snorkel trip ($26 round-trip, reservations essential). Note that the boats to the keys only run November through May; and expect mosquitoes to be fierce year-round, so bring everything you'll need.

Listings

Listings

⑩

Accommodation

iami's increasingly a place for splashing out on suites in swanky boutique hotels, though there are still some smart, budget-conscious bargains to be found amid the five-star palaces. Prices for hotels start around $120 in South Beach, but rocket in **high season** (January–March) or when major conventions are in town. A smart alternative is to come in May or December – rates will be much lower and, although the weather can be variable, it should be beachworthy most days. Also, if you're hoping to see Miami without renting a car, it makes most sense to stay Downtown or on South Beach, as connections by bus are most regular to these areas.

Unsurprisingly, a huge percentage of the hotels and guesthouses are clustered together on **South Beach**, most of them lining two streets, Ocean Drive and Collins Avenue – in fact, there are almost fourteen thousand rooms available on the beach. Increasingly, though, former budget hotels are being converted into luxury hot spots or even condos, so it's getting harder and harder to score a bargain in high season – budget accordingly. Sticker shock aside, bedding down in South Beach is money well spent, given the thrill of staying in one of the many photo-ready Deco masterpieces. Remember, however, that Deco hotels were built in a different era, and rooms can be tiny.

Heading north, the enormous 1950s hotels in **Central Miami Beach**, like the *Fontainebleau* and the *Eden Roc*, make fun, kitschy places to stay for any would-be Rat Packer. There's a smaller selection of pleasant places in **Coconut Grove** and **Coral Gables**, though no incredibly compelling reason to stay in either neighborhood. Otherwise, **Downtown** is crowded with sub-par or overpriced chain hotels, while Little Havana is not yet geared to providing visitor accommodation; steer clear of all the modernist motels along Biscayne Corridor for now – sadly, no one's snapped any up yet to transform them from crack dens or hourly rentals into haute hotels.

If you're planning on spending a few days in Miami before heading down to the Keys, it's worth considering one of the guesthouses around **Homestead** or **Florida City**, although be aware that the trip to South Beach is quite a hike (at least an hour's drive plus the inevitable traffic jams).

Throughout this chapter we have given **prices** for rooms. They reflect the lowest listed price for a standard double room **in high season** (which, in Miami, is January through March). Depending on availability and season, you may end up paying twice as much, or you might pay half the listed price by snagging a great deal online. Note, too, that there's an additional hotel tax of 12.5 percent added to rates, charged by the hotel and paid to the county.

▲ A balcony view of South Beach from The Setai hotel

Hotels and guesthouses

Downtown

The Four Seasons Miami 1435 Brickell Ave ☎ 305/358-3535 or 1-800/819-5053, ⓦ www. fourseasons.com/miami. Right on Brickell's main drag, this sleek, business-minded 70-story condo-hotel is known for the impressive modern art scattered through the common areas, as well as the visiting sports teams, who often stay here because of its enormous onsite Sports Club LA facility and the three-pool complex on the roof of the sixth floor. The bathrooms with standalone tubs and showers are especially roomy. $475.

Holiday Inn Marina Park – Port of Miami 340 Biscayne Blvd ☎ 305/371-4400 or 1-800/526-5655, ⓦ www.holiday-inn.com. Conveniently located near all the major attractions and public transport, this is an above-average option – especially given the rather ratty other chain outposts Downtown – with clean, large rooms close to the waterfront. $150.

InterContinental 100 Chopin Plaza ☎ 305/577-1000 or 1-800/327-3005, ⓦ www.interconti-nental.com. What distinguishes this high-rise from other Downtown chain hotels is its location: right on the edge of Biscayne Bay

and the Port of Miami, with appropriately gawp-worthy views (though you'll pay for the privilege). The rooms themselves are stylishly furnished, with good amenities for business travelers, like power outlets built into the desktops. $410.

Mandarin Oriental 500 Brickell Key Drive ☎ 305/913-8288 or 1-866/888-6780, ⓦ www.mandarin-oriental.com. Vying with the *Four Seasons* for the title of Downtown's top luxury hotel: the *Mandarin* certainly has a spectacular setting – on its own island just off the main business district. The infin-ity-edged pool is a lush place to lounge, as is its private bayfront beach. The rooms are large, with a vaguely Asian theme (as befits the hotel's name), but the snooty staff is a major letdown. $510.

South Beach

Albion 1650 James Ave ☎ 305/913-1000, ⓦ www.rubellhotels.com. A sensitive conversion of a classic Nautical Deco build-ing houses one of the best hotels in the city; even better it's only two blocks from the beach. It's a great-value choice, thanks to the huge, simple rooms (recently done over but maintaining their minimalist white bed-and-walls vibe) plus one of the best pools in town: in a whimsical touch befitting the hotel's ocean liner-riffing architecture, it's elevated above ground and has portholes cut into its sides so you can spy on swimmers from the side. $225.

Anglers Resort 660 Washington Ave ☎305/534-9600, ⊛www.theanglersresort .com. An understated luxury addition to South Beach's hotel strip. Spread across four villa-style buildings, the Anglers Resort has a leafy, Florida Keys atmosphere: the 49 rooms have mod cons (plasma TVs, WiFi) but are decked out in a throwback style – the private duplexes have rooftop decks and outdoor showers. Ask for one of the 25 rooms in the 1920s Mediterranean Revival building for maximum glamour. Highly recommend, with the one caveat that the onsite pool is postage stamp-small. $250.

Aqua 1530 Collins Ave ☎305/538-4361, ⊛www.aquamiami.com. This motel conversion has preserved little other than the original Sea Deck sign out front. The superb, spartan-chic rooms have raw concrete floors with tart tangerine and bright blue accents – IKEA-inspired and funky. All rooms look over a tranquil courtyard, and there's a private sundeck, too. $185.

Best Western South Beach 1050 Washington Ave ☎305/674-1930 or 1-888/343-1930, ⊛www. bestwestern.com. A cluster of four historic hotels (the *Kenmore*, *Taft*, *Bel Aire*, and *Park Washington*) that are owned and operated by Best Western as a single property. This is one of the few remaining cheaper options on the beach. The rooms have been renovated to remove all character, but amenities have been added – ask for a room with a kitchenette, as there's no extra charge for the convenience. $140.

Catalina 1732-1756 Collins Ave, South Beach ☎305/674-1160, ⊛www.catalina hotel.com. High style at thrift store prices, this standout bargain-priced hotel spreads across three buildings: in each, expect simple white rooms crammed with luxe touches like flatscreen TVs and marble bathrooms. The differences: the Catalina building has a bamboo-filled 'zen courtyard' for meditating while the Maxine's rooms are larger, and there's an outdoor pool. For a slight premium, around $40 per night, book a room in the newest addition, the Dorset building: the suites here are huge and there's a rooftop pool with bar and lush cabanas. $90.

Delano 1685 Collins Ave ☎305/672-2000 or 1-800/697-1791, ⊛www.morgans hotelgroup.com. Thanks to the twin star power of owner Ian Schrager and designer Philippe Starck, Delano was one of the first high-profile celebrity hang-outs on the beach. It fell out of fashion for a few years, but thanks to new owners and a thorough refit – including everything from plasma TVs to new mattresses – it's regaining some of its glossy glitz; the addition of the Lenny Kravitz-helmed Florida Room (see p.161) didn't hurt either. Even better, now that it's strictly Schrager-free, the staff have retained their model good looks but lost most of the attitude. $525.

▼ The Delano

Doubletree Surfcomber 1717 Collins Ave ☎305/532-7715 or 1-800/445-8667, ⊛www. surfcomber.com. A fashion and media favorite, this unassuming hotel has direct beach access, a full-sized pool, and spacious, airy rooms. Camera crews often use its terrace to film TV shows, and – always a good vote of confidence – it's one of the places that locals will lodge their relatives when they visit. $270.

Essex House 1001 Collins Ave ☎305/534-2700 or 1-800/553-7739, ⊛www.essexhotel.com. The *Essex House* has bland, corporate-style rooms that are luxurious but could be anywhere. The building, though, is a gem, with a superbly restored Egyptian Deco lobby full of ziggurats – plus, the management is friendly. $165.

(10)

Gansevoort South 2377 Collins Ave, ☎ 305/604-1000, ⓦ www.gansevoortsouth.com. The Manhattan hotel's new Florida outpost is housed in the radically overhauled former Roney Palace building. It clones the New York spot's signature rooftop pool area, this time making it a huge space with coco palm trees and cabanas; a second elevated oceanfront 'Pool Plaza' has a Jacuzzi, bar and cafe. The charcoal grey-walled rooms are a nod to Miami's heyday, with 1940s pin-up photos on the wall and large, tan-friendly balconies. Rates from $425.

The Hotel 801 Collins Ave ☎ 305/531-2222, ⓦ www.thehotelofsouthbeach.com. Designer Todd Oldham oversaw every element in this hotel's renovation, using zesty colors on everything from the lobby to the bathrobes. The luxurious rooms are like a millionaire's tropical hideaway, their stylish look only part of a thoughtful aesthetic of smart improvements – for example, the shower control is not under the shower head, so you won't have to scald yourself every time you turn on the water. Expensive, but a treat. For a review of *The Hotel*'s rooftop bar, *The Spire*, see p.161. $385.

The Loft Hotel 952 Collins Ave ☎ 305/534-2244, ⓦ www.thelofthotel.com. A sleek low-rise building converted from apartments, the *Loft* has a chic, rather LA feel with modern, wrought-iron furniture and an airy garden filled with lush trees. Its rooms all have down comforters, kitchenettes, and DVD players. $140.

Mondrian 1100 West Ave ☎ 305/672-2662, ⓦ www.morganshotelgroup.com. Marcel Wanders' $60 million conversion of a residential tower on the bay side of the beach has become the *Mondrian*, a sister hotel to the *Delano*. Nearing completion at the time of writing, the roomy suites have a monochrome color scheme but an organic, ornate feel (think a lacey patterned sofa and crystal chandelier over the dining table). Private yachts can be berthed at the 40-slip onsite marina. Expect rooms to start at around $500.

The Park Central 640 Ocean Drive ☎ 305/538-1611 or 1-800/727-5236, ⓦ www.theparkcentral .com. One of the first hotels to be reborn during the South Beach renaissance of the early 1990s, the 127-room *Park Central* was looking rather careworn until a recent upgrade, which has made the hotel one of the better bargains on the beach. The

makeover retained its colonial safari feel, a retro effect boosted by the black and white photographs throughout the hotel, a nod to the time when *The Park Central* was the Miami hotel of choice for Rita Hayworth and Clark Gable. There's also a roof deck for sunbathing and sightseeing. $245.

Pelican Hotel 826 Ocean Drive ☎ 305/673-3373 or 1-800/773-5422, ⓦ www.pelicanhotel.com. Owned by the Italian jeanswear company Diesel, the *Pelican* injects a welcome touch of campy humor into the earnest coolness of South Beach. Each room is themed, with either refurbished flea-market finds or specially constructed furniture: try No.307, the "Deco(cktail)" room, for a touch of Twenties glamour, or No.215, the "Best Little Whorehouse" room, with deep red wallpaper and plenty of lush black lace (the rooms are constantly renovated, with new designs and themes swapping in seasonally – check the website for the latest selection). You'll also be given two chairs and an umbrella to use on the beach opposite the hotel. $280.

🏃 **The Raleigh** 1775 Collins Ave ☎ 305/534-6300 or 1-800/848-1775, ⓦ www.raleighhotel.com. Once languishing in dusty if elegant dotage, the *Raleigh* has been transformed after a sensitive refurbishing by Andre Balazs (also owner of the *Standard*, see p.136) that retained signature touches like the huge garden, curvy pool – where many 1920s synchronized swimming movies were shot – and the dark, wood-paneled bar; with its cream sofas and colonial feel, it's very Gable and Lombard. The rooms, though, are where the difference really shows, with orthopedic beds and sumptuous linens. Highly recommended for a splurgey stay. $425.

🏃 **The Ritz-Carlton South Beach** 1 Lincoln Rd ☎ 786/276-4000 or 1-800/241-3333, ⓦ www.ritzcarlton.com. The former *DiLido* hotel was another Morris Lapidus confection – see the *Fontainebleau* (p.137) – and its new owners have spruced the place up. The design of the lobby is exactly as it was in its 1950s heyday, though using more durable materials, such as cherry wood instead of stucco on the walls. The rooms themselves are large but bland; try to snag one overlooking the pool where you'll likely spot one of the hip-hoppers who have adopted this hotel as their homebase during recording sessions at local studios. The hotel is co-owned by the Lowenstein family

▼ The Ritz-Carlton South Beach

of local gallery fame; its modern art collection – heavy on Latin names like Miró and Dario Basso – is scattered throughout the common areas. Rooms from $615.

Royal Hotel 763 Pennsylvania Ave ☏ 305/673-9009 or 1-888/394-6835, ⓦ www.royalsouthbeach.com. Fantastic 42-room bargain hotel housed in a beautiful Streamline Moderne building. There's a candy-colored lobby covered in Art Deco posters; the room decor, though, is all white and Jetson-inspired – marble floors with injection-molded plastic bedframes and a swirly love seat with TV stand built in. There are microwaves, coffee makers, and even free toothpaste in the bathrooms. Note that the entrance is behind the hotel's main facade on Washington Avenue. $150.

Royal Palm 1545 Collins Ave ☏ 786/276-0177, ⓦ www.royalpalmmiamibeach.com. Overlooked, great-value-for-the-location hotel named after one of Henry Flagler's pioneering B&Bs (though that's all they have in common). There are three towers here and the 400-odd rooms vary wildly – the one-bedroom suites in the Lanai Bungalow are priciest – though the regular rooms in the main building are fine with large bathrooms, power showers and bright, if a bit dated, décor. $190.

Sagamore 1671 Collins Ave ☏ 305/535-8088 or 1-877/242-6673, ⓦ www.sagamorehotel. com. A low-key luxury hotel, with 93 enormous rooms decorated in muted shades of chocolate and taupe, each of which was recently renovated with marble floors and plasma TVs. There's a beachfront pool, where you can swim a few laps then climb out straight onto the sands. Even if you aren't staying here, stop in to the lobby to gawp at the stunning modern artwork dotted around the public areas, including works by Cindy Sherman and Cathy de Monchaux or grab a cocktail at the video garden by the pool, with lounge-worthy sofas and screens showing highlights of the owner's video art holdings. $385.

The Setai 2001 Collins Ave ☏ 305/520-6000, ⓦ www.setai. com. Specially constructed condo tower-cum-hotel that's known for its celeb-heavy clientele (Lenny Kravitz is said to have his own recording studio in the building) as much as for its high priced, vaguely Asian-themed rooms. Save up to stay here for snob value and the best views on the beach – pity the service is so patchy. $715.

The Shelborne 1801 Collins Ave ☏ 305/531-1271 or 1-800/327-8757, ⓦ www.shelborne. com. Site of the early Miss Universe pageants, the *Shelborne* offers all the usual amenities (free onsite fitness center, pool) and is well located at the northern end of the beach, right on the ocean. The rooms are unremarkable in decor, but have small kitchenettes, DVD players, and Internet access. With 200 rooms, this is one of the larger hotels on the beach, so often has space in peak season when other smaller properties are booked up. $235.

Hotel Shelley 844 Collins Ave ☏ 305/531-3341 or 1-877/762-3477, ⓦ www.hotelshelley.com. A budget boutique hotel, the *Shelley* is stylishly spartan, with the usual all-white rooms. There are some great comp add-ons, like a free open bar every night from 6 to 10pm and discounted gym passes, but there's no elevator, so don't stay here unless you are traveling light. High-season rates are often reduced on negotiation and can even be slashed in half during the summer. $125.

The Shore Club 1901 Collins Ave ☏ 305/695-3100 or 1-800/697-1791, ⓦ www.shoreclub. com. Ian Schrager swooped in to save this high-end hotel when it floundered only months after opening and turned it into *the* place to stay on the beach – Schrager's gone and so has some of the buzz but the *Shore Club*'s still a swanky berth. Rooms are small and minimalist in style, decorated in bright colors rather than all-white, but you

ACCOMMODATION | Hotels and guesthouses

probably won't spend long inside when you can be lounging with the beautiful people in the poolside *Sky Bar* (see p.161). $525.

South Beach Plaza Villas 1411 Collins Ave ⊤ 305/531-1331, ⊛ wwww.southbeachplazavillas .com. Formerly the *Brigham Gardens Guesthouse*, this hotel is actually a hamlet of buildings holding 23 rooms crowding around a shady courtyard. It's one of the best low-cost options in the area, with friendly management and an onsite laundry. The quirky rooms have an eccentric, Caribbean feel thanks to delightfully mismatched furniture; fully equipped kitchenettes in the studio rooms are worth the extra $30 expense. $150.

The Standard Miami 40 Island Ave, Belle Isle ⊤ 305/673-1717, ⊛ www.standardhotels. com/miami. The Miami outpost of hip hotelier Andre Balazs' cheaper *Standard* chain is hit and miss. The pluses: the spa-themed hotel has signs asking guests to mute cellphones, the rooms are kitted out in a wood-and-cotton Zen-inspired color scheme and the onsite spa occupies the entire third floor with treatment rooms, a gym, and a unisex hammam (Turkish steam room). The minuses: its location on the opposite side of the sandbar from the beach, the small size of its motel-style rooms and the paper-thin walls (bring earplugs). $300.

The Tides 1200 Ocean Drive ⊤ 305/604-5070 or 1-800/439-4095, ⊛ www.thetideshotel.com. Spectacularly situated on Ocean Drive, with enormous floor-through rooms (some of the largest on the strip) each with ocean and city views, the Tides has just undergone major renovations paid for by its deep-pocketed new owner, the KOR group. Designer Kelly Wearstler's re-do seems to have taken inspiration from *The Mummy Returns*, with a 1930s, Cairo-by-the-Sea vibe including front-door flanking caryatids and reproduction ebony-like busts. $545.

Townhouse 150 20th St ⊤ 305/534-3800 or 1-877/534-3800, ⊛ www.townhouse-hotel.com. Many boutique hotels promise much but deliver little – *Townhouse* is an exception. Stark, white (of course) rooms are well-thought-out and comfortable; the staff is attentive but laid-back, and there's an indulgent roof deck filled with crimson waterbeds for sybaritic sunbathing. It sits on the beachfront behind the *Shore Club*, a two-minute walk to the water. $265.

Hotel Victor 1144 Ocean Drive ⊤ 305/428-1234, ⊛ www.hotelvictorsouthbeach.com. This lavish hotel, despite its name, is actually a hush-hush *Hyatt* project. The decor's apparently inspired by jellyfish – there's a tank-full in the lobby – and it's intended to be a clubby, Ibiza-style spot, complete with in-residence DJs spinning daily until midnight. The rooms all have deep-soak tubs, LCD TVs, and even a hot button on the phone to Neiman Marcus in Bal Harbour for last-minute shopping urges. $480.

Villa Paradiso 1415 Collins Ave ⊤ 305/532-0616, ⊛ www.villaparadisohotel.com. More basic and retro than its sibling the *Loft* (see p.134), *Villa Paradiso* features *Miami Vice* decor and leather futons. However, the place is clean, the rooms are large, and all have their own kitchenettes; there's also an onsite coin laundry. Good discounts for longer stays. $140.

The Wave 350 Ocean Drive ⊤ 305/673-0401 or 1-800/501-0401, ⊛ www.wavehotel.com. Nestled in the increasingly buzzy SoFi area below 5th Street and close to *Prime 112* (see p.150, "Restaurants"), this hotel has small but fully equipped rooms, each with a mood machine so you can drift off to sleep to the sound of crashing waves. The huge free breakfasts are a major plus. $150.

Whitelaw Hotel 808 Collins Ave ⊤ 305/398-7000 or 1-877/762-3477, ⊛ www.whitelawhotel. com. Another terrific bargain option from the South Beach Group, which also owns the *Shelley*, *Catalina* and a clutch of other local cheapies, The *Whitelaw* has stylish, if over-designed, all-white rooms complete with CD players and some good add-ons are offered, too, such as free airport pick-up and an open bar in the hotel every night. $150.

The Winterhaven 1400 Ocean Drive ⊤ 305/531-5571 or 1-800/553-7739, ⊛ www.winterhaven hotelsobe.com. The *Winterhaven* offers rooms that are standard and comfortable enough. The real draw, though, is the lobby, restored to an identical replica of its original design – notice especially the antique etched mirrors and *terrazzo* floor – though the chairs were tweaked to accommodate more generous modern proportions. $200.

Central Miami Beach and north

Circa 39 3900 Collins Ave ⊤ 305/538-4900, ⊛ www.circa39.com. Another mid-range Miami Beach hotel given the boutique makeover: the 82 rooms here are, predict-

ACCOMMODATION | Hotels and guesthouses

ably, all white with pale blue accents, and feature CD players and flat screen TVs. The common areas are more playful, with mismatched Modernist furniture scattered through the lobby as well as a handy, well-priced onsite café, *Bistro@39*. $180.

Days Hotel Thunderbird Resort 18401 Collins Ave ⊕305/931-1700, ⓦwww.dezerhotels. com/thunderbird. No frills, but handy for both Miami and Fort Lauderdale; it's popular with families and has amenities like an onsite laundry. As in most other hotels in Sunny Isles Beach, you can step straight out of your room into the pool or onto the beach. The biggest bonus is the chance to admire its fabulously retro facade close-up. $105.

Eden Roc 4525 Collins Ave ⊕786/276-0526 or 1-800/327-8337, ⓦwww.edenrocresort. com. At time of writing, this Morris Lapidus-designed, 349-room MiMo icon – known for its steamship chimney-inspired roof and a sleek, showy lobby – just reopened after a $110 million makeover. The once garish rooms have been turned into breezy, minimalist pods, with warm cherrywood finishes, white linens and mod furniture; the renovation also added tech treats like plasma TVs and modernized the outdated bathrooms. The owners plan to add a second, contemporary tower that will house almost 300 more rooms by end of 2008. Rack rates from $700.

The Fontainebleau 4441 Collins Ave ⊕305/538-2000 or 1-800/548-8886, ⓦwww. fontainebleau.com. Once the ground zero of cool in the 1950s (see p.70), this hotel hosted Lucille Ball, Frank Sinatra, and Elvis, among others. Like its sibling-cum-rival hotel the *Eden Roc*, also designed by Morris Lapidus, this hotel's new owners have ambitious plans to return the place to such trendy heights and have sunk enormous chunks of cash (one estimate puts it at $1 billion and counting) into modernizing the 22-acre campus. Gone are the mismatched lobbies and fiberglass octopus named Cookie on the kiddie pool; instead, there are infinity pools, waterside cabanas, 11 restaurants, and nightspots run by the team behind Las Vegas' glitzy *Pure*. As for the 1500 rooms, they're now a reflection of the hotel's heritage: geometric patterned chairs sit alongside lush, enormous beds and spindly, midcentury-inspired dressers. Note that Lapidus' original Chateau building is now surrounded by contemporary towers, including the brand new Sorrento: rooms in these towers are a little larger, but lack any historical cachet. $320.

Little Havana

Miami River Inn Bed & Breakfast 118 SW South River Drive ⊕305/325-0045 or 1-800/468-3589, ⓦwww.miamiriverinn.com. The charming, off-beat *Miami River Inn* is a cluster of old buildings set around a secluded courtyard and small pool – rooms are furnished in a floral country style, with antique beds and dressers, and there's a self-service home-made breakfast every morning. As it's somewhat off the beaten path, though, you really need a car to stay here. $100.

Coral Gables

Best Western Chateau Bleau 1111 Ponce de Leon Blvd ⊕305/448-2634, ⓦwww.hotel chateaubleau.com. Don't let its oddly spelled, old-world name mislead you – this place is a 1960s-style concrete-box motel. However, it's great value if you're not worried about prettifying extras; there's an onsite, kidney-shaped pool, every room has a balcony and some have kitchenettes. Ask for a room at the back, if you're a light sleeper. $160.

The Biltmore 1200 Anastasia Ave ⊕305/445-1926 or 1-800/915-1926, ⓦwww.biltmorehotel. com. Miami's first grand hotel has been thoroughly restored – rooms are luxurious but unremarkable, though the giant chevron-shaped pool and onsite golf course are major pluses. The rooms themselves are reminiscent of a Spanish island villa, with lots of gauzy drapes in peach and cream tones. For a more in-depth account of the *Biltmore* and its history, see p.104. $375.

The Gables Inn 730 South Dixie Hwy ⊕305/661-7999, ⓦwww.thegablesinn.net. Coral Gables' version of a budget hotel, the *Gables Inn* is Mediterranean Revival in style, with arched walkways painted a deep ochre, and *Biltmore*-lite rooms: plenty of bottle green and dark wood, but this time with a linoleum floor. One of the few cheaper options in the area, it's located directly on Hwy-1 (or the South Dixie Hwy), so it can be noisy. $110.

Hotel Place St Michel 162 Alcazar Ave ⊕305/444-1666 or 1-800/848-4683, ⓦwww. hotelplacestmichel.com. Country-style rooms in a small, charming hotel minutes from the center of Coral Gables. There are gold fixtures, mixed antiques, and overstuffed sofas in each room – even the elevator is vintage, complete with a sliding grill and hand operation. Ask for a suite if you can; the added expense is more than worth it for the extra room. $250.

Westin Colonnade Hotel 180 Aragon Ave ⊤305/441-2600, ⓦwww.westin.com. The mahogany-decorated rooms here are all minisuites: a bedroom plus a sitting area filled with overstuffed, rather over-floral sofas. The multi-million dollar renovation when Westin took over in summer 2007 did upgrade the blandish rooms, though, and included installing the chain's aptly named Heavenly Bed in each suite. As for the building, it's a historic spot – George Merrick's original rotunda-capped sales office on the Miracle Mile – and today the hotel is equally commerce-minded, geared as it is to be close to Coral Gables business district. One upside: rates often plummet at weekends. $310.

Coconut Grove

Doubletree Coconut Grove 2649 S Bayshore Drive ⊤305/858-2500 or 1-800/222-TREE, ⓦwww.doubletree.com. Formerly the *Coconut Grove Hotel*, this place has now been grandiosely reinvented, all dark wood and deep carpets. The rooms are large and nondescript – many look out over the bay, while some have balconies and small kitchenettes. $290.

Hampton Inn 2800 SW 28th Terrace ⊤305/448-2800, ⓦwww.hamptoninncoconutgrove.com. Basic but bright accommodation geared to the budget business traveler. Free local calls, onsite coin laundry, and complimentary continental breakfast make this a good base for exploring away from the beach. $220.

Mayfair Hotel and Spa 3000 Florida Ave ⊤305/441-0000 or 1-800/433-4555, ⓦwww.mayfairhotelandspa.com. Groovy hotel in the heart of the Grove, intended as a spa or retreat spot; it's tucked into the back of the Shoppes of Mayfair shopping center, hence the name. There are quirky touches everywhere – from the free *mojito* and scented towel on check-in to the iPods on loan by the rooftop pool. The best feature, though, is undoubtedly the two-person tubs on the balconies of every room. $230.

Ritz-Carlton Coconut Grove 3300 SW 27th Ave ⊤305/644-4680, ⓦwww.ritzcarlton.com. Much like the MiMo-inspired *Ritz-Carlton South Beach* (see p.134), this tiny hotel – just over 100 rooms – is a boutique operation: the decor of the common areas is Vizcaya lite, with lashings of marble and moldings, though the atrium's a surprisingly pleasant place to linger, especially in the evenings when there's live jazz. The rooms are large, with separate marble tubs and showers. There's even a waterfall in the grounds. $400.

Key Biscayne

Ritz-Carlton Key Biscayne 455 Grand Bay Drive ⊤305/365-4500 or 1-800/241-3333, ⓦwww.ritzcarlton.com. This enormous family-friendly hotel – its 400 or so rooms decked out in the usual chintzy Ritz décor – has its own beach and several onsite restaurants (including the outstanding *Cioppino*; see p.156). Of the two pools, the large southern one is for families; the smaller northern one is adults only, with iPods and cocktails, plus a new beachfront bar-restaurant. Pack some whites, too: the onsite tennis center's a nod to Key Biscayne's obsession with the sport – book a session with a pro, or just whack a ball or two around with your partner. $520.

Silver Sands Beach Resort 301 Ocean Drive ⊤305/361-5441, ⓦwww.key-biscayne.com/accom/silversands. There's little to recommend this bland motel, other than the fact that it's on the inexpensive side as far as Key Biscayne goes. It also huddles right on the beach – the pricier oceanfront rooms allow you to step right out of your door onto the sand. $170.

South of the city

Best Western Gateway to the Keys 411 S Krome Ave, Florida City ⊤305/246-5100 or 1-888/981-5100, ⓦwww.bestwestern.com. One of the most comfortable if bland places to stay around here; all rooms have coffee makers, microwaves, and fridges. The location's the handiest thing: Florida City's a good stop-off en route to the Keys. All rooms are non-smoking. $130.

Greenstone Motel 304 N Krome Ave ⊤305/247-8334, ⓦwww.greenstonemotel.com. Smack in the middle of Homestead and within walking distance to the stores and eateries of downtown, this motel is a quirky oddity. Linking with the local ArtSouth complex next door that aims to bring the arts to the masses, it has recruited local creative types to customize the bedrooms. If their styles put you off, there are also plain rooms available with full motel amenities. $50.

Grove Inn Country Guesthouse 22540 SW Krome Ave, Homestead ☎ 305/247-6572 or 1-877/247-6572, ⓦ www.groveinn.com. On an old fruit farm, the *Grove Inn* makes for a comfortable South Miami base, with friendly, knowledgeable owners and an informal atmosphere. $85.

Redland Hotel 5 S Flagler Ave ☎ 305/246-1904 or 1-800/595-1904, ⓦ www.redlandhotel.com. A historic inn, where every unit is named after a pioneer family, in the center of old Homestead. The decor's comfy, country florals with all modern conveniences, and there's a welcoming bar in the hotel. $100.

At the airport

Hampton Inn-Miami Airport 777 NW 57th Ave ☎ 305/262-5400 or 1-800/HAMPTON, ⓦ www.hamptoninnmiamiairport.com. Branch of a good-value hotel chain two miles from the airport, offering some of the best rates in the area with free breakfast, Wi-Fi and all the usual *Hampton Inn* amenities. Twenty-four-hour courtesy bus available to airport. $220.

MIA Miami International Airport ☎ 305/871-4100 or 1-800/327-1276, ⓦ www.miahotel.com. There's no excuse for missing your plane if you stay here; this fully equipped, if bland, hotel is located inside the airport. At time of writing, it's midway through a renovation, which has shuttered the amenities on the 8th floor (including its rooftop pool) while the building's upgraded. Walk-ins can book a day rate for rooms if you have a long layover and want to shower and relax between flights, pending availability ($95). $210.

Hostels

Clay Hotel and Hostel 1438 Washington Ave, South Beach ☎ 305/534-2988 or 1-800/379-2529, ⓦ www.clayhotel.com. Located in a landmark building on the corner of Española Way, the *Clay* has both private and dorm rooms at budget rates. It's a great place to meet other travelers, and has a fully equipped kitchen, but unfortunately, some rooms are cleaner than others: ask to see one before you commit. Dorms from $29 YHA members or $30 nonmembers; rooms from $130.

Jazz on South Beach Hostel 321 Collins Ave, South Beach ☎ 305/672-2137, ⓦ www.thesouthbeachhostel.com. Spiffy new space for an old local hostel, one block from the beach and a major improvement on its former digs: every room, kitted out in blond wood furniture, now has a private bathroom and there's free breakfast and WiFi, as well as an onsite bar raging until 5am. Dorms $15–20, private rooms $100.

Ocean Hotel and Hostel 236 9th St, South Beach ☎ 305/534-0268, ⓦ www.oceanhotelmiamibeach.com. The great location, just blocks from the beach, has always been the biggest selling point of this hostel. A recent spruce-up and name change has improved the rooms dramatically and the rates haven't risen much. There's free breakfast and a rooftop sundeck, though why guests wouldn't stumble a few yards to the beach rather than bake there is anyone's guess. Dorms from $25, private rooms from $80.

The Tropics Hotel & Hostel 1550 Collins Ave, South Beach ☎ 305/531-0361, ⓦ www.tropicshotel.com. The private rooms are cheap but unappealing, though that's no matter as the real reason to stay here is the hostel accommodation: it's sparse yet clean, and each room sleeps four with a private bath. Dorms from $29, rooms from $105.

Cafés and light meals

From a quick Cuban coffee to a filling Jewish knish, Miami has plenty on offer in the way of **cafés**, snacks, and **light meals**. Two unmissable local specialties are the Cuban sandwich, made with pickles, cheese, smoked ham, and roast pork – all crammed into a fluffy roll that's toasted in a press – and the toxically sweet *cafecito*, a thimble-sized jolt of caffeine and sugar that's addictively energizing.

In addition, the city features New York–style pizza joints, vintage diners, home-style bakeries, and a range of cheap, filling breakfast spots – plus plenty of sidewalk cafés good for nursing a coffee while watching the crowds go by. The city has also produced an impressive string of casual cafes with branches popping up across the city; the best of these chainlets include the Japanese-Thai joint *Sushi Siam*, French bakery *La Provence*, hot-dog grill *Dogma* and *gelateria Dolce Vita*. We've listed some of the best options below; all are fairly inexpensive. For listings of places more appropriate for a sit-down dinner, see "Restaurants," beginning on p.146.

Downtown

Garcia's Seafood Grille 398 NW North River Drive ☎305/375-0765. This lunch-only riverside fish café is bustling and efficient, serving tasty fresh fish at reasonable prices, with a small counter in the front and racks of waterfront picnic tables out back. The dolphin sandwich (actually mahi mahi) is delicious, as is the house special, lemon-grilled grouper.

Karlo Bakery 1242 SW Coral Way ☎305/858-1080. The European-style food at this bakery is delicious, especially the buttery soft croissants and frothy *café au lait*. The rich desserts are delicious, too, and just right for an indulgent picnic – smuggle them into Vizcaya's waterfront grounds a couple of blocks away.

La Paris Cafeteria 251 SE 1st St ☎305/374-0988. Packed with office workers at lunchtime, *La Paris* is one of the better Cuban diners, serving basic dishes at rock-bottom prices (sandwiches $4, entrees $5). The place is absolutely without frills and there's limited counter seating, but the food is hearty and appetizing.

Las Palmas 209 SE 1st St ☎305/373-1333. Although there are plenty of similar Cuban lunch-counter cafés around Downtown serving sandwiches and deep-fried treats at breakfast and lunchtime, *Las Palmas* is clean and the staff friendly.

Perricone's Marketplace 15 SE 10th St ☎305-374-9693. Nestled in a leafy tropical garden, this eighteenth-century barn was shipped down wholesale from Vermont to take up a permanent perch in Miami's skyscraper-filled Brickell district. It's run by Stephen Perricone, a partner in *Michy's* (see p.152), so it's little wonder that the food is so good. There are cakes and muffins at breakfast, hot and cold sandwiches like steak with sautéed mushrooms come lunchtime ($8–10), and simple mains for dinner like grilled ahi tuna and veal Milanese, breaded and pounded thin ($20–25) It's easy to forget you're downtown when sitting on the verandah by the rough hewn wooden bar.

Raja's 33 NE 2nd Ave ☎305/539-9551. This no-nonsense restaurant serves South Indian staples like a *masala dosa* (potato pancake) accompanied by tangy *sambhar* (hot-and-sour soup). Prices hover around

$6 per dish, and the portions are generous. Lunch only.

Soya & Pomodoro 120 NE 1st St
T 305/381-9511, W www.soyaepomodoro.com. Tucked into a brightly painted historic arcade, this old-world Italian café's an appealing downtown pitstop. The slogan here is "Simple Food Made with Love," so expect gnocchi, spaghetti with Bolognese sauce, tiramisu and a few steaks; you'll struggle to pay more than $10 for most dishes. Breakfast & lunch daily, dinner Thursday evenings only to accompany the weekly live music sessions.

Top Hat Deli 150 W Flagler St T 305/381-6337. Well-priced for the neighborhood, this café offers filling sandwiches for around $7 and has plentiful outdoor seating overlooking the Metro-Dade Cultural Center. Service can be rather slow, but it's a convenient stop-off when sightseeing.

South Beach

A La Folie Café 516 Española Way T 305/538-4484, W www.alafolie.com. Run by French expats, this trendily dilapidated café serves authentic, tasty crêpes and salads from $6 and is well-stocked with European magazines. It's a refreshing respite from the tourist traps and conga music elsewhere on Española Way, and you're likely to sit beside locals rather than other visitors.

Balans Lincoln Road 1022 Lincoln Rd T 305/534-9191. An outpost of a small British chain of gay restaurants, *Balans* serves its stylish brunches to visitors and locals alike – don't expect warm service, but it's a great place to see and be seen on Lincoln Road. Good weekday breakfast specials (budget around $12 per person), and don't miss the chunky, crunchy *Balans* potatoes.

Books & Books Café 933 Lincoln Road T 305/695-8898, W www.booksandbooks.com. The sister spot to the effortless Coral Gables café has a thriving lunch and dinner scene – grab one of the six shaded tables spilling out onto Lincoln Road if you can. Lunch is standard sandwiches (around $8) with fresh-brewed coffee while dinner's more elaborate, featuring Floribbean dishes like scallops in coconut-shrimp sauce.

David's Café 1058 Collins Ave T 305/534-8736. At this original outpost of the famed Cuban restaurant, expat businessmen sit alongside brassy teenagers. Try the great, filling Cuban sandwiches for around $8, along with a delicious *cafecito* (60 cents), or head to the Meridian Ave branch – *David's Café II*, at no. 1654 (T 305/672-8707) – for swanky dining-room seating and pricier food like *ropa vieja* for around $15.

Fratelli La Bufala 437 Washington Ave T 305/532-0700, W www.fratellilabufala.com. Don't be fooled by its out-of-the-way location – this is where expat Italians come for a fix of authentic wood-fired pizzas. It's like a true rustic Neapolitan trattoria, with most ingredients flown in from Italy; fine, except for the time the plane was late so the restaurant couldn't open. Allow no more than $20/head for a bellyful.

Front Porch Café 1418 Ocean Drive T 305/531-8300. Despite its over-touristed location, this really is where the locals go for breakfast. Portions are supersized: gigantic omelets, wholemeal pancakes as big as Frisbees, and doorstop sandwiches are all well-priced ($6–8 for most entrees). Come here early with a newspaper and check out the morning crowd.

Gino's 731 Washington Ave T 305/673-2837. Open 24 hours a day, *Gino's* serves true New York–style pizza to shift workers and clubbers alike: each slice comes with a free, buttery garlic knot.

Icebox Café 1657 Michigan Ave
T 305/538-8448, W www.iceboxcafe.com. Owner Robert Seigmann was a ballet dancer and Wall Streeter before turning to baking. He now runs a small, gay-friendly café-bakery with industrial décor, beefy waiters and a terrific, dinerish menu: expect meat loaf and kobe burgers at dinner, pina colada pancakes at the packed brunch. He's best known for cakes, though, and Oprah recently anointed his the best in the country. The 3-course $35 prix-fixe menu (Mon–Thurs 6–11pm) is a steal.

Jerry's Famous Deli 1450 Collins Ave T 305/532-8030. This 24-hour deli, housed in a converted cafeteria, offers a menu so vast that you'll find almost anything you're craving (try the salad served in a pizza crust – it's better than it sounds). Sure, it's overpriced, but as a late-night pitstop it's almost unbeatable.

La Sandwicherie 229 W 14th St T 305/532-8934. Don't be put off by the pretentious name; open until 5am, this place serves serious sandwiches starting at around $6 from its open-air lunch counter. Each giant

French loaf could make two meals – if you can fit it in your mouth, that is – crammed with fresh, crunchy greens and cold cuts.

Le Provence 1627 Collins Ave ☎305/538-2406, ⓦwww.laprovencemiami.com. This French bakery close to the beach is a terrific place to stock up on baguettes and brioches before a day on the sands. The croissants are outstanding, as are the jewel-like fruit pastries. Daily 7am–7:45pm. There's another branch at 2300 Ponce de Leon Boulevard, Coral Gables (☎305/476-5694).

News Café 800 Ocean Drive ☎305/538-6397. The food may be nondescript, but its location at the corner of 8th and Ocean Drive has made the *News* ground zero for the South Beach scene since the early Nineties. Enjoy the fact that its brasserie approach lets you sit all afternoon over a single coffee without being shooed away. Branch: 5582 NE 4th Court in 55th Street Station, Biscayne Corridor.

Pizza Rustica 863 Washington Ave ☎305/674-8244, ⓦwww.pizza-rustica.com. This is a cheap beach stop serving huge slices of pizza for only $4.50. Un-Italian toppings like barbecue chicken combined with tangy tomato sauce make delicious snacks, and each slice is cut into six bite-sized pieces while still hot from the oven. Try the Rustica, piled high with artichoke, olives, ham, and sun-dried tomatoes. Though there are new branches across the city every year, the pizzas at this, the original location, are consistently the best. Other locations includes 1447 Washington Ave, South Beach (☎305/538-6009); 667 Lincoln Road, South Beach (☎305/672-2334); 250 SW 8th Street, Brickell (☎786/621-4300).

Puerto Sagua 700 Collins Ave ☎305/673-1115. Larger and much cheaper than *David's*, this Cuban hang-out, with brown wood-effect Formica tables, has a decor that's unchanged since the late 1970s. Thankfully the traditional food is filling – try the hefty portions of rice and beans.

Taystee Bakery 1450 Washington Ave ☎305/538-4793. Join the elderly clientele for breakfast from 6am in this super-cheap neighborhood bakery, serving old-fashioned kosher breads, pastries, and *empanadas* with various fillings at a couple of Formica tables tarted up with bright red tablecloths.

Van Dyke Café 1637 Jefferson Ave ☎305/534-3600. Newsstand-cum-café serving pastries and cappuccinos in a space with squish sofas, low tables, and plenty of reading material: the wall of magazines, both domestic and foreign language, is the best selection on the beach. Daily 7am–3am.

Central Miami Beach and north

Arnie & Richie's Deli 525 41st St ☎305/531-7691. In the bosom of Miami Beach's Jewish neighborhood, this deli serves standbys like pastrami sandwiches, knishes, and whitefish salad without fuss or fanfare – if you eat in, be prepared to share a table with the gaggles of local old ladies who stop in regularly or grab a meat-crammed sandwich ($8–9) to go. The fruit *rugelach* are also delicious.

Buenos Aires Bakery 7134 Collins Ave ☎305/861-7887. This gourmet Argentine bakery in North Beach serves mostly glistening handmade tarts and candies, as well as coffee and a small selection of ice cream by the cone.

Laurenzo's 16385 West Dixie Hwy ☎305/945-6381. A local institution in North Miami Beach, the diner counter inside this Italian-American supermarket serves *zitti*, lasagna, and garlic-laced spaghetti for cheap and filling lunches. It's hardly the funkiest restaurant around, but the pasta portions are good value if you're in the neighborhood visiting the Old Spanish Monastery.

Miami Juice 16120 Collins Ave ☎305/945-0444. A welcome healthy alternative amid the diners and fast-food joints that cluster along this stretch of Collins Avenue in Sunny Isles. It's also good for Middle Eastern specialties like falafel and hummus.

Santa Fe News & Coffee Bal Harbour Shops complex, 9700 Collins Ave ☎305/861-0938. An unremarkable café that's notable simply as one of the few places to grab a quiet coffee in Bal Harbour, and the only eatery in the mall that isn't as premium-priced as the stores – coffee's just $1.85. There are magazines for sale, as well as gooey pastries and simple sandwiches ($6).

Yakko-San 17040 W Dixie Highway, North Miami Beach ☎305/947-0064. An undiscovered gem, this Japanese joint serves more than just blah California rolls. The clean-lined tiny restaurant serves tapas-style small plates (budget no more than $10/dish) with adventurous but authentic ingredients like monkfish liver, chrysanthemum leaf tempura, and a pork and tofu hotpot. Even better, it's open late (3.30am at weekends, 2am weekdays). A hike from most hotels, but well worth it.

North along the Biscayne Corridor

A Café 4582 NE 2nd Ave ☎ 305/572-9902. This bohemian bolthole on the mainland is a refreshing change from the seen-and-be-seen culture elsewhere in Miami: it serves organic food like venison and wild boar to an artsy crowd. Even better, it's BYOB with no corkage charge, though since ice isn't served (too shocking for the system, apparently) get used to a glass of lukewarm water.

Adelita's Cafe 2804 NE 2nd Ave ☎ 305/576-0331. With a tiny kitchen and the daily menu scribbled on a whiteboard, this Honduran hole-in-the-wall shares a Wynwood store-front with the local laundry. Sit down at the counter amid the washing machines and enjoy tasty soups like black bean or crispy fried savory treats for less than $5 a portion.

Dogma 7030 Biscayne Blvd ☎ 305/759-8433. Hipsters make pilgrimages to this stylish Little Haiti hot-dog stand on a sketchy part of Biscayne Boulevard. Sit at red and white tables and munch on cheap,

filling dogs – try the best-selling chili dog (slathered with chili flown in specially from Los Angeles) or more exotic inventions like the Athens, topped with feta, oregano, and cucumber (both under $4). There's a branch at 899 NE 125th Street, North Miami (☎ 305/893-6462).

Lakay Tropical Ice Cream 91 NE 54th St ☎ 305/751-2912. This tiny shop in Little Haiti produces outstanding home-made ice cream, using exotic and familiar fruits as flavoring – try the pineapple or the guava. Two large scoops cost a paltry $1.50, and there's also a small selection of flaky Haitian pastries.

Lost and Found Saloon 185 NW 36th Street, Miami ☎ 305/576-1008, ⓦ www.thelostand-foundsaloon.com. Cheapie Southwestern joint with more than a whiff of the Old West – thanks to its location, it's popular with local artists (much buzzed-about Bhakti Baxter dashed off the sunset-and-moun-tains mural in the alcove on the right of the door). The menu has classics like tacos and burritos with hip additions like a tofu *chipotle* melt – all for around $8. Eclectic artisanal beers are served in mason jars until late.

Out of the Blue 2426 NE 2nd Ave ☎ 305/573-3800, ⓦ www.outoftheblueca-fe.net. The delightful owner Carmen Miranda presides over this coffee shop in a convert-ed house, with mismatched 1960s furniture, a shady patio and emerging artists' work tacked to the walls. The menu includes sandwiches and salads (around $7), house-made soups and smoothies (from $4.25), and the usual coffee drinks. Breakfast and lunch only, closed Sunday. Free WiFi.

The Secret Sandwich 3918 N Miami Ave ☎ 305/571-9990. Spy-themed café in the Design District, with a massive world map spread across one wall, serving hearty sandwiches for around $8: try the flavorful Mata Hari (lime-marinated chicken with car-amelized onions) and the deliciously creamy flan. It closes whenever the food's run out, usually around 4pm.

Sushi Siam Inside the 55th Street Station complex, 5592 NE 4th Court #1 & 2 ☎ 305/751-7818. Another local chainlet, this time fusing Thai and Japanese dishes. This branch – decked out like a Big Easy brothel with bright red walls, black lacquered chairs and huge glittery crystal lampshades – is busiest at lunchtime when there's a superb special:

▼ Dogma

CAFÉS AND LIGHT MEALS | North along the Biscayne Corridor

a dozen dishes with chicken, pork, beef or vegetable for $12. Branches at 647 Lincoln Road, South Beach (☎305-672-7112); 632 Crandon Boulevard, Key Biscayne (☎305-361-7768).

Little Havana

La Bodeguita Martinez 833 SW 29th Ave ☎305/649-9313. When a savvy businessman snapped up the right to the name Bodeguita del Medio in the US – Hemingway's favorite spot in Havana – this café had to become La Bodeguita Martinez to avoid a lawsuit. Whatever it's called, the café's worth a pilgrimage to the back corner of a shopping center for superb Cuban classics ($9–15) like *Tasajo* (beef jerky) served Criolla style in tomatoes, onions and peppers, and *pollo cacerola* (chicken baked casserole style). There's live Cuban music most nights.

Nuevo Siglo 1305 SW 8th St ☎305/854-1916. The pick of the many grocery-store cafés on Calle Ocho, this lunch counter along the back wall serves excellent *café cubano* as well as delicious pressed Cuban sandwiches with sweet pork, pickles, and ham.

Los Piñarenos 1334 SW 8th St ☎305/285-1135. Enormous *fruteria* sprawling along the southern side of Calle Ocho: for around $2 you'll snag a flagon of juice squeezed to order. Even better, you'll rub elbows with the old-timers from the neighborhood who hang out here during the day. Breakfast and lunch only.

El Rey de las Fritas 1821 SW 8th Street, Little Havana ☎305/644-6054. New location for an old neighborhood favorite – the name's a nod to its specialty, a Miami confection that's also nicknamed the Cuban hamburger (think of it as a regular sandwich, extra crispy from frying and with a richer, butterier taste). Gulp it down with some of the café's ultra-thin French fries. Dirt cheap and delicious.

Coral Gables

Books & Books Café 265 Aragon Ave ☎305/448-9599. A low-key oasis off the Miracle Mile, this café serves crusty French-loaf sandwiches starting at $7, as well as rich, buttery pastries and sweets produced by a local bakery – try the fresh strawberry cheesecake. There's live music every Friday from 7:30–10pm.

Burger Bob's 2001 Granada Blvd ☎305/567-3100. Tucked away in the clubhouse of the public Granada Golf Course is one of Coral Gables' gems: this homely café, with its green Formica chairs, white plastic tables, and yellow mustard bottles, is where local politicos power breakfast alongside pensioners looking for a deal. The home-made chili's a steal at $2.50, but the reason to come here's as much for the vibe as the food. Breakfast and lunch only.

Chocolate Fashion 248 Andalusia Ave ☎305/461-3200. What started out as a stall at the local Farmers' Market has become this appealing café-bakery off the Miracle Mile with mirrored walls and minimal wooden furniture. There are glass cases full of the French chef-owner Georges Berger's glistening confections (try the chocolate mousse or raspberry tart) and crusty breads, all made onsite; for savory treats, there are sandwiches and salads like caprese or tuna on focaccia, as well as weekend breakfast specials (all around $9).

Giardino 30 Giralda Ave, Coral Gables ☎305/460-6010, ⊛www.giardinosalads.com. Local take on the gourmet salad-to-order trend in a bare-bones concrete space with a few tables if you want to linger. The enormous 30-choice menu's surprisingly eclectic, with everything from panzanella (cucumbers, tomatoes, red onions and vinaigrette-soaked croutons) to the sweet potato, pecan and feta-crammed Harvest. Salads cost $5.75 (small), $7.75 (medium) and $9.75 (large); baked sweet or standard potatoes with salad-style toppings cost $5. Lunch only.

Nena's 3791 Bird Rd. No phone. Nena's is the lunchtime hub of Miami's power Cuban scene: within a derelict-looking building two lunch counters and a couple of tables, with whiteboards on the wall describing the day's offerings – the *croqueta preparada* (Cuban sandwich) is juicy and delicious.

Sacha's Café 2525 Ponce De Leon Boulevard ☎305/569-1300. Tucked into an office building behind the Miracle Mile, this lunchtime joint with white chairs and metal tables looks like the in-house cafeteria of a particularly groovy design firm. The menu's small but impressive, including the like of a chicken spring roll asian salad or roast beef and gruyère sandwich on pantoufle for around $9. There are a few tables outside in the shady colonnade.

Miami's vices

Miami's appeal is 24/7. Plenty of people seek out the wide white sands here for tanning and a dip in the Atlantic Ocean; but just as many are lured to the city for its after-dark appeal, with buzzing bars, throbbing nightclubs, and trendy restaurants all jostling for space like a disco ball-lit one-stop shop. Even the earliest-to-bed visitor should take a siesta one afternoon and brave the scene: there's no better snapshot of Miami's shameless hedonism than a bar on South Beach at

Mojitos ▲

Miami after dark

Oddly, no one can fully explain what turned Miami from a retirement hideaway twenty years ago to a raging nightlife mecca. In part, it was the gay pioneers who revived South Beach in the late 1980s and early 1990s; tucked away in forgotten South Florida, they partied at iconic nightclubs like long-shuttered *Warsaw Ballroom* on Washington Avenue (it's now *Jerry's Deli* – open 24/7, of course). Soon, trendy straight visitors joined them and cloned their anything-goes, dance-until-dawn lifestyle for the masses.

Celebrities were another factor. While LA and New York were full of nosy journalists and long-lensed paparazzi, Miami was a surprisingly private place… at least until the last few years. Kate Moss could come here, misbehave a little (or at least behave like a real person might) and not fret that gossip columns or magazines would report her antics. Of course, that's all changed and now Miami's a regular stop on the party circuit as much for shutterbugs as the celebrities they dog.

Glass nightclub ▲

The Pawnshop Lounge ▼

But the origins of Miami's 24/7 culture might lie overseas from – and a lot earlier than – South Beach's 1990s revival; and specifically, in Miami's links with Cuba. Pre-Castro Havana was the hedonistic hub of the world – it was a daring trip for thrill-seeking Americans, hitting the steamy dancefloors of its nightclubs and watching burlesque live shows, knocking back freshly made *mojitos* and smoking hand-rolled cigars. When those Cubans were expelled by the dictator, they brought their culture, and late-night revelry, with them to Miami; clubs in Little Havana were throbbing at 3am long before anyone even thought to open *Velvet* or *The Spot*, two more iconic South Beach clubs also long shuttered.

Best festivals

Three annual events best showcase Miami's nightlife. First comes the Winter Music Conference in late March (Ⓦ www. wmcon.com), bringing producers and DJs from across the world to play at venues in and around the beach – if you're a light sleeper, don't book a room here that week. Hotel rooms are at a similar premium during early December's Art Basel Miami Beach (Ⓦ www.artbaselmiamibeach. com). This spin-off of the pricey Swiss art show matches the original's artistic laurels but adds a slew of lavish parties: 2007's schedule included a staggering 92 events. Finally, there's New Year's Eve, a single night during which Miami's gang of club promoters can make up to half of their annual income – no wonder, when top price tickets at the *Setai* luxury hotel's recent bash cost a wallet-blistering $1500 per person.

▲ Winter Music Conference

▼ Art Basel Miami Beach

Five top clubs and lounges

The Florida Room The *Delano Hotel*'s hip basement lounge was the brainchild of the interiors firm owned by Lenny Kravitz. See p.161.

Mansion The likeliest place to party alongside Paris Hilton and other pseudo-celebs. See p.163.

Mokaï Jewel box-like boîte with capacity for barely 200 – make it in here, and you'll rub shoulders with whatever A-listers are in town. See p.163.

Nikki Beach Yes, a little past its prime, but worth a visit to see the birthplace of the champagne-and-bikini lifestyle. See p.164.

Set Party here under a Swarowski chandelier that's Phantom of the Opera-style grand. See p.164.

▼ Mokaï

South Florida fashion

One inevitable byproduct of Miami's focus on the good life? A fashion scene with a gold-tinged aesthetic that shuns the seasonality of *Vogue* for a more stable mantra: if in doubt, show more skin. Miami has a shamelessly glitzy fashion culture, with heels and short skirts more a uniform than a choice come nightfall; one local radio station's recent straight-faced promotion even offered listeners the chance to win $1000 vouchers from a cosmetic surgery clinic towards the procedure of their choice.

But the city's reputation for tanning and too-tight tees isn't entirely fair. In fact, there's a thriving high-end fashion scene here: Julian Chang and Rene Ruiz are two local designers with gowns that are red carpet regulars – Kimora Lee Simmons and Paris Hilton are often spotted in the latter's stretchy, crystal-studded dresses. Miami's brightest fashion hope, though, is Esteban Cortazar; aged just 18 (by some accounts – Cortazar's chronology can be hilariously hazy) when he showed his namesake collection at New York's Fashion Week in 2002, Esteban recently ditched South Beach for a gig helming the fabled Ungaro label.

Arrive Boutique ▲
Base ▼

Though Esteban doesn't have a standalone store in Miami, most of the big name brand names are present at the two major luxury malls, the Village at Merrick Park and Bal Harbour (see p.182). Miami branches of high-end retailers consistently jostle with their Las Vegas counterparts for the right to claim status as most-profitable-per-square-foot worldwide. The artfully curated concept store has arrived in Miami too, with boutiques like Arrive, Base and Culture Kings showing an eclectic mix of clothes, gadgets, ornaments and adults toys.

Titanic Brewery 5813 Ponce de Leon Blvd
☎305/667-2537. Unpretentious pub food served in a friendly bar just outside Coral Gables. The hamburgers are especially good and start around $6, and there are gourmet beers on tap. In addition, the *Titanic* hosts regular performances by local bands (see p.160, "Drinking").

Coconut Grove

Dolce Vita Gelato 3462 Main Highway
☎305/461-1322, ⓦ www.dolcevitagelato. com. Glorious sorbets and ice creams are sold at this modernist *gelateria*, staffed by Italians who give the place a laid-back, European feel. Ask for a sample before you order – the *frutti di bosco* (fruits of the forest) and *zuppa inglese* (trifle) are staff favorites. There's also a small counter for a quick *caffè*. Branches: 26 E Flagler Street, Downtown (☎305/577-2423); 18288 Collins Ave #3, Sunny Isles Beach (☎305/933-9990); 1655 Collins Ave, South Beach (☎305/604-0104).

Daily Bread Marketplace 2400 SW 27th St
☎305/856-5893. Just over Hwy-1 from Coconut Grove proper, this Middle Eastern grocery store and cafeteria serves delicious lunches like falafel, *tabbouleh*, and ground-lamb pitta kebab in a hurry.

Greenstreet Café 3110 Commodore Plaza
☎305/444-0244. The *Greenstreet's* terrific breakfasts of fragrant fruit pancakes and hefty omelets make this café a real scene at weekends. There are also a large number of outdoor tables where you can dawdle undisturbed over a coffee.

Scotty's Landing 3381 Pan American Drive
☎305/854-2626. Though hard to find, tucked away on the water near City Hall, and service can be slow, there are few better places to taste local flavor than at *Scotty's* – sit out on the water at the Marina, order a fish sandwich (around $9), and join the locals for lunch.

Key Biscayne

Donut Gallery 83 Harbour Drive ☎305/361-9985. Open at 5.30am, this old-time diner is an untouched classic on Key Biscayne, with its red vinyl stools, faded Formica tables, and sweet, greasy donuts. Breakfasts start around $4.

South to Homestead and Florida City

El Toro Taco 1 South Krome Ave, Homestead
☎305/245-8182. This bring your own beer Mexican restaurant in the historic district of downtown Homestead has been family run for more than twenty years. It's one of the best choices if in the mood for authentic *fajitas* or *chile relleño*, made to please the immigrant residents drawn here to service the fruit-picking trade.

Moreno's Tortilla Shop 439 West Palm Drive. No phone. Neighborhood café primarily catering to the large number of migrant Mexican workers in Florida City. Worth stopping by, though, for its excellent and authentic hand-made *tamales*.

Robert Is Here 19200 SW 344th St
☎305/246-1592. Started in the mid-1950s, when his farmer father put young Robert in charge of an impromptu roadside cucumber stall, this fruitstand is now a ramshackle institution. Part farmers' market, part café, Robert and his team sell fruity milkshakes, preserves, and tropical salad dressings. Close to the main entrance of Everglades National Park.

Soli Organic Ice Cream 7209 SW 59th Ave, South Miami ☎305/663-9399, ⓦ www.soliorganic.com. This suburban ice-cream store is dedicated to all-natural ingredients: milk from vegan-fed cows, pesticide and chemical-free ingredients for flavoring, and low calorie agave-nectar sweetener subbing for sugar. Flavors are still reassuringly indulgent, including coconut almond chocolate chunk and baked apple pecan. Cones start at $4.75, sundaes at $6.50 while a to-go pint is $9. There's fair trade coffee and free WiFi as well.

CAFÉS AND LIGHT MEALS | Coconut Grove • Key Biscayne • Further south

⑫

Restaurants

With cuisine from nearly every corner of the globe, including hearty dollops of Cuban, Haitian, Italian, and French, eating in Miami is an endless pleasure. This is the realm in which Miami's cosmopolitan, cobbled-together history produces plenty of flavor with none of the friction.

The dominant ethnic food is, of course, **Cuban** – though it's not for the weak-hearted: many of the tender meat dishes are fried, and glorious desserts like *tres leches* are artery-clogging. Cuban menus also often feature Spanish staples such as paella and black beans and white rice, known as Moros y Cristianos (literally, "Moors and Christians"). The ethnic style most in vogue in Miami, though, is **Haitian**: restaurants like *Tap Tap* in South Beach have opened outside the borders of Little Haiti, and the dishes – which place emphasis on ingredients like starchy tubers and goat, much like in Jamaican cooking – are hearty and satisfying.

The 1990s were the era when a true local cooking style evolved: it's now known variously as **Floribbean**, **Nuevo Cubano**, or **Tropical Fusion**. The concept was simple: Miami's chefs took much from Cuban cooking (hearts of palm, avocados, and guava) then used those same ingredients in unusual combinations, often adding light but spicy tastes like ginger or bonnet peppers. Now mainstream in many local mid-priced and upscale restaurants, many of the Floribbean dishes use heaps of fresh fruit and, since the key is to keep flavor high but fat low – a popular combination in body-conscious Miami – seafood is more common than meat.

As an antidote to all that slenderizing freshness, recent years have seen a rash of openings of flashy, clubby **steakhouses** both in South Beach and the mainland; we've listed our pick of them below. **Sushi**, once a cheapie staple in the city and often a disappointing, tasteless facsimile of the real Japanese recipe, has improved drastically, largely thanks to the arrival of several new, upscale restaurants.

As for where to go, **South Beach** unsurprisingly holds the largest grouping of trendy restaurants. Many of these establishments serve excellent food that lives up to the hype – though unfortunately, so do the prices. As with hotels, restaurants in South Beach are increasingly catering to an upscale, moneyed clientele rather than the poor and trendy types who first recolonized the place years ago. Rent hikes have priced out many older restaurants, though there are still a few budget-friendly finds that we've listed and plenty of the cafés reviewed in the previous chapter also serve well-priced evening meals. Whatever you do, beware of Ocean Drive, filled as it is with so-so eateries staffed by carnival-barking waitresses who lasso unsuspecting passers-by into eating the food – skip anywhere other than the handful of places we've highlighted. Back on the mainland, **Coral Gables** is the other chichi place to dine – restaurants here are less sceney than their counterparts in South Beach, though often more formal. And the **Biscayne Corridor** renaissance is most evident in the profusion of trendy new restaurants that have sprung up over the past two years; it's one of the best options away from the beach.

Away from these two areas, though, the pickings thin out: **Coconut Grove** has only a small cluster of restaurants at its center, while in **Little Havana** stick to Calle Ocho as there are plenty of authentic choices on every block. When it comes to **Downtown**, north of the river is virtually bereft of good eateries, and those worth trying all tend to close early (plan to dine before 9pm); south of the river, in Brickell, though, a clutch of new restaurants have sprung up to cater to its increasing residential population. Back on Miami Beach, Collins Avenue offers a few clusters of restaurants as it snakes northwards, notably around 41st Street and 71st Street. For the best Mexican food around, head south to **Homestead**, where several cheap canteens cater primarily to the migrant workers who staff the fruit farms each season.

Downtown

Big Fish Mayami 55 SW Miami Ave ☎305/373-1770. Known for its crab cakes, this riverside shack offers a taste of the Florida Keys without leaving Miami for around $20 per person. The atmosphere is casual and the design ramshackle – the bar is built around an enormous banyan tree.

Grimpa Steakhouse 901 S Miami Ave, Brickell ☎305/416-9355, ⊛www.grimpa.com. The first foray outside Brazil for this all-you-can-eat steakhouse chain, serving meat *rodizio*-style – carved off sword-like skewers to order at the table ($30 per person at lunchtime, $45 at dinner and all day Sat and Sun). There are 17 different cuts, from beef to seafood, all grilled over natural charcoal, plus a self-serve salad bar. A showy glass staircase and chandelier form the centerpiece of the restaurant though it's really the 500-strong wine list that's more gasp-inducing.

La Loggia 68 W Flagler St ☎305/373-4800, ⊛www.laloggiaristorante.com. A casual Italian pasta café with terracotta floors and plenty of Chianti bottles for decoration – the food's fine enough, and it's one of the few evening options in the CBD. There's bar and restaurant seating, plus a varied wine list. Entrees start around $10.

Los Ranchos Bayside Marketplace, 401 Biscayne Blvd N-100 ☎305/375-0666. As this chainlet of Nicaraguan steakhouses has grown, its food has become more Americanized, but steak specials like *churrasco con chimichurri* (steak with spicy herb salsa) are tender and delicious, while the *cuatro leches* dessert outdoes the traditional Cuban *tres leches*. Allow at least $50/head.

Morton's Steakhouse 1200 Brickell Ave ☎305/400-9990, ⊛www.mortons.com. Clubby old-world steakhouse in the midst of skyscraping banks, serving juicy slabs

of aged beef to an upscale clientele – try the Porterhouse or double filet mignon for around $40. One of the few places in Downtown to remain lively during the evening.

Rosa Mexicano 900 S Miami Ave, Brickell ☎786/425-1001, ⊛www.rosamexicano.com. Miami branch of the impressive countrywide Mexican chain, nestled in the Mary Brickell Village development. It has the usual bright colored but modernist interior, and the same menu standouts as its sister restaurants – tableside guacamole *en molcajete* and *chili ancho relleno* (chili peppers with chicken picadillo). Gulp down a signature pomegranate margarita ($8.50), delicious and much less sweet than most frozen versions. Entrees run $15–23.

Rosinella 1040 S Miami Ave ☎305/372-5756. At this outstanding family-run restaurant, you'll find classic Italian comfort food at reasonable prices (around $20 for a two-course meal). Even though all the bread and pasta are made on site, Mama Rosinella is best known for her soft, floury gnocchi. Another location is at 525 Lincoln Rd (☎305/672-8777).

Tobacco Road 626 S Miami Ave ☎305/374-1198, ⊛www.tobacco-road.com. This bar and live music venue (see p.157, "Drinking") also serves surprisingly hearty and fresh American diner food to a mix of slumming yuppies and bikers. The burgers are juicy, and there are regular bargain specials like lobster for $15 – just don't come here if you're in the mood for a romantic dinner.

Tutto Pasta 1751 SW 3rd Ave ☎305/857-0709. A small Italian restaurant, *Tutto* is one of the cluster of eateries that have colonized the emerging residential neighborhood in southwestern Downtown. There's outdoor seating and the menu features standard Italian classics for around $10/dish. It's not the place for a foodie's pilgrimage, but still a strong option if you're in the area.

South Beach

Afterglo 1200 Washington Ave, South Beach ☎305/695-1717. Overlook the over-the-top souk-style décor and gimmicky concept here (every dish is supposedly 'beautritional' or good for your health) and chow down on delicious, unexpected treats like the Way To Glo salad of carrot rods, daikon, and watercress served with a shot glass of fresh papaya juice, or one of the crispy flatbread pizzas for around $45/head. It's just a pity the service is so slow.

Ago Shore Club, 1901 Collins Ave ☎305/695-3226, ⓦwww.shoreclub.com. The first of the *Shore Club*'s two celebrity eateries, this is an LA transfer, co-owned by Robert DeNiro, and is sceney if not especially celeb studded – for that, you'll have to head to *Nobu* next door (see p.150) Even so, the pricey Italian food is tasty enough, especially the home-made ravioli ($26) and crispy wood-fired pizzas ($16–21).

Barton G The Restaurant 1427 West Ave ☎305/672-8881, ⓦwww.bartong.com. Quirky mid-priced food (entrees start at $18) from the flamboyant local caterer Barton G. He's known for his food and drink-related trickery: witty, bizarre dishes like 'disco' crab (chilled and served with a trio of dips) or lobster pop tarts (sandwiched between flaky pastry) and even nitrogenized vermouth swizzle sticks made using dry ice. It may seem gimmicky at first, but the food's delicious and the vibe on this emerging strip on South Beach's western reach very friendly. It's especially popular with an older singles crowd.

Big Pink 157 Collins Ave ☎305/532-4700, ⓦwww.bigpinkrestaurant.com. This cartoonish diner, decked out in pink lucite and alumi-

num, is famous for its TV dinners served on vintage trays ($14). The cheap and huge menu offers good versions of traditional burgers and salads, as well as ample desserts; the cafeteria-style tables make the diverse crowd more intimate. Open till 5am weekends with a beer and food happy hour on Thursday evenings.

Bond St Townhouse Hotel, 150 20th St ☎305/398-1806. The Miami outpost of a chic New York scene eatery that is smaller but otherwise identical to its sibling: glamorous people, same sleek menu (the vegetarian sushi roll with sun-dried tomato and avocado for $6 is excellent) and same signature cocktail, the Saketini.

Casa Tua 1700 James Ave ☎305/673-1010, ⓦwww.casatualifestyle.com. The priciest place to eat on the beach – it's technically a members-only club, but the restaurant is open to outsiders and a good hotel concierge should be able to wrangle a table. Hidden behind a high hedge, this lounge-restaurant is a gourmet experience; the portions of Italian food are tiny, so don't come hungry, and most entrees will set you back close to $80. The sumptuous ingredients – truffles, artisanal cheeses – make it almost worth it, since Italian chef Sergio Digala's so picky about his ingredients. He's known for his organic rice risotto with chanterelles, tuna tartare, and a booze-laced tiramisu.

DeVito South Beach 150 Ocean Drive, South Beach ☎305/531-0911, ⓦwww.devitosouthbeach.com. Yes, that Danny DeVito. And he's managed to make his Chop House-meets-rustic Italy eatery one of the splashiest, hottest tables in town. The chandelier-decorated interior is intended to ape classic designer Dorothy Draper, while the menu's Italian-American: gooey lemon chicken served in a skillet with rich caramelized sauce ($28), fresh flown-in *burrata* with thick Balsamic drizzle ($22), and cheesy popovers that sub for a bread basket. Very pricey, especially if you guzzle a bottle of wine or two, but worth it – ask for a table upstairs.

Eleventh St. Diner 1065 Washington Ave ☎305/534-6373. Housed in a 1948 Art Deco–style diner car, specially shipped to South Beach from Pennsylvania, the feel here is local, diverse, and friendly. Open 24 hours, it has terrific down-home food for

▼ Big Pink

RESTAURANTS | South Beach

148

less than $10 a dish – the spinach salad is particularly good – chatty staff, and happy-hour specials from 5 to 7pm and again from 10pm to midnight on Monday to Friday.

Joe's Stone Crab 11 Washington Ave ☏ 305/673-0365, ⓦ www.joesstonecrab.com. Synonymous with South Beach for decades, this packed, pricey restaurant serves fresh, steamed stone crabs to those prepared to wait up to three hours for the pleasure – though it's popular as much out of tradition than tastiness these days. The stone crab claws are market price, but other seafood dishes run $17-24. To avoid the wait and save some cash, do as locals do and grab a portion to go from the take-out window next door.

Kobe Club 404 Washington Ave, South Beach ☏ 305/673-5370. Miami outpost of the expense account-busting steakhouse from New York known for its namesake beef, the butter-soft steaks produced only by Wagyu cattle (this spot serves cheaper Australian- and American-raised options, as well as the pricey Japanese original – a taster portion of the trio runs up to $200). There's also a raft of steakhouse standards, including super-sized crab cakes and an iceberg/blue cheese wedge salad. The décor's said to be inspired by a samurai sword – there are 2000 of them dangling on one wall – though the thousands of shoelace-thin leather straps that dangle in the bar area are both off-putting and bizarre. Dinner only.

🏃 Kung Fu Chu Catalina Hotel, Dorset Building, 1732-1756 Collins Ave ☏ 305/534-7905, ⓦ www.catalinahotel.com. Handy, funky cheapie on this upscale strip, which serves both Japanese and Chinese dishes (there's a sushi chef and a Cantonese wok-master on duty at all times). Ask for a rough-hewn wood table out front on the patio to gawp at the stiletto-clad club goers teetering along the sidewalk. Sushi costs $2–6, rolls $4–13; try the flambéed orange with mixed seafood, an unusual, creamy mix swirled with miso and mirin that arrives tableside engulfed in blue flames ($8).

Macaluso 1747 Alton Rd ☏ 305/604-1811. Nestled in a strip mall by the canal at the northern end of South Beach, *Macaluso's* NY-born chef-owner Michael D'Andrea serves unpretentious Italian-American food that's far better than many of the chic, overpriced Italian restaurants around Lincoln Road. Try his 70-year old family recipe meatballs, the punchy, tomatoey chicken parmigiana, or a portion of the home-made sausages; the next door gourmet market, Macaluso's & Co, sells these sausages as well as other take-home gourmet treats. Don't try to book – d'Andrea never answers the phone: just turn up early and charm your way into a table.

Madiba 1766 Bay Road ☏ 305/695-1566, ⓦ www.madibarestaurant.com. This huge South African restaurant and bar is a satellite branch of the original in Brooklyn, New York (the name, Nelson Mandela's nickname, means "son of Africa"). The hard to find whitewashed building is stark and simple inside – raw concrete floors, wooden tables – and the menu's intended to ape the townships' social halls. Unusual-sounding combinations make for a delicious payoff: try the hearty *bobotie* (curried, baked mince) or a chicken *breyani* (rice and lentil stew). Most mains cost around $16. There's live music most nights.

Maison d'Azur Anglers Resort, 634 Washington Ave ☏ 305/534-9600, ⓦ www.maisondazur.net. Delightful, St Tropez-inspired restaurant (think crushed velvet sofas and chill-out DJ), with indoor seating and a few poolside tables. The menu (entrees $22–72) is French-Mediterranean, heavy on seafood (including raw bar treats like the straight-from-Brittany langoustines at market price and mussels or whole sole prepared table-side). The tiny bar is a romantic place for a glass of wine and some snacks.

La Marea Tides, 1220 Ocean Drive ☏ 305/604-5070. The hyped up renovation of this classic restaurant continues the hotel's 1930s theme – the accent wall here is covered in faux tortoiseshells. The Mediterranean menu features classics like fettuccine with lobster, snapper and dover sole, as well as slightly too-sweet popsicle martinis swizzled with a frozen sucker. Pastas cost $18–31; other mains $24–45. The best tables are the ones with the enormous, retro leather chairs with pod-like hoods that allows for almost complete privacy.

Miss Yip Chinese Café 1661 Meridian Ave ☏ 305/534-5488, ⓦ www.missyipchinesecafe.com. Owned by the same woman who helps run *Bond St*, this casual café serves Cantonese food, with *dim sum* offered at lunchtime ($5–7) and staples like moo shu pork at night ($14). The décor, however, is more exotic, its bent wood chairs, tiled floor, and statuary oozing the decadence of a swanky café in Shanghai's 1930s heyday.

149

Nobu Shore Club, 1901 Collins Ave ☎305/695-3232, ⓦ www.shoreclub.com. Still the top celeb-spotting place on the beach, sibling to the famous sushi restaurant in New York. Chef Nobu Matsuhisa and his onsite protégé, Brit Thomas Buckley, serve up a similar menu here, offering his offbeat Japanese/Peruvian dishes alongside a selection of sushi, sashimi, and rolls. The black cod with miso may be a cliché now, but for good reason – it's superb ($26); and the fried rock shrimp with spicy mayonnaise is like tangy, savory popcorn ($20).

OLA Sanctuary Hotel, 1745 James Ave, ☎305/695-9125, ⓦ www.olamiami.com. This is the third location for this restaurant from local wunderkind Douglas Rodriguez – it started out as a pioneering spot on Biscayne Boulevard, switched to South of Fifth and is now holed up in the *Sanctuary Hotel*. Despite its many sites, the menu remains the same: fish-heavy, pan-Latin selections (hence the name: Of Latin America) that jump from tapas-sized ceviches (try the Ecuadorian shrimp) to fusion appetizers such as *foie gras* and fig empanadas. Appetizers run $12–18, entrees $26–40. Wash it down with a killer mojito ($13).

Prime 112 112 Ocean Drive ☎305/532-8112, ⓦ www.prime12.com. A clubby 80-seat steakhouse housed in a Miami Beach hotel that dates back to 1915: despite the crowd of slick-haired expense-account businessmen, the waiters in butcher's aprons, dark wood walls, and a Sinatra-heavy soundtrack all give the place an old-school feel. The menu is equally traditional, featuring dry-aged prime beef in all its cuts and a vast raw bar; the $20 Kobe beef hot dog is a signature dish as is the four-cheese truffled mac'n'cheese. Make a reservation well in advance, and if you do get in try to snag one of the handful of spots on the patio out front to avoid the crowded dining room.

Quattro Gastronomie Italiane 1014 Lincoln Rd ☎305/531-4833, ⓦ www.quattromiami.com. Nicola Siervo – the man behind the club *Mokaï* (see p.163) – also owns this upscale Italian eatery, so expect his regular crowd of A-listers to be hogging the best tables most nights. Thankfully the restaurant is more relaxed than his velvet roped nightspots, with mirrored walls and comfy banquettes. The food is knockout authentic Northern Italian – don't miss the ravioli stuffed with fontina and drenched

in truffle oil, the barley risotto with *taleggio* cheese, or the *vitello glassato* (braised veal glazed with vermouth).

Social Miami Sagamore Hotel, 1671 Collins Ave ☎786/594-3344. If you can't face a cab ride across the causeway to sample superstar chef Michelle Bernstein's food at her hideaway *Michy's* (see p.152), hit *Social* instead: she was the "consulting chef" at this sleek, all-white-and-silver bar-cum-restaurant on the right side of the hotel's rear lobby. It specializes in tapas-style small plates, each of them with Bernstein's signature offbeat simplicity like lobster nachos, chicken lollipops Korean-style, or fried minced lamb cigars ($15–19).

Sushi Samba Dromo 600 Lincoln Rd ☎305/673-5337, ⓦ www.sushisamba.com. At *Sushi Samba Dromo*, the cuisine and space fuse Tokyo with Rio: brightly colored tiles meet black lacquered wood while the sushi chef prepares sashimi and the samba chef whips up ceviche. It has a great vibe, thanks more to its central location, which attracts plenty of Lincoln Road evening strutters than the food: the sushi can be disappointing, but dishes like crispy whole red snapper work better. Allow at least $40/head for a filling meal.

Table 8 Vincci Hotel, 1458 Ocean Drive, ☎305/695-4114, ⓦ www.table9la.com. South Beach clone of Govind Armstrong's groovy and eclectic Los Angeles restaurant. It's tucked inside the *Vincci* hotel (note that while the hotel's entrance is on Collins Avenue, the restaurant opens onto Ocean Drive). The bar/lounge/restaurant sprawls across the entire first floor, but try to get a seat in the lively bar area instead of the stuffy restaurant proper as the menus are the same. Standout dishes include a bouillabaisse-style calamari in a peppery vermouth broth as an appetizer ($12) and the butter soft Kobe-style beef entree ($30).

Talula 210 23rd Street ☎305/672-0778, ⓦ www.talulaonline.com. Husband and wife owners Frank Randazzo and Andrea Curto run a romantic, out-of-the-way bistro with an appropriately homey, understated vibe. The menu's modern American, from lavender and peppercorn-crusted venison to deep-fried Chesapeake Bay oysters with a punchy watermelon salsa.

Tantra 1445 Pennsylvania Ave ☎305/672-4765, ⓦ www.tantrarestaurant.com. Modern Indian cuisine with a Mediterranean slant served in a dense, sexy environment, where every element is designed to be sensual – there's grass on the floor, enormous embroidered cushions, plus hookahs and belly dancers. It may sound gimmicky, but it works as the food is extremely good, if pricey (allow $60/head); if it's on the menu, try the Saffron Saigon Stew, with market seafood and lashings of coconut.

Tap Tap 819 5th St ☎305/672-2898. One of the few restaurants outside Little Haiti that serves authentic, cheap Haitian food, *Tap Tap* often features intriguing specials – say, goat in a peppery tomato broth or a mango, avocado, and watercress salad – and the drinks are cheap. Worth stopping by for the Caribbean art displayed on the walls or the live Haitian folk music every Thursday and Saturday.

Taverna Opa 36–40 Ocean Drive ☎305/673-6730, ⓦwww.tavernaoparestaurant.com. This massive Greek restaurant – with its frantic table-dancing, loud music, and Mediterranean-themed decor – might at first seem like a tourist trap, but it's an absolute gem. Skip the forced bonhomie inside and grab a table on the patio out back; the food is delicious, and well priced – the tapas-style *meze* dishes run $3–5.

Toni's Sushi 1208 Washington Ave ☎305/673-9368. *Toni's*, which claims to be the oldest sushi bar on the beach, is especially good for vegetarians, boasting a wide selection of vegetable and noodle dishes. There's classic sushi and sashimi as well as funky new options; try the Miami Heat roll, with tuna and peppery sesame oil ($12). The staff is notoriously gruff, although the bartenders in the small bar can be friendlier.

Wish The Hotel, 801 Collins Ave ☎305/674-9474, ⓦwww.wishrestaurant.com. Daring Floribbean food, heavy on fruit, fish, and unexpected ingredients. Dinner here may not be cheap, but it's good value for a rare treat – though the cranked-up muzak can get rather overwhelming. Chef Michael Bloise is known for his Australian barramundi with summer peaches and a daring tangerine-barbecue duck leg.

Central Miami Beach and north

Café Prima Pasta 414 71st St ☎305/867-0106. Everyone raves about this North Beach place, and for good reason: the pasta's home-made ($16–20), the tiny main room charming, and the prices reasonable – it's

no surprise, then, that the wait for a table can be on the long side, so come early with a newspaper or two.

The Food Gang 9472 Harding Ave ☎786/228-9292, ⓦwww.thefoodgangcompany.com. The modernist space stands out from its drab Surfside surroundings thanks to details like its bright orange awnings, geometric fixtures and a huge white glass communal dining table. The bilingual menu is a nod to the Gallic background of the gourmet restaurant's owner, a onetime Remy Martin exec (sadly, the somewhat snooty service has a Gallic whiff, too); the food is more pan-Mediterranean, like a moist and fragrant pizzette with white truffle essence ($13) or a tangy tuna tartare ($16). There's a handy gourmet market attached for take-home treats.

The Forge 432 41st St ☎305/538-8533, ⓦwww.theforge.com. Dining at this Middle Beach institution, owned by Shareef Malnik, is an unmissable experience, not for the staggeringly huge wine cellar (available for tours if you ask nicely), the theatrics (each dish is flourishingly presented in a silver cloche), the hearty steakhouse food, or the kitschy gilt décor. Rather, it's the sizzling scene that draws most people here: expect to find hip locals eating the likes of goat-cheese-crusted rack of lamb, smoked Scottish salmon in brown sugar and *chipotle* cure or bone-in filet mignon alongside sixtysomething Miami Beachers. Malnik's A-list address book also means there's usually a celebrity somewhere in the restaurant, from Sharon Stone and Tom Cruise to local resident Jennifer Lopez.

Lemon Twist 908 71st St ☎305/868-2075. Midrange French-Mediterranean spot on Normandy Isle known for its live music most nights and the owner's generosity with free shots of tangy limoncello liqueur. Try the spinach lasagne with salmon.

Mr Chopstik 4020 Royal Palm Ave ☎305/604-0555, ⓦwww.misterchopstik.com. Chinese-Japanese casual restaurant with an unexpected bonus – it's kosher-friendly and closes on Shabbat. The menu of pork-free Chinese classics, like mu shu beef and orange chicken, is supplemented with Japanese treats like a California roll with imitation crab meat. Another nod to the locale: pastrami in egg rolls, low mein and chow mein. Chinese mains and tempura rolls run around $13.

Rascal House 17190 Collins Ave ☎305/947-4581, ⓦwww.rascalhouse.com. Make a pilgrimage to this vintage standby, where portions of mid-priced standard diner fare are huge, and breakfast is accompanied by dozens of baked treats, such as bagels, *rugelach*, and muffins. The kvetching, black aproned staff are throwbacks to Sunny Isles old days – there's not a Botox shot or facelift among them – as are the old fashioned display cases filled with mouthwatering slabs of jewel-colored fruit pies.

Tamarind Thai 946 Normandy Drive ☎305/861-6222, ⓦwww.tamarindthai.us. This smallish restaurant's run by two Thai expats and cookery-book authors who whip up delicious, tangy dishes like *gratong mee krop* (crispy noodles with sweet tamarind for $7) or *Ped makham (*roast duck in tamarind sauce for $19).

North along the Biscayne Corridor

Bin #18 1800 Biscayne Boulevard ☎786/235-7575. A tapas-style spot run by local chef Alfredo Patiño, where a filling meal's only around $20: make sure to order a warm fig brûlée (fruit grilled with blue cheese) and a bocadillo sandwich with manchego.

▼ Bin #18

The homely space has raw concrete floors and comfy sofas plus walls that act as a rotating art gallery. Patiño's sommelier/waiter brother's a great source of wine pairings.

Domo Japones 4000 NE 2nd Ave ☎305/573-5474, ⓦwww.domojapones.com. Run by Amir Ben-Zion, a refugee from South Beach's Bond Street, *Domo* is housed in the old neighborhood post office. But this 70-seat space is no basic sushi spot; rather, it's a 'Japanese bistro' serving sashimi with a twist (toro with edamame-wasabi puree or octopus with plum sauce), plus specials like slow braised short ribs. Budget around $25/head for lunch and double that for dinner. There's also a lounge-worthy bar, with a sushi bar, on the upper floor, plus an outdoor deck for smokers. Dinner served until 2am daily.

Enriqueta's 2830 NE 2nd Ave ☎305/573-4681. This local diner bustles all day, serving no-frills Cuban sandwiches and massive steaks. Sit at the counter and watch the squad of old ladies who staff the kitchen nonchalantly preparing an assembly line of pressed sandwiches – try a Cuban sandwich, jammed with ham, pork, Swiss cheese, and pickles, for $4.

Michael's Genuine Food & Drink Alta Plaza, 130 NE 40th Street, Design District ☎305/573-5550, ⓦwww.michaelsgenuine. com. Michael Schwartz – the chef behind *Afterglo* (see p.148) – opened this casual eatery in 2007 and it's been filled with a mix of gallery-toiling intelligentsia and glitzy beach scenesters ever since. The indoor/outdoor space has an industrial aesthetic: best to eat solo at the bar or snag a table on the plaza under an umbrella. The menu is eclectic modern American: Schwartz is especially known for two dishes, his crispy beef cheek in a Scharffenberger chocolate reduction and a bunch of tomatoes roasted on the vine, served with a hunk of blue cheese and grilled bread. Lunch runs around $20 per person plus drinks; for dinner, allow at least $50.

Michy's 6927 Biscayne Boulevard, Biscayne Corridor ☎305/759-2001. Local-girl-made-good, Michelle Bernstein owns and runs this homey, neighborhood spot with her husband; it's cheerily kitted out like a 1960s beach house, with bright floral wallpaper and whitewashed thrift store chairs. Though the lunchtime menu's standard, at dinner every dish is offered in full or half portions, so you can graze on as many of her creations as you fancy – try the meat mixed fish ceviche or conch served escargot-style drenched in garlic. One staple on the rotating menu is guaranteed to be her melt-in-the-mouth blue cheese and ham croquetas with fig marmalade. Unlike many namebrand chefs, Bernstein really is often found in the kitchen so you might well taste her stunning cooking first-hand.

Soyka 5556 NE 4th Court ☎305-759-3117. Soyka – the man behind the *News Café* on South Beach (see p.142) – is the mastermind of this large, cavernous space in Little Haiti, with its distressed concrete walls and simple wood furniture. The food is Mediterranean-American: huge salads and crispy thin pizzas ($10–12), served alongside Italian touches like polenta and fried calamari. It's a cheaper option to stop by for lunch than dinner.

Little Havana

Ayestaran 706 SW 27th Ave ☎305/649-4982. This unpretentious restaurant serves Spanish-Cuban food in a family-style setting – the sandwiches are good and daily lunchtime specials keep prices low, so you shouldn't spend more than $20/head. Try the *arroz con mariscos* (rice with prawns).

Casa Juancho 2436 SW 8th St ☎305/642-2452, ⓦwww.casajuancho.com. Oddly reminiscent of either a Swiss chalet or Disney's idea of Old Cuba, this upscale Calle Ocho restaurant offers hearty, Spanish-inflected dishes, notably the fish. It's one of the few posh restaurants in the neighborhood, and makes for good people-watching.

Casa Panza 1620 SW 8th St ☎305/643-5343. Less formal and more Iberian than many of the other Spanish restaurants hereabouts, with tapas, *raciones*, and main dishes prepared primarily in a Madrid style. Above-

average prices ($18–30), but you get to watch free flamenco on Tues and Thurs–Sat from 8pm onwards.

El Cristo 1543 SW 8th St ☎305/643-9992. Casual café, with mismatched brown Formica furniture indoors, a lunch counter, and a few white garden chairs propped up on the sidewalk. Come here for huge helpings of tangy ceviche for only $6 or *palomilla* steaks for just $7. There are around ten different daily specials, too.

El Fogon 5401 NW 79th Ave ☎305/468-6608. This out-of-the-way restaurant serves massive Mexican dinners at minimal prices ($10 or less): try the house special of *cochinita pibil* (shredded marinated pork) in one of its many preparations, or order real Mexican fajitas.

Guayacan 1933 SW 8th St ☎305/649-2015. Tasty, fresh Nicaraguan food served either at the counter or in the small, unfussy dining room to the back: it's known for its soups, with a different recipe served every day – and somehow, the unfriendly staff doesn't detract from the place's charm. Mains start at $13.

Habana Vieja 3622 Coral Way ☎305/448-6660. In a sprawling cream building with a tiled red roof, this restaurant's known for its *vaca frita* ($10) and *fufu de plantano* (mashed plantains), $23. High-spirited and friendly, the staff makes even non-Spanish speakers feel welcome.

Hy Vong 3458 SW 8th St ☎305/446-3674. Glorious Vietnamese gem, tucked away on the western end of Little Havana. The decor's simple – bright lights, varnished pine tables without cloths – but the food is sumptuous: try *banh cuon* rolls made with home-made rice papers as an appetizer or beef and fresh rice noodle as an entree (prices hover around $15). The other major plus is an extensive beer list, taking in selections from Australia, the Bahamas, Jamaica, and, of course, Vietnam.

Sergio's Cafeteria 3252 Coral Way ☎305/529-0047. Loud, noisy, and fun, *Sergio's* is a Cuban diner with plenty of attitude, welcoming late-night diners and offering a wide menu at fair prices. A great place to finish up a long Friday night and chow down on one of the best Cuban sandwiches in town. There's another branch at 13600 SW 152nd St, South Miami (☎786/242-9790).

▼ Michael's Genuine Food & Drink

▼ Yambo

Versailles 3555 SW 8th St ☎305/445-7614. This local legend has retained its 1960s decor and mirrors despite several renovations. Come here for the homestyle Cuban food, and watch a cross-section of Miami's Cuban community come together to enjoy it with you. Traditional, delicious dishes like *ropa vieja* and *vaca frita* should be followed with *tres leches*. Low-fat devotees will find little to eat here.

Yambo 1643 SW 1st St ☎305/642-6616. This 24-hour Nicaraguan restaurant is one of Miami's treasures, with plentiful outdoor seating that's covered in mosaics and a bevy of bizarre items. Entrees like *puerca asada* (grilled pork) or fried whole snapper go for around $5 – grab them from the counter, then seat yourself – and

expect to be offered videos or CDs by itinerant peddlers who thread through the crowd. There's little English spoken here.

Coral Gables

Bugatti's 2504 Ponce de Leon Blvd ☎305/441-2545. An Italian restaurant run by a German in the heart of Cuban Coral Gables, *Bugatti's* food is surprisingly impressive – make sure to try the buffalo mozzarella, as well as the tender gnocchi. The only downside is the sometimes-sniffy service.

Caffè Abbracci 318 Aragon Ave ☎305/441-0700. For a taste of local life in Coral Gables, visit this upscale Italian trattoria, which serves traditional pastas ($17–25) alongside more unusual combinations (try the pumpkin ravioli or the hearty lentil soup). There's a good wine list, too.

Canton 2614 Ponce de Leon Blvd ☎305/448-3736. Chinese restaurant that offers a greatest-hits-style menu, with Cantonese, Mandarin, and Szechuan favourites – it's especially known for huge portions of honey garlic chicken wings ($6). There's a good sushi bar as well.

Chef Innocent at Restaurant St Michel Hotel St Michel, 162 Alcazar Ave ☎305/446-6572, ⓦwww.chefinnocent.com. Inside the B&B-like hotel, this new steakhouse – open for breakfast, lunch and dinner – is run by the namesake Nigerian-born chef Innocent Utomi. Expect riffs on dry-aged beef plus steakhouse classics like lobster bisque, duck à l'orange, oysters Rockefeller and Caesar salad. Save

A brief Cuban food glossary

Aguacate Avocado
Ajo Garlic
Arepas Cornmeal pancake
Arroz con pollo Chicken and yellow rice
Buñuelos Cuban donuts
Cabra or **chivo** Goat
Camarones Prawns
Chorizo Spicy, greasy sausage
Churrasco Marinated and grilled beef tenderloin
Empanada Ground beef in a tortilla, either fried or baked
Escabeche Pickled fish
Langosta Florida lobster
Maduros Sweet, fried plantains

Mariscos Seafood
Moros y Cristianos Black beans and white rice
Paella Spanish dish, incorporating saffron rice with seafood or chicken
Papa Potato
Queso Cheese
Ropa vieja Literally "old clothes": shredded beef, fried with vegetables
Sesos Brains
Tostones Mashed, fried plantains
Tres leches Super-sweet custard-like dessert, made from condensed, evaporated, and fresh milk, sometimes served with sweet caramel
Vaca frita Beef fried with onions

room for one of the slab-like desserts (the apple crepe's delicious). Mains start at $20 and there's live music Friday nights.

Christy's 3101 Ponce de Leon Blvd ☎305/446-1400, ⓦ www.christysrestaurant.com. Upscale restaurant with old-fashioned decor and a robust, steak-filled menu for carnivores only – if you dare splash out on the filet mignon ($36), it won't disappoint; the Caesar salad, too, is tangy and delicious. Clubby, rather formal, and very Coral Gables.

Gables Diner 2320 Galiano St ☎305/567-0330, ⓦ www.gablesdiner.com. Fresh and unpretentious compared with many of the posh eateries around the Miracle Mile, this bistro serves good meatloaf, alongside standard sandwiches and salads, for around $10.

The Globe 377 Alhambra Circle ☎305/445-3555. Yes, it's a rabid pick-up joint, but still good fun: the bar is lively at weekends, packed with a twentysomething Cuban crowd. The food is gimmicky but adventurous, drawn (as per the restaurant's name) from across the world: for an appetizer, try the Cajun egg rolls.

Havana Harry's 4612 LeJeune Rd ☎305/661-2622. The homestyle food here comes in large, cheap portions and is authentically Cuban – try the *pollo a la plancha* (marinated grilled chicken) or the *vaca frita* (fried beef with onions). The space is tiny, though, so be prepared to wait at dinnertime.

House of India 22 Merrick Way ☎305/444-2348. Quality catch-all Indian food including some excellently priced lunch buffets ($9 weekdays, $12 weekends). Not the chicest place, but terrific value.

Les Halles 2415 Ponce de Leon Blvd ☎305/461-1099, ⓦ www.leshalles.net. Almost too cozy, this packed French bistro serves excellent classics like steak tartare ($16.50) and *moules frites* ($17). The decor's a little overdone in its desperate attempts to reproduce every element of a true French restaurant, but the food makes up for it.

Miss Saigon Bistro 148 Giralda Ave ☎305/446-8006, ⓦ www.misssaigonbistro.com. Sushi aside, it's challenging to find much good Asian food in Miami, but this family-owned Vietnamese restaurant hits the mark (even more so, given the rockbottom, less-than-$20-a-head prices). The food's light and zesty – the noodles with lemongrass and chicken are particularly tasty, as are the spring rolls; what's more, the staff is welcoming and great fun.

Mykonos 1201 Coral Way ☎305/856-3140. Greek food in an unassuming atmosphere, with prices for main dishes $9–12 at dinner,

a couple of bucks less at lunch. *Spanako-pita* (cheese and spinach filo pastry pie), lemon chicken soup, gyros, *souvlaki*, and huge Greek salads are among the offerings, along with good vegetarian options.

Ortanique on the Mile 278 Miracle Mile ☎305/446-7710, ⓦ www.cindyhutsoncuisine.com. Another chic eatery in downtown Coral Gables, *Ortanique* serves innovative, adventurous Tropical Fusion food in a lush tropical setting. Deliberate as the atmosphere may be, the food's sumptuous and creative (mains $21–40), there are always reliable fish specials, while the chocolate mango tower is a heavenly dessert.

Coconut Grove

Baleen Grove Isle Hotel, 4 Grove Isle Drive ☎305/857-5007. The food at *Baleen* – like the house special, lobster "martini" served on truffled roast potatoes – is good but too expensive (appetizers around $16, mains $30 and up). The views, however, are priceless: situated on a private island just off Coconut Grove, the waterfront patio looks out over Biscayne Bay, making this one of the most romantic dining spots in town.

Bizcaya Grill Ritz-Carlton Coconut Grove, 3300 SW 27th Ave ☎305/644-4670. Sure, it's inside a hotel on the mainland but this buzzy restaurant deserves its excellent reputation. It's all down to the fantastic food; best described as simple but flavor-packed – try the lobster risotto or crispy organic chicken (mains run $18–32). There are cute touches to the venue, too – every woman's handed a "purse stool" specially designed for her handbag to rest on while she eats.

Café Tu Tu Tango Inside CocoWalk, 3015 Grand Ave ☎305/529-2222. This gimmicky restaurant offers Brazilian and belly dancers, onsite tarot-card readers, and even in-residence artists daubing every day from 1.30pm. But forget all that and come just for the reliable, tasty food: the pizzas ($7–10) are terrific, especially the tomato with roasted garlic and shallot puree, as are the "sticks and bones" selections of skewers, chops, and ribs.

Cielo 3390 Mary Street ☎ 305/490-9060, ⓦ www.cielorestaurant.com. This glammy club/restaurant draws a heavily Hispanic crowd, thanks to its inventive but authentic takes on classic Lain dishes, in both small tapas-sized plates and larger entrees. Highlights include a seafood stew simmered in cilantro and corn broth, and ravioli stuffed with black bean puree smothered in goat cheese sauce (finish off with a cigar from the onsite locker). There's live music or a DJ, including local legends Spam AllStars, most nights of the week.

Jaguar 3067 Grand Ave ☎305/444-0216, ⊛www.jaguarspot.com. Try the vast range of ceviche at this large restaurant, either single servings on a mouthful-sized spoon for $2 or a plateful for $15: the verde (octopus and shrimp with lemon, lime, orange and avocado) and the oriental (yellowfin tuna with ginger, soy and lime) are standouts. There's also a grill (mains $17–23) and some Mexican classics like tamales. The décor's casual: wooden tables and brightly colored accents like a Santa Fe café, and outdoor seating is available.

Le Bouchon du Grove 3430 Main Hwy ☎305/448-6060. Ramshackle chic with its designer-dilapidated signage, *Le Bouchon* is a treasure at the heart of the Grove – funky but posh, it's a restaurant that the locals still love, serving French favorites at fair prices (allow $40 person at dinner) like chicken *en papillote* and home-made patés in a brasserie atmosphere that lets you linger.

Señor Frog's 3480 Main Hwy ☎305/448-0900, ⊛www.senorfrogsfla.com. Don't be put off by the name – the food here is terrific, tasty, and affordable, with most entrees hovering around $16 for a plate piled high with Tex-Mex standbys like burritos and enchiladas. The cavernous ceilings stifle any atmosphere, unfortunately. There's another branch at 616 Collins Ave ☎305/673-5262.

Key Biscayne

Cioppino Ritz-Carlton Key Biscayne, 455 Grand Bay Drive ☎305/365-4500, ⊛www.ritz-carlton.com. The large, family-friendly *Ritz-Carlton* on Key Biscayne may seem an odd spot for a superb restaurant, but don't be put off—it's worth a detour wherever you're staying. A deluxe take on a traditional Tuscan trattoria, *Cioppino* has a warm, homey vibe and most of the menu features ingredients fresh off the plane from Italy – try the namesake, soupy seafood stew ($28).

Lighthouse Café Bill Baggs Cape Florida State Park, 1200 S Crandon Blvd ☎305/361-8487. Tucked away in the Cape Florida State Park, this is a casual beachside café by the historic lighthouse. With plenty of outdoor seating, it's worth the trip for the tasty fresh fish, Cuban specials, and, of course, the views.

Tango Grill 328 Crandon Blvd, suite 112

☎305/361-1133. A small Argentine grill in one of the Key Biscayne Village strip malls, *Tango Grill* serves superb *bife de chorizo* (sirloin steak) and other South American specialties to a heavily Latin crowd.

Yagé Bay Club 3301 Rickenbacker Causeway ☎786/399-3454, ⊛www.yagekeybiscayne.com. This combo restaurant/lounge/marina is a waterfront hotspot on increasingly tony Key Biscayne. The views of downtown are spectacular from the restaurant (dine on staples like jumbo crab cakes or popcorn shrimp for around $15) and there's a huge outdoor Tiki Hut Lounge for seaside cocktails, complete with live DJs spinning most days and gauzy curtained cabanas. Oh, and that weird name? It's a hallucinatory vine from South America.

South to Homestead and Florida City

Captain's Restaurant & Seafood House 404 SE 1st Ave, Homestead ☎305/247-9456. Preview a Florida Keys dinner before hitting the highway and pitstop here: it's a no-nonsense restaurant serving stone crabs and conch fritters as well as more unusual treats like a killer lobster reuben.

Rosita's Restaurante 199 West Palm Drive ☎305/246-3114. Located off Hwy-1 at the junction for the Everglades and Biscayne National Park, *Rosita's* serves glorious Mexican food at budget prices, accompanied by spicy salsa, creamy refried beans, and tangy cheese toppings. There's canteen-style seating at basic Formica tables, all set to a backdrop of loud Hispanic talk radio. Well worth the detour south.

Sango Jamaican and Chinese Restaurant 9485 SW 160th St ☎305/252-0279. Somewhat of an offbeat combination (and the Caribbean food is far better than the Chinese confections), this is still a worthwhile stop in South Miami, especially given its low prices (there's barely a dish that costs more than $11) Try the curried goat and jerk chicken. Mainly a take-out joint, but there are a few tables if you want to linger.

Shorty's Bar-B-Q 9200 South Dixie Hwy, South Miami ☎305/670-7732. A log-cabin institution, *Shorty's* is now more than fifty years old, with a perennial line outside waiting for the splendid, rich barbecue. A piled high platter of brisket's just $8.50; even better, the golden fries served up alongside are crinkly and have a deliciously smoky flavor (Gorge on an extra portion for just $1.30).

13

Drinking

O ddly enough, Miami is not a hard-drinking town. There's little distinction between bars, clubs, and restaurants and in most places you'll be able to eat dinner – or at least snack heartily – with your cocktails. There's also a thriving **hotel bar scene**, some highlights of which we've included in the box at the end of this chapter.

As you might guess, **South Beach** is the place to head first for a night of drinking: there are plenty of options, and its compact, walkable center means you won't need to designate a driver for the evening. Weeknights here are just as good as weekends for going out, if not better: locals haughtily dismiss the so-called "Causeway Crowds" from across the bridges who flood the beach on Friday and Saturday nights, often clogging up smaller lounges. While there are still plenty of South Beach's signature lounges to choose from, the vogue at the moment here is for dive bars, whether ersatz upscale newcomers or rediscovered old gems; an added plus is that prices here tend to be much lower, too.

Beyond South Beach, the scene **along the Biscayne Corridor** is exploding, as hip new bars and night spots open every month, powered by the option of a 24-hour liquor license **Downtown**; while **Coral Gables** has a less trendy selection of places to drink, but is a great destination for a quality beer. There are a couple of detour-worthy spots on **Key Biscayne**, yet **Coconut Grove**, which once hoped to swipe South Beach's crown in funky nightlife, has admitted defeat – bars here are less sceney, to the point of being disappointingly quiet (except at weekends).

Licensing hours vary by neighborhood: South Beach spots are usually serving until 5am, although the incumbent mayor's campaigned – so far, unsuccessfully – to tighten licensing laws so reveling would end three hours earlier. Expect mainland spots to shutter by 2am at the latest, except in the club hub of Park West (see p.162), where there's an experiment in 24-hour licensing. Miami is also a hotbed of bottle service, where swankier clubs reserve seating only for those willing to shell out upwards of $175 for a single bottle of liquor, so be prepared to stand at these places if you're on a tighter budget.

All bars are open to those 21 and over only, so remember always to bring photo ID.

Downtown

Tobacco Road 626 S Miami Ave ☎305/374-1198, ⓦ www.tobacco-road.com. This late-night dive bar lives off its reputation: it purportedly received the city's first liquor license in 1912, and the place is gloriously gritty. The bar food is standard American – burgers and fries – but the drinks list is more adventur-

ous. There are also two stages where nightly live acts (primarily blues and traditional R&B) perform.

South Beach

The Abbey Brewing Company 1115 16th St ☎305/538-8110, ⓦ www.abbeybrewingcompany.com. A hops-fueled antidote to the South

Beach scene, *The Abbey* is as close to a neighborhood pub as the area gets. The tiny space is themed on a church – hence the wooden pew seating – and the homebrewed range of beers is superb: try the popular Oatmeal Stout or one of twelve other varieties on tap.

Automatic Slim's 1216 Washington Ave ☎305/695-0795, ⓦwww.automatic-slims. com. A loud, velvet-rope-free locals' favorite: come here to down cheap beers (only $2 4–8pm), dance to classic rock or 80s hip-hop, and ogle the foxy bartenders who gyrate on the bar throughout the evening. Refreshingly unpretentious spot amid the swanky lounges of South Beach.

Buck 15 707 Lincoln Lane ☎305/534-5388, ⓦwww.buck15.com. Artsy lounge above *Miss Yip's* (see p.149) that's a hybrid bar/gallery – the décor's thrift store chic (look for the bar salvaged from a 1970s high-rise condo) and most of the street art on the wall comes from Jenny Yip's own collection.

▼ Buck 15

🏃 **Club Deuce 222 W 14th St** ☎305/531-6200. Grimy, noisy grunge bar, this remnant from pre-fabulous South Beach is equally fabulous in its own way. This is one of Miami's premier dive bars: drinks are cheap, plus it features a dartboard and pool table and stays open until 5am every night.

Lario's on the Beach 820 Ocean Drive ☎305/532-9577. The sole reason to come to Gloria Estefan's restaurant on the beach is its mojitos, the signature Cuban concoction of crushed mint and rum – most people concede that *Lario's* serves the best mojitos on the beach.

Lost Weekends 218 Española Way ☎305/672-1707. Divey sports bar that's popular with backpackers from the nearby *Clay Hostel*. There are more than 100 different beers on

offer from around the world, as well as every bar game, from foosball and billiards to air hockey.

Love/Hate lounge 423 Washington Ave ☎305/695-8616, ⓦwww.lovehatelounge.com. Run by the celebrity tattoo artists behind the TV show *Miami Ink*, this is another rock-inflected spot – think tattoo-inspired décor (pin-up girls, fast cars and classic Americana), metal bar stools and live rock – with a hipster edge. Try the hair-stiffening house special drink, the lethal and mysterious Ami's Attitude, a nod to co-owner Ami James' notoriously pricky mien.

Macarena 1334 Washington Ave ☎305/531-3440, ⓦwww.macarenaweb.com. Ignore its odd location – attached to a grimly overpriced Latin eatery – and its awful name: this bar/club is popular with the Estefan set (it's where Ricky Martin held an album release after-party) and the quality of live performers most nights is impressive; there are regular flamenco shows on Friday and Saturday nights and a rotating cluster of singers and guitarists at 10pm most other evenings.

Privé 136 Collins Ave ☎305/531-5535, ⓦwww.theopiumgroup.com. Attached to the *Opium Garden* nightclub, this lounge is tucked away in a back alley. The door policy is one of the tightest around, especially on Friday nights, so make sure to sashay like a VIP if you want to sip with the A-list behind the silk curtains.

Purdy Lounge 1811 Purdy Ave ☎305/531-4622, ⓦwww.purdylounge.com. This groovy, out-of-the-way lounge is big enough that you should be able to grab a table without too long a wait, no matter the night. The vibe's overwhelmingly local (especially during the hilarious monthly adult Spelling Bee contests – winner gets free drinks all evening) and the decor vaguely Arabian with minaret-shaped seat backs in a sludgy gold and purple color scheme. It's the pool tables and late license that really matter – *Purdy* stays open until 5am every night.

Rok Bar 1905 Collins Ave ☎305/674-4397, ⓦwww.rokbarmiami.com. Just three years after opening Tommy Lee's upscale dive bar recently received a facelift, though it's still a sweaty box of a place with barely any seating and a thrashing, 80s rock soundtrack on loop. Dress like a groupie to party like a rockstar – and expect a tough door.

The Room 100 Collins Ave ☎305/531-6061. The Miami outpost of a minimalist New

York bar, with raw concrete floors, industrial metal tables, and low lighting. One wall's lined with high leather banquettes and metal tables; the other's home to the large bar. The low-key crowd's generally a mixed selection of locals and tourists.

Ted's Hideaway South 124 2nd St ☎305/532-9869. Twice-daily happy hours (from noon–7pm and again from 1–3am) keep this local spot popular: the atmosphere's basic and homely, and the cheap beer really is the only draw.

Vino Miami 1601 Washington Place, South Beach ☎786/207-8466, ⓦwww.vinomiami.com. Onetime Coconut Grove mainstay that recently defected to the beach, and a refreshing change from the bottle-driven lounges. The concrete-floored, stark wine bar – easily missed on a side street next to a parking garage – offers a choice of 50 or so small batch vintages by the glass ($9–12), and flights of three tasting tipples ($16–20), plus a tapas-style bar snacks menu.

Wet Willie's 760 Ocean Drive ☎305/532-5650, ⓦwww.wetwillies.com. Frat boy central, this raucous Ocean Drive bar has its own upstairs terrace packed with youngish tourists from lunchtime on. The frozen drinks are served from washing-machine-sized mixers – be sure to try a rumrunner – and, at only $9, each giant helping is a bargain.

Central Miami Beach and north

Glass at the Forge 432 41st St ☎305/604-9798, ⓦwww.theforge.com. The onetime *Jimmy'z* space has been renamed and renovated into *Glass*, a sleek lounge/club that's popular with lithe models and the permatanned men who love them. The décor's all-white with over-stuffed leather sofas and contemporary art dotted around as an upscale distraction.

North along the Biscayne Corridor

Boteco 916 NE 79th Street, Biscayne Corridor ☎305/757-7735, ⓦwww.botecomiami.com. Banging Brazilian bar/cafe, with a lively, eclectic schedule of events – free samba classes most Mondays, happy hour with free snacks weekdays 5–8pm, monthly Full Moon parties with jam bands, and *feijoada* (pork and black bean stew) feasts the first Sat of each month. Expect a healthy mix of expats and curious locals.

Churchill's Hideaway 5501 NE 2nd Ave ☎305/757-1807, ⓦwww.churchillspub.com. Emblazoned all over with the Union Jack, this utterly out-of-place bar set deep in the heart of Little Haiti is home away from home for Miami's expat Brits. It serves good tap beer, and satellite soccer and rugby matches are beamed into the main bar; check out the live band performances, too.

Circa 28 2826 N Miami Ave, Wynwood ☎305/722-1858, ⓦwww.circa28.com. New bar that's an instant classic: maybe it's the unfussy décor downstairs (simple raw wood bar, chandeliers and velvet-upholstered seating), the cheap drinks ($10 a cocktail), the artsy crowd made up largely of refugees from the galleries and studios nearby, or even the disco ball-equipped dancefloor upstairs with bands or DJs most nights. Closed Sun & Mon.

Magnum Lounge 709 NE 79th St Causeway ☎305/757-3368. This out-of-the-way Biscayne Corridor restaurant-bar feels more like a bordello or a speakeasy, with its lush red

Cocktails in Miami

Don't miss the chance to try one of Miami's signature **cocktails**. Potent and flavorful, they're often made with fresh ingredients and, of course, rum – yet another nod to Cuba's dominant influence in the city. Even if you're a confirmed cosmopolitan drinker, stray a little and sample something local, like the drinks listed below – it'll be worth it.

Cuba Libre A fancy name for rum, coke, and a splash of lime juice.

Mojito A sumptuous Cuban cocktail. Mint is pounded to release its full flavor, then stirred with sugar syrup, rum, lime juice, and soda water: many claim that *Lario's on the Beach* serves the best in town (see review, opposite).

Rumrunner Another rum-based cocktail, combined with a variety of fruit flavors, often banana or blackberry: whatever the combination, expect it to be heavily alcoholic. Though the classic place to sample a Rumrunner is Key West (see p.233), bars in Miami often mix a mean version, too.

banquettes and hidden entrance. The food's so-so, but the campy sing-alongs around the piano and stiff cocktails make it a fun detour for a drink or two.

Mike's at Venetia 9th floor, 555 NE 15th St, Omni ☎305/374-5371 ⊛www.mikesvenetia. com. Welcoming and divey, this Irish sports bar and restaurant has cheap martinis, a superb juke box that takes in rap, vintage country and jangle pop, a friendly staff and an out-of-the-way location (on the 9th floor of a condo complex by the Venetian Causeway) that keeps it full of regulars, especially after Wynwood gallery openings.

The Pawn Shop Lounge 1222 NE 2nd Ave ☎305/373-3511, ⊛www.thepawnshoplounge. com. Park West's *Pawn Shop Lounge* is a massive, converted pawn shop with an exterior unchanged since its seedier days and interior best described as Alice in Wonderland on acid. Inside, there's a whole school bus, its innards gutted and replaced with comfy banquettes; while boots and chandeliers dangle side by side from the ceiling, and a retro playlist heavy on 1980s classics throbs from the speakers.

PS14 28 NE 14th St, Biscayne Corridor ☎305/358-3600, ⊛www.ps14.com. Named after a public school in New York, this bar has a downtown Manhattan dive bar vibe. Sit on the couches and nurse a beer or two, dance to the rockish DJs on the patio (the sound system's impressive) or play a game or two of pool; there's also a diner-style menu of pizzas, salads and the like. Popular with the artsy crowd from nearby Wynwood.

Stop Miami 3533 NE 2nd Ave, Wynwood ☎305/576-0900, ⊛www.stopmiami.com. Another locals-aimed hole in the wall in Wynwood, this closet-sized gem has rotating art exhibits, a terrific wine list, and a friendly clientele. There's pleasantly schizophrenic live music programming most nights, from funk and Britpop to reggaeton.

Coral Gables

The Globe 377 Alhambra Circle ☎305/445-3555. On weekends, the bar at this popular restaurant is the place to be in Coral Gables, as it's invariably packed with a lively, twenty-something Cuban crowd; on Saturday, there's usually live jazz. Just don't go for a quiet drink or a date – it becomes a raucous pick-up joint by the end of the evening.

John Martin's 253 Miracle Mile ☎305/445-3777, ⊛www.johnmartins.com. Run by two Irishmen,

John Martin's is refreshingly authentic. In the restaurant section, the food includes potato soup and other hearty Irish staples; in the bar, it's all dark green drapes and wood paneling, where a wide mix of people down pints of Guinness in a relaxed atmosphere that seems a world away from tony Coral Gables.

Titanic Brewery 5813 Ponce de Leon Blvd ☎305/667-2537, ⊛www.titanicbrewery.com. The *Titanic* brewpub offers its own terrific beers – try the Boiler Room brown ale or the amber known as Captain Smith's; it's also recently invited the 50-strong Miami Area Society of Homebrewers (MASH) to 'guest curate' custom batches, so ask about the latest flavors. All the beers here are served with deliciously greasy bar food, and often accompanied by live music. Since it's right next to the University of Miami, expect a youngish, mainstream vibe.

Coconut Grove

Monty's Raw Bar 2550 S Bayshore Drive ☎305/856-399. Come to *Monty's* for the views: this outdoor tiki bar overlooks Biscayne Bay and offers stunning panoramas, especially at dusk. Drink prices are reasonable, and the vibe is more partying than posing – though when the house reggae band starts up it's often too loud to chat comfortably.

Tavern in the Grove 3416 Main Hwy ☎305/447-3884. Down-to-earth locals' haunt with a bouncy jukebox and easygoing mood – TVs play the latest football game, and there's a popular dartboard. The real draw, however, is the rock-bottom drinks prices – beer is only $2/bottle every day until 8pm.

Key Biscayne and Virginia Key

Jimbo's Inside the park at Virginia Key Beach ☎305/361-7026. More like a junkyard with a place to drink attached than a real bar, *Jimbo's*, on Virginia Key, is rundown, ramshackle, and renowned throughout Miami. Help yourself to a beer from a wheelbarrow full of ice and settle down on a broken plastic chair in the shade: a bit self-consciously stagey, but good fun nonetheless.

Rusty Pelican 3201 Rickenbacker Causeway ☎305/361-3818. The views from the terrace of Key Biscayne's *Rusty Pelican* are superb – an unbroken panorama of Downtown Miami's glittering skyscrapers. Buy a drink and settle back to watch one of Miami's sensational sunsets from the deck.

You might normally associate **hotel bars** with middle-aged business travelers nursing a lonely Scotch, chatting wearily with the bartender. But in Miami, especially on South Beach, many of the funkiest spaces these days are inside hotels. We've listed a few suggestions below, but check *Street Miami* and the *New Times* for one-off events at other hotel bars thrown by local promoters.

The Coral Bar *The Tides Hotel*, 1220 Ocean Drive, South Beach ☎305/604-5070. The VIP hideaway at the re-imagined *Tides* is named after the coral and stained-glass medallion that dominates the space. Pull up one of the twenty or so seats and try one of the hotel's signature popsicle martinis – a kicker of liquor stirred with a frozen popsicle – as well as a killer selection of rums.

The Florida Room *The Delano Hotel*, 1685 Collins Ave, South Beach ☎305/675-2000. Tucked in what was once the basement gym, this retro bar/lounge – its design overseen by Lenny Kravitz, no less – is intended to ape a speakeasy in 1950s Havana, with its smoked mirror ceilings and crystal chandeliers (the Lucite piano's a replica of Lenny's own). There's a small dancefloor when DJs are playing. Note that the entrance is via a side door on 17th Street by the pool; capacity's barely more than 200 so expect a stiff door policy. Recommended.

M-Bar *Mandarin Oriental Hotel*, 500 Brickell Key Drive ☎305/913-8288. This high-rise hotel bar boasts astonishing views across Biscayne Bay, as well as a martini list with more than 250 different options – try the Ruby Slipper, made from cranberry vodka & juice, gin, and sour mix. The snack menu is heavy on sushi and rolls. There's also a delightful sandy bar-beach area known as the *Oasis* that often hosts sunset parties at the weekend.

Raleigh Bar *Raleigh Hotel*, 1775 Collins Ave, South Beach ☎305/534-6300. This beautifully restored wood-paneled bar is a chic, elegant place to grab a cocktail to a soundtrack of jazz and 1940s classics: try the bartender's namesake concoction Crispy's Pink Lady, made from Absolut citron, 7UP, cointreau, and cranberry juice. Alternatively, grab a cocktail and saunter out back to the sexy figure-of-eight pool behind the hotel.

RumBar *Ritz-Carlton Key Biscayne*, 455 Grand Bay Drive, Key Biscayne ☎305/365-4286. New lobby bar that's a recreation of Hemingway-era Havana – overstuffed leather seats, B&W pics, and sultry ceiling fans – serving 50-plus different rums, caches, and piscos both neat and in cocktails (try a Millionaire's Mojito made with $750-a-bottle Rhum Clement XO). There's a cigar humidor and live music from a five-piece Latin band Thurs–Sat.

The Spire Bar *The Hotel*, 801 Collins Ave, South Beach ☎305/531-2222. New rooftop bar, designed, like *The Hotel*, by fashion icon Todd Oldham. The overstuffed white couches are a muted touch, and there's zingy color everywhere else from bright red cushions to candy-striped floorboards. The small bar nestles in the shadow of the neon-lit sign: make sure to order the bartender's mojito ($15). Open Thurs–Sun only.

Sky Bar *The Shore Club*, 1901 Collins Ave, South Beach ☎305/695-3100. Sprawling outdoor bar arranged around the hotel pool, with giant overstuffed square seats and a Moroccan theme thanks to desert-tent-like cabanas made from billowy gauze curtains. It's hottest on a Thursday night, but the velvet rope is restrictive, so dress to impress. Once inside, check out the smaller *Sand Bar* attached to it, with fine views of the beach and ocean.

The Standard *The Standard Hotel*, 40 Island Ave, Venetian Islands ☎305/673-1717. This spa hotel has no license for outdoor music, making the waterfront bar a reliably sedate, soothing place to sip a mid-afternoon cocktail while reading by the pool or at one of the tables looking out across the bay. Bar bonus: kitschy bingo games held Sunday nights – call for schedules.

(13)

DRINKING | Hotel bars

14

Nightlife

or a city with a hard-partying image like Miami, it's surprising how few true nightclubs there are. Instead, most **nightlife venues** tend toward the hybrid bar-lounge-dancefloor, where you can choose to stand and sip a cocktail, kick back and relax with friends, or dance – or, conveniently, all three. And although the whiplash from the velvet rope at some bars may be painful, most nightclub spaces are less snooty. That said, it's always worth looking sharp for an evening out in style-conscious Miami: doormen are very label-conscious and intolerant of anyone scruffy. As in any city, it's best to dress up, smile, and arrive in a well-mixed male-female group early in the evening.

Certainly, Miami's nightlife scene has sobered up slightly since its debauched and celebrity-studded heyday of the early Nineties, but there's still plenty of choice and – especially away from the beach – some intriguing options. The hotter new clubs are located in and around **Park West**, a warehouse district just north of Downtown; the cavernous empty spaces here and lack of residents to object to early hours partying has combined to produce a clutch of new clubs. Earlier in the evening, you're better off sticking to **South Beach** and one of the better bars for dancing, like *Mokaï*. The playlist is increasingly likely to lean on hip-hop – house nights are growing less common, replaced with harder R&B and rap.

One boon for nightlife has been a renewed focus on Miami by the music industry, thanks to locally based producers like the Neptunes' Pharell Williams and hip hop maestro Scott Storch, plus state-of-the-art studios like the Sound Factory. Together, such talent and technology has drawn bona-fide superstars like Beyoncé and Justin Timberlake to record tracks in the afternoon and then spend the evenings holed up in VIP booths at many of the clubs listed below; they often test-market tracks anonymously with DJs here.

As for **live music**, the Miami scene is – unsurprisingly – strongest with regard to Latin clubs, and there are some good spots for salsa, merengue, and modern Latin fusion. The rock'n'roll scene is less exciting; there are a few rock-centric spots like *Churchill's Hideaway*, but otherwise, as a rule, don't expect world-class quality in the performers, and you'll have fun.

Clubs

Most clubs in Miami keep hours **from 10pm to 5am**, although thanks to less restrictive liquor licenses, many of the newer Downtown spaces are open even later than that – some even 24 hours a day.

The larger spaces tend to open only at the weekends, but you can usually hit the mid-sized and smaller venues during the week – a bonus, as that's when the crowd will be most local, especially on South Beach. Generally, **cover charges** will be

$15–20, although early in the evening they may be waived. Note also that many clubs in Miami are alcohol- and age-conscious, so you're likely to have problems if you're under 21: call individual venues to check.

Finally, as parties and promoters change frequently, clubs-of-the-moment come and go overnight; be sure to peruse the latest line-ups in the *New Times*, or call the phone numbers and check the websites in the reviews below.

Downtown and the Biscayne Corridor

Metropolis 950 NE 2nd Ave, Park West ☎305/415-0000, ⓦwww.metropolisdowntown. com. Thurs–Sat 10pm–9am. Gigantic 50,000 square foot mega-club: the interior's carved into five separate mini venues, each of them hosting a different musical style (there's hip-hop in the Egypt-themed Nile and Spanish rock in Azucar). Even better, you can stay out past dawn thanks to the club's 24 hour liquor license. $20 and up.

Nocturnal 50 NE 11th St ☎305/576-6996, ⓦwww.nocturnalmiami.com. Fri & Sat 10pm–10am. Park West's *Nocturnal* is as much about high tech as hard house: the rooftop terrace has a 360-degree IMAX-style screen where trippy images can be projected all night, while staff are equipped with wireless PDAs so they can not only summon a bottle to your table in around 5 minutes, but also send for your car via valet without a wait. As for the music space, it's the standard dark and cavernous dancefloor. $20.

Space 34 NE 11th St ☎305/372-9378 or information line ☎ 305/375-0001, ⓦwww.clubspace. com. Fri 10pm–Sat 10am, Sat 10pm–Sun 10am. One of the pioneers of the nightlife scene downtown and still the place most likely to draw a brandname international DJ, *Space* is housed in a sprawling complex with rough décor and a reassuringly illicit ambience (think acres of concrete and spartan bathrooms). Most people migrate to the three dancefloors when the other venues shut down; there's a lusher chill-out patio on the roof. $15–20.

🏃 **Studio A** 60 NE 11th St ☎305/358-7625, ⓦwww.studiomiami.com. Daily 6pm–4am. Hurrah – at last, a club in Miami that isn't house- or rap-obsessed and is refreshingly music-focused. This club spotlights rock, jangle pop and experimental music, often with live performances on huge main stage (the excellent sound system's a major plus). The décor's vaguely goth – comfy banquettes and chandeliers – and there's a bizarre glass box overhead for "performance art" happenings. $12 and up.

South Beach

Blue 222 Española Way ☎305/534-1009. Daily 10pm–5am. This small bar/club is a surprising find on South Beach: the underground DJs spin an impressive house/techno mix, the crowd's mostly residents and their house guests, and if there's a dress code, it's "comfy." No cover.

Cameo & Vice 1445 Washington Ave ☎305/672-8084, ⓦwww.crobarmiami.com. Weds–Sat 10pm–5am. *Cameo* – which takes its name from the marquee out front, when the building was once an Art Deco movie theater – is a huge, disco-inspired spot complete with giant glitterball on the main floor. It's run by the crobar team from Chicago so expect hard-partying, serious music and plenty of drag queens. A smaller satellite space in the same building, *Vice* is a rock-themed lounge with a guitar-heavy playlist. From $20.

The Fifth 1045 Fifth St ☎305/300-3922, ⓦwww. thefifth.com. Wed, Fri & Sat 10pm–5am. Overseen by nightlife pasha Gerry Kelly (former czar of iconic clubs, *State Level* and *Bash*), this is a sister spot to the namesake original in Toronto. The enormous and loft-like two-level space – converted from a onetime strip club – sticks to a glammy, mainstream playlist and it's aimed strictly at the bottle service crowd so budget accordingly. The VIP suites upstairs have their own hotel-style mini bars – and binoculars to scan the crowd below and check out the hottest talent.

Mansion 1235 Washington Ave ☎305/531-5535, ⓦwww.mansionmiami.com. Weds–Sat 11pm–5am. At three years old and counting, this movie theater-turned-nightclub is still buzzing – an impressive feat in any club-land, let alone South Beach. Thank the setting, a 40,000 square foot super club with six VIP areas, nine bars and five dancefloors that cater to schizophrenic tastes simultaneously. Cover $20 & up.

Mokaï 235 23rd St ☎305/531-4166, ⓦwww. mokaimiami.com. Tues, Thurs–Sat 10pm–4am. Nicola Siervo, once of *Mynt*, defected to open this tiny boite (there are just 22 tables) aimed squarely at the VIP crowd. It's a

▼ Mokaï

bar earlier in the evening, but morphs into a clubby elite dancing spot by midnight – there's a postage stamp-sized dancefloor by the DJ booth at the rear. Bypass the ferocious door policy by booking a table for bottle service, with the bonus that you'll also land a free parking spot in the lot next door. No cover.

Mynt Lounge 1921 Collins Ave ☎ 305/532-0727, ⓦ www.myntlounge.com. Wed–Sat 11pm–5am. *Mynt* reigned as the tightest door and hottest club on the beach for several years after opening in 2000. It's lost some of its luster, but new owner Romain Zago recently sunk $1m into a refit, improving the sound and lighting system and spiffing up the bar. It's a welcome improvement, and the place is still worth checking out, but you'll need to dress to impress. $20.

Nikki Beach 1 Ocean Drive ☎ 305/538-1111, ⓦ www.nikkibeach.com. Mon, Fri, Sat 11pm–5am, Sun 3–11pm. The worldwide phenom (14 outposts and counting, plus a clothing line, magazine and a hotel in Panama) actually started in Miami with this branch – and it's still the best. *Nikki Beach* is an engagingly ersatz recreation of St Tropez with a glitzy, only-in-Miami edge; it's one of the few places on South Beach where it still almost feels like 1995. Sway and sip here at the bar which spills onto the white-teepee-dotted private beach; Sunday afternoon's Indio Loco party is the hottest scene, but remember to wear your skimpiest bikini. From $10. Branch: Nikki Coconut Grove, 2889 McFarlane Road, Coconut Grove ☎ 305/476-3600.

Opium Garden 136 Collins Ave ☎ 305/531-5535, ⓦ www.theopiumgroup.com. Fri & Sat 11pm–5am. A massive open-air complex

with a vaguely Asian theme – Chinese lanterns and a smattering of golden Buddha statues – *Opium Garden* plays fierce, if populist, house. The central dancefloor is enormous and there are plenty of private booths scattered around when it's time to rest the toes. Up to $20.

Set 320 Lincoln Rd ☎ 305/531-2800, table reservations ☎ 786/303-5872, ⓦ www.setmiami.com. Thurs 10pm–5am, Fri & Sat 11pm–5am. The latest addition to the Opium Group's roster (*Mansion*, *Opium Garden*) is surprisingly small, and all the better for it. The main floor is dominated by a DJ booth, hydraulic go-go dancer-crowned platforms and giant chandelier, and usually plays mainstream house; the upstairs lounge at the front is always hip-hop. The best place to be is the VIP room, a 20-person jewel box, decorated like a hunting lodge, that's hidden behind a two-way mirror above the bar. From $20.

Snatch & Suite 1437-1439 Washington Ave ☎ 305/604-3644, ⓦ www.snatchmiami.com and ⓦ www.suiteloungemiami.com. Fri & Sat 10pm–5am. Two clubs-in-one – *Snatch* downstairs is a pseudo dive bar, with lingerie dangling from the ceiling, a mechanical bull and a sweaty rock soundtrack. Upstairs, swankier *Suite* is a more a traditional bottle service-and-house place. Expect a tough door policy at both clubs, though *Snatch* is a little less impossible for mortals to penetrate. $20 and up.

Coconut Grove

Oxygen Lounge Basement of the Streets of Mayfair, 2911 Grand Ave ☎ 305/476-0202, ⓦ www.oxygenlounge.biz. Daily 10:30pm–4am. Enormous lounge-restaurant-club in an unprepossessing setting, with futuristic decor and funky staff uniforms, as well as an onsite waterfall. Although there's a live DJ every night, it's clubbiest on weekends with a house night on Friday and a Middle Eastern fusion DJ on Saturdays. The crowd's dressy and a little self-conscious. Up to $20.

Live music

Unlike the club scene, which focuses on South Beach and the after-hours strip Downtown, **live music venues** are scattered throughout the city: the indie rock club *Churchill's* and boho hangout *One Ninety* are hidden away in Little Haiti while one of the best Latin clubs, *Café Nostalgia*, is stashed in a onetime dive bar space behind an unremarkable hotel midway up Miami Beach.

Cover charges vary widely – up to $20 or more for bigger names, while local pub bands will run you around $5. Call the numbers or visit the websites we've listed below for up-to-date schedules, or check with the *New Times*.

Latin, Caribbean, and reggae

Bayside Seafood 3501 Rickenbacker Causeway, Virginia Key ☎305/361-0808. Daily 11am–11pm. A rundown restaurant that's worth heading out to on weekends, when there's live pop/rock music with a minimal cover: no big names, but groovy enough. The views of Biscayne Bay are great, too. $10–20 cover.

Café Nostalgia Versailles Hotel, 3425 Collins Ave, Middle Beach ☎305/531-8838, ⓦwww.cafenostalgia.com. Wed–Sat 8pm–5am. This itinerant and legendary Cuban club looks to have confirmed a permanent home. It's now ensconced in Miami Beach in what was once *Paco's*, an alt-Latin rock lounge. Earlier in the evening, the older crowd listens to live music from established bands, but come 1am it morphs into a Latin hip-hop spot for twentysomething locals. $20.

Casa Panza 1620 SW 8th St, Little Havana ☎305/643-5343. Mon & Wed 11am–11pm, Tues & Thur–Sun 11am–2am. A yuppiefied restaurant with a large dancefloor attached, *Casa Panza* is liveliest on Tuesdays and Thursdays when there are flamenco shows and a live guitarist. Otherwise, it's open to diners and drinkers every night for salsa and merengue; weekends are low-key. No cover.

Club Típico Dominicano 1344 NW 36th St, Little Havana ☎305/634-7819. Daily 11pm–5am. This restaurant transforms into a salsa and merengue club at the weekends; don't be put off by the low cover – the music's authentic and the crowd enthusiastic. Up to $15.

Hoy Como Ayer 2212 SW 8th St, Little Havana ☎305/541-2631. Wed–Sat 9pm–4am. Former home of *Café Nostalgia*, this dark space – a low-slung terracotta building with unfussy décor and an almost ratty interior – is one of the most reliable venues in the city for inventive Cuban-fusion music, featuring old-time performers jamming alongside second-generation expats. $7 and up.

Mango's 900 Ocean Drive, South Beach ☎305/673-4422, ⓦwww.mangostropicalcafe.com. Daily 11am–5am. Shamelessly tacky and gloriously over-the-top, *Mango's* offers nightly live pop music and dance shows by the waiters: the blaring music spills out onto the sidewalk, and so does the crowd. Cheesy, but fun, especially on weeknights when the crowd's a little more local. Free–$20.

One Ninety 26 NE 54th St, Little Haiti ☎305/758-7085. Wed–Thurs 6pm–midnight, Fri & Sat 6pm–1am. While this cafe has bounced around venues from its original home at 190 46th Street in the Design District (hence the name), owner Alan Hughes has finally found what looks like a permanent perch near his original location. The restaurant is still delicious, the boho vibe intact, and its live music programming as eclectic as ever – expect everything from jazz to bossa nova, and if you're lucky Hughes himself on guitar. Recommended.

Tap Tap 819 5th St, South Beach ☎305/672-2898. Wed–Sun 5pm–11pm, Fri & Sat 5pm–1am. Known for its excellent restaurant (see p.151), gallery of brightly colored native art, and regular live Haitian music, usually without a cover – phone ahead for details.

Rock, R&B, and jazz

Churchill's Hideaway 5501 NE 2nd Ave, Little Haiti ☎305/757-1807, ⓦwww.churchillspub.com. Daily 11am–5am. Unmissable, if inconveniently located, rock venue that's nurtured emerging and local talent for twenty years: both Marilyn Manson and the Mavericks played here in their early days. While the bill is sometimes hit-or-miss, it's still an authentic glimpse at Miami's underground music scene; Monday open-mic night for jazz and rock bands is usually a highlight. $3–15.

If you're looking to catch **big-name acts** on world tours, the following venues are likely where they'll be playing. Miami also offers a chance to catch stadium shows from some Latin superstars who don't tour across the rest of the US. At time of writing, the city's other big concert venue, Downtown's Miami Arena at 721 NW 1st Ave, was undergoing a major renovation, with no confirmed reopening date.

American Airlines Arena 601 Biscayne Blvd, Downtown. Info ☎786/777-1000, box office ☎786/777-1250, ⓦ www.aaarena.com.

James L. Knight Center 400 SE 2nd Ave, Downtown. Info ☎305/416-5970, tickets ☎305/358-5885, ⓦ www.jlkc.com.

Pro Player Stadium 2269 Dan Marino Blvd, sixteen miles northwest of Downtown Miami. ☎305/623-6100, ⓦ www.proplayerstadium.com.

The Fillmore at the Jackie Gleason Theater 1700 Washington Ave, South Beach ☎305/674-1040. ⓦ www.livenation.com. Concert behemoth Live Nation took over this venue when its theater productions defected to the Arsht Center and now runs it as a mid-sized concert space for the likes of Ricky Martin and Fall Out Bay, as well as marquee comedians such as Sarah Silverman. From $20.

Jazid 1342 Washington Ave, South Beach ☎305/673-9372, ⓦ www.jazid.net. Daily 9pm–3am. The only R&B and jazz venue in the heart of club-obsessed South Beach. A welcome alternative, if only it had a little more edge. Granted, there's nightly music in both the jazzy downstairs space and upstairs in the DJ-driven sleek, modern section, but both decor and music are bland and toothless – in other words, *Jazid's* won't please jazz fanatics. $10.

John Martin's 253 Miracle Mile, Coral Gables ☎305/445-3777, ⓦ www.johnmartins.com. Mon–Sat 11.30am–1am, Sun 11.30am–11pm. This expat-run Irish pub (see review, p.160) hosts regular live music – often Irish folk – that's surprisingly enjoyable and high-quality for a pub space. No cover charge.

Luna Star Café 775 NE 125th St, North Miami ☎305/799-7123, ⓦ members.aol.com/luna-13star. Closed Sun & Mon. There's an open-mic night on Saturday, poetry readings during the week, and occasional folk concerts at this largely vegetarian café. Phone before you go as it has erratic opening hours. No cover.

Scully's Tavern 9809 Sunset Drive, South Miami ☎305/271-7404, ⓦ www.scullystavern.net. Mon–Thurs 11am–1am, Fri & Sat 11am–3am, Sun noon–1am. *Scully's*, an unremarkable sports bar in South Miami, hosts local rock bands at 10pm every Friday and Saturday night without a cover – decent, although *Churchill's Hideaway* (see p.165) is more worth the pilgrimage.

Soho Lounge 175-193 NE 36th St, Design District ☎ 305/576-1988 ⓦ www.soholoungemiami.com. Wed–Sat 10pm–5am. Four-room, multi-level space with different live music and DJs in each section: there might be a hard house DJ in one and a jangly local band in another. The programming's interesting, though the space has lost the trendy luster it had a couple of years ago (not always a bad thing). Unusual in that it welcomes 18 year olds and up. From $5.

Tobacco Road 626 S Miami Ave, Downtown ☎305/374-1198, ⓦ www.tobacco-road.com. Daily 11.30am–5am. This gritty, rather shabby Downtown bar features two stages where nightly live acts perform. The tunes are mostly blues and R&B, and the place occasionally snags biggish names – so check listings for upcoming performances. On a regular night, the cover's around $7.

Van Dyke Café 846 Lincoln Rd, South Beach ☎305/534-3600, ⓦ www.thevandykecafe.com. Sun–Thurs 8am–midnight, Fri & Sat 8am–2am. Aside from the main restaurant, there's an upstairs jazz lounge with a full bar and high-quality performances seven days a week. Don't come to chat, as enthusiasts will quickly let you know if you disrupt the music. $5–10.

⑭

NIGHTLIFE | Live music

15

Performing arts and film

The new Arsht Center, a one-stop warehouse for cultural browsing that's siphoned off the highest calibre local companies into a single venue, has made a predictably large impact on Miami's **performing arts** scene. While it hasn't quite been the success its overly hopeful civic champions had promised, the programming has been impressive. The monolith hasn't elbowed out smaller local companies – its only casualty so far has been the ineptly managed Coconut Grove Playhouse – and impressive outfits like the New Theatre continue to thrive. Still, if you're looking for truly edgy, avant-garde performance troupes, they're surprisingly scarce for a city of this size; the best such option is Miami Light Project.

Arguably it's in **film** that Miami's art scene is strongest: there are plenty of alternative theaters dotted around, like the Miami Beach Cinemathèque, as well as a thriving Spanish-language circuit, plus megaplexes shilling Hollywood blockbusters and appealing local oddities like Movies on the Green. Annual events like the Miami Gay and Lesbian Film Festival (see p.173, "Festivals and events") add to the selection.

When it comes to **dance**, the nationally known Miami City Ballet – which now performs at the Arsht Center – is the city's major draw; fringe Latin American troupes help add interest. **Classical music and opera** offerings are only average, although the New World Symphony in South Beach often delights with the quality of its performances thanks to iconic artistic director Michael Tilson Thomas.

Comedy and other **spoken word** performances are the city's weakest link: there are few venues, and the existing companies are hit-and-miss at best.

Getting tickets

For **tickets** to most performing arts shows, contact the ubiquitous Ticketmaster (☎305/358-5885, ⊛www.ticketmaster.com) or the venues directly – you're unlikely to have problems finding tickets for anything other than one of the pre-Broadway shows that occasionally surface at the Actors' Playhouse. Pick up the *Miami Herald*'s Friday edition for details of the following week's concerts or the essential freesheet *New Times*. Check these listings, too, for sporadic performances at other venues, like the Barnacle in Coconut Grove (see p.110), which hosts magical moonlit concerts on its bayfront lawn each month.

Most of the city's performing arts offerings are clustered on the mainland, but if you're staying in South Beach and want to browse alternatives within walking distance, check the well-maintained ⓦ www.mbculture.org.

Theater

Actors' Playhouse 280 Miracle Mile, Coral Gables ☎ 305/444-9293, ⓦ www.actorsplayhouse.org. Built as a movie theater, this extensively restored building holds three performance spaces: a large auditorium with room for 600 downstairs, a smaller, 300-seat theater upstairs, and a 100-person capacity black raw space on the third floor for experimental work. Many Broadway productions stop off here, and there's an in-house children's theater workshop that performs regularly.

African Heritage Cultural Arts Center 6161 NW 22nd Ave, Liberty City ☎ 305/638-6771. This community center offers classes in ethnic dance, drama, and art, and features sporadic performances – often community productions – in its Wendell A. Narasse Theater, a tiny black-box venue with 200 seats.

Colony Theater 1040 Lincoln Rd, South Beach ☎ 305/674-1040. Originally a moviehouse, this rehabbed Deco building was converted to a theater with a 500-seat auditorium. Programming is a mixed bag of famous comedians, dance concerts, and performances by local theater groups; it's also home to the Miami Gay & Lesbian Film Festival each spring. A recent renovation restored the original facade and lobby design.

GableStage Biltmore, 1200 Anastasia Ave, Coral Gables ☎ 305/445-1119, ⓦ www.gablestage. org. Formerly known as the Florida Shakespeare Theater, this company shuttled around Coral Gables for years before settling into a permanent home in the *Biltmore*; the hotel, though, has long agitated to wrest the space back, so call before stopping by. Artistic director Joe Adler is a local legend, known for producing accessible and exciting shows. Performances take place Thursday–Sunday, and the season usually includes classic plays alongside Florida premieres of Off-Broadway hits.

The Lyric Theater 819 NW 2nd Ave, Overtown ⓦ www.theblackarchives.org. Owned and run by the Black Archives (see p.48), this Overtown landmark has been mired in planning problems as it tries to perform a major renovation. If and when it's completed, programming within the 400-seat auditorium will focus on African-American acts – whether jazz, gospel, or theater – both national and from Miami. Check the website for updated details.

🏃 **Miami Light Project** 3000 Biscayne Blvd, Biscayne Corridor ☎ 305/576-4350, ⓦ www.miamilightproject.com. Miami Light Project (MLP) is an umbrella organization that brings avant-garde theater, music, and dance to various city venues, including the Gusman Center Downtown. Expect banner performers like Laurie Anderson and Kenny Muhammad, as well as less-well-known hip-hop groups or performance troupes. February's Here & Now festival, hosted onsite at MLP's own Light Box theater, is a showcase for new works by local performers.

The New Theatre 4120 Laguna St, Coral Gables ☎ 305/443-5909, ⓦ www.new-theatre.org. This 100-seat theater is an artsy gem providing high-quality, adventurous theater: it's dedicated to putting on edgy productions, whether by well-known dramatists like Tony Kushner, of *Angels in America* fame, or by new, local playwrights – the Pulitzer Prize–winning *Anna in the Tropics* was commissioned here.

Teatro Avante 744 SW 8th St, Little Havana ☎ 305/445-8877, ⓦ www.teatroavante. com. This two decade-old Spanish-language theater company produces one major production each year (with English supertitles), as well as the International Hispanic Theater Festival each June, with performances at various venues around town – check the website or call for schedules.

Classical music and opera

Coral Gables Congregational Church 3010 DeSoto Blvd, Coral Gables ☎ 305/448-7421, ⓦ www.coralgablescongregational.org. Built in the Mediterranean Revival style, this church has a dark interior with fine acoustics, perfect for classical music performances from local groups.

🏃 **Lincoln Theater** 541 Lincoln Rd, South Beach ☎ 305/673-3330, ⓦ www.nws.

The Arsht Center

Officially called **The Adrienne Arsht Center for the Performing Arts of Miami Dade County** (Biscayne Boulevard between 13th & 14th streets, OMNI; ☎305/949-6722, Ⓦ www.carnivalcenter.org; tickets start at $15), this long-awaited arts hub opened in 2006 after years of delays. Initially lumbered with the awkward name of Carnival Center for the Performing Arts, thanks to a multi-million dollar cash injection from a local cruise giant, it's now saddled it with an equally sponsor-driven moniker in honor of the local banker-cum-philanthropist.

The swooping, gleaming center houses a 2400 seat ballet and opera house, a 2200-capacity concert hall, and a black-box studio theater for two hundred, all spread between two main buildings linked by an elegant road-spanning bridge.

Those three venues are the new home hubs for two longstanding local cultural organizations: the Concert Association of Florida and the Florida Grand Opera, whose five annual productions are now staged here. Two other local arts mainstays also make use of the center: the Miami City Ballet and New World Symphony will now not only perform at their current homes on the beach but also here on the mainland.

More mainstream programming at the Arsht Center comes in the form of the always sold-out Best of Broadway season, which brings in high profile touring shows. Edgier offerings in 200-seater include an eclectic roster of jazz concerts, experimental theater and stand-up comedy; tickets start at only $25.

Designed by Cesar Pelli, the splashy building is more than just an architectural statement; the flawless technical specs make it an impressive spot for even the pickiest of audiophiles. Still, management and programming issues in its first year led to massive losses and the ouster of the original team; at time of writing, a new and more commercially minded group was in charge. For more on the building's architecture and its somewhat tortured genesis, see p.80 .

edu. One of the best venues in the city, Lincoln Theater is the current home base for the New World Symphony, composed of graduate students from across the country who endure rigorous auditions to secure a place in the Symphony's three-year fellowship program. It's a training ground for future orchestral superstars, and the quality of the performances is superb – no surprise given that the resident artistic director is classical legend Michael Tilson Thomas. Ticket prices vary, but can be as low as $10.

Olympia Theater Gusman Center, 174 E Flagler St, Downtown ☎305/374-2444, Ⓦ www.gusmancenter.org. This kitschy performance space is home to a highbrow but eclectic program: there's classical music, dance, and offbeat touring productions, though it's suffering slightly after the loss of the Florida Philharmonic as its home company. The Olympia isn't all earnest worthiness, though – one of its biggest hits was a season of *Sing-A-Long Sound of Music*.

Dance

Ballet Gamonet Maximum Dance Company ☎305/259-9775, Ⓦ www.balletgamonet.org. This impressive dance company, run by former Miami City Ballet choreographer Jimmy Gamonet de los Heros, was formed in 2005 when Gamonet's troupe merged with the high calibre but cash starved Maximum Dance Company. The quality program features mostly original choreography by Gamonet set to Mahler and Stravinsky-style classical music. It performs at the Gusman Center downtown and the Colony Theater on the beach. Tickets from $25.

Miami City Ballet 2200 Liberty Ave, South Beach ☎305/929-7010, Ⓦ www.miamicityballet.org. Miami City Ballet, founded by onetime New York City Ballet star Edward Villela, is among the largest regional companies in the country and the quality of performances is consistently exceptional. The more than 20 year-old company splits its time between two performance spaces: its original home on South Beach, a specially

169

▼ Miami City Ballet

designed space that allows passers-by to gawp at ongoing rehearsals, and the new Arsht Center on the mainland.

Miami Hispanic Ballet 900 SW 1st St, Downtown ⊤305/549-7711, ⓦwww.miamihispanicballet.com. MHB is best known for producing the International Ballet Festival every September at venues across the city including the Gleason and Tower theaters; companies are brought in from across the world to perform under artistic director Pedro Pablo Peña. He also produces classical and contemporary productions throughout the year.

Momentum Dance Company ⊤305/858-7002, ⓦwww.momentumdance.com. This troupe performs around the city throughout the year at various festivals and events; its repertoire is all kinds of contemporary dance, with special emphasis on productions for children. Momentum is also the driving force behind the Beach Dance Festival each April; most of the performances are at the Byron Carlyle Theater, 500 71st St, North Beach. This troupe's offices are in Coconut Grove; for $12 aspiring Pavlovas of all ages can pirouette with the professionals – check the website or call for updated details.

Film

AMC CocoWalk 16 3015 Grand Ave, Coconut Grove ⊤305/448-6305 **AMC Sunset Place 24** 5701 Sunset Drive, South Miami ⊤305/740-8904. Two of the many mall-based megaplexes in the city, these are both reasonably close to central Miami. Both have the usual stadium seating and booming speakers to go along with all the latest releases.

Bill Cosford Cinema University of Miami Memorial Building, University of Miami campus, Coral Gables ⊤305/284-4861. Named after the long-time film critic at the *Miami Herald*, this is an artsy, surprisingly plush cinema that specializes in foreign-language and indie films. The program is set by University of Miami professors, so expect an academic slant to its schedule.

Living Room Theater, The Living Room Building, 4000 Miami Ave ⓦwww.livingroomtheaters.com. At time of writing, this indie movie house had just been announced as the flagship tenant within a long-empty building (see p.84). The complex is set to include eight screens, screened-off rooftop parking, and a restaurant/bar, with an opening date planned in early 2009.

Miami Beach Cinematheque 512 Española Way, South Beach ⊤305/673-4567, ⓦwww.mbcinema.com. Tucked away on the western end of Española Way, this fifty-seat rep house is home to the Miami Beach Film Society. The regular fare of movies is impressive, taking in arthouse classics – like Fellini, Martino and Baino-directed Italian cult faves – plus artsy newbies as well as low-profile documentaries.

Movies on the Green 1777 Kane Concourse at 96th Street, Bay Harbor Island ⊤786/355-7785, ⓦwww.moviesonthegreen.com. Run by the Bay Harbor Islands Art & Culture Foundation, this outdoor movie theater shows indie and foreign language films on the second Sat of each month (check the website or call for schedules). Adult tickets are $8, with kids free; bring a blanket or chair, and snacks. There's complimentary parking at 97th street.

Regal South Beach 18 1200 Lincoln Rd, South Beach ⊤305/674-6766. Massive multiplex on South Beach showing the usual range of Hollywood blockbusters; it was hugely controversial when constructed as several old buildings were demolished to make way for this gleaming (and rather garish) new structure. It's well located for the nearby municipal parking at 17th Street. One of its 18 screens is always set aside for artier indie fare.

Tower Theater 1508 SW 8th St, Little Havana ⊤305/649-2960. A landmark Deco building, this cinema was purchased by the city of Miami to show Hollywood movies with Spanish subtitles as a cultural service to Little Havana. Now run by Miami-Dade College, it only sporadically opens for mainly Spanish-language films.

Comedy

The Improv Comedy Club 3390 Mary Street, Coconut Grove T 305/441-8200, W www.miami-improv.com. Miami branch of a nationwide supper/comedy club: the food's mediocre, but the talent is not. One of the few places to see quality, big-name comics like Dave Chappelle in the city.

Just The Funny 3119 Coral Way, Coconut Grove T 305/693-8669, W www.justthefunny.com. A local rarity, this homegrown comedy improv troupe has landed at its own venue after years of shuttling from venue to venue. There are usually two shows Friday & Saturday evenings ($10 for 9pm show; $5 for 11pm show).

Spoken word venues

Churchill's Hideaway 5501 NE 2nd Ave, Little Haiti T 305/757-1807, W www.churchillspub.com. Daily 11am–5am. Renowned for supporting breakout local bands, *Churchill's* is also a place to catch spoken word performances – the program's the most varied of all venues, mixing everything from story slam-style long-form rants to hip-hop-inspired rhymes.

Literary Café 12325 NE 6th Ave, North Miami T 786/234-7638 W www.myspace.com/literarycafe. Opened by a poetry-loving ex-con, this offbeat spoken word venue is modelled directly after New York's legendary *Nuyorican Poets Café*: it's intended as a community gathering spot where local freestyle poets can perform throughout the week alongside aspiring newcomers on open-mic nights.

16

Gay Miami

For more than two decades, Miami has been viewed as one of the top **gay destinations** in the country. There's certainly a gay-friendly vibe in Miami proper, and the **South Beach** is still the epicenter of gay life in the area, but things have slowed since the frantic, muscle-bound party atmosphere of the early 1990s. In fact, gays have merged so much with the mainstream here that it was barely remarked on that the recently elected Miami Beach city commissioner, Michael Gongora, is openly gay.

Much as in Key West – whose anything-goes gay vibe is gradually vanishing (see p.246) – the downshift in gay good-lifeing has largely happened thanks to increasing numbers of straight tourists filling hotel rooms here. Though Miami Beach has been long been popular with trendy straight travelers, the city's aggressive marketing campaign to attract beach-seeking families in the late 1990s helped change the tourist profile here and push many gay locals to the mainland, notably to the impressive old apartment complexes and homes in the **Morningside District near 79th street along Biscayne Corridor**, and a short jaunt up I-95 to **Fort Lauderdale** (for gay and lesbian listings in Fort Lauderdale, see p.213). Another emerging neighborhood is **Normandy Isle**, where a cluster of renovation-ready mid-Century buildings, cheaper prices and friendly vibe has proved to be an irresistible draw to those loathe to leave the sandbar. The one time where gay life still utterly subsumes straight life in the city is the mammoth, hedonistic HIV fundraiser known as the **White Party** held each November. For the rest of the year – and certainly away from the beach – there's a limited number of clubs and bars for such a mythic gay hot spot.

Information and resources

There are plenty of free **newspapers and magazines** illuminating happenings in the gay and lesbian scene around Miami. For events around town, the standard resource is *TWN* (W www.twnonline.org), a well-known, newsy freesheet. The glossy *Hot Spots* (W www.hotspotsmagazine.com) and *Outlook* (W www.outlook-mag.com) cover the whole of Florida, with a heavy focus on the party scene; a local counterpart is the freesheet *The Wire*, which spotlights South Beach almost exclusively. *The Express* (W www.expressgaynews.com) is geared to gay tourists and residents across the whole of South Florida. For women, the large-format glossy women-oriented *She* (W www.shemag.com) spotlights the lesbian scene in the Sunshine State, and local newbie *girL magazine* (W www.girl-magazine. com) has a rather home-made feel but up-to-date listings.

The Winter Party Early March

A huge week-long event, the Winter Party is the springtime counterpart to November's White Party, with special nights at most major South Beach venues. The festivities climax with an outdoor club on the beach at 14th St and Ocean Drive. ☎305/571-1924, ⓦwww.winterparty.com.

Pride South Florida March

Pitifully, Miami's Pride celebrations collapsed a couple of years ago, so you'll need to head up the coast to celebrate Pride South Florida in Fort Lauderdale, which is larger and livelier. ☎954/561-2020, ⓦwww.pridesouthflorida.org.

Miami Gay and Lesbian Film Festival Late April

The Colony Theater in South Beach features two weeks of gay-themed film programming, a mixture of amateur and professional movies, in both documentary and drama genres. ☎305/534-9924, ⓦwww.mglff.com.

Aqua Girl Mid-May

One of the few women-oriented events in the city, this four-day party of cocktails and clubbing – essentially, the first circuit party targeted at girls – raises money for the Women's Community Fund, an NFP that supports lesbian rights. ☎305/532-1997, ⓦwww.aquagirl.org.

The White Party Thanksgiving

The godfather of all circuit parties, this is a week when what few clothes people wear must be white. Hotels and bars across South Beach take part, but don't miss the debauched, surreal White Party itself when the neo-Italian Villa Vizcaya is transformed into gay Miami's fabulous answer to the Venice Carnival, all to raise funds for local HIV-related charities. ⓦwhiteparty.net.

The *Miami Herald* is unusual in having a reporter assigned to cover gay and lesbian issues – but if you really want to find smart coverage of gay news and politics in Miami, visit ⓦwww.outinmiami.com online.

The **Lambda Passages Bookstore**, 7545 Biscayne Blvd (☎305/754-6900), is a gay and lesbian bookstore that also acts as an unofficial community center: it's a little out of the way, but alongside a wide range of books and a library of classic films, you can pick up all the freesheets and flyers for gay events around town. For any other questions, contact the **Miami–Dade Gay & Lesbian Chamber of Commerce** at ☎305/573-4000 or ⓦwww.gogaymiami.com.

Accommodation

There's plenty of **accommodation** in Miami specifically geared to gay and lesbian travelers, especially on South Beach. You'll also find that most mainstream hotels are gay-friendly: those listed below are especially so.

Gay accommodation

European Guesthouse 721 Michigan Ave, South Beach ☎305/673-6665, ⓦwww.european guesthouse.com. This secluded, 12-room clothing-optional B&B is rather out of the way on the western side of the beach. The rooms are eclectically furnished but comfortable. Amenities include an outdoor hot tub, leafy pool, buffet breakfast, and even a massive

flat-screen TV. It's very male-dominated and women may prefer to stay elsewhere. Shared bath from $100, private bath from $140.

The Island House 1428 Collins Ave, South Beach ☎305/864-2422 or 1-800/382-2422, ⓦwww. islandhousesouthbeach.com. Nothing special, the *Island House* is notable only as one of the larger gay guesthouses in the area. Rooms are standard, if a little shabby, but rates are excellent. $104.

SoBe You Tropical Bed and Breakfast 1018 Jefferson Ave, South Beach ☎305/534-5247 or 1-877/599-5247, ⊛www.sobeyou.us. The ten rooms in this lesbian-owned historic Art Deco house are tastefully decorated with a motley assortment of antiques and each room has a TV/DVD and CD player. There's a free cocktail hour every evening and a healthy breakfast's included in the overnight rate; the free parking's a plus. $125.

Gay-friendly accommodation

Doubletree Surfcomber 1717 Collins Ave, South Beach ☎305/532-7715 or 1-800/222-TREE, ⊛www.surfcomber.com. The hotel is an active supporter of the White and Winter parties, so book well ahead if you want to stay during those times; for more, see review on p.133. $245.

Grove Inn Country Guesthouse 22540 SW Krome Ave, Homestead ☎305/247-6572 or 1-877/247-6572, ⊛www.groveinn.com. Gay-owned and -operated, this is a charming guesthouse that makes a welcome – if inconveniently

located – alternative to the South Beach scene. It's a good base for many of the city's outer district attractions, though there's little nightlife nearby. $85.

Hotel Ocean 1230 Ocean Drive, South Beach ☎305/672-2579, ⊛www.hotelocean.com. Rooms in this French-owned hotel are offbeat, charming, and feature tiled floors, mismatched antique furniture, and light switches that only operate when you insert a room key; breakfast is included in the rates. Its location opposite the primarily gay 12th Street Beach section makes it a convenient choice, although it's a little over-priced for the amenities it offers. $275.

The Shelborne 1801 Collins Ave, South Beach ☎305/531-1271 or 1-800/327-8757, ⊛www. shelborne.com. Site of the early Miss Uni-verse pageants, for some reason, this main-stream hotel's now popular with queens of a different type: there are a few nods to gay travelers (gay porn on the hotel pay-per-view channels, for instance) but the rooms themselves are unremarkable. $235.

Bars and clubs

Inevitably, most of the gay bars and clubs can be found in **South Beach**, although, as the local gay population's migrated to gentrify the shabby but historic **Biscayne Corridor**, a new raft of night spots has opened nearby.

Anthem ⊛www.anthemsundays.com. Sunday's legendary gay mecca run by über-pro-moter Michael Tronn is an astonishing two decades old: once synonymous with the beach, it now hopscotches around venues downtown – most recently, at the Pawn Shop Lounge. Check the website for latest listings; cover is usually $20.

Boy Bar 1220 Normandy Drive at 71st Street, Normandy Isle ☎305/864-2697 New owners have expanded and revitalized this long-struggling, cruisey bar – cutting down on the sleaze and amping up the fun (think drag shows and strip contests). There's a friendly Sunday tea dance on the outdoor patio; a bonus, thanks to its off-South Beach location, is the 5am close.

Club Boi 726 NW 79th St, Little Haiti ☎305/836-8995, ⊛www.clubboi.com. A refreshing change from the circuit-boy scene on South Beach, this largely black club plays Hi-NRG hip-hop, house, and old-school R&B every Tuesday, Friday, and Saturday night. $5–12.

Halo 1625 Michigan Ave, South Beach ☎305-534-8181, ⊛www.haloloungemiami.com. New glossy lounge (a sister spot to a bar in DC) on a side street off Lincoln Road. The wavy walls and pink neon look like a 1960's Bond Girl's boudoir while the cocktail-heavy list (whether a pineapple mint *caipirinha* or a mind-bogglingly wide list of potential ingre-dients to Build Your Own Bloody Mary) is a change from the light beer and vodka-sodas that dominate elsewhere. One of the gay bars to spot celebs – Lance Bass and Nar-ciso Rodriguez both stopped by in its first few weeks of opening.

Laundry Bar 721 Lincoln Lane, South Beach ☎305/531-7700. Stylish, glass-fronted laundromat-bar, where you can sip a beer while your bedlinens dry. The clientele here is young and pretty, and it's one of the few places that has a good mix of girls and boys.

Magnum Lounge 709 NE 79th St Causeway, Little Haiti ☎305/757-3368. Not strictly a gay bar, but this campy restaurant-lounge is popular with gay locals, mostly for its sing-alongs around the piano. The crowd's a little older than on the beach, but very friendly and low-key – on a quiet night, Jeffrey, the owner, often passes out free after-dinner glasses of port.

Martini Tuesdays ☏ 305/535-6696, ⊛ www.sobesocialclub.com. Gay promoter Edison Farrow runs this roaming party, which shuttles between different venues each Tuesday from 9pm–1am. The crowd's youngish and friendly, making most of the parties great fun. He also hosts similar events throughout the week, including SugarDaddy Sundays – check the freesheets or website for venues.

O'Zone 6620 SW 57th Ave (Red Road), South Miami ☏ 305/667-2888. A huge suburban club with a sunken dancefloor and a predominantly Latin muscle-boy crowd, *O'Zone* is grooviest at the weekends when there's salsa and house music, as well as drag shows. Cover $5–15.

The Palace 1200 Ocean Drive, South Beach. ☏ 305/531-7234. This restaurant and bar opposite the gay beach is more welcoming than most on the South Beach circuit, with a diverse clientele – old and young, buff and less so. The food's so-so but the circular bar that looks out onto the sidewalk's a pleasant place for a martini or two – look for the $4 drinks specials.

Score & Crème 727 Lincoln Rd, South Beach ☏ 305/535-1111, ⊛ www.scorebar.net. This decade-old local video bar has been spruced up. The front area's open from 1pm: it's decked out with red and black Starckian furniture and free WiFi, making it a great place to grab a coffee or beer and watch the Lincoln Road runway. The rear

▼ Score & Crème

area's now been given over entirely to a dancefloor, where you can expect housey, Hi-NRG DJs each weekend. Upstairs is the standalone *Crème*, a gay riff on Miami's dominant lounge culture – lower key music, martinis and surprisingly affordable bottle service (less than $200).

Twist 1057 Washington Ave, South Beach ☏ 305/538-9478, ⊛ www.twistsobe.com. A labyrinthine bar that keeps expanding: there are two dancefloors, video screens in the main lounge downstairs, and a garden bar out back. The all-male crowd's friendly and more diverse than most South Beach watering holes. Open 1pm–5am daily, with two-for-one drink specials from 1–9pm; go-go boys perform in the garden bar Friday, Sunday, and Monday nights. No cover.

Gyms and saunas

If you're going to spend any time at all on Miami's body-conscious beaches, best to stay in shape at one of the local gyms – we've listed the two best known (the gay workout mecca, glass-fronted Idol's Gym on Lincoln Lane, recently shut down) plus the city's most popular sex club-cum-sauna.

Lesbian Miami

Most of the nightlife in Miami is aimed strictly at gay males. The last attempt to launch a fully-fledged lesbian joint on South Beach, Jade Bar, sputtered out of business within months, as did Anam's in Coral Gables. The best options for girl-heavy nightlife are the weekly roving one-nighters at the beach's clubs, most overseen by Pandora & Ultra Events (⊛ www.pandoraultra.com), whose website lists a full upcoming schedule.

Club Body Center 2991 Coral Way, Little Havana ☎ 305/448-2214, ⓦ www.clubbodycenter. com/miami. The best-known sauna/gym/sex club in town. There's super-cruisey nude sunbathing by the pool, a rough-hewn timber bar known as the KY Corral (complete with flogging stations), and plenty of social events to help encourage mingling – plus it's open 24 hours year-round.

David Barton Gym 1510 Bay Road, South Beach ☎ 305/674-5757, ⓦ www.davidbartongym.com.

The musclebound sparkplug owner's the best ad for this gym. Now, the gym has two locations – one bayside and another inside the *Gansevoorth South* hotel (see p.134)

SoBe Sports Club 1676 Alton Rd, South Beach ☎ 305/531-4743, ⓦ www.sobesportsclub.net. Massive gym on the west side of South Beach, less sceney than others and with extensive classes available: a day-pass costs $25.

Gay beaches

There are no officially designated gay beaches in the city – however, look for the densest crowds on the South Beach seafront, and you'll find the **12th Street Beach**, a popular gay hang-out that stretches for several blocks of sand. In addition, the northern reaches (stations 27–29) of the nude beaches at Haulover Park (see p.75) are less predominantly gay but, oddly, cruisier. There are also several predominantly gay sections along the beach in Fort Lauderdale (see p.213).

Shopping

M iami provides plenty of opportunities to drop your dollars **shopping** for clothes, music, souvenirs, and beauty treatments – though the pickings are fairly conventional. The biggest disappointment in Miami's retail landscape is its dearth of bookstores, pitifully few for a city this size. At least most shops generally stay open late, especially at the beach, so you can browse well into the evening – expect outlets along Lincoln Road, for instance, to be open until 10pm or later most nights.

For a city as fashion conscious as Miami, trendy boutiques used to be far and few between. In the past few years, though, that's changed: stalwart Base has doubled in size, new concept stores like Arrive, Tomas Maier and Culture Kings have opened, and New York mainstays such as Atrium have cloned a sunnier second outlet, no doubt to cater for the number of refugee New Yorkers who flee here on winter weekends for a break from the bitter cold up north.

Where to shop

South Beach is undeniably the place to head if you're looking for quirky, smaller boutiques; its outdoor spaces are a welcome antidote to overly air-conditioned malls. Collins Avenue and Lincoln Road hold the largest number of stores, while further north on the beach, **Bal Harbour** is home to the city's densest selection of designer names, albeit in an unflattering setting.

Check out **Coconut Grove** for some unusual gift stores, especially in the triangle made by Commodore Plaza, Grand Avenue, and the Main Highway; otherwise, its much-ballyhooed shopping centers are rather disappointing. **Coral Gables'** reinvigorated downtown shopping strip is known as the Miracle Mile: after languishing for several years as a musty retail dead end, local efforts have drawn cafes, wine shops and much groovier stores to its small, vintage shopfronts. Around the city, a large number of **suburban malls** essentially replicate one another's offerings with branches of The Gap, Express, and Victoria's Secret.

In **Little Havana**, all the retail action aligns Calle Ocho: come here for cigars and Cuban knickknacks, as most of the other storefronts house mini-markets or cafés. Along the **Biscayne Corridor**, there are notable housewares stores on 40th Street in the Design District, and a burgeoning fashion scene further north along Biscayne Corridor en route to Little Haiti.

Finally, **Downtown Miami** is barren except for an odd assortment of a dozen or so fabric peddlers, plenty of cheap shoe stores, and numerous electronics outlets, blaring music onto the sidewalk and hooking bystanders with deals that seem too good to be true – and they are.

Books

It's surprisingly hard to find a good bookstore in the city; listed below are all the major ones close to the center – the most bookish neighborhood for browsing is undoubtedly Coral Gables, and Fifteenth Street Books there is the only outlet with a sizeable selection of secondhand titles.

Barnes & Noble 152 Miracle Mile, Coral Gables ☎ 305/446-4152, ⓦ www.bn.com. Located in the heart of downtown Coral Gables, this is the only central branch of the book mega-chain – it stocks the usual wide selection of books and music, plus a large Spanish-language section of both novels and nonfiction.

Books & Books 933 Lincoln Rd, South Beach ☎ 305/532-3222, ⓦ www.book sandbooks.com. The city's signature book-store turned 25 in 2007. Though smallish and filled with coffee-table books, it's the only place on the beach for reading material other than the rundown Kafka's Kafé. Another much more impressive branch – with ample stock and an appealing court-yard café – is at 265 Aragon Ave, Coral Gables (☎305/442-4408), plus there's a satellite spot inside the Bal Harbour Shops, 9700 Collins Ave (☎305/864-4241).

The Bookstore in the Grove Shoppes at Mayfair in the Grove, 2911 Grand Ave, Coconut Grove ☎ 305/443-2855. This old Borders location has morphed into an indie outlet, though sadly, it's not necessarily an improvement: a large part of the store's now taken up by a so-so café and there's a surprisingly limited selec-tion of mostly bestselling titles. Still, it's the only bookstore in the area and will make do in a pinch.

Borders Village of Merrick Park, 358 San Loren-zo Ave, Coral Gables ☎ 305/529-4567, ⓦ www. borders.com. Megastore chain offering good discounts on new hardcovers and has a strong selection of local-interest books. It also sells CDs and hosts author readings – call or drop by for schedules.

Downtown Book Center 247 SE 1st St, Down-town ☎ 305/377-9939. This tiny Downtown bookstore is particularly strong in popular fiction, thrillers, and romance in both Span-ish and English.

Eutopia 1627 Jefferson Ave, South Beach ☎ 305/532-8680. This small bookstore stocks first editions and rare books – not exactly

beach reading, but a joy for connoisseurs. Open Tues–Sat 2–8pm.

Fifteenth Street Books 296 Aragon Ave, Coral Gables ☎ 305/442-2344, ⓦ www.fifteenthstreet-books.com. While it may not be a bargain hunter's paradise, Fifteenth Street Books is well stocked with art books and old hard-covers in top condition. The knowledgeable, friendly owner was the original founder of nearby Books & Books.

Kafka's Kafé 1464 Washington Ave, South Beach ☎ 305/673-9669. Don't come here looking for anything specific as the filing system for this rather ratty selection of used books is erratic. The budget paperbacks are good beach throwaways; on the plus side, there's a wide selection of magazines, and Kafka's is open until midnight.

Ninth Chakra 530 Lincoln Rd, South Beach ☎ 305/538-0671, ⓦ www.9thchakra.com. New-age bookstore and gift shop that's rather out of place in the strutting retail palace of Lincoln Road. There's a wide selection on everything from *reiki* healing to regression; though it's a pity about the disinterested staff.

Clothes: new

The **high fashion** zone in Miami stretches along Collins Avenue on South Beach, between 5th and 8th streets, and on the newly re-energised Lincoln Road nearby. On either of these stretches, elbow to elbow, you'll find many of the big-name, mid-price designer names: the upscale stuff is in the Bal Harbour shops or Vil-lage of Merrick Park. Strangely for a town as funky and fashion-conscious as Miami, there are few homegrown designers – two of the best-known names are Julian Chang and Rene Ruiz as well as emerging talent Karelle Levy of Krel.

Adidas 226 8th St, South Beach ☎ 305/673-8317. Boutique for the reborn sportswear brand that stocks not just its core col-lection of shoes, but some harder-to-find limited-editions styles, including the Y-3 range produced under the direction of Yohji Yamamoto.

American Apparel 720 Lincoln Rd, South Beach ☎ 305/672-1799, ⓦ www.americanapparel.net. Sweatshop-free clothes churned out from the company's own factory in downtown LA: workers have full healthcare benefits and can even make or receive phone calls on the factory floor. The well-priced product's tees, sweats, and sports-inspired casual wear in sherbet colors for boys and girls.

Arrive Miami 100 16th Street, South Beach ☏ 305/604-5818, ⓦ www.arrivemiami.com. Former creative director of Sean John, Dao-Yi, teamed up with local nightlife fixture Max Pierre to open this store: the sleek, all-white space looks like a 1970s bachelor pad and specializes in togs for the dude-about-town, with fashions from Margiela and Marc Jacobs, rare sneakers from Nike and vintage sunglasses. There's a small selection of womenswear.

Atrium 1931 Collins Ave, South Beach ☏ 305/695-0757, ⓦ www.atriumnyc.com. The cutting-edge boutique from downtown New York opened its Miami outpost in the retail space tucked under the Shore Club. It has some of the smartest, most trend-savvy buyers in the rag trade, so the sprawling selection of men's and women's gear here is well worth browsing: this selection's heavy on denim from the likes of J Brand, Blue Blood and Ksubi plus accessories from YSL, Y-3 and Stella McCartney.

Banana Republic 1100 Lincoln Rd, South Beach ☏ 305/534-4706. The reason to come to this outlet of the national chain isn't the clothes – they're fine, if a little bland – but the building. It's an old bank that has been sensitively converted to a clothing store using many of the original features; the fitting rooms, for instance, are in the old vault, complete with huge, swinging metal door.

Barneys Co-op 832 Collins Ave, South Beach ☏ 305/421-2010, ⓦ www.barneys.com. The younger, funkier offspring of upscale New York designer department store, Barneys, this dual-level space houses jeans – usual suspects like Earl and Juicy are alongside lesser known, rotating names – as well as sportswear and accessories for both men and women. Pricey, but unbeatable.

Base 939 Lincoln Rd, South Beach ☏ 305/531-4982 ☏ 305/695-4026, ⓦ www.baseworld.com. Concept store with books, magazines and accessories plus urban clothes for men (with a few women's products thrown in), conceived by British

choreographer-turned-designer Steven Giles. Labels rotate regularly, but expect the likes of Tsubi, Westwood, Margiela, and Y-3. The new Base Annex a few doors down (927 Lincoln Road, Suite 118) in a onetime lawyer's office is devoted to home, tabletop and furniture (Fornasetti, Tobias Wong) – each eye-popping room's devoted to a singe color scheme.

▼ Base

Club Monaco 624 Collins Ave, South Beach ☏ 305/674-7446, ⓦ www.clubmonaco.com. Mostly monochromatic unisex basics from this Canadian mid-price chain now owned by Ralph Lauren. Expect preppy sweaters for guys, great white shirts, and fun accessories for women.

Culture Kings 4300 NE 2nd Ave, Design District ☏ 305/573-2399, ⓦ culturekings.blogspot.com. There's a huge white wall of hard-to-find sneakers, graphic tees and jackets plus Banksy or WK Interact-style books at this new store, which also invites a different artist to take over each month, creating work on canvas, on shoes or on both.

Earl Jean 1008 Lincoln Rd, South Beach ☏ 305/695-7301, ⓦ www.earljean.com. Countrified designer denim brand for men and women – stronger on hard-wearing, high-quality pants for around $200 than on its odd, somewhat overpriced separates.

Energie denim 826 Lincoln Road, South Beach ☏ 305/672-9457, ⓦ www.energie.it. The Italian men's denim and casualwear line – the sibling collection to skin-cinching Miss Sixty – has a standalone store here. The outlet sells its usual selection of vaguely retro, often ornamented jeans (perfect for local clubbing), as well as graphic tees and 80s-inspired accessories.

Green Glass Clothing & Art Boutique 54 SW 10th Street, Brickell ☎305/373-7423. Another sign of Brickell's residential upswing, this unisex gallery-cum-boutique run by husband-and-wife team Claudia and Carlos Sanz stocks ethereal women's goodies from Trina Turk and Miguelina, as well as tees and button downs for men. There's a rotating selection of pop art on the walls, too.

Hiho Batik 6909 Biscayne Blvd, Biscayne Corridor ☎305/754-8890, ⊛www.hihobatik.com. Local designer Julia Silver spent years knocking out tour shirts for the likes of Carlos Santana and has now launched her own label of hand-dyed, hand-painted clothes: they're much more stylish and inventive than you might expect – the prices aren't bad either.

Hip.e Boutique 359 Miracle Mile, Coral Gables ☎305/445-3693, ⊛www.hip-e-boutique.com. This girly boutique's decked out like a boudoir with Murano chandelier and red lacquer mirrors; it stocks starlet-ready labels like Nicky Hilton's Nicholai, C&C and Cynthia Steffe. Bored boyfriends can chug a free flute of champagne or espresso while their girlfriends browse.

Intermix 634 Collins Ave, South Beach ☎305/531-5950, ⊛www.intermixonline.com. This New York boutique's Miami outpost hosts the same quirky, youthful mix of women's designers alongside wardrobe staples: think Theory, Matthew Williamson, J Brand and Earnest Sewn.

JFishKicks 225 Collins Ave, South Beach ☎305/535-1715, ⊛www.jfishkicks.com. Another of Miami's new crop of footwear emporia, though this one stands out: for $300–2000 you can buy a pair of custom-ized sneakers (Air Force One's the standard) made to order in five days by eight different designers. Sneakerhead snobs should opt for laser stitching of hip hop heavyweights like Diddy and Kanye by Absoleute.

Julian Chang 6667 Biscayne Blvd, Biscayne Corridor ☎305/751-8900, ⊛www.julianchang.com. The go-to gown maker for skin-baring local socialites and Latina celebs like firm fan Gloria Estefan, Chang churns out skimpy, flashy eveningwear and showy casual sepa-rates, often featuring brocade. He also produces a capsule men's line of rockstarrish pants plus a few shirts and ties.

Krel 180 NW 25th Street, Wynwood ☎305/576-7465, ⊛www.krelwear.com. Paris-born designer Karelle Levy, who once toiled as a costumer at the Florida Grand Opera, now helms her own label: the studio where she works is open to the public weekdays 11am–7pm, where you can browse her two womenswear collections. Krelwear's cheaper line, with mostly stretchy, body-conscious designs (sweaters, dresses, skirts and a few legwarmers) in candy colors; Krel is pricier, custom-made one-off knits.

Morgan Miller Shoes 1634 Euclid Ave, South Beach ☎305/672-6658, ⊛www.morganmill-ershoes.com. New made-to-order women's shoe mecca: pick a sole (cork wedge or kitten heel, for example) then add a strap from more than 100 different designs (yes, there's python) and add jewels or buckles to taste. Two fittings later, they're ready for the Lincoln Road strut. Prices from $150.

Penguin clothing 925 Lincoln Road, South Beach ☎305/673-0722, ⊛www.originalpenguin.com. The reborn Munsingwear line features a nerdy-cool collection of mid-century sweat-ers, slacks and shirts for boys and 1950s starlet-style threads for girls. The retro accessories selection is especially strong.

Rasool Sportswear 6301 NW 7th Ave #B, Liberty City ☎305/759-1250. Spectacular and bizarre menswear bazaar crammed with zoot suits for $200 and rack after rack of brightly colored spats and shoes, from yellow and mustard to baby blue, in leathers including ostrich and gator ($120–400).

Rebel 6669 Biscayne Blvd, Biscayne Corridor ☎305/758-2369, ⊛www.rebelmiami.com. Trendy twentysomething store that's Miami's answer to LA's Kitson boutique (think Paris Hilton slouchy-glam style). Owned by Andrea Love, it stocks Juicy Couture, Rebecca Beeson, and anything else you'd need for a lazy sun-drenched afternoon by a five-star pool.

Rene Ruiz Couture 2700 Ponce de Leon Boulevard, Coral Gables ☎305/445-2352. Ruiz is a local fashion designer, known for his lycra-packed, stretchy gowns for women and sequined, glitzy accessories at couture prices. He's just moved to this huge space from his tiny store on the Miracle Mile: Ruiz renovated the entire building himself, adding glass floors and mother-of-pearl walls.

17

Rosa Cha by Amir Slama 830 Lincoln Rd, South Beach ℡ 305/673-3665, 🌐 www.rosa-cha. com. Tiny, closet-sized store stocking tiny, skimpy beachwear and bikinis from Brazil (plus a few men's shorts). You may have to have a killer body to carry off these mostly acid-colored designs, but there's nothing hotter for the beach.

Sabrina Monte Carlo 530 Collins Ave, South Beach ℡ 305/672-9950. Monaco-based boutique owner Sabrina Monteleone's namesake spot is like a Gallic riff on girly mecca Intermix, with twentysomething must-haves from the likes of Jenny Packham, Pucci, Blumarine, Sonia Rykiel and beach-ready threads from Monteleone's namesake in-house label.

Santini Mavardi 935 Washington Ave, South Beach ℡ 305/538-6229, 🌐 www.santinimavardi. com. For the South Beach Cinderella, this store stocks a small line of clothes, but is best known for its glitzy shoes – they run the gamut from rhinestone-studded to super-stiletto-heeled.

🏃 **Tomas Maier** 1800 West Ave, South Beach ℡ 305/531-8383, 🌐 www. tomasmaier.com. Bottega Veneta svengali Tomas Maier quietly opened his namesake store here in a converted 1930s apartment building; the interconnecting showrooms are intended to cater to the Florida lifestyle – think bikinis and lightweight cashmere – while showcasing Maier's own mens- and womenswear as well as homewares and gifts. Pricey but irresistible for browsing.

Transit 7301 Biscayne Blvd, Biscayne Corridor ℡ 305/754-2866, 🌐 www.transit.it. This outpost of Italian mens- and womenswear casual label is housed in what was once the lobby of the *Vagabond Motel*. At time of writing, owner Eric Silverman, a developer and former Dolce & Gabban exec, has plans to transform the rest of the landmarked motel site into a high-end mall.

Y-3 150 40th Street, Design District ℡ 305/573-1603 🌐 www.adidas.com/y-3. Yohji Yamamoto's Y-3 returned the 80s favorite to fashion relevance – it's a minimalist take on men's and women's sportswear produced in collaboration with Adidas. It was an endorsement of the area when the designer chose to open his standalone Miami boutique in the Design District rather than over on the beach.

Clothes: vintage and thrift

There's a good selection of **vintage shops** in South Beach, but true retro devotees should make the pilgrimage to Liberty City. There, you'll find half a dozen warehouses piled high with heap bargains – there's even a strip mall housing nothing but **thrift stores**.

Beatnix 1149 Washington Ave, South Beach ℡ 305/532-8733. Alongside the vintage clothes, Beatnix keeps technicolor wigs, enormous feather boas, and plenty of rubber clubwear – half drag, half dress-up, and definitely fun.

🏃 **C Madeleines** 13702 Biscayne Boulevard, North Miami Beach ℡ 305/945-7770. Iconic and enormous local vintage store which draws namebrand fashionistas like Kate Spade and Marc Jacobs who trawl for inspiration here; Sex and the City costumer Pat Field's also a regular. No bargains, but the place to find that Dior cocktail 1950s cocktail dress you've always wanted.

Consign of the Times 1635 Jefferson Ave, South Beach ℡ 305/535-0811. Miami's obsession with designer labels pays off here – locals offer their Gucci cast-offs for sale, splitting the profits with the store. Granted, there's plenty of flashy trash, but also the occasional find if you're prepared to sift through the racks.

Douglas Gardens Thrift Store 5713 NW 27th St, Liberty City ℡ 305/638-1900. One of several vast warehouses clustered together, there's an enormous selection at rock-bottom prices – in fact, chichi vintage stores from New York and LA regularly arrive with vans to scour for stock. Keep in mind that this isn't the greatest part of town, so it's best to visit by car or not at all.

Fly Boutique 650 Lincoln Road, South Beach ℡ 305/604-8508. This vintage bolthole's known for its slinky and sexy cast-offs – expect edgier old threads from older Pucci dresses to Versace men's shirts. PETA-shunning fashion types will also rifle enthusiastically through the wide range of well-priced furs, starting around $150.

Recycled Blues 1507 Washington Ave, South Beach ℡ 305/538-0656. The largest thrift store on the beach, this shop has a great selection of cool merchandise (especially denim). Its biggest drawback, however, is the premium prices they charge.

⑰

SHOPPING | Clothes

Department stores and malls

Miami has a large number of **malls**, both traditional and open-air – though all tend to house the standard crop of shops and department stores. The two most noteworthy are the duelling designer meccas of old favorite Bal Harbour Shops and upstart newcomer Village of Merrick Park.

Aventura Mall 19501 Biscayne Blvd, Aventura ☏305/935-1110, ⊛www.shopaventuramall. com. North of Miami, just off I-95 (take the Miami Gardens Drive exit and follow the signposts), you'll find Aventura, the local megamall that essentially sprouted a town around it. There are several department stores here, as well as an enormous food court and the usual branch shops.

Bal Harbour Shops 9700 Collins Ave, Bal Harbour ☏305/866-0311, ⊛www.balharbour shops.com. The Bal Harbour Shops house every well-known designer name, plus an enormous Saks Fifth Avenue. The indoor-outdoor mall itself is singularly unappealing, housed in a clunky concrete building, but the range and variety of stores is impressive, including upscale barber Art of Shaving, Lacoste, Vilebrequin, and Sergio Rossi.

Bayside Mall 401 N Biscayne Blvd, Downtown ☏305/577-3344, ⊛www.baysidemarketplace. com. This waterfront complex features stores much like any other: there's a large branch of the upscale jeanswear company Guess?, funky teen shoe store Skechers, and a Sharper Image.

CocoWalk 3015 Grand Ave, Coconut Grove ☏305/444-0777, ⊛www.cocowalk.com. When it opened in the early 1990s, this shopping center revitalized Coconut Grove. Now, the pleasant but unremarkable Mediterranean Revival architecture, with its covered walkways and plenty of eateries, houses usual names like Victoria's Secret and The Gap.

The Falls Shopping Center 8888 SW 136th St, South Miami ☏305/255-4570, ⊛www.shop-thefalls.com. Enormous open-air shopping complex, sporting a waterscape punctuated with falls, and a funky sculpture by Romero Britto. It has more than 100 stores and is a little more upscale than most suburban malls: there's a massive Bloomingdales, plus stylish homewares from Crate & Barrel, Pottery Barn, and Williams-Sonoma – and sexy women's wear from BCBG and Bebe.

Macy's 22 E Flagler St, Downtown ☏305/577-2312, ⊛www.macys.com. The former flagship branch of Florida's signature department store, Burdine's, has been rebranded by its current owners. The tattered Downtown branch sells home-wares, clothes from the usual designer names, and plenty of perfume. The outpost at 1777 West Ave in South Beach (☏305/825-7351) is smaller and more architecturally interesting, complete with ornamental palm trees.

Shops at Sunset Place 5701 Sunset Drive, South Miami ☏305/663-0482, ⊛www.simon.com. A mammoth outdoor mall in South Miami that's notable for its large Niketown, as well as substantial branches of Barnes & Noble and Urban Outfitters.

Shoppes at Mayfair in the Grove 2911 Grand Ave, Coconut Grove ☏305/448-1700, ⊛www.mayfairinthegrove.com. Positioned as Coco-Walk's posher sister, this oddly designed and unappealing mall – blame it on bad taste in 1979 when it was built – has never really managed to find a niche and has as many empty lots as tenants (some of the original retail was converted to apartments). Aside from the onsite hotel, the *Mayfair* (see p.138), the remaining stores include branches of The Limited, United Colors of Benetton, Bath & Body Works and the Bookstore in the Grove.

Village of Merrick Park Ponce de Leon and Hwy-1, Coral Gables ☏305/529-0200, ⊛www.villageofmerrickpark.com. Recent upscale rival to long-established Bal Harbour Shops: amid the open-air walkways, you'll find a branch of the sumptuous Elemis Spa, as well as fashions from Burberry, Diane von Furstenberg, and Jimmy Choo.

Ethnic specialties and crafts

Stores across the city claim to sell authentic souvenirs of Miami's two dominant immigrant cultures – Cuban and Haitian – but the ones listed below offer the real thing.

El Credito Cigar Factory 1106 SW 8th St, Little Havana ☏305/858-4162. It's easy to understand why this is the best-known smoke-shop in the city. Here, you'll see rows of *tabaqueros* (cigar rollers) making fat cigars by hand, using top-quality tobacco – it's generally agreed that this store's La Gloria Cubana cigar is one of the best available.

Haitian Art Factory 835 NE 79th St, Little Haiti
℡305/758-6939, Ⓦwww.haitianartfactory.com.
This eccentric shop, attached to a doctor's
office, carries fine woodcarvings and crafts
from Haiti – admittedly alongside plenty of
tat. Call ahead to see if it's open, as hours
can be erratic.
Halouba Botánica 101 NE 54th St, Little Haiti
℡305/751-7485. One of many *botánicas* on
the *voudou* strip, this store is spacious and
a little less daunting than some of the others. There's a large temple on site, which
holds regular ceremonies ministered by the
husband-and-wife team running the store.
**La Casa de las Guayaberas 5840 SW 8th St, Little
Havana** ℡305/266-9683. The specialty here is
the unmistakably Cuban *guayabera* shirt
– cool in the tropical heat and billowy in the
wind. The tailor-owner is one of the earliest
Cuban-American refugees, and everything is
hand-sewn by his team: he offers inexpensive options starting at $15 to $20, as well
as pricey, custom-made designs starting
at $250.
**La Casa de las Piñatas 1756 SW 8th St, Little
Havana** ℡305/649-4711. Gaudy *piñatas* in
any shape or size are sold here. Hundreds
hang from the ceiling, and if your Spanish is good (and you've time and money)
you can even commission custom-made
shapes.
**Libreri Mapou 5919 NE 2nd Ave, Little
Haiti** ℡305/757-9922, Ⓦwww.libre-
rimapou.com. The place to go if you want
to dig deeper into Little Haiti, offering a
wide selection of books on the history and
politics of the Caribbean nation, as well
as Haitian novels in English, French, and
Kreyol, magazines, and Haitian newspapers.

Food and drink

You don't have to splurge on every meal
if money's tight – there are branches of
the supermarket chain Publix everywhere in the city. There are also plenty
of liquor stores, although note that
local ordinances limit the sale of alco-
hol after 10pm on the beach.

Epicure Market 1656 Alton Rd, South Beach
℡305/672-1861. A gourmet market offering
expensive, high-quality foodstuffs like hand-
made biscotti, plus fresh fish and meats.
There's an interesting beer selection, as well
as a small flower stand.
Whole Foods Market 1020 Alton Rd, South Beach
℡305/532-1707, Ⓦwww.wholefoodsmarket.
com. Delicious and healthy, this enormous
supermarket offers more than just granola
and tofu – among other things, there are
freshly baked cakes, exotic juices, and
organic produce. A terrific picnic lunch stop-
off. There's a another branch at 6701 Red
Road, Coral Gables (℡305/421-9421).
**Wolfe's Wine Shoppe 124 Miracle Mile, Coral
Gables** ℡305/445-4567, Ⓦwww.wolfeswines.
com. Miracle Mile gem selling a superb
selection of hard-to-find wines – plus
glassware, corkscrews and other accoutre-
ments – in a faux industrial setting with raw
concrete floor and slashed-open cardboard
cases. The knowledgeable staff is a major
plus.

Galleries

Most of Miami's best **galleries** are in
Wynwood, lured by both the aggressive marketing of the area by landlords
and its low rents (for more on the area's

Farmers markets

A more interesting option than ploughing through Publix is checking out one of sev-
eral local **farmers markets** held in various neighborhoods around the city; expect
freshly made snacks, plants, and produce for sale, much of it organic.
Coconut Grove Every Saturday year-round 11am–7pm ℡305/238-7747, junction of
Grand Avenue and Margaret Street
Coral Gables Every Saturday January–March 8am–1pm ℡305/460-5311, between
Coral Gables City Hall and Merrick Park
North Beach Every Saturday year-round 8am–8pm ℡305/531-0038, Normandy Vil-
lage Fountain Plaza at 71st Street and Rue Vendome
South Beach Every Sunday year-round 8am–8pm ℡305/531-0038, Lincoln Road
between Washington and Pennsylvania avenues

resurgence, see p.81). Off the mainland, check out the combination studios/gallery space of the Art Center of South Florida on South Beach's Lincoln Road (see p.59).

Ambrosino Gallery 2628 NW 2nd, Wynwood & 7769 NE 125th St, North Miami ℡305/891-5577, ⊛www.ambrosinogallery.com. Longterm local art fixture Genaro Ambrosino has been showing the likes of Carol Brown and James Lecce for almost ten years: his shows are reliable, intelligent and less gimmicky than many of his competitors. There's also has a satellite project space opposite MOCA in North Miami.

Diana Lowenstein 2043 N Miami Ave, Wynwood ℡305/576-1804, ⊛www.dlfinearts.com. Lowenstein started her business in Argentina almost twenty years ago, popping up in Miami as its art world boom began. Unsurprisingly, her roster's heavy on Latin talent like Carlos Betancourt; her family also owns the Ritz-Carlton South Beach so she consults on art shows there, too.

Dorsch 151 NW 24th St, Wynwood ℡305/576-1278, ⊛www.dorschgallery.com. Art world renegade Brook Dorsch hosts parties and exhibitions in equal measure, with a mission to showcase works across media. Not the edgiest or most exciting art perhaps, but always a hot spot.

🏃 **Galerie Emmanuel Perrotin** 194 NW 30th Street, Wynwood ℡305/573-2130, ⊛www.galerieperrotin.com. Housed in a boxy midcentury building that once was home to a refrigeration company, this Miami outpost of the Parisian gallery was a major arrival on the local art scene when it opened in 2005. Perrotin reps Vuitton's favorite designer Takashi Murakami (the artist's onetime right-hand man, Gen Watanabe, runs this outpost of the gallery) as well as France's most recent entrant in the Venice Biennale, Sophie Calle.

Kevin Bruk Gallery 2249 NW 1st Place, Wynwood ℡305/576-2000, ⊛www.kevinbrukgallery.com. South African-born Bruk's an anomaly among galleristas – he's passionate about old-fashioned painting: at this space, a former taco factory, Bruk displays stunning canvases from his two-dozen strong contemporary roster which includes Richard Butlet and Tom Wesselman.

Locust Projects 105 NW 23rd St, Wynwood ℡305/576-8570, ⊛www.locustprojects.org. This space is run by a charitable collective,

so expect shows with a political slant. The upside is that prices are uniformly low, making this a good place to actually buy a piece or two.

Snitzer 2247 NW 1st Place, Wynwood ℡305/448-8976, ⊛www.snitzer.com. Fred Snitzer is one of the most famous local galleristas, and when he moved a couple of years ago from a comfy perch in Coral Gables to this Wynwood spot, it was a boon for the area. Snitzer specializes in 2-D contemporary art, both painting and photography, including local superstars Bhakti Baxter and Hernan Bas.

Spinello Gallery 2294 NW 2nd Ave, Wynwood ℡305/576-0208, ⊛myspace.com/spinellogallery. Wunderkind gallerista Anthony Spinello was barely 22 when he first converted his apartment into a public art space in 2005: he just decamped to a larger, more traditional location giving more space to show his unorthodox roster of artists. Offbeat, but worth browsing.

Twenty Twenty Projects 2020 NW Miami Court, Wynwood ℡786/217-7683, ⊛www.twentytwentyprojects.com. Founder Scott Edward Murray trained with Kevin Bruk and Frederic Snitzer, before opening his experimental space in late 2006: he taps a rotating roster of guest curators, including local artist Daniel Arsham, to helm shows, mostly group bashes featuring emerging local talent.

Gifts and oddities

Britto Central 818 Lincoln Rd, South Beach ℡305/531-8821, ⊛www.britto.com. Local artist Romero Britto paints colorful, cartoonish images on everything from ties to handbags, available at this store/gallery. There's something sweet, trashy, and deliciously Miami about his work.

🏃 **KidRobot** 630 Collins Ave, South Beach ℡305/673-5807, ⊛www.kidrobot.com. Boys' toys boutique, selling their own brand of apparel – mostly graphic tees and hoodies with a Japanese edge – as well as ironic desktop action figures that look like manga cartoons come to life. Best known for its plastic Munny figurine, sold blank so you can customize it with pens and paints at home.

Me & Ro Inside the Shore Club, 1901 Collins Ave, South Beach ℡305/672-3566, ⊛www.meandrojewelry.com. Famous as Julia Roberts' favorite jeweler, this pair of New Yorkers (Robin and Michelle – hence the name) churn out high-priced, vaguely ethnic baubles, often featuring small, bead-like clusters of semi-precious stones – big rings, jangly bracelets, and necklaces.

Miami Ink/305 Ink 1344 Washington Ave, South Beach ☎305/531-4556. Fans of Ami James and Chris Nuñez's tattoo-based reality show can come to this parlor for a permanent take-home souvenir: the artists featured on the show are usually booked, but walk-in work by the rest of the staff is welcome. Expect a line, and try to come early – it's open 7pm–midnight weekdays, and noon–midnight weekends.

Pop 1151 Washington Ave, South Beach ☎305/604-9604, ⊛www.popsouthbeach.com. An eclectic mix of toys, greeting cards, and a few clothes, all chosen with the same wacky sense of style and humor. Pop is a great place for unusual gifts – check out the bootleg CDs from local circuit parties, as well as pristine 1980s memorabilia.

The Seybold Building 36 NE 1st St, Downtown ☎305/374-7922. Miami's diamond merchants are all housed in this one building in the heart of Downtown: here, more than 300 different jewelers, selling everything from simple gems to glitzy watches, are crammed together in one space. Not many obvious bargains, but it's well worth haggling.

Sex&... 743 Washington Ave, South Beach ☎305/604-0119. The mirror-heavy black-walled décor creates a fittingly decadent setting for this upscale raunch store. Members only (pay the $100 annual fee and gain fingerprint-recognition entry), it has 11 different rooms, decked out with glitzy chandeliers and custom chairs, and each assigned to one specialty, from lingerie to evening gowns or luxury gifts. It also runs 'Sex Academy' sessions for seduction training, like striptease and pole dancing lessons.

Toy Town 260 Crandon Blvd, Key Biscayne ☎305/361-5501. Forget Toys'R'Us and F.A.O. Schwarz – this is a traditional, family-owned toy store that's the best in the city. It sells simple, nostalgic toys like train sets, board games, and stuffed animals, perhaps as novel to today's kids as it is familiar to their parents.

Health and beauty

Brownes & Co. Apothecary 841 Lincoln Rd, South Beach ☎305/538-7544, ⊛www.brownesbeauty.com. Stock up on sumptuous skincare lines like Fresh, as well as top-name make-up brands here. The Some Like It Hot salon (☎305/538-7544) upstairs is renowned for great, if pricey, manicures.

Kiehl's 832 Lincoln Rd, South Beach ☎305/531-0404. The Miami outpost of the once-cultish Manhattan skincare range. Make sure to ask for free samples – Kiehl's is known for its generosity with testers.

Ricky's NYC 536 Lincoln Rd ☎305/674-8150, ⊛www.rickys-nyc.com. Saucy, sexy drugstore from New York, that stocks any and every lotion or potion possible, as well as wigs, feather boas, and drag-queen-worthy cosmetics. There's a campy salon at the rear called, naturally, The Birdcage. Upstairs, discreetly stashed behind a bead curtain, is an Adults Only room with sex toys and a wall full of condoms.

Russian & Turkish Bath Castle Hotel, 5445 Collins Ave, Miami Beach ☎305/867-8313. The facilities here are a little less lush than at other spas, but it's a place utterly devoid of attitude; there's a gym, steam rooms, and a salt-water Jacuzzi. $23 for a day-pass.

Housewares

The main **housewares** drag is along 40th Street in the Design District, although you'll find as much furniture as ornaments on this and the surrounding blocks. If you do fall in love with something large, most stores will be happy to ship it to you anywhere in the world – at a price, of course.

Holly Hunt 3833 NE 2nd Ave, Design District ☎305/571-2012, ⊛www.hollyhunt.com. Beyond chic, this showcase for multiple homeware lines is the last word in classic design. There's little that's daring or avant-garde (and definitely no bargains), but it's a sumptuous space with luxurious furniture – great for browsing.

Jonathan Adler 1024 Lincoln Rd, South Beach ☎305/534-5600, ⊛www.jonathanadler.com. New York–based potter Adler is known for his chic, understated homewares – expanding from simple vases in muted tones like beige and cream to soft goods and rugs in geometric patterns. Pricey, but luscious.

Marimekko 1671 Meridian Ave, South Beach ☎305/496-0449, ⊛www.marimekkomiami.com. An entire store devoted to the Scandinavian brand known for its dayglo prints of poppies and flowers: the chirpy range includes Marimekko-branded and -printed shirts, trays and homewares plus quirkier treats like slippers and disposable coasters.

Museum stores

There's little imaginative buying at most **museum gift shops**, but those listed below are fun enough places to browse.

Art Deco Welcome Center 1001 Ocean Drive, South Beach ℡305/672-2014, ⓦwww.mdpl. org. This lobby store is a treasure trove of offbeat trinkets, from unique embossed metal postcards to a wide range of gifts and books on all things Deco.

Miami Art Museum Gift Shop Metro-Dade Cultural Center, 101 W Flagler St, Downtown ℡305/375-1700, ⓦwww.miamiartmuseum.org. Superb Downtown gift shop with a funky edge. Alongside the usual books and artsy cards, you'll find design-conscious housewares at better prices than in most rarefied museum stores.

Music

For dance and club **music** in the city, there's nowhere to beat the stores on South Beach. If your taste is a little more eclectic, there are superb no-name closet-sized stores in Little Havana and Little Haiti that sell rare or hard to find Caribbean and Latin American music.

Casino Records 2290 SW 8th Street, Little Havana ℡305/642-7522, ⓦwww. casinorecordsmiami.com. The city's best spot for browsing any Latin music, whether it's obscure salsa or Gloria Estefan's latest album. The staff at the surprisingly large, decades-old outlet speaks English as well as Spanish, though the website is monolingual in the latter.

Do-Re-Mi Music Center 1829 SW 8th St, Little Havana ℡305/541-3374. Come here for astonishingly wide selections of Latin music from merengue and salsa to modern pop, including an encyclopedic assortment of obscure Spanish-language artists.

Grooveman Music 1543 Washington Ave, South Beach ℡305/535-6257, ⓦwww.groovemanmusic .com. A DJ's dream, this store stocks underground house and trance – kept dark during the day and night, the place throbs with loud music and is usually packed with local club kids.

Uncle Sam's Musiccafe 1141 Washington Ave, South Beach ℡305/532-0973, ⓦwww.uncle samsmusic.com. Standard record store with an ample selection of popular music, as well as a secondhand section, posters for sale, and mountains of flyers and freesheets – a good place to check out what's happening music-wise in the next few weeks around the city. The weird name owes itself to an attached café that's since closed.

18

Sports, fitness, and ocean activities

Miami's climate makes it ideally suited to most outdoor **sports**, and there's plenty on offer, whether you want to stay fit by playing or just lounge around and watch. The city hosts franchises from three major professional sports – football's Miami Dolphins have been around the longest and been the most consistently successful, while the Miami Heat draw the hoops crowd and the Florida Marlins the baseball fans. College football is fanatically followed, thanks to the past success of the University of Miami Hurricanes; college basketball and baseball less so. In addition, Miami hosts top-name tennis and golf tournaments on its numerous, quality, facilities, probably best in Key Biscayne – and most greens and courts are open to the public.

For those who don't just like to watch, biking is popular, as is rollerblading, the patron sport of South Beach. In addition, many people casually fish off the jetties at the beach; a better, though pricey, option is a charter deep-sea fishing trip. There are also plenty of shops that run diving and snorkeling outings but, other than the coral reef in Biscayne National Park, the best regional diving spots are dotted along the Keys less than two hours away.

An authentic local experience is to watch (or even attempt) a game of jai alai, a fast, frenzied sport that arrived in Miami from Spain via Cuba. Alternatively, take in a day at the greyhound track, undeniably an experience.

Baseball

One of the youngest teams in Major League Baseball, the **Florida Marlins** played their first season in 1993 and, incredibly, managed to win two World Series in their first decade of play (1997 and 2003). After both wins, however, the team's top stars were sold off almost immediately, alienating an already dwindling fan base. Attendance for games remains low, and due in large part to the perception of negligent ownership there is little passion in the region for the squad.

The baseball season runs April to early October, and ticket prices range from $29 to $108. For now, the Marlins play at Dolphin Stadium, at 2269 Dan Marino Blvd, sixteen miles northwest of Downtown Miami on the Dade-Broward county lines (information ☏305/623-6100 or 1-877/MARLINS, tickets ☏305/350-5050, Ⓦwww.flamarlins.com). Tickets can also be bought in person from the satellite ticket office at 3701 SW 8th Street, Coral Gables (Mon–Fri 9am–5pm).

187

SPORTS, FITNESS, AND OCEAN ACTIVITIES

The college team, the University of Miami **Hurricanes**, has won a number of championships, too, and produced some top pros; games are on the UM Campus at Mark Light Stadium, 6201 San Amaro Drive in Coral Gables (tickets $8; ☎1-800/GO-CANES)

Basketball

Founded in 1988, the NBA's relatively new **Miami Heat** have been defined in large part by larger-than-life coach/general manager Pat Riley, who joined the team in 1995 and stuck around until 2008. While the team failed to win a championship with him at the helm his first go around as coach, as general manager Riley engineered the addition of one of the sport's biggest stars, Shaquille O'Neal, in 2004. The team prospects were immediately improved, its local profile – and the fan hysteria – raised meteorically with the addition of rising superstar Dwayne Wade. With Riley back as head coach, the Heat won the NBA Championship in 2006.

To see Wade – both O'Neal and Riley are no longer with the team – in action, the regular season runs from October to April. Ticket prices start at $30 and can reach $200–350. The Heat play at the American Airlines Arena, 601 Biscayne Blvd, Downtown – call ☎786/777-4328 for tickets, or visit ⓦwww.nba.com/heat.

College basketball is also popular in Miami, and the UM **Hurricanes** attract a good following, if one less fanatical than their football team. They play in the most competitive conference in the nation, so go as much to see the opponents' skills as to root on the locals. The hoops season runs from November to March at the BankUnited Center on the UM Campus, 1234 Dauer Drive, Coral Gables (☎305/284-2263, ⓦwww.hurricanesports.com).

Beaches and swimming

Most of the notable **beaches** and **swim spots** are, of course, on Miami Beach. **Surfers** will find the best waves off South Pointe at the end of South Beach, where there's a handy pier and jetty (daily 24hr; ☎305/673-7730), but for more of a seafront scene, head to Lummus Park between 6th and 14th streets (daily 24hr). It's the best known of all the city's beaches, with full facilities and a **gay section** around 12th Street. Further up Miami Beach, Haulover Park – notorious as a **nudist enclave** – actually has the most appealing sands of all, not to mention full facilities and several **volleyball courts** (daily sunrise to sunset; ☎305/944-3040). Continuing north, the beaches in Sunny Isles may look lavish and wide – it's cosmetic, as much of the sand was pumped from the sea floor – but thanks to vicious undertow and currents, swimming can be tricky and dangerous here (☎305/947-0606).

For **families**, head to 3rd Street on Miami Beach, where there are lifeguards, restrooms, picnic tables, and showers. Another family-friendly spot is on Key Biscayne: Crandon Park at the northern end of the island has more than three miles of sand, but even so can be packed with people at weekends (daily 8am–sunset; $5 per car; ☎305/361-5421, ⓦwww.miamidade.gov/parks/parks/crandon_beach.asp).

The other noteworthy beach nearby is Virginia Key Beach, where blacks were banished in times of segregation and which still retains its popularity among the local African-American community (daily 8am–sunset; free parking; ☎305/575-5256, ⓦwww.virginiakeybeachpark.net).

▲ Beach volleyball

A terrific, if landlocked, option for a day in the water is the artfully landscaped **Venetian Pool** in Coral Gables – see p.103 for details. For a professional-quality pool, head to Fort Lauderdale's International Swimming Hall of Fame (see p.210).

Biking and rollerblading

Downtown Miami is configured only for the bravest of **bikers** – there are few cycle lanes, and the slipknot of freeways that crisscross the city make it even tougher on two wheels. A bike is a good option, though, in South Beach, where car parking is both pricey and congested; even better are the cycle routes in Coconut Grove (a fourteen-mile path down to South Miami) and Key Biscayne, which is especially worthwhile: not only are the parks beautiful, but scant public transport makes getting around any other way almost impossible.

As for **rollerblading**, it's arguably Miami's signature sport: the payoff for days spent perfecting your body in the gym is a couple of hours cruising along the beach on a pair of blades. Don't be put off, though, even if you're a neophyte – rollerblading through South Beach's oceanfront parks is a glorious way to see the sight and is well worth the occasional tumble.

Rental and repair shops

Electric Rentals 2745 Collins Ave, South Beach ☏ 305/532-6700. Scooter rental is $50 for 24hrs; bikes cost $25 for 24hrs. Daily 11am–8pm.

Fritz's Skate, Bike & Surf 730 Lincoln Rd, South Beach ☏ 305/532-1954. Blades and bikes for $10/hr, $24/day. Daily 10am–10pm.

Mangrove Cycles 260 Crandon Blvd, in the Square Shopping Center, Key Biscayne ☏ 305/361-5555. Cycles at $15/2hrs, $20/ day. Tues–Sat 9am–6pm, Sun 10am–6pm, closed Monday.

Miami Beach Bicycle Center 601 5th St, South Beach ☏ 305/674-0150. Rates are $24/24hr. Mon–Sat 10am–7pm, Sun 10am–5pm.

SPORTS, FITNESS, AND OCEAN ACTIVITIES

Diving and snorkeling

Much is made of **diving** and **snorkeling** in Miami, and most hotels will offer some form of aquatic trips. However, locals agree that diving in Miami comes a far second to dive sites in the Keys like Looe Key or the more remote but spectacular Dry Tortugas (see p.244). The one exception is the reef at Biscayne National Park near Homestead, a massive underwater park with fantastic coral formations. When booking a trip, ask whether it's better for snorkelers or scuba divers – some trips may head out to deep waters, making observation from the surface difficult. The operators below are both reliable and arrange trips at reasonable rates.

Dive operators

South Beach Divers 850 Washington Ave, South Beach ☎305/531-6110 or 1-888/331-DIVE, ⓦwww.southbeachdivers.com.

Tarpoon Lagoon 300 Alton Rd at Miami Beach Marina, South Beach ☎305/532-1445, ⓦwww.tarpoondivecenter.com.

Fishing

Tearing into your own fresh catch for dinner is a satisfying experience, and plenty of anglers come to Miami for the **fishing** – although, as with underwater sports, the Keys are probably a better bet for variety and volume of fish (for details, see p.225)

If you've more money or less experience, a great option is a day out on a boat **deep-sea fishing**: expect to pay around $500–700 for a half-day, and $750–1000 for a full day of private charter, including bait, supervision, and fish-gutting. For confident anglers, there are public boats, which cost $40 and up for the ride only.

Boat operators

Mark the Shark Biscayne Bay Marriott Marina, Downtown ☎305/759-5297, ⓦwww.marktheshark.com.

Reward Fishing Fleet 300 Alton Rd at Miami Beach Marina, South Beach ☎305/372-9470, ⓦwww.fishingmiami.com.
Sonny Boy Sportfishing Key Biscayne Marina ☎305/361-2217, ⓦwww.sonnyboysportfishing.com.

Football

The Miami **Dolphins** have a storied past, closely associated with (now-retired) star Dan Marino, one of the league's all-time great quarterbacks, and ex-coach and local legend Don Shula, who led the team to the NFL's sole perfect season in 1972. Unfortunately, the team has not appeared in the Super Bowl since 1985.

The season runs from September to January, and ticket prices range from $29 to $108. The Dolphins play at Pro Player stadium when the Marlins are out of season – call ☎305/573-8326 for tickets, or visit ⓦwww.miamidolphins.com. Tickets can also be purchased in person at Gate F onsite at the stadium (Mon–Fri 8.30am–5:30pm, Sat 10am–2pm).

On the collegiate level, the UM **Hurricanes** had one of the top football programs in the country before falling onto hard times in recent years. Still, local devotion to them is as passionate as to the Dolphins. The regular season runs September through November, and ticket prices start at $15. The 'Canes, as they're known, have just decamped from their long-term historic home at the Orange

SPORTS, FITNESS, AND OCEAN ACTIVITIES

Bowl for the Marlins' long-term home of Dolphin Stadium at 2269 Dan Marino Blvd almost into Broward County (☏305/284-2263, ⓦwww.hurricanesports. com).

Golf

Miami's large enough and warm enough to mean that there are plenty of options for **golf** in and around the city. Greens fees vary widely – anything from $15 to $250 – as does the experience. Note that some of the places below are resorts or hotels, but nonguests/nonmembers can play too, usually for a higher fee than those staying there. An alternative option for less talented greens-goers is the new Back No.9 mini golf course, 7244 Biscayne Boulevard ($5 for adults, $3 for kids; ☏305/984-3231, ⓦwww.uppereastgarden.com) with its nine artist-designed mini holes.

Courses

Biltmore Golf Course 1210 Anastasia Ave, Coral Gables ☏305/460-5364, ⓦwww.biltmorehotel. com. Luxurious, historic course, with the prices to match, at $172 (Mon–Thurs) and $192 (Fri–Sun) including cart.
Crandon Park 6700 Crandon Blvd, Key Biscayne ☏305/361-9129. A top-ranking public course that's the site of the Royal Caribbean Classic. A round costs from $60 to $150.
Doral Golf Resort & Spa 4400 NW 87th Ave on the mainland ☏305/592-2030, ⓦwww.doral

golf.com. Lushest and best-known course in Miami (actually five courses on site), and home to the Ford Championship; $75 to $275 for 18 holes.
Normandy Shores Miami Beach, 401 Biarritz Drive at 71st St ☏305/868-6502, ⓦwww.geo cities.com/normandyshoresgc. Like the Bilt-more, quite a venerable course that's been recently spiffed up, with cost to match. $200.
Palmetto Golf Course 9300 SW 152nd St, South Miami ☏305/238-2922. The best choice for those on a budget, but out in the suburbs a bit. Fees $15–36.

Gyms

Miami has no shortage of **gyms** for South Beach body-toning, or just general fitness; the following all offer day-pass memberships for around $25 – remember to bring two forms of ID, including one with a photograph, and dress appropriately.

Crunch 1259 Washington Ave, South Beach ☏305/674-8222, ⓦwww.crunch.com. With a boxing ring, yoga studio, dance studio, large open gym and 90 or so classes a week, this is a terrific option.
David Barton Gym 1510 Bay Rd, 8th Floor, South Beach ☏305/674-5757 **and inside the Gansevoort South Hotel, 2377 Collins Ave,** ☏305/604-1000, ⓦwww.davidbartongym.com. The trendiest of all the local gyms – the brand new *Gansevoort Hotel* outpost is a celeb-heavy favorite.

Downtown Athletic Club 200 S Biscayne Blvd, 15th floor, Downtown ☏305/358-9988, ⓦwww. miamihealthfitness.com. Unfussy, no-non-sense spot with more than just weights – there's a climbing wall and basketball court onsite too.
The Standard 40 Island Ave, Belle Isle ☏305/673-1717, ⓦwww.standardhotel.com. *The Standard*'s wellness center is more New Age than pumping iron, but a $25 fee gets you a yoga class and all-day access to the onsite hammam, cedar sauna and soaking tubs.

Jai alai

Derived from the Basque game of *pelota*, **jai alai** (pronounced "high-uh-lie," meaning "merry festival" in Basque) arrived in Cuba from Spain late in the nineteenth century. It quickly made the leap across the water to Miami, and there are now more jai alai frontons (or courts) in Florida than anywhere else in the world. It's a brutal, breakneck sport: a bullet-hard ball ricochets around the court at speeds up to 150mph, and players try to catch it in a *cesta* (basically a lacrosse basket attached to a baseball mitt). Until a star player suffered an accident in the late 1960s, helmets weren't even mandatory, and each fifteen-minute match is a thrilling, if dangerous, spectacle. The Miami Jai Alai is where the pros play: it's located at 3500 NW 37th Ave, near the airport, where you can watch matches daily except Tuesday noon to 5pm and Friday, Saturday, and Monday 7pm to midnight. General admission is $1, reserved seating $2; ⊕305/633-6400.

Tennis

The climate in Miami suits **tennis** as much as it does golf, and there are plenty of public courts. Most of them operate on a first-come, first-served basis and charge only nominal fees – the list below is by no means exhaustive: for other options in different neighborhoods, contact the City of Miami Parks & Recreation Department (Mon–Fri 8am–5pm; ⊕305/416-1308, ⊛ www.ci.miami.fl.us) or the City of Miami Beach Parks & Recreation Department (Mon–Fri 8.30am–5pm; ⊕305/673-7730, ⊛ www.ci.miami-beach.fl.us).

One of Miami's major sporting draws, the **Sony Ericsson Open** (⊕305/446-2200, ⊛ www.sony-ericssontickets.com), in late March, attracts marquee players to the fifth largest tennis tournament in the world. It's held on Key Biscayne at the Crandon Park Tennis Center and tickets start at $50.

Courts and fees

Crandon Park 7300 Crandon Blvd on Key Biscayne ⊕305/365-2300. Wide range of surfaces: hard $3 per person/hr daytime, $5 per person/hr night, grass and clay $10 per person/hr.

Flamingo Park 1100 Jefferson Ave, South Beach ⊕305/673-7761. $8 per person/hr.

Haulover Park 10800 Collins Ave, Bal Harbour ⊕305/940-6719. More courts than Flamingo Park; $2.30 per person/hr.

Kids' Miami

lorida's one of the prime family vacation destinations in the US, thanks mostly to the flawless, if soulless, mecca of Orlando's Disney World, a four-hour drive away north along Florida's Turnpike. If you're looking for a more cosmopolitan experience in addition to the good weather, Miami's also a smart option. Not only is there a more varied choice of attractions from art museums to animal sanctuaries, but there are also dozens of sandy and clean seaside beaches.

After its club-hopping renaissance of the late 1980s, Miami recognized its beaches were a prime family draw and worked hard for several years to market itself as a family-friendly destination. Its aggressive advertising highlighted those clean sandy stretches and modern hotels. Though the city's tourism tactics may have shifted back in recent years – emphasizing once more the city's chic sexiness – Miami's still a city that caters well to kids and adults alike. Indeed, newer attractions like the Children's Museum mean it's luring more families than ever. We've highlighted below the best museums and activities for kids of all ages, as well as suggested the best beaches and hotels for families.

The weather's one of the most appealing aspects, though make sure to slather little ones in **sunscreen**, especially during the winter high season when the sunshine's relentless. The fact that you can walk, rather than drive, around South Beach is also appealing: kids don't have to be cooped up in the car all day to enjoy themselves, and there are plenty of cafés close to the beach for quick snack breaks. Other than the swankiest five-star eateries, most restaurants in town will either offer a children's menu or be more than happy to cater to kids.

Nevertheless, if you do want to leave the kids behind for an evening out, **babysitting** can be arranged through Nanny Poppinz Child Care Services (T 1-877/262-6694, W www.nannypoppinz.com), or ask at your hotel – most of the larger ones in the city have an extensive list of qualified, on-call sitters.

Family-friendly accommodation

Most of the boutique hotels in **South Beach** are geared to young singles or couples, with few nods to families; rooms are often so small that extra beds aren't possible. Better, in fact, to stay further up in **Middle Beach**: even after its glitzy Vegas makeover, the enormous *Fontainebleau* (see p.137) has kid-friendly amenities and sits smack on the beach. Otherwise, many families opt to stay on **Key Biscayne**. It's a smart move: the Seaquarium's close by, there are ample beaches, and most of the hotels can easily cater to kids.

One caveat: don't be tempted to stay in **Sunny Isles Beach**, despite the family-friendly packages at its new crop of towering luxury hotels. The trip to any attraction's a long haul, and the treacherous undertows in the sea make it risky for little ones.

Museums, aquariums, and zoos

The **Children's Museum** on Watson Island is the most obvious family-focused attraction: the exhibits here are jazzy and interactive, including a "design your own money" station and a play hospital. Note, though, that they're firmly geared toward pre-schoolers, and the relentless corporate branding may be off-putting to some parents. Parents of older kids might prefer to head across the street to **Jungle Island**: it's a safe place to let them explore solo, and the ornery, idiosyncratic birds will entertain for hours. See pp.64–66 for more info on both attractions.

Elsewhere in the city, the **Museum of Science and Planetarium** in Coconut Grove is amusing, if a little old-fashioned, and better for older children; when it moves to its new Downtown site (no earlier than 2012, and likely later; see p.115), expect radical improvements. The **Historical Museum of South Florida** has several interactive exhibits, including dress-up boxes with period clothes, all designed to bring the area's history to easily digestible life. Key Biscayne is home to the **Miami Seaquarium**, which showcases performing sea creatures, like Lola the acrobatic killer whale, with a thumping dance-music soundtrack. In fact, the most appealing parts of the seaquarium are its conservation efforts – kids of all ages will be captivated by the rangers' chats on the endangered manatee (see p.117).

Heading south of the city brings you to the **Miami Metrozoo** and **Monkey Jungle** (see p.123 and p.124). The zoo's well designed, with its humane enclosures and informative plaques that detail each species' survival status (those endangered are highlighted); children hoping for opportunities to feed the animals (albeit behind cage bars) will find Monkey Jungle unmissable. Another possible pitstop is **Pinecrest Gardens**, the former home of the aviary now known as Jungle Island: when the tenants decamped, the site was left intact and is now run as a free park by the local city council – there's a huge kids' playground and lots of trails and lawns for energy-burning running-around (see p.122)

Activities

⑲

KIDS' MIAMI

If you're in town on the second Saturday of the month, head to Downtown's **Miami Art Museum** (see p.41). It boasts a stunning collection for adults, but even better, from 1 to 4pm, entrance is free for families, and the museum hosts storytellers, guides, and art programs for younger kids under 7. Older children might better enjoy the **Lowe Art Museum** in Coral Gables (see p.106): two or three times a month, there are Art Adventures, docent-led introductory tours on Saturday or Sunday at 2pm. These aren't specifically aimed at children, but they're usually immensely accessible and great fun.

Don't miss the chance to catch a performance at the **Actors' Playhouse**; its Theater for Young Audiences series ($15), usually on Saturdays at 2pm, features shows ranging from traditional fairytales to modern work, but all are smart, engaging, and thoroughly satisfying (see p.168).

The **Venetian Pool** in Coral Gables (see p.103) is a dazzling place to dawdle for an afternoon: there are full-time lifeguards, a small artificial beach-cum-sand-pit and plenty of nooks and crannies in the landscaped lagoon. The only downside is that children under 3 are not permitted.

A killer new addition to the family circuit is the campy mini golf course **Back No.9** (see p.86): the $5 adult entry includes a free piña colada, while the booze-free kid price is $3. It's a fun but cultural afternoon, knocking balls around a course designed by a clutch of emerging local artists.

As for **tours**, most in the city are rather heavy going for anyone with a limited attention span, children or otherwise: the best option is one of the **Miami Cultural Tours** (see p.25) which focus as much on sense of place – stopping and tasting Haitian food, for instance – as on history.

Beaches

The best place for families on **Miami Beach** is the sands around 3rd Street: there are lifeguards, restrooms, picnic tables, and showers. The beach at **Bal Harbour** provides few facilities and frankly isn't that appealing; its one draw is that its sands are packed with shells, so it's the best place to spend an afternoon looking for take-home treasures.

Over on Key Biscayne, you'll find the city's de facto family beach: **Crandon Park**. In addition to the standard amenities, there are changing facilities, outdoor grills, soccer and softball courts, and more than three miles of seafront. It can get a little busy at weekends, but during the week is an ideal place for kids (see p.118). The marina at **Matheson Hammock Park** in South Miami encloses a man-made lagoon that flushes naturally with the tides of Biscayne Bay and is popular with young children (see p.121).

Festivals

Many of Miami's high-profile events are decidedly adult affairs, but there are some that not only welcome but cater to the entire family.

In winter, head over to the **Coral Gables Farmers Market** (Jan–March Sat 8am–1pm; ☎305/460-5311), where, in addition to the produce on sale, there's a range of kids' activities, usually including face painting and storytelling. Then there's the **Carnaval Miami** in early March (☎305/644-8888, Ⓦ www.carnaval-miami.com), when Little Havana's Calle Ocho is transformed into a riot of color, noise, and cooking smells, all celebrating Cuban heritage – it's a terrific way to introduce little ones to Miami's Latin influence.

A short drive from Miami proper, the surreal and splashy **Great Sunrise Balloon Race** in May (☎305/596-9040, Ⓦ www.sunrisegroup.org) is held at Kendall-Tamiami airport. Spectators are welcome to watch dozens of hot-air balloons as they compete for charity. Bookish kids will enjoy the **Harvest Festival** on the weekend before Thanksgiving (☎305/375-1492, Ⓦ www.hmsf.org). It's overseen by the Historical Museum Downtown and celebrates South Florida's heritage – there are activities, stalls, and even historical re-enactments.

Festivals and events

M iami is always looking for an excuse to party, and plenty of **festivals and events** cater to that need throughout the year. The greatest number of events take place during peak season, from January through April; the only time when there's little, if anything, on offer is during the sticky summer months of July and August. When it comes to accommodation scarcity and price hikes, there are three major events to anticipate: the Boat Show in February, the Winter Music Conference in March, and Art Basel Miami Beach in December.

The list below is by no means comprehensive, but includes a range of widely different activities – for detailed information, call the phone numbers listed or check the websites. Otherwise, contact the Greater Miami Convention and Visitors Bureau, 701 Brickell Ave (Mon–Fri 8.30am–6pm; ☎305/539-3000, ⊛www.gmcvb.com). Another option is to check the usual freesheets like *New Times*, for listings and events; there's also a handy, if unofficial, guide at ⊛www.festivalsmiami.com or call the Greater Miami Festivals & Events Association at ☎305/651-9404.

January

Three Kings Day Parade Early January ☎305/447-1140. This celebration of the Three Wise Men is one of the biggest Latin events in the country, with crowds of up to half a million. It all takes place along Calle Ocho between 4th and 27th avenues.

Martin Luther King Day Parade January 16 ☎305/635-4454. A march through Liberty City commemorating the slain civil rights leader; there's a fair with music, stalls, and food in the MLK Memorial Park, at 61st and NW 32nd Court.

Scottish Festival and Games Mid-January ☎954/460-5000, ⊛www.sassf.org. This festival includes country dancing and an evening ceilidh, as well as Scottish pipe bands and Highland food. It takes place at various sites around South Florida, often in the nearby towns of Pembroke Pines or Fort Lauderdale satellite suburb Coral Springs. Entrance fee is $15.

Art Deco Weekend Third weekend in January ☎305/672-2014, ⊛www.artdecoweekend.com. Ocean Drive is completely taken over with booths and bands for this celebration of all things Deco. As part of the festival, the Miami Design Preservation League (⊛www.mdpl.prg) arranges tours of the historic district.

Taste of the Grove Late January ☎305/461-5506, ⊛www.coconutgrove.com. Coconut Grove's lively restaurants join together to stage this event in Peacock Park, each with a booth that offers samples from their menus. There's also live music.

Homestead Championship Rodeo Late January ☎305/245-2935, ⊛www.homesteadrodeo.com. Here you can see professional rodeo cowboys competing in steer-wrestling, bull-riding, calf-roping, and bareback-riding competitions. Tickets cost $15, $12 in advance.

Miami International Film Festival Late January to early February ℡305/237-3456, Ⓦwww.miamifilmfestival.com. Run by Florida International University, this festival includes arthouse and mainstream films from the USA and abroad, especially Cuba. Films are shown in three locations – the Colony Theater and the Regal Cinema on South Beach, and the Gusman Center in Downtown.

February

Miami International Boat Show Mid-February ℡954/441-3220, Ⓦwww.miamiboatshow.com. A massive luxury exhibition at the Miami Beach Convention Center showcasing top-range boats for potential buyers from around the world – a great place to gawp at local million-dollar lifestyle essentials. Tickets $16–30.

Coconut Grove Arts Festival Mid-February ℡305/447-0401, Ⓦwww.coconutgroveartsfest.com. Fittingly eccentric for Coconut Grove, you're as likely here to find alternative crafts – such as talking mirrors – as you are traditional painting; a lively, fun festival.

March

Toyota Indy 300 Early March ℡305/230-5000 for information or 305/409-RACE for tickets, Ⓦwww.homesteadmiamispeedway.com. The season opener for the Indy Racing League, the Toyota Indy 300 – better known as the Miami Grand Prix – takes place at the Homestead track, south of Miami. Tickets cost $25–45.

Carnaval Miami Early March ℡305/644-8888, Ⓦwww.carnavalmiami.com. This nine-day celebration of Latin culture, held across the city, culminates in a parade at the Orange Bowl Stadium, while a Little Havana off-shoot showcases Cuban arts, crafts, and cooking along Calle Ocho.

Asian Arts Festival Early March ℡305/247-5727. This festival at the Fruit and Spice Park (see p.124) features Asian crafts, cuisine, and martial arts, as well as fashion shows and acrobatic displays.

Key Biscayne Art Festival Mid-March ℡305/361-6016, Ⓦwww.key-biscayne.com. Crandon Boulevard hosts a small but fun party where more than 100 local artists display and sell works in every medium, from acrylic and oil to folk crafts and stained glass.

Winter Music Conference Late March ℡954/563-4444, Ⓦwww.wmcon.com. Producers, managers, and promoters convene at the Miami Beach Conference Center for one of the highlights of the electronic music industry's year. Performances at South Beach clubs by scores of top-name DJs draw a huge crowd, and hotel space is often tight.

▼ Carnaval Miami

FESTIVALS AND EVENTS

April

FedEx Polo World Cup Mid-April ⓦwww.miamipolo.com. On the sand between 20th and 22nd streets outside the *Setai* hotel in Miami Beach, the glitziest players of the Sport of Kings gather for its fiercest contest. Expect a champagne swilling, socialite-heavy crowd clad in Gucci and flown in private jet from Argentina and Brazil, instead of the more staid, Lily Pulitzer-draped regulars at the winter matches further up the coast.

The Great Sunrise Balloon Race Mid-April ☎305/596-9040, ⓦwww.sunriseballoonrace.org. A surreal and spectacular race, where dozens of brightly colored balloons compete for charity at Kendall-Tamiami airport.

Miami Gay and Lesbian Film Festival Late April ☎305/534-9924, ⓦwww.mglff.com. Overseen by the director of the classic gay documentary *Beyond Stonewall*, this festival usually takes place at the Colony Theater in South Beach, and features amateur as well as professional submissions.

May

Hip-Hop Weekend Memorial Day weekend. Recent years have seen an unofficial Hip-Hop Festival held on South Beach during Memorial Day weekend – expect plenty of makeshift clubs, big-name DJs, and personal appearances by a handful of well-known performers.

June

Goombay Festival Early June ☎800/891-7811, ⓦwww.goodmbayfestivalcoconutgrove.com. This celebration of Bahamian culture takes over Peacock Park in Coconut Grove with colorful stalls and music.

Tropical Agriculture Fiesta Mid-June ☎305/247-5727, ⓦwww.tropicalag.org. A chance to sample dozens of different varieties of mango, as well as other exotic fruits at the Fruit and Spice Park (see p.124).

July

International Hispanic Theater Festival July ☎305/445-8877, ⓦwww.teatroavante.com. Held at The Miracle Theater in Coral Gables, this festival marks Hispanic achievement in the theater arts with performances by companies from around the world.

America's Birthday Bash July 4 ☎305/358-7550, ⓦwww.bayfrontparkmiami.com. Independence Day features fireworks and a laser show, with a three-stage music concert at Bayfront Park. The *Biltmore* hotel in Coral Gables also hosts a July 4th celebration, which is pricey but spectacular.

September

International Ballet Festival of Miami Early September ☎305/549-7711, ⓦwww.miamihispanicballet.com. Ballet's big stars come to town for a two-week-long program that is spread among the Colony and Jackie Gleason theaters in South Beach, and the Manuel Artime Theater in Little Havana. It's overseen by the Miami Hispanic Ballet, so expect a strong Latin American slant.

Festival Miami Mid-September to mid-November ☎305/284-2438, ⓦwww.music.miami.edu. The University of Miami sponsors this festival, with almost two months of mostly classical concerts in and around Coral Gables.

October

Columbus Day Regatta Early October ⓦwww.columbusdayregatta.net. Held on the weekend nearest Columbus Day, this two-day race begins at Dinner Key Marina in Coconut Grove and heads out to Elliott Key in Biscayne National Park.

Sportsman Fishing Show Mid-October ⓣ813/839-7696, ⓦwww.floridasportsman.com/shows/miami. Held in the Dade County Fairgrounds, this show features nearly everything to do with angling, from cat-netting

and fly-casting demonstrations to actual fishing seminars. Entrance fee for visitors is $8.

Lincoln Road Halloween October 31. Although there's little officially organized for Halloween in the city, the place to see the wildest costumes (and most outrageous behavior) in Miami is along Lincoln Road on South Beach. Grab a spot at one of the outdoor cafés and watch the impromptu parade.

November

Miami Book Fair International Early November ⓣ305/237-3258, ⓦwww.miamibookfair.com. Enormous fair attracting every publisher you could name to set up stalls for the weekend on the campus of Miami-Dade Community College in Downtown.

Harvest Festival Weekend before Thanksgiving ⓣ305/375-1492, ⓦwww.hmsf.org. Organized by the Historical Museum, this festival celebrates the agricultural traditions of South Florida. There are stalls, quilting demonstrations, and even historical re-enactments at the Dade County Fairgrounds in West Dade.

The White Party Late November ⓣ305/673-5282, ⓦwww.whiteparty.net. Centered on South Beach, this is one of the largest HIV/AIDS fundraisers in America – a largely gay, six-day extravaganza of clubbing and cocktail parties where white clothing is de rigueur. It peaks with the decadent ball at Villa Vizcaya, where the white costumes are almost all elaborate, skimpy affairs. Tickets for events start at $20, while tickets for the ball start at around $150.

December

Art Basel Miami Beach Early December ⓣ305/674-1292, ⓦwww.artbasel.com/Miami_beach. The pre-eminent modern art dealers of the world descend on Miami's Convention Center to hawk their clients – the quality's spectacular, though prices are high. For more affordable alternatives, hit satellite fairs like PULSE (ⓦwww.pulse-art.com) or cheapest of all, NADA (ⓦwww.newartdealers.org). There's also an emerging parallel design exhibition over in the Design District (check ⓦwww.designmiami.com for more info).

Art Miami December ⓣ305/573-1388 or 1-866/727-7953, ⓦwww.art-miami.com. Thanks to Miami's vibrant art scene, this massive

exhibition at the Wynwood Art District often showcases interesting and innovative work by local artists; entrance fee is $15.

Indian Arts Festival Late December ⓣ305/522-8365, ⓦwww.miccosukeeresort.com. The Miccosukee Village in the Everglades plays host to Native American artists from across America who come to show and sell their work. Tickets cost $10.

King Mango Strut Late December ⓣ305/401-1171, ⓦwww.kingmangostrut.org. Begun twenty years ago by a rejected would-be marcher in the Orange Bowl Parade, the Strut is a campy parade through Coconut Grove, whose participants take aim at topical events with their bizarre costumes.

FESTIVALS AND EVENTS

South Florida

South Florida

21

Fort Lauderdale

fter a long beach-party hangover, **Fort Lauderdale**, just forty minutes drive north from Downtown Miami, is slowly developing a distinctive, more sophisticated atmosphere. Its Historic District along the waterfront downtown, centered around some pioneer homes, has been aggressively revived; while the mod and modish mid-Century houses and condo towers by the beach have been gussied up, largely by the city's influx of gays. Admittedly, despite constant predictions, Fort Lauderdale has yet to swipe Miami's cachet as the coolest city in South Florida. However, it's notable that the St Regis chain chose here, rather than Miami Beach, for its first hotel in the area; more megabuck waterfront hotels, from Donald Trump and Starwood, are on the way and should raise both the city's profile and, less happily, its room rates.

It's a far cry from Fort Lauderdale's former reputation as the site of what seemed like the whole of America's college **spring break**; or indeed its origins, when the settlement began as a military fortification against a Seminole Indian attack (the commanding officer was a Major William Lauderdale). By the end of the nineteenth century, Lauderdale's one-time fort had grown into a thriving trading post; but it wasn't until the 1930s, when swimming teams began coming here for meets, that the town's hard-partying reputation was born. That legend was cemented by the 1960 film *Where the Boys Are*, starring Paula Prentiss and a young George Hamilton (see p.271, "South Florida on Film")

That movie made Fort Lauderdale synonymous with college students' spring break for more than twenty years until the mid-1980s, when numbers grew so unmanageable that the local council wrote to universities across the country expressly asking them to dissuade students from coming on vacation. This anti-student initiative, coupled with the aggressive upgrading of beach facilities, proved effective by the late 1990s and helped Fort Lauderdale slough off its somewhat tawdry image.

Now, as Miami grows more popular, trend-chasers and bargain-minded gays attracted by the potential of Fort Lauderdale's mid-Century homes are scoping out the city. The swanky restaurants here are also a little cheaper and less intimidating than their sister spots down the coast. A further draw in comparison with Miami is Fort Lauderdale's laid-back vibe – think board shorts and flip-flops instead of heels and a thong.

▲ ❶, ❷ &❸ ▲ Wilton Manors ▲ ❹, ❺ &❻ ▲ ❼, ❽, ❾, ❿, Ⓐ, Ⓑ & Pompano Beach ▲

FORT LAUDERDALE

0   400 yds

ACCOMMODATION		EATING		The Four Rivers	12	DRINKING & NIGHTLIFE	
Backpacker Beach	Pineapple Point	Blue Moon	8	Galanga	5	Blue Martini	15	Elbo Room	18
Hostel	E Guesthouse E	Café Martorano	7	Kilwin's	17	Boom	2	Georgie's	
Green Island Inn B	The Riverside	Canyon		Kitchenetta	4	Cero	G	Alibi	3
Orton Terrace D	Hotel H	Southwest Café	14	La Spada's	10	The Copa	13	Kalahari Bar	6
Pier 66 I	The Royal Palms C	Dogma Grill	20	Sublime	11	Coyote Ugly	16	Sidelines	1
The Pillars F	St Regis G	The Floridian	19	Tarpon Bend	16	Dude's	9		

Arrival, information, and getting around

Fort Lauderdale–Hollywood International Airport (FLL) is becoming an increasingly popular choice for access to both Fort Lauderdale and Miami, thanks both to the hellish disorganization at MIA and this airport's popularity with budget domestic carriers like JetBlue and Spirit Airlines (☎954/359-1200, ⓦwww.broward.org/airport/). There are ample car rental desks on site and plenty of cabs; expect to pay $12 one-way to the beach.

All the long-distance public-transport terminals are in or near downtown: the Greyhound **bus station** is at 515 NE 3rd St (☎954/764-6551), while the **train**

▲ Water taxi on the Intracoastal Waterway

and Tri-Rail station is two miles west at 200 SW 21st Terrace (Amtrak ☎1-800/USA-RAIL, ⓦwww.amtrak.com; Tri-Rail ☎1-800-TRI-RAIL, ⓦwww.tri-rail.com), linked to the center by the regular bus #22.

The downtown **Convention and Visitors Bureau** is at 100 E Broward Blvd at SE 1st Ave, Suite 200 (Mon–Fri 8.30am–5pm; ☎954/765-4466 or 1-800/22-SUNNY, ⓦwww.sunny.org). Otherwise, pick up a copy of the free *CityLink* magazine or *New Times* (available throughout the city) to find out what's going on.

The handiest service offered by the thorough **local bus** network (BCT ☎954/831-4000, ⓦwww.broward.org/bct) is the #11, which runs twice hourly along Las Olas Boulevard between downtown Fort Lauderdale and the beach; **timetables** are available from Governmental Center (at the corner of Andrews Avenue and Broward Boulevard), the bus terminal directly opposite, or from libraries and check-cashing centers. If you are using the buses, remember to buy an **All-Day Pass** ($3), which allows unlimited travel on the buses throughout Broward County – otherwise it's $1.25 a journey and there are no transfers. There's also a hop-on/hop-off **trolley service** (50¢) that loops through Himmarshee every day (Mon–Wed 7:30am–6pm, Thurs 7:30am–11pm, Fri 7:30am–11pm, Sat 10am–11pm).

More expensive than buses – but more fun – are the **water taxis** (daily 10:30am–midnight; ☎954/467-6677, ⓦwww.watertaxi.com); a series of small boats pick up and deliver passengers almost anywhere along Fort Lauderdale's many miles of intracoastal waterfront, from Broward up to Seventeenth Street Causeway. These taxis are without a doubt the best way to see the city, and an all-day pass, allowing unlimited usage, costs only $11 (single tickets are $9).

If you'd rather have a structured **water tour** of the city, try the riverboat cruise-cum-cabaret show on the campy but fun *Jungle Queen Riverboat*, moored at Seabreeze Boulevard at Hwy-A1A (daily 6pm; $35 including dinner; ☎954/462-5596, ⓦwww.junglequeen.com).

Accommodation

Accommodation prices in Fort Lauderdale tend to be reasonable year-round and you'll often get more for your money staying here than in Miami, especially in the motels or B&Bs that hug the interior of the Intracoastal Waterway like *The Pillars*. An exception, of course, is a room at one of the cluster of new luxury hotels rimming the seafront: already open at time of writing was the *St Regis* (see below) soon to be joined by a megalithic *W*, a Mandarin Oriental and a glitzy Trump-branded high rise.

Backpacker Beach Hostel 2115 N Ocean Blvd at NE 21st St, beachside ☎954/567-7275, ⓦ www.fortlauderdalehostel.com. This clean, friendly hostel has plenty of free pluses: parking, food (bread, tea, coffee, pasta), Internet access, laundry, and even pick-up from the airport, bus, or train station during the day. There's also a pleasant rooftop patio and no curfew. Dorm beds $20.

Green Island Inn 3300 NE 27th St at NE 33rd Ave, beachside ☎954/566-8951 or 1-888/505-8951. This charming, family-run inn features two dozen bright, homely rooms (each named after a different island in the Caribbean) and kitchenettes, set around a leafy garden. There's a small pool, and ample parking. $70.

Pier 66 2301 S.E. 17th Street, beachside t954/525-6666, ⓦ www.pier66.com. This beloved local landmark – the spike-topped tower and jagged balconies stand out on the skyline – has been recently upgraded, including a relandscaped pool area and made-over rooms in bland-but-tasteful all-beige (the closets are unusually huge). Rates are higher than before, but the $12 resort fee tacked on isn't the usual con – it includes free transfers to the beach (a 2-minute ride from its almost-on-the-causeway location), local/long distance calls, and WiFi. $220.

The Pillars 111 N Birch Rd at Sebastian St, beachside ☎954/467-9639, ⓦ www.pillarshotel.com. A former private house turned upscale B&B, this beach bolthole has 22 large, antique-crammed rooms, and a breakfast patio overlooking the Intracoastal Waterway. There's also a shady, tree-lined pool – ideal for an alfresco massage – and a water-taxi stop nearby. $265.

The Riverside Hotel 620 E Las Olas Blvd at 7th St, downtown ☎954/467-0671, ⓦ www.riversidehotel.com. The best option if you want to stay downtown, the *Riverside* is a historic inn with a 110-room modern addition. Suites in the 1992 addition may be larger, but the older building's much more charming – the rooms there are filled with raffia furniture and tropical-print, Tommy Bahama–style bedspreads. The main entrance and check-in is at the rear, close to the Stranahan House, rather than on Las Olas. $240.

St Regis Fort Lauderdale 1 North Fort Lauderdale Beach Boulevard, beachside ☎954/465-2300, ⓦ www.stregis.com/fortlauderdale. The white, airy interior of this exclusive chain resort is a nod to the Florida climate, from the soothing marble lobby to equally bright, huge rooms that include a sitting area and guest bath for maximum entertaining potential. Bonus points for its prime beachfront locale, endearing luxury touches like a chilled bottle of water from the valet when he hands over car keys, and the huge in-room bathtubs. $370.

The Town

The private yacht-clogged Intracoastal Waterway splits Fort Lauderdale roughly in half, between **downtown** and **beachside**. Each area has its own north–south artery: Hwy-1 (also known as the Federal Highway), which cuts through the center of the city; parallel to this along the beachfront is the drag known usually as Hwy-A1A (don't be confused by the various local designations it collects along the strip, like Fort Lauderdale Beach Boulevard or Ocean Boulevard). East–west, the handiest roads are Sunrise and Las Olas boulevards, both of which run the length of the city to the sea.

Downtown and the Historic District

Tall, anonymous, glass-fronted buildings may make an uninspiring first impression, but **downtown Fort Lauderdale** – a thin rectangle bounded by NW 7th Avenue to the west, NE 8th Avenue to the east, Broward Boulevard to the north, and Las Olas Boulevard to the south – has an outstanding modern art museum and a pleasant pedestrian area along Las Olas Boulevard where there are affordable shops and restaurants, mostly between the Federal Highway and NE 11th Avenue.

The Museum of Art

Fort Lauderdale's **Museum of Art** (Wed–Mon 11am–7pm; $10; ℡954/525-5500, Ⓦwww.moafl.org) is housed at 1 E Las Olas Blvd in a Post-modern building shaped like a slice of pie. It has one of the most impressive permanent collections in the state, and thanks to the work of executive director Irvin Lippman, it's begun attracting attention-grabbing temporary shows, among them art from the Vatican collection as well as commemorations of the likes of Princess Diana.

Year-round, it displays a rotating choice from its permanent collection, including household names like Andy Warhol, plus plenty more Pop Art. It's best known, though, for its exhaustive survey of work from the short-lived CoBrA movement of the early 1950s – the acronym derives from the three cities (Copenhagen, Brussels, and Amsterdam) where its artists were most active. With a desire to create without inhibitions, the CoBrA clique's Abstract Expressionism is marked by a focus on intense color, making their canvases an eye-popping, if acquired, taste; look for marquee names like Asger Jorn, Carl Henning-Pedersen, and Karel Appel.

Himmarshee

Millions were spent gussying up the oldest part of downtown into a new development known as **Riverwalk**, a shopping center and park complete with pedestrian walkways and waterfront cafés. At the end of the Riverwalk, at 401 SW 2nd St, is the creative, fun **Museum of Discovery and Science** (Mon–Sat 10am–5pm, Sun noon–6pm; $15 including admission to one IMAX film; ℡954/467-6637, Ⓦwww.mods.org). The interactive exhibits are engaging and educational for kids and tweens, including "Gizmo City" on the second floor, which explains the principles of physics through everyday machines; and the "Florida EcoScapes" exhibition near the atrium, which houses native Everglades critters such as fish and turtles, plus a huge living coral reef. There's also an **IMAX theater** on site that shows a rotating schedule of 3-D films; call for showtimes and current movies (℡954/463-4629).

The Riverwalk development, in which the museum sits, brackets two different areas: one is the Historic District (see below). The other, known variously as the **Performing Arts District** or **Himmarshee** (HIM-uh-shee), is the site of bars and restaurants that hum with people most Friday and Saturday nights. It's also where you'll find the only road tunnel in sodden Florida, scooped under downtown in 1960 to ease traffic congestion on the Federal Highway Bridge.

The Historic District

Fort Lauderdale's **Historic District** (℡954/463-4431, Ⓦwww.oldfortlauderdale.org) comprises a small collection of buildings located around SW 2nd Street and SW 3rd Avenue.

The city's first tourist hotel, the 1905 **New River Inn**, 231 SW 2nd Ave (Tues–Sat 10am–5pm, Sun noon–5pm; $7 self-guided visit, $10 guided visit), is now home to the Old Fort Lauderdale Museum of History. It showcases a varied collection of documents and artifacts on the city's history. The sports room is especially good, crammed with quirky ephemera, as is the video that shows clips from the dozens of movies – including *Porky's* and *Body Heat* – that were filmed or set locally. Next door, at 229 SW 2nd Ave, there's the **King-Cromartie House** (tours by appointment only Tues–Sat 10am–4:30pm, Sun noon–4:30pm), built in 1907 and housing an unremarkable museum of early settler life. The building itself, though, is more interesting: when contractor Edwin T. King built it, this home boasted then-astonishing amenities like indoor running water. Its design – it was originally a bungalow made with termite-resistant Dade County pine and a large, airy porch – set a template for other pioneers to follow. The **Hoch Heritage Center**, 219 SW 2nd Ave, is essentially a resource for amateur local historians, with extensive archives to trawl through; it's of little use or interest to the casual visitor (Tues–Fri 10am–4pm, Mon & Sat noon–4pm).

The Stranahan House

East from the Historic District stands a more complete reminder of early Fort Lauderdale life: the **Stranahan House** (Oct–May Wed–Sun 1–3pm, compulsory tours begin every 30 minutes; $12; ℡954/524-4736, ⓦwww.stranahanhouse .org), at 335 SE 6th Ave. With a lovingly restored interior that belies its unprepossessing exterior, this was the home of Frank Stranahan, so-called Father of Fort Lauderdale, who set up the first trading post with the Seminoles here and accrued substantial wealth. The Florida frontier-style house gives a good idea of what life was like for early settlers with money, crammed as it is with antique ephemera. Frank's life – along with that of his yoga-loving, eccentric wife, Ivy – is lovingly detailed by the knowledgeable and chatty docents. The wraparound porch, raised from the ground but open on all sides much like a *chickee* (Seminole hut), is where Native Americans would spend the night during trading expeditions to the area.

Beachside

The main route to the Fort Lauderdale **beaches** is Las Olas Boulevard, lined with shops and reasonably priced restaurants; the drive leads past the swanky residences of **the Isles**, spindly finger-shaped islets that allow its rich residents to park their boats at the end of the back garden. Once across the bridge that spans the Intracoastal Waterway, you've reached **beachside** Fort Lauderdale.

It may be less brash than it was in its spring-break heyday, but there are still plenty of theme restaurants and rowdy bars, especially around the unappealing shopping center known as **Beach Place**. As for the beach itself, it's hemmed in by swaying palm trees and a swirling white wall that's one of the city's signature sights (though the wall's broken, in-built strip of neon lighting is still awaiting funds for repair). It's usually easy to stake out a spot in the sun or rent a beach chair, and even better since the water here's been certified Blue Wave for its cleanliness and safety; if the crowds are heavy head south – the beach widens in that direction. There are facilities dotted along the stretch of sand: showers at the end of Las Olas Boulevard, and restrooms plus picnic tables a little further north at the end of Sunrise.

▲ Lifeguard hut on Fort Lauderdale's beach

The Bonnet House

The **Bonnet House**, at 900 N Birch Rd (Oct–Aug Tues–Sat 10am–4pm, Sun noon–4pm, closed Sept; obligatory tours hourly on the half hour until 90min before closing time; $20 house and garden visit, $10 gardens only; ⊤954/563-5393, Ⓦwww.bonnethouse.org), and its surrounding gardens are one of Fort Lauderdale's major cultural draws, a pioneer oddity nestled among the towering beachside condos. Built by amateur artist-collector Frederic Clay Bartlett, whose family made millions as hardware merchants in Chicago, the place is named after the yellow water-lily that grows in abundance on the estate. Bartlett snagged the land here when he married another wealthy Midwesterner, Helen Birch, whose father Hugh had snapped up swathes of land in southern Florida in the late nineteenth century; this chunk was a wedding gift. Helen died not long after, and Frederic found a second, even wealthier bride, in Evelyn Fortune Lilly – ex-wife of medicine magnate Eli. Together Frederic and Evelyn set about building their dream home.

The low-slung, pioneer-style house is set around a central courtyard, with no indoor stairways or walkways; it forms a simple backdrop to the Bartletts' vast but unexceptional trinket collection. It's a tribute more to acquisitiveness than taste, full of whimsical carved animals and menageries culled from merry-go-rounds. Bartlett was unable to resist decorating almost every surface, whether smothering woods in a cheap faux-marble finish, or with more appealing, brightly colored murals on some ceilings. The one noteworthy object is the dazzling porcelain sculpture by Lombardi in the music room; it's a virtuoso example of a mourning bust, where the artist has depicted translucent fabric of a widow's veil in china.

Evelyn donated the house to the state in 1983, with the proviso that she be able to winter here until her death – she didn't pass away until fourteen years later, at the astonishing age of 109. Her longevity ensured that by the time the home passed into government hands, the structural problems here were clearly evident.

Visitors are free to explore the gardens alone: the paths are clearly marked and points of interest signposted. For a sweat-free, more leisurely option, pay $2 to ride the electric tram that trundles slowly through the 35 acres of greenery; it leaves from just outside the gift shop on a sporadic schedule, with greater frequency during the winter season. The park itself is mostly sea grape trees and mangrove swamp, but look for several quirky buildings stashed around: most notable are the orchid house and thatched tiki-style Island Theater, a waterbound hut Bartlett built as a home moviehouse and to which he charged guests an entrance fee of two matched shells from the nearby beach.

Hugh Taylor Birch State Park

Hugh Taylor Birch was a lawyer from Chicago who handled legal work for Henry Flagler at the Standard Oil Company – and from whom he heard raves about Florida. It cost Birch only $1 an acre when he bought an enormous estate here to flee the boom in his hometown after the World's Fair of 1893; Birch's surprisingly modest house still stands. He deeded a chunk of his original holdings to son-in-law Frederic Bartlett, and then left the rest on his death to the state.

Today, that land is known as the **Hugh Taylor Birch State Park**, at 3019 East Sunrise Blvd (daily 8am–dusk, visitor center Sat & Sun 10am–5pm; $4 per vehicle or $1 per pedestrian; ☎954/564-4521, ⓦwww.floridastateparks.org). It's packed with sea grape and tropical hardwood trees, and centered on a shady freshwater lagoon, an ideal alternative to baking on the beach. There are also picnic facilities and basic campsites – for overnight reservations, contact the visitor center.

The International Swimming Hall of Fame

The threadbare **International Swimming Hall of Fame**, at 1 Hall of Fame Drive at Seabreeze Blvd (daily 9am–5pm; $8; ☎954/462-6536, ⓦwww.ishof. org), supposedly showcases great swimmers and divers from every country across the world. Once inside, though, visitors may feel as if time stopped ten years ago; there's no mention of any Olympic Games since Seoul in 1992, or any sign of recent record-breakers like Australian Ian Thorpe. If this alone didn't render the whole place rather anachronistic, the almost creepy tribute to past titans like Johnny Weismuller and Mark Spitz are decisive, thanks to the lifelike dummies that form their centerpiece (Spitz's likeness is especially odd; while the mannequin looks at least twenty years old, its hands are brand new, donated – as noted in a large accompanying plaque – by a company that specializes in producing such prosthetics). In short, there's little here for anyone other than a dedicated swimmer with a gothic imagination.

Lighthouse Point and Hillsboro

It's worth driving north along Highway A1A, past the tourist spots and snazzy 1960s condo towers of Lauderdale-by-the-Sea, into the areas known as **Lighthouse Point** and **Hillsboro**. This is a hushed, tony enclave, whose zoning laws forbid high-rises and whose residents are as likely to own a boat as a car. Tooling around the leafy streets here, lined by architecturally eclectic old mansions, is a reminder that the moneyed elite Fort Lauderdale's seeking to lure back with its flashy new hotels never really left.

Eating

The handiest selection of **eateries** lines Las Olas Boulevard downtown or in Himmarshee, though there are plenty of appealing options on the beach or along Wilton Drive in the largely gay district of Wilton Manors. Increasingly, the options and quality here rival that in Miami, though prices are refreshingly reasonable.

Cafés

Dogma Grill 900 South Federal Highway, downtown ☎954/525-1319, ⓦ www.dogmagrill. com. Satellite branch of the Miami original, with a larger air-conditioned interior – still painted cheery red and white – and kitchen that doles out classic hot dogs and quirky innovations (the feta and cucumber-slathered Athens Dog is delicious) for $3–5. Wash it down with some refreshing home-made mint-lemonade.

Kilwin's 809 E Las Olas Blvd at 9th, downtown ☎954/523-8338. Old-fashioned chocolate shop on downtown's main strolling drag: wait for the smell to hit you on the sidewalk and be lured in for hunks of fudge, hand-dipped chocolate marshmallows, or pecan turtles, as well as gooey ice cream – all for less than $5.

La Spada's 4346 Seagrape Drive, Lauderdale-by-the-Sea ☎954/776-7893. Yes, it's a trek, but the food at this legendary local sub shop is superb. Expect doorstop-sized sandwiches on home-made rolls for around $7; each is crammed with sliced-to-order slabs of beef, ham or turkey, plus piles of vegetables. Don't expect smiley service, but the lashings of food more than make up.

Restaurants

Blue Moon 4055 W Tradewinds Avenue, Lauderdale-by-the-Sea ☎954/267-9888, ⓦ www.bluemoonfishco.com. The views from the terrace here are delightful, looking out across the Intracoastal waterway – it's usually full of local families gorging on fish specials like lobster and shellfish panroast ($32–38). Pricey, but a worthwhile treat.

Café Martorano 3343 E Oakland Park Boulevard, beachside ☎954/561-2554. ⓦ www. cafemartorano.com. A local institution which serves unapologetically Italian-American grub, like pasta with spicy Sicilian sausages or fettucine alfredo for $30 a platter or so – there are no reservations and no menu, either, so just ask the server. It's noisy with mirrored walls and a DJ, who's often owner/chef Steve Martorano.

Canyon Southwest Café 1818 E Sunrise Blvd at NE 18th Ave, Victoria Park ☎954/765-1950. Swanky eatery outfitted in Southwestern shades of burnished bronze, navy, and mustard tones plus crisp white tablecloths and gauzy curtains billowing round the booths. The pricey but delicious food's worth splashing out for (entrees hover around $25) – try the spicy tuna tartare or pork with Gorgonzola – but save room for the white chocolate and berry bread pudding. Even if not eating, stop in at the bar for a signature prickly-pear margarita, made in-house from fresh cactus steeped for three days in tequila.

The Floridian 1410 E Las Olas Blvd at 14th, downtown ☎954/463-4041. Old Fort Lauderdale at its finest: 1980s vintage Formica furniture, peeling autographed pictures lining the walls, and outstanding diner food at rock-bottom prices (belly-filling breakfasts for $10). Unpretentious and enormous, which means never having to wait for a table.

The Four Rivers 1201 N Federal Highway ☎954/616-1152. Astonishingly good upscale (entrees $25–33) Thai run by a couple who once worked at *Galanga* (see below): the interior looks like a loungey nightclub, with dark, minimalist furniture and a granite bar, plus a raised central pool always strewn with flowers. Try the peppery wok-tossed beef tenderloin as an appetizer ($10) and avoid filling up on the garlic crackers with peanut dipping sauce served gratis instead of bread.

Galanga 2389 Wilton Drive at NE 9th Ave, Wilton Manors ☎954/202-0000 ⓦwww.galangarestaurant.com. Mixed gay/straight neighborhood favorite, worth seeking out for its northern Thai dishes – try crab fish rools or *panang* curry, with lime leaf and peanuts ($12–17 depending on protein). The atmosphere's casual, with low candelight, rattan furniture, and overstuffed cushions.

Kitchenetta 2850 North Federal Highway ☎954/567-3333, ⓦwww.kitchenetta.com. Grab a tasty pizza at this modern Italian spot with raw concrete floors, a red-and-yellow tiled open kitchen and dayglo bright furniture – the mozzarella's made fresh daily onsite and the flour flown in specially from Naples. Pizzas and pastas, served in huge family-style portions, start around a bargain $14.

Sublime 1431 N. Federal Highway ☎954/539-9000, ⓦwww.sublimeveg.com. An unexpected find, this all-vegan, all-organic eatery in a strip mall has a sleek, soothing interior – there isn't a whiff of hippiedom about the place – and a menu even meat-lovers will devour, like portabella mushroom "tenderloin." It's all for a good cause: owner Nancy Alexander donates her profits to animal charities and will usually be found cajoling diners for donations in the restaurant.

Tarpon Bend 200 SW 2nd St at SW 2nd Ave, Himmarshee ☎954/523-3233. Appealing, airy sports bar that serves up flagons of beer in glasses chilled so much that it freezes solid on the sides. There are several TV screens, as well as chalkboards showcasing local and IGFA fishing records. There are stacks of different chili sauces on each table; the American menu is comprised mostly of sandwiches and salads ($7–13).

Drinking and nightlife

Despite Fort Lauderdale's gentrification, **nightlife** along Hwy-A1A on the beach tends to revolve around chugging mixing-bowl-sized margaritas: the *Elbo Room* bar, which co-starred with Prentiss and Hamilton in *Where the Boys Are*, still stands at the corner of Las Olas Boulevard and Hwy-A1A (☎954/463-4612, ⓦwww.elboroom .com). If this isn't your scene, head inland to the drag of no-nonsense drinks spots along Himmarshee: there's a branch of the Hooters-with-attitude club/bar *Coyote Ugly*, at 220 SW 2nd St at SW 3rd Ave (☎954/764-UGLY, ⓦwww.coyoteuglysaloon .com) here, as well as similar frat-heavy but fun pubby bars. For slightly more upscale drinking, thirty-somethings can sip in more chic surroundings in some of the restaurants along Las Olas, like *Blue Martini* at 2432 E Sunrise Blvd in the huge Galleria Mall (☎954/563-2583), which serves bar snacks and cocktails as well as offering live jazz each night. The bar attached to the *St Regis'* (see p.206) new restaurant, *Cero* is

Sawgrass Mills

Forty minutes west of Fort Lauderdale's beachfront lies the discount retail palace of **Sawgrass Mills**, 12801 W Sunrise Blvd in Sunrise (Mon–Sat 10am–9.30pm, Sun 11am–8pm; ☎954/846-2300, ⓦwww.sawgrassmillsmall.com). It claims to be the world's largest designer outlet mall, and alongside the usual factory stores from Gap and Levi's, it's crammed with higher-end discounters like Neiman Marcus, Last Call, and Saks Off Fifth, making a worthwhile detour, even for non-shopaholics, as everyone is likely to find bargain or two. It's also home to a superb kids' attraction, Wannadoo City – forgive its wince-inducing name and focus on the fact that it's like a career-themed Disney World; pre-teens can try out jobs like pilot, nurse and TV anchor in the indoor, miniature town. Take heart if the building's layout seems confusing – it's all in honor of local wildlife, as the mall was planned to mimic the shape of an alligator. Sawgrass Mills can be reached from the city via interstates 75 or 595; from either turn off at the Sawgrass Expressway exchange – it's a longer drive (at least 30 minutes or so from the beach) than you'd expect.

also buzzy with young professionals, especially at weekends, though drinks prices can be gasp-inducing; the restaurant itself is rather overpriced and disappointing. Worth a detour is the intriguingly exotic *Kalahari Bar*, 4446 NE 20th St at Floranada Road on the north side of town (☎954/493-5371, ⓦwww.kalaharibar.com), run by an expat South African couple and decked out with artifacts from their homeland; it claims to be the only such bar in the whole USA.

Fort Lauderdale's oddly deficient in South Beach-style nightlife or clubs – in fact, the closest real option is the **Seminole Hard Rock Casino**, several miles inland near to Florida's Turnpike at 1 Seminole Way (☎954/327-7625, ⓦwww.seminolehardrockhollywood.com), where there's a choice between a new Florida outpost of long-time New York nightlife fixture, *Pangaea* (☎954/581-5454, ⓦwww.pangaea-lounge.com), with its vague safari theme plus brand-name DJs, or the flashier *Gryphon* nightclub (☎1-866/502-7529).

Gay Fort Lauderdale

As Miami, and especially South Beach, has grown more expensive and straight in the last couple of years, Fort Lauderdale's gay and lesbian population has swelled with refugees from it as well as older "gayby boomers" looking to retire in the sun. That isn't to say that the scene here is now glitzy and hedonistic – far from it; rather it's retained a welcoming, laid-back vibe.

For up-to-date **information** on what's happening call or stop by the Gay and Lesbian Community Center of South Florida at 1717 N Andrews Ave at Sunrise (Mon–Fri 10am–10pm, Sat & Sun noon–5pm; ☎954/463-9005, ⓦwww.glccsf.org), or pick up one of the flyers at the noticeboard inside the *Pride Factory* shop-café at 850 NE 13th St (☎954/463-6600, ⓦwww.pridefactory.com); reliable local **freesheets** include *Scoop*, *Hotspots*, and *The 411*. We've listed gay-specific accommodation and nightlife below. As for **gay beaches**, there are unofficial spots along A1A at Sebastian Street and the quieter, less cruisey patch at NE 18th Street.

Accommodation

There are over thirty **guesthouses and B&Bs** aimed at gay men in the city: there's a large cluster together on the beach around Terramar Street at the Intracoastal Waterway. Pick of the bunch is undoubtedly *The Royal Palms,* 2901 Terramar St at Orton Ave, beachside (☎954/564-6444, ⓦwww.royalpalms.com), with rooms from $200. Expect Frette linens, rainhead showers, and an ultra-private clothing-optional pool – not to mention safe-sex kits under every pillow. On the mainland, try the *Pineapple Point Guesthouse* at 315 NE 16th Terrace at NE 3rd Court, Victoria Park (☎954/527-0094 or 1-888/844-7295, ⓦwww.pineapplepoint.com), with rooms from $270, tucked away in an upcoming neighborhood with a lush tropical garden, pool, and Jacuzzi. A cheaper option, *Orton Terrace*, with simpler rooms and more basic facilities, 606 Orton Ave at Terramar St, beachside (☎954/566-5068 or 1-800/323-1142, ⓦwww.ortonterrace.com), has rooms from $130.

Drinking and nightlife

More than ever, Fort Lauderdale's selection of gay and lesbian **nightlife** shames Miami's meager offerings – local freesheets have the full listings, including one nighters at different clubs. Standouts include *Georgie's Alibi* at 2266 Wilton Drive at NE 22nd St, Wilton Manors (T954/565-2526, Wwww.georgiesalibi.com), with a few pool tables, a short bar menu, and a friendly crowd, which is unusual in including gays, lesbians and gay-friendly straights. Nearby are the bar/club *Boom* – go for drinks early evening, but expect a loud DJ and pumping dance floor after dinner – at 2234 Wilton Drive (T954/630-3556) and jockish sports bar *Sidelines* at No. 2031 (T954/563-8001, Wwww.sidelinesport.com). Otherwise, there's *Dude's*, 3720 NE 33rd St at A1A, beachside (T954/568-7777, Wwww.dudesbar.com), which has go-go boys most nights.

As for all-out **clubs**, *The Copa*, 2800 S Federal Hwy in Port Everglades (T954/463-1507, Wwww.copaboy.com), is a local institution, open for more than thirty years. It's a warehouse-like space with a dancefloor, terrace, and video room – note the crowd doesn't arrive until midnight or so most nights. Circuit-style parties usually take place at *Coliseum*, 2520 S Federal Hwy, in Port Everglades (T954/832-0100, Wwww.coliseumnightclub.com); for all-out cruising in saunas, there's the busy *The Club Fort Lauderdale* at 11 NW 5th Avenue ($6 one-time entry, $17 locker rental; T954/525-3344, Wwww.the-clubs.com).

The Everglades

"The Everglades is a test. If we pass, we get to keep the planet."

Environmentalist Marjory Stoneman Douglas

ittle more than an hour from the condos and clubs of Miami, expansive **Everglades National Park** is breathtakingly wild. Although the land is on the same latitude as the Sahara, more than one third of the park is made up of marine areas and underwater estuaries, and sawgrass covers nearly four million acres of swampy prairie. Both water and land teem with wildlife, from rare crocodiles and alligators to raccoons, as well as dozens of species of bird.

Despite this raw vastness, the Everglades exist in a delicate and endangered ecosystem. The area was originally formed by natural water drainage from the region around Orlando, flowing south to collect on the oolitic limestone table of Florida's swampy tip. In the last half-century, though, developers have diverted this precious water source east to cities like Miami, Fort Lauderdale, and Palm Beach, leaving the Everglades ecosystem not only thirsty but shrinking.

Coconut Grove-based environmentalist Marjory Stoneman Douglas was one of the first local lobbyists against such eco-vandalism – in fact, many say that her book *The Everglades: River of Grass* kickstarted the conservation movement in South Florida in the late 1940s (Douglas was crusading until her last breath in 1998, at the astonishing age of 108). Now, of course, there are dozens of organizations dedicated to safeguarding this unique ecosystem – though of course none could prevent the wreckage caused by Hurricane Andrew; even 15 years later, some northern portions of the park, notably **Big Cypress**, are only now beginning to regain their pre-hurricane flora.

When exploring the Everglades, the worst thing to do is rush around. Although the speed limit on most roads is 55mph, you'll see and enjoy far more if you travel slowly and look for nature's subtleties: notice, for example, that the water everywhere is tea-brown, thanks to the tannic acid that leaches out of fallen leaves. In the northwest region of the park, around **Everglades City**, all activities are aquatic: there's good fishing, boat tours, and canoeing. Conversely, at **Shark Valley**, in the northeastern corner of the park, there's a trail too long to hike in its entirety, but accessible via bike or tram. Further south, **Flamingo** offers something for everyone: superb saltwater fishing and excellent birdwatching sites, plus boat tours, canoeing, kayaking, and hiking. As for wildlife spotting, early in the morning is the best time; during the dry season, make it a point to come during the week, as busy weekends on the waterways drive animals under cover during the day.

Note that though **airboat tours** are an image synonymous with the park, they're an iffy prospect; a reputable operator will cause no environmental damage, but there are dozens of less scrupulous types whose gas and oil pollute the rivers and whose constant use of the same routes scars the land. If in doubt, it's much better

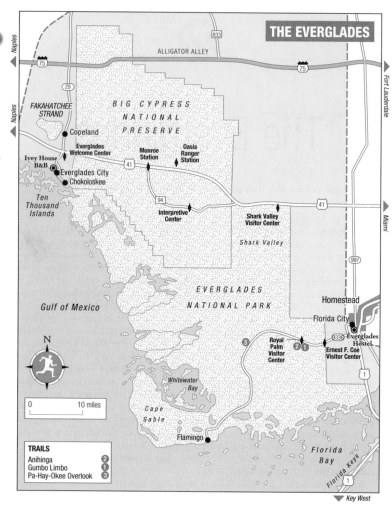

ALLIGATOR ALLEY

Naples

75

29

FAKAHATCHEE
STRAND

BIG CYPRESS

NATIONAL

PRESERVE

Copeland

Naples

Everglades
Welcome Center

Monroe
Station

Oasis
Ranger
Station

Ivey House
B&B

41

Everglades City
Chokoloskee

94

Ten
Thousand
Islands

Interpretive
Center

Shark Valley
Visitor Center

41

Shark Valley

Fort Lauderdale

Miami

997

Gulf of Mexico

EVERGLADES

NATIONAL PARK

Homestead

Florida City

9336

Everglades
Hostel

N

Royal
Palm
Visitor
Center

3

2 1

Ernest F. Coe
Visitor Center

1

0   10 miles

Whitewater
Bay

Cape
Sable

Flamingo

Florida
Bay

Florida Keys

1

TRAILS

Anihinga   2
Gumbo Limbo   1
Pa-Hay-Okee Overlook 3

Key West

to take a trip with one of the boat operators recommended on p.220 than to opt for an airboat.

Getting there

The park is almost impossible to reach without a **car**, as there's no public transport to or within the Everglades. The pricey day-trips offered by numerous operators in Miami are rushed and not terribly enjoyable – if you want to see the park, splash out and hire a car for a few days. See p.26 for details on car rental.

There are three **entrances** to the protected area: **Shark Valley** in the northeastern corner and **Everglades City** in the northwest are both served by the busy Hwy-41 (also known as the Tamiami Trail) – follow Calle Ocho through Little Havana and out of Miami until it morphs into this highway. Out in the countryside, the road cuts through the top half of the park and provides direct access, though don't expect much scenic beauty until you enter the park itself.

The third, and most popular, entrance, which leads to the settlement of **Flamingo** is much tougher to reach. Drive south through Homestead; once out of the city center, either look for the poorly signposted Rte-9336 or just turn left at the ramshackle "Robert is Here" fruit stand. This road leads to the Ernest F. Coe Visitor Center at the main entrance, from where it's a 40-minute drive through a windy, two-lane road to Flamingo. All entrances are open 24 hours a day except Shark Valley (daily 8.30am–6pm).

Information and permits

There are four **visitor centers** in the park: the **Ernest F. Coe Center** at the main entrance is the largest and most informative (daily 9am–5pm; ☎305/242-7700, Ⓦwww.nps.gov/ever/), and a likely first stop-off for anyone arriving here from Miami. There are satellite offices at **Flamingo** (Nov–April daily 8am–4.30pm; ☎239/695-2945), **Shark Valley** (daily 9am–5pm; ☎305/221-8776), and the **Gulf Coast** near Everglades City (Nov–April daily 8am–5pm; May–Oct daily 9am–5pm; ☎239/695-3311).

A seven-day general **permit** costs $10 per vehicle and $5 per person for cyclists. **Backcountry permits** are also available from any visitor center December to April, and are $10 per permit plus $2 per person for up to two weeks; backcountry campgrounds throughout the park are little more than tended clearings, unless marked as a *chickee* (raised platform with a roof, open on all sides) on the map available from the visitor center.

Accommodation

Unless you're camping, in-park **accommodation** is problematic. The only option, the already bare-bones *Flamingo Lodge* motel, was pummeled by two hurricanes in

---

Everglades practicalities

Most people come during the **dry season** (late Nov–April), when the park is at its most active, and the mosquitoes at their least. At this time, there are larger numbers of birds, and receding water levels leave the animals a reduced number of watering holes, thus concentrating wildlife activity; plus, there are more activities for people offered by the park and its concessionaires. The only downside, of course, is that accommodation prices will be steeper.

A visit in **wet season** (May to early Nov) is only for the dedicated: the park receives at least sixty inches of rain each year, ninety percent of which falls between May and early November, and insects abound – especially if the preceding winter was very dry, killing off the fish that eat bug larvae. Campsites at this time are virtually uninhabitable, and there are few birds to be spotted, so think hard before planning a trek.

As for the **shoulder season** (late April to early May or late Oct to early Nov), it's a risk: the weather may still be poor, but there will be fewer crowds.

What to bring

Whatever and whenever your plans, bring plenty of **insect repellent** and long pants. Year-round the mosquitoes are numerous, and especially ferocious during the summer wet season. If camping, you might also encounter sand gnats, or "no-see-ums," tiny insects that inflict painful bites. There's also little shade, so **sunblock** (plus sunglasses and hat) is essential. For backcountry camping, bring flashlights, a compass, and water in hard containers – raccoons can (and will) tear through soft cartons. Remember that there's only one restaurant inside the park – an unremarkable café in Flamingo – so bring some **food**, too.

▲ A Snowy Egret on the Anhinga Trail

2005, and remained shuttered at the time of writing. However, the National Park Service has indicated it will be seeking tenders from new operators to renovate and reopen the place as an eco-tourism spot – check ⓦwww.nps.gov/ever for updates. If you don't want to camp, it is feasible to use Everglades City or Florida City as overnight bases provided you don't mind a little extra driving.

Everglades Hostel 20 SW 2nd Ave, Florida City ☎305/248-1122 or 1-800/372-3874, ⓦwww.evergladeshostel.com. A clean, budget option in Florida City with the usual amenities (laundry room, kitchen, Internet access) that also runs various excursions into the park. Dorm beds $25/night, private rooms $65.
Ivey House Bed & Breakfast 107 Camellia St, Everglades City ☎239/695-3299, ⓦwww.

iveyhouse.com. A charming B&B with reasonable rates, especially in its older building where the simple rooms share baths; the new addition has plusher rooms with private baths. Family-style dinners are also served each evening, and the owners also rent canoes/kayaks and run regular paddle tours into the park. From $140. Open Nov–April.

Route 9336: the road to Flamingo

Just southwest of Homestead, **Route 9336** enters the park at the main visitor center (open 24 hours; see p.217), leading to some of the best and most accessible sights in the Everglades, before eventually arriving at **Flamingo**, the only settlement inside the park proper. This southerly section of the park is known as Pine

Camping

Rangers will tell you that *Long Pine Key* campground – west from the Ernest F. Coe Visitor Center and south from Rte-9336 – has the fewest bugs, but that it's worth braving the mosquitoes at **Flamingo** campground for its views and its facilities, such as hot and cold showers. Camping at all sites is $16 per night, and reservations (☎1-800/365-2267 or ⓦhttp://reservations.nps.gov) are recommended from November to April.

Island; and for a casual visitor, a few days spent here are an ideal way to glimpse all the elements that make the Everglades unique. Dotted along the 38-mile road to Flamingo are several trails, most of which are manageable for even the most inexperienced hiker; many are former roads, while others are specially constructed boardwalks.

One mile after entering the park, take a turn south toward the **Royal Palm Visitor Center**: two very different but equally intriguing brief trails start here. The **Anhinga Trail** is a half-mile concrete path through sawgrass marsh that's a dependable site for wildlife viewing. It's especially reliable for seeing alligators: remember, though, that this isn't a zoo, and the seemingly harmless and lethargic animals splayed within feet of the path can be vicious if they feel threatened. The trail's named after the anhinga bird, a black and white cormorant-like creature known for sunbathing on rocks after diving for fish. If you'd prefer an animal-free trek, try the **Gumbo Limbo Trail** for a glimpse of the Paradise Key hardwood hammock packed with strangler figs, royal palms, and, of course, the gumbo limbos with their flaky red bark.

Back on the main road, before Rte-9336 takes an unexacting turn south, the **Pa-hay-okee viewing platform** is a tall outlook, nestled in the middle of a stretch of dwarf cypress – it's worth stopping for a quick stroll from the car up a few steps to catch panoramic views across the sawgrass plain.

Heading further south, you'll come to **Paurotis Pond**. Unremarkable for much of the year, it's a stunning sight in January when the place becomes a wading-bird rookery, with egrets, woodstorks, and occasional spoonbills coming to breed. Continue on until you hit **Nine Mile Pond**, a manageable canoe trail choice for amateurs. Conversely, **Hells Bay Trail**, about five miles from here, is a well-sign-posted adventure for more experienced canoeists – maps of these and other canoe trails are available from the visitor center.

The rest of the sights on the final stretch to Flamingo are aimed largely at the flocks of birdwatchers who make up the Everglades' most loyal tourists: try **Snake Bight Trail** (just watch for the armies of mosquitoes) or **Mrazek Pond**, particularly appealing in February when the receding waters concentrate the fish population and draw dozens of hungry birds to feed. If you're not a birdwatcher, skip these and carry on to Flamingo, where you'll find the **Eco Pond Trail** just past the Flamingo Visitor Center. It leads to a freshwater pond, where there's a good variety of wildlife spotting, and is equipped with a proper viewing platform if you want to lurk and wait.

Flamingo

The only settlement inside the park proper, **Flamingo** began as a nameless nine-teenth-century pioneer village, home to a few families and plenty of renegades. It finally took a name in 1893 in order to build a post office; settlers voted for Flamingo in honor of the pink birds that were commonplace in the area. Of course, they weren't flamingoes; it's more likely they were roseate spoonbills. Fittingly, Flamingo has been dependent on birds throughout its history. Today, birdwatchers flock to watch them, but back then, it was hunters who clogged the town, keen to illegally harvest egret feathers for the millinery trade (indeed a game warden employed by the bird-friendly Audubon Society was famously murdered near the town in 1905 while trying to protect nests from plume hunters).

There isn't much in Flamingo other than a campground for visitors and wardens' accommodation; during the winter season, the Marina Store (Nov–April daily 6am–8pm) here sells sandwiches and fixings for meals. Otherwise, this marina (☏239/695-3101) is the departure point for the **boat tours** run into the back

▲ Everglades alligator

country of Pine Island; the two-hour Pelican Backcountry Cruise (daily 10am, 1pm, 3pm, fewer trips out of season; no service Tues and Wed; $18) journeys into Coot Bay and offers plenty of reptile spotting. You can also rent canoes ($32 full day) and fishing skiffs (from $100 for half a day).

Shark Valley

Highway 41 enters the northeastern corner of the park near the **Shark Valley Visitor Center**: this spot's not only the best place to understand how vast the sawgrass plain truly is but also the clearest testimony of how Miami's explosive development has drained the park of water – the growing, arid patches of land here are the scars.

There's only one lengthy **trail** from here, a fourteen-mile-long loop that's off-limits to cars and a tough hike: it's paved, though, so it makes for a pleasant, if shadeless, cycling trip. Rent bikes from the Shark Valley Tram Tour Company (daily 8.30am–4pm, last rental 3pm; $6.25/hour; ℡305/221-8455) and head for the 50-foot observation tower at the trail's mid-point. A more leisurely way to see the trail is on a **tram tour** (daily 9am–4pm on the hour, fewer trips out of season; $14.50; ℡305/221-8455), where park rangers point out notable wildlife and stop regularly for viewings – alligators and turtles are plentiful, and the birdwatching is truly spectacular.

Those determined to set out on foot can enjoy two short rambles from the visitor center: the **Bobcat Boardwalk** runs through sawgrass marsh, and the rough limestone **Otter Cave trail** snakes into tropical hardwood hammock.

Big Cypress National Preserve

The huge swathe of protected land in the northern reaches of the park known as **Big Cypress National Preserve** is not a must-see stop – rather, this is a functional designation by the government to stop the draining and development that was wrecking the waterlogged earth here thirty years ago. The cypress trees and wood storks that were once abundant here suffered a further blow with Hurricane Andrew in the early 1990s – a casual visitor is better off speeding through here along US-41 to reach Everglades City.

Everglades City

Though Flamingo is the only settlement within the preserve's boundaries, there is another town that serves the Everglades – Everglades City, just outside the Everglades' northwestern corner. It's yet another example of a Florida pioneer's overenthusiastic optimism; the place was purchased and named in the 1920s by an advertising executive dreaming of setting up his own fiefdom. Today, the year-round population hovers around five hundred or so.

The reason to come here is to use the town and its facilities as a base for exploring the **Ten Thousand Islands**, where the park's coastline shatters into mangrove island shards that are excellent fishing sites. To reach **Everglades City**, leave Hwy-41 at Rte-29 and head three miles south. Continue through the city to the end of Rte-29 until you reach the dock at Chokoloskee Causeway, site of the official visitor center and boarding point for most **boat trips**.

Everglades National Park Boat Tours is one of the few park-sanctioned operators (daily 9.30am–5pm; ⓣ239/695-2591 or 1-800/445-7724), offering two trips: the 90-minute Ten Thousand Islands Tour ($26), which heads for the outer islands bordering the Gulf of Mexico, or the 2-hour Mangrove Wilderness Tour ($35), which journeys inland through the winding red mangrove waterways. Boats leave every half-hour year-round from the docks at Chokoloskee. Canoes can also be rented from the same company (daily 8.30am–5pm; $25/day). This chunk of the park is a kayaking and canoeing hub, thanks to thousands of islands that form handy waterways – and so in turn become marked trails. The especially active can even plan a week in the wilds paddling the 100-mile trail known as the Wilderness Waterway that snakes through the backcountry here all the way south to Flamingo; contact the *Ivey House Bed & Breakfast* (see p.218) for rental and tour information.

The Florida Keys

T he **Florida Keys** are a dash of the Caribbean in America, as distant from the US in attitude as geography. Beginning with the small islands in Biscayne National Park and ending with the Dry Tortugas, the Keys form a broken necklace of land that stretches for more than two hundred miles from Florida's southern tip. Roughly 125,000 years ago, they were a living coral reef, created when water levels rose dramatically, flooding low-lying areas. As the waters gradually receded, the upper reaches of reef were exposed, and limestone islands were formed from the dying coral. At the same time, the lower areas of the reef to the west survived, making for spectacular snorkeling and diving.

Aside from the shipping hub in Key West and a short-lived settlement on Indian Key, the islands remained sparsely populated by European settlers until well into the twentieth century, in part owing to harsh, humid summers and legions of insects. However, after Henry Flagler's railroad connected the Keys with Miami in 1912, communities grew up in clusters, supported mostly by fishing and smuggling – indeed, the narcotics trade here was endemic until well into the 1980s, as in the 1984 case of the so-called Big Pine 29, when almost thirty sheriff's deputies were arrested for drug smuggling. (Even now, it's not unusual for blocks of marijuana and cocaine to wash up along the western coast; locals call them square groupers.) Today, though, both fishing and smuggling have given way to tourism as the overwhelming local industry.

The Keys are more or less divided into three sections. The **Upper Keys**, which include the towns of Key Largo, Tavernier, and Islamorada, are used as bases for fishing and diving in the John Pennekamp State Park – though there's a definite uneasiness in the locals' relationship with tourism, and the famously laid-back local attitude is less prevalent here. Centered on the settlement of Marathon and the remarkable Seven Mile Bridge, the **Middle Keys** are more welcoming. Marathon has good amenities, plus access to clean beaches and well-stocked fishing sites nearby: for the casual traveler, this is the best base for exploring the area. South from here, the **Lower Keys**, beginning at Big Pine Key, are rewarding for landlocked wildlife-watching – most notably, the rare Key Deer.

The prime target for most visiting the Keys, of course, is fabled **Key West**. Old Town is now a feast of wooden colonial houses and winding streets, less blighted by tourism than some contend, and with much of the sleepy grace that first attracted visitors thirty years ago; it's also one of the gayest towns in America, owing to liberal local attitudes plus pure chance.

Arrival, information, and getting around

Greyhound runs a limited **bus** service connecting Miami and Key West, a roughly five-hour trip with stops in major centers along the route ($38.50 one way; depar-

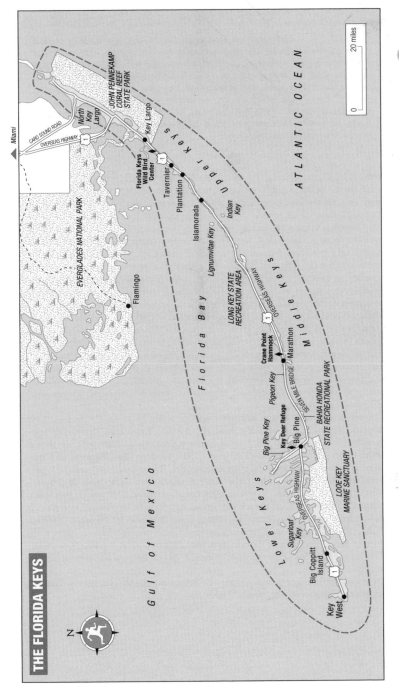

THE FLORIDA KEYS

0 _____ 20 miles

Miami

CARD SOUND ROAD

OVERSEAS HIGHWAY

North Key Largo

JOHN PENNEKAMP CORAL REEF STATE PARK

Key Largo

EVERGLADES NATIONAL PARK

Florida Keys Wild Bird Center

Tavernier

Plantation

Islamorada

Lignumvitae Key

Indian Key

Upper Keys

ATLANTIC OCEAN

Flamingo

Florida Bay

LONG KEY STATE RECREATION AREA

OVERSEAS HIGHWAY

Gulf of Mexico

Crane Point Hammock

Marathon

Middle Keys

Pigeon Key

SEVEN MILE BRIDGE

BAHIA HONDA STATE RECREATIONAL PARK

Big Pine Key

Key Deer Refuge

Big Pine

LOOE KEY MARINE SANCTUARY

Lower Keys

OVERSEAS HIGHWAY

Sugarloaf Key

Big Coppitt Island

Key West

N

Flying to Key West

One savvy option that maximizes time in the Florida Keys is a **fly-drive** combo: hop a puddle jumper to Key West then drive the return along Highway 1. The advantages are two-fold: firstly, you'll only have to deal with US-1 traffic once and secondly, the aerial views of islands are spectacular, notably on the smaller (12 seats or less), lower-flying planes. Flights are operated by Delta, Continental/Cape Air and American from various cities in Florida (see p.21 for contact details); there are regular connections from Miami and Fort Lauderdale for around $100 one way, and several brand name rental car firms at the Key West International Airport (℡305/296-5439, ⓦwww.keywestinternationalairport.com).

tures at 12.35pm, 6.50pm; ℡1-800/231-2222, ⓦwww.greyhound.com). Even so, since there's no local public transportation, it's almost impossible to see or enjoy most of what the Keys have to offer without a **car** (see p.26 for rental information). Driving is easy, as the islands are joined by a single road – **Hwy-1**, also known as the **Overseas Highway**, which connects Key West with Florida City (see p.125), continuing on up the East Coast. To avoid tourist traffic, do as the locals do and branch off from Hwy-1 south of Homestead onto Card Sound Road, also known as Hwy-905A ($1 toll). It's slightly longer, but after passing through the desolate southeastern section of the Everglades, this route gives soaring views of the mangrove-dotted waters of Florida Bay (where a long wait and a lot of luck might be rewarded with the sight of a rare American crocodile) – and a glimpse of the Keys as they would all have looked long ago before commercialism took hold.

Addresses in the Keys are given using the Mile Marker (MM) system, which begins with 0 in Key West at the junction of Whitehead and Fleming streets and ends just south of Homestead. In theory, there's a sign marking each mile, but don't rely on it. The only islands large enough to require street addresses in the Keys (aside from Key West) are Big Pine and Marathon. We've also followed the local convention of indicating whether buildings sit north (Bayside) or south (Oceanside) of the freeway.

There are several **visitor centers** scattered along Hwy-1. The largest is the **Florida Keys Visitor Center** at MM 106-Bayside, Key Largo (daily 9am–6pm; ℡305/451-4747 or 1-800/822-1088, ⓦwww.keylargochamber.org), which provides information on the Keys in general. The **Islamorada Chamber of Commerce** is unmissable in its bright red roadside caboose and good for the Upper Keys, at MM 83.2-Bayside (Mon–Sat 9am–5pm, Sun 9am–3pm; ℡305/664-4503 or 1-800/FAB-KEYS, ⓦwww.islamoradachamber.com); while the **Marathon Chamber of Commerce** has ample information on the Middle Keys at MM 53.5-Bayside, Marathon (daily 9am–5pm; ℡305/743-5417 or 1-800/262-7284, ⓦwww.floridakeysmarathon.com). Further along Hwy-1, there's the **Lower Keys Chamber of Commerce**, MM 31-Oceanside, Big Pine Key (Mon–Fri 9am–5pm, Sat 9am–3pm; ℡305/872-2411, ⓦwww.lowerkeyschamber.com).

Finally, don't forget to bring plenty of **insect repellent**: ravenous mosquitoes are plentiful whatever the time of year.

The Keys rightly lure outdoorsy types with their wide range of **water activities** – some more taxing than others, from a day lolling on a boat with a fishing rod to a bracing kayak jaunt round one of the outlying mangrove swamps. The only letdown, especially after Miami Beach, are the **beaches** – the sand strips in the Keys are small and mostly man-made; we've listed the pick of them below.

Beaches

Hands down, the best Keys beaches are all in **Bahia Honda State Recreational Park** (see p.231); otherwise, snatch some time sunbathing at **Sombrero Beach** near Marathon and **Anne's Beach** just west of Islamorada. Around Key West, there are few options – the best is probably the beach at **Fort Zachary Taylor Historic State Park**.

Snorkeling and diving

The **John Pennekamp State Park** (see p.226) has several notable reefs and is very popular; however, there's livelier wildlife and more to see at **Looe Key Marine Sanctuary** (see p.232) or at **Biscayne National Park** (see p.126). **Fort Jefferson** in the Dry Tortugas has spectacular coral formations and plenty of fish less than 100 yards off its western shores.

Tour operators include the Coral Reef Park Company at the John Pennekamp Visitor Center (daily 8am–5pm; ☎305/451-1621, ⊛www.pennekamppark.com), which runs glass-bottomed-boat tours at 9.15am, 12.15pm, and 3pm for $22, or snorkel trips at 9am, noon, and 3pm for $34, including equipment. Its branch in Bahia Honda State Park runs snorkeling trips to Looe Key (daily 8am–5pm; ☎305/872-3210, ⊛www.bahiahondapark.com) at 9.30am & 1.30pm (year-round—call for summer times) for $35.

In the Lower Keys, the friendly staff at Underseas, MM 30.5-Oceanside, Big Pine Key (snorkel trips start at $30; ☎305/872-2700 or 1-800/446-5663, ⊛www.flkeysdiving.com), run enjoyable trips out to Looe Key – a good choice for first-timers. The leisurely alternative for coral viewing is by glass-bottomed boat: try the two-hour trip on the *Key Largo Princess*, MM 100-Oceanside (daily 10am, 1pm, 4pm; $30; ☎305/451-4655, ⊛www.keylargoprincess.com).

You can only visit the Looe Key reef on a trip organized by one of the many diving shops throughout the Keys; the nearest is the neighboring Looe Key Dive Center (snorkel and diving trips start at $40; ☎1-800/942-5397, ⊛www.diveflakeys.com).

Fishing

A good independent **bait shop** is the World Class Angler, at MM 50-Bayside, Marathon (☎305/743-6139), where the staff is knowledgeable, and can make good local fishing recommendations. The deluxe option is to take a personal **charter trip** – in Marathon, try Captain Tina Brown ($425/four-hour trip, $475/six-hour trip; ☎305/896-2560, ✉tina824us@yahoo.com), who's renowned for her helpfulness with less experienced anglers, or Captain Brian Yates (☎305/393-2308). In the Upper Keys, Robbie's, at MM 77.5-Bayside, Islamorada, runs larger group trips (9.30am–1.30pm and 1.45–5.45pm for $35, plus $3 rod rental; 7.30pm–12.30am for $40, plus $4 rod rental; ☎305/664-8498, ⊛www.robbies.com).

Kayaking

Florida Keys Kayak & Ski at Robbie's Marina, MM 75.5-Bayside, Islamorada (☎305/664-4878), runs escorted **kayak tours** to Indian and Lignumvitae keys, as well as the chance to see wildlife in the mangrove swamps nearby (from $60). Kayak rentals without a guide start at $55 for four hours. In the Lower Keys, try Sugarloaf Marina, MM 17-Bayside, Sugarloaf Key (☎305/745-3135, ⊛www.sugarloafkeymarina.com), where rental starts at $15/hr or $35/day.

The Upper Keys

Driving south along Hwy-1, **Key Largo** is the first of the **Upper Keys'** three major communities you'll come to. It's perhaps the most unappetizing of all the settlements in the Keys, and there's little reason to spend much time here. Nearby is the 80-acre underwater coral reef in the **John Pennekamp State Park**, as well as the **Florida Keys Wild Bird Center** further south in Tavernier, the second major community and notable mostly as the one-time first stop on Henry Flagler's pioneering railway.

The third, **Islamorada** (pronounced eye-lah-more-RAH-dah), is actually a chain of four small islands: Plantation, Windley, and Upper and Lower Matecumbe. It's one of the larger fishing hubs in the Keys, and makes a good base for exploring both **Indian Key** and **Lignumvitae Key**.

Key Largo

Essentially a hub of gas stations, fast-food outlets, and shopping plazas, **Key Largo** lives in the shadow of two things: the 1948 film *Key Largo* and the coral reef at **John Pennekamp State Park**. The film, starring Humphrey Bogart and Lauren Bacall, was shot entirely in Hollywood – it was so named because the title evoked the exotic tropics. So successful was its suggestiveness, in fact, that savvy locals changed their town's name in 1952 from Rock Harbor to Key Largo – *Cayo Largo*, meaning Long Island, was originally applied to the entire Keys by early Spanish explorers. For some reason, the rickety boat used by Bogie and Katharine Hepburn in *The African Queen* is moored at the *Holiday Inn* here; sadly, it's no longer used for trips but simply decoration at MM 100-Oceanside.

John Pennekamp State Park

The enormous, underwater **John Pennekamp State Park**, at MM 102.5-Oceanside, Key Largo (daily 8am–sunset; $3.50 for a single-occupancy vehicle, $6.00 for double-occupancy vehicles, 50 cents per additional passenger; ℡305/451-1202, Ⓦwww.floridastateparks.org/pennekamp) is, frankly, a little overrated – the beaches are far better at Bahia Honda (see p.231), while the coral formations more spectacular in Biscayne National Park (see p.126) or the Dry Tortugas (see box, p.244).

However, it's worth a detour for **wreck diving** – particularly around horseshoe-shaped **Molasses Reef**. Two coastguard cutters were deliberately sunk here in 1987 since the coral was in such a bad state that authorities intervened to provide divers and tourists with other appealing sights. The best visibility for diving is a few miles northeast of Molasses at **the Elbow** – the reef closest to the cleansing Gulf Stream, which keeps the waters clear. There are a number of intriguing, barnacle-encrusted nineteenth-century ships here for dive-based exploration.

Otherwise, head for the waters just off **Cannon Beach**, where you'll find the remains of an early Spanish shipwreck; of course, like most of the Keys' diveable wrecks, it too was deliberately brought here to bolster tourism in the Seventies, which lessens the allure somewhat and means you definitely won't find any treasure.

Arguably one of the weirdest sights in the Keys is the algae-soaked **Christ of the Deep** statue, a nine-foot bronze memorial to sailors who lost their lives at sea, which lies 20 feet down at Key Largo Dry Rocks – visible only by snorkelling or scuba diving. It was donated by an Italian industrialist and sports fisherman, and is a replica of Guido Galletti's *Christ of the Abyss*, similarly submerged off the coast of Genoa, Italy.

Swimming with dolphins

Dolphins are still a common sight around Miami and the Florida Keys – go out into the deeper waters on a charter and you should spot one at some point during the day. To find out why so many people rave about the animals (and often claim some sort of nonverbal communication with them), schedule a session to swim alongside a dolphin or two. The Keys is a handier place to try this than Miami, with two facilities in Key Largo that rarely book up (it's still wise to call in advance and schedule a session). **Dolphins Plus** is just south of MM 100-Oceanside at 31 Corrine Pl (daily 8am–6pm; ☏1-866/860-7946, ⊛www.dolphinsplus.com). It's an education and research facility where you can indulge in a dolphin encounter with one of twelve friendly creatures in the ocean. The price of a structured, half-hour swim is $165 (8.30am, 12.45pm, and 3pm; to observe only $10, under-17s $5, under-5s free), and there is also a "natural" swim with wild dolphins for $125 – though with the latter, contact is not guaranteed (9.30am & 1.30pm).

The other venue is **Dolphin Cove**, a five-acre marine environment research center at MM 102-Bayside (daily 8am–5pm; ☏305/451-4060). If you have a swimsuit, a towel, and $165, you can join sessions that run daily at 9am, 1pm, and 3.30pm (weekends only March to mid-Dec) – plan to book around four weeks in advance. The dolphins here live in a small inlet that opens directly onto the sea, so the experience is a little more authentic than swimming laps in a pool. There's also a "natural" swim for $125 (9.45am & 1.45pm). If you can't afford a close encounter, $20 (under-16s $15) gets you in as a non-swimming observer.

There are various ways to see the park's different reefs, all run by the same park concessionaire (☏305/451-6300, ⊛www.pennekamppark.com): **snorkeling tours** (daily 9am, noon & 3pm; 2hr 30min; $29, plus $5 for equipment), a **guided scuba dive** (daily 9.30am & 1.30pm; 1hr 30min; $50; diver's certificate required), or for the lazy, a two-and-a-half hour **glass-bottomed-boat-tour** (9.15am, 12.15pm & 3pm; $22).

Aside from the wrecks, there are nature trails through hardwood hammock and mangrove swamps here, as well as two man-made beaches – of the two, Far Beach close to the visitor center is better for sunbathing and paddling. It's sheltered by a well-concealed artificial seawall and there's a pavilion nearby with vending machines.

Florida Keys Wild Bird Center

Just south along Hwy-1 from the John Pennekamp State Park is the **Florida Keys Wild Bird Center**, 93600 Overseas Hwy-Bayside (daily 8.30am–5.30pm; $3; ☏305/852-4486, ⊛www.fkwbc.org). Located on the northern outskirts of small, homely Tavernier, this hospital and sanctuary receives wounded birds from around the Keys; many have flown into telephone wires or choked on fishing hooks. The staff nurses most until they can be returned to the wild, while those too badly injured remain in specially constructed habitats. A visit here is a great way to get close to local species, including the gaggles of pelicans waddling around. An eco-friendly walkway made from recycled materials snakes through the aviary, and many long-term residents are tame enough to approach.

Islamorada

Workaday **Islamorada** is best known for the WPA-funded, Art Deco **Florida Keys Memorial** in the center of town at MM 82-Oceanside. The Hurricane

Monument commemorates the Labor Day storm in 1935 that swept through the Middle Keys with winds of up to 200mph and the lowest barometric reading on record. Loss of life and property was severe; the cremated remains of the 425 people who died were placed in the memorial in 1937. It's recently been spruced up after decades of disrepair – look for the sparkling mosaic showing a map of the Middle Keys and the stone relief of coconut palm trees bending ominously in the wind. Along with hosting the best local accommodation options, Islamorada is also worth a stop for both a wide range of fishing charters and **Anne's Beach**, a terrific man-made strip that's small but clean. Though there are no concessions or ocean activities on offer here, there are picnic areas and a grassy lawn rimming the narrow beach itself.

Indian Key Historic State Park

Further south along Hwy-1, a trip to the wilderness of **Indian Key Historic State Park** (daily 8am–sunset; free; ☏305/664-2540, ⓦwww.floridastateparks. org/indiankey) reveals the ruins of what was once the last inhabited outpost on the journey down to Key West. This is an evocative, if crumbling, reminder of early settler life in the Keys – take special note of the grassy paddock that was once the town square. Seek out the observation tower, too, which gives spectacular views across the island's lush and jumbled foliage.

Much like the vegetation here, Indian Key's history is jumbled. In 1831, a rogue wrecker named Jacob Houseman, driven out of Key West in disgrace, bought this island to build his own fiefdom. He succeeded, racking up $30,000 and furnishing the eleven-acre key with streets, a post office, a resort hotel, and even a bowling alley; its population numbered around fifty. Houseman was frequently accused of deliberately running ships aground on the reef using misleading lanterns on the island's shore; eventually he did lose his license for salvaging from an anchored boat. Indian Key was eventually sold but a brutal Seminole attack in 1840 leveled the town, ending the island's habitation as quickly as it had begun.

Lignumvitae Key Botanical State Park

On the north side of Hwy-1, roughly opposite Indian Key on the south side, the **Lignumvitae Key Botanical State Park** (Thurs–Mon 8am–5pm; free; ☏305/664-2540, ⓦwww.floridastateparks.org/lignumvitaekey) is the best remaining example of original Florida Keys tropical hammock. It's named for the medicinal hardwood *lignumvitae* (meaning "wood of life") tree, abundant in the Caribbean but whose habitat stretches no further north than this island.

This island was purchased for $1 by billionaire William Matheson in 1919 in order to further his research into tropical plants. It's now primarily used as a research facility by the University of Miami and other like-minded groups. There's a small caretaker's house, originally built by the Mathesons in the 1930s then blown away by a hurricane in 1935 but reconstructed, though it holds little of interest other than some trinkets and ephemera. Rather, focus on the exotic vegetation – knowledgeable rangers lead 60-minute **tours** ($1; Thurs–Mon 10am & 2pm) that provide thorough background on all the indigenous plants that flourish here: there are also a large number of sizeable spiders, such as the golden orb, that spin webs across the paths. The island is ravaged by **mosquitoes**, so bring long sleeves and long pants plus plenty of repellent if you decide to make the trip.

Upper Keys practicalities

The easiest way to reach Lignumvitae Key is by **boat** from Robbie's Marina, located at MM 75.5-Bayside, Islamorada (Thurs–Mon 10am & 2pm; $20; ℡305/664-9814, Ⓦwww.robbies.com). Indian Key's a little trickier – the dock there was destroyed in a recent hurricane and has yet to be rebuilt, so tours were suspended at time of writing; it's still possible to visit, though, if you kayak out to the island instead.

The best **accommodation** options for the Upper Keys are in Islamorada, though don't expect to snag a room for much less than $90, especially in high season. The popular *Holiday Isle Beach Resort*, MM 84-Oceanside (℡305/664-2321 or 1-800/327-7070, Ⓦwww.holidayisle.com; $145), is a psychedelic trip: vivid citrus-colored plastics and tiki huts fill this vacation village. The atmosphere is young and friendly, and the hotel itself is very comfortable. A cheaper option, the *Key Lantern/Blue Fin* at MM 82.1-Bayside (℡305/664-4572, Ⓦwww.keylantern.com; $55), has basic, if a little frayed rooms. If you have a choice, take a room in the *Blue Fin*, as these were redone more recently.

As for **eating**, try the *Islamorada Restaurant & Bakery*, MM81.6-Bayside (℡305/664-8363), famous locally for its gooey cinnamon buns; there are some tables inside and out if you want to linger. The *Hungry Tarpon*, at MM 77.5-Bayside, Lower Matecumbe Key (℡305/664-0535), serves superb fish from local recipes in a converted 1940s bait shop, as well as hearty breakfasts; while *Squid Row* at MM 81.9-Oceanside (℡305/664-9865) is a large, low-slung fish restaurant with comfortable booths and long-serving waitresses – the bargain three-buck margaritas are a plus. The smartest option for budget eating, though, is in Tavernier. Despite its dismal exterior, the *Sunshine Supermarket*, at MM 91.8-Oceanside (no phone and no English spoken), is a hidden gem. At its small café inside, you can get a top-notch *cafecito* for $1 and piled-high plates of Cuban food; a plate of rice and beans is only $4.

The Middle and Lower Keys

Between Islamorada and Key West lie the **Middle** and **Lower Keys**, split in half at the western end of the **Seven Mile Bridge**. The one major settlement in the Middle Keys is **Marathon**, an appealingly blue-collar town with ample amenities that makes a terrific base for exploring; **Bahia Honda State Recreational Park** is just twelve miles south from here.

The Lower Keys are much larger, and heavily residential: it's worth pausing here before racing on to Key West, especially on Big Pine Key for the **Key Deer Refuge**, as well as trips out to the **Looe Key Marine Sanctuary**. Aligned north–south (rather than east–west) and resting on a base of limestone (rather than a coral reef), these islands have flora and fauna that are very much their own: the reason is that this limestone erodes more easily than coral rock, leaving hollows to fill with rain water that will sustain **animals**. Species like the Key Deer, the Lower Keys Cotton Rat, and the Cudjoe Key Rice Rat – all of which are endangered – live here, though mainly tucked away miles from the Overseas Highway.

Marathon

Named after the back-breaking shifts workers endured as they raced against Henry Flagler's failing health to finish the Seven Mile Bridge, which begins just south of here, **Marathon** is the liveliest town in the Middle Keys, with ample food and lodging options at all prices. It wasn't always so busy – by 1926, the population here was only 17; rather, the sportfishing craze of the 1950s revived the town after a moribund few decades. It's located on Key Vaca, so named by the Spanish because the natives they encountered here ate manatees, or sea cows, as staples in their diet – the endangered animals are now as rare round here as they are in and around Miami.

If you don't wish to explore the ocean and countryside in and around Marathon, spend the day at **Sombrero Beach** (daily 7.30am–dusk). Follow the signs for Sombrero Beach Road off the Overseas Highway near MM 50-Oceanside: at the promontory, there's a slender, well-kept strip of sand, with full facilities including showers and picnic tables, and ample shade from lush palms.

Crane Point Hammock

The tropical hardwood hammock is one of the most ecologically precious areas in the Keys, and this 63-acre woodland, known as **Tropical Crane Point Hammock** (Mon–Sat 9am–5pm, Sun noon–5pm; $8; ☎305/743-9100, ⓦwww.cranepoint. net), surprisingly in the heart of Marathon, is a good place to see it up close. You'll find the entrance by turning north onto 55th Street at MM 50.5-Bayside (opposite the K-Mart). The entry fee includes a booklet with details of the trees found along the easy one-mile **nature trail**. Also on the trail is one of the last examples of Bahamian architecture in the US: the **Adderley House**, built in 1903 by Bahamian immigrants, gives a vivid impression of what life was like for them, with its simple construction and bare-bones amenities. The detailed **Museum of Natural History of the Florida Keys** gives an overview of both the geological and political histories of the Keys, including the wrecking of *HMS Looe* (see p.232), as well as a raft made of inner tubes that carried four Cuban refugees across ninety miles of ocean in the early 1990s.

The hammock's resident **mosquitoes** are a painful nuisance, so consider buying bug spray at the pharmacy directly opposite.

The Seven Mile Bridge

Connecting Marathon to the Lower Keys is the **Seven Mile Bridge**, a stunning feat of engineering when built in 1908 and equally impressive a century later. Eschewing landfill to preserve the deep Moser Channel for commercial shipping, Henry Flagler sought to bridge the unthinkable seven-mile gap between Key Vaca and Bahia Honda Key, thereby providing a course for extending his railroad. At one point, every US-flagged freighter on the Atlantic was hired to bring in materials while floating cranes, dredges, and scores of other craft set about a job that eventually cost the lives of seven hundred laborers. Using his own technicians, Flagler oversaw the completion of the bridge in only four years (a year ahead of schedule) at a staggering cost of $22 million. Although the railway was soon wiped out by the hurricane of 1935, the bridge itself held. (For more on Flagler, see p.253 "Contexts: History")

By 1982, though, it was superseded by a wider, modern structure, built to better allow trucks passage back and forth along the highway; sadly, the newer bridge's walls are just high enough to obscure the fabulous views. Moreover, Flagler's bridge, built with imported German concrete chemically impervious to salt water seepage, is as strong as ever though abandoned; while the cheaper, bigger, modern bridge is already corroding and in need of repair less than thirty years after its construction.

Pigeon Key

A flat, treeless island left to the pigeons by early European settlers (hence its name), **Pigeon Key** (daily 10am–4pm; $11; ☎305/289-0025, ⓦwww.pigeonkey.net) was developed during the mammoth construction of Flagler's Miami–Key West railway and served as a camp from 1908 to 1935. Houses were built for the immigrant workers from the Bahamas, Cuba, and Puerto Rico who'd replaced Northeastern laborers who'd fled the heat, mosquitoes, and malaria soon after arriving. The island was bought by the University of Miami in the middle of the last century and used for scientific experiments, before being leased to a nonprofit foundation that has restored the buildings and runs residential courses for local teens to learn about marine biology.

Cars are not permitted access to Pigeon Key, which contributes to the serene atmosphere of the place. Access to the island is via one of two ways: the simplest is on foot, strolling along a short span of Flagler's old bridge, though small ferries also leave from the visitors' center on Knight's Key (daily 10am, 11.30am, 1pm, 2.30pm; reserve on ☎305/743-5999). Once on the island, there's a tiny museum on the island itself with pictures of former residents and revealing census data, but aside from that there's little to do other than wander around and imagine what life must have been like for those early laborers.

Bahia Honda State Recreational Park

Once you leave the soaring new Seven Mile Bridge, you've entered the Lower Keys. **Bahia Honda State Recreational Park** at MM 37-Oceanside (daily 8am–sunset; $3.50 for single-occupant vehicle, $6 for double, 50 cents per additional passenger, $1.50 pedestrians; ☎305/872-2353, ⓦwww.floridastateparks.org/bahiahonda) marks the division between the Upper and Middle Keys, comprised largely of coral rock, and the Lower Keys from here on, which are made of limestone.

Most visitors stop for the park's **beaches**, including a glorious two-mile-long strip of white sand, one of the few natural beaches in the Keys. Closest to the park entrance, delightful Sandspur Beach has all the usual amenities and scattered plants growing in the sand, while Calusa and Loggerhead beaches at the western tip are more family-friendly, each with a specially marked swimming area and marina, though the ripe ocean smells and sea-grass debris may be off-putting to some. If you want to find a solitary spot to sunbathe, pick through the undergrowth to the two-story **Flagler Bridge**, immediately south of which lies a gloriously isolated strip of golden sand. The unusually deep waters here (Bahia Honda is Spanish for "deep bay") made this the toughest of the old railway bridges to construct, and widening it for the road proved impossible: the solution was to put the highway on a higher tier. It's actually far safer than it looks, and there's a fine view from the top of the bridge over the Bahia Honda channel toward the forest-coated Lower Keys if you clamber up.

Take care when swimming in the deep waters off the park's southern tip here, as currents can be strong. If you're **snorkelling** here – there's no reef but plenty of marine animals – there's a concession at the marina that rents equipment ($10 per person for masks, fins, and snorkels; ☎305/872-3210, ⓦwww.bahiahondapark. com); they also rent kayaks and run reef dive-trips.

Otherwise, the park's known for its rare and unusual plants, such as the endangered silver palms, and there's a pleasant nature **trail** that weaves along the coast through the tropical hardwood hammock; self-guiding leaflets are available at the entrance. If you want to **spend the night**, there's a choice of camping or one of three raised cabins on the waterfront ($120 per night, sleeps up to six people): for these, book well ahead, as they're very popular in season – call ☎1-800/326-3521 or visit ⓦwww.reserveamerica.com for reservations.

Key Deer Refuge

The 8400-acre **Key Deer Refuge**, at MM 33-Bayside (park open daily sunrise–sunset, visitor center in Big Pine Shopping Center open Mon–Fri 8am–5pm; free; ⊤305/872-0774, ⓦwww.fws.gov/nationalkeydeer), stretches across Big Pine and adjacent No Name Key and is the only home of the **Key Deer**, a rare subspecies of white-tailed deer.

The deer, no bigger than large dogs, arrived long ago when the Keys were still joined to the mainland; they provided food for sailors and Key West residents for many years, but hunting and the destruction of their natural habitat led to near-extinction by the late 1940s. The **National Key Deer Refuge** was set up here in 1954 to safeguard the animals – one refuge manager went so far as to burn the cars and sink the boats of poachers – and their population has now stabilized between 250 and 300. Don't feed them (it's illegal), and be cautious when driving – signs alongside the road state the number of road-kills to date during the year.

The best time to spot the deer is at sunrise or sunset, when they take advantage of their sharp eyesight and come out to forage in safety. Don't miss the **hiking trails** here, either – Blue Hole is a large freshwater lake that's home to plenty of soft-shelled turtles and alligators, and a good place for bird spotting.

Nearby **No Name Key** is home to a few settlers, living with solar power and septic tanks. It's notable as the staging ground for the Bay of Pigs invasion; it was here that Cuban patriots practiced before their disastrous attempt to dislodge Castro and the remnants of the decaying airstrip can be made out in a clearing on the south of the Key. It's also the site of one of the quirkiest restaurants in the Keys – the *No Name Pub* (see opposite).

Looe Key Marine Sanctuary

Named after the British frigate *HMS Looe* that sank here – just off Ramrod Key – in 1744, there's no Looe Key landmass. Instead, the **Looe Key Marine Sanctuary** (Mon–Fri 8am–5pm; ⊤305/292-0311, ⓦfloridakeys.noaa.gov/) consists of five square miles of protected coral reef that makes for some of the best and easiest snorkeling in all the Keys; if you make one dive trip along the route to Key West, make it here. The water ranges in depth from 8 to 35 feet, so it's ideal for both novices and experienced snorkelers, and like the Elbow in John Pennekamp State Park, it's cleansed by the Gulf Stream, which keeps water clearer. The coral formations on the Y-shaped reef are enormous – look for showy elkhorn and star coral, not to mention deadly but shortsighted barracuda. Don't come to see a sunken ship, though: the *HMS Looe* has long since disintegrated, and all that's left are a few hard-to-spot ballast stones. For snorkel tour operators here, see the box on p.225.

Middle and Lower Keys practicalities

In the Middle and Lower Keys, Marathon is your best bet for **accommodation**. *Banana Bay*, MM 49.5-Bayside (⊤305/743-3500 or 1-800/BANANA-1, ⓦwww.bananabay.com; $145), is a lush, palm-crowded resort with airy, tropical rooms and good onsite amenities, popular with holidaymaking British families. The *Flamingo Inn*, MM 59.3-Bayside (⊤305/289-1478 or 1-800/439-1478, ⓦwww.theflamingoinn.com; $95), is an old-style motel with big, clean rooms engagingly painted in lurid pinks and greens, while the *Sea Dell Motel*, MM 49.8-Bayside (⊤305/743-5161 or 1-800/648-3854; ⓦwww.seadellmotel.com; $130), features spotless, simply furnished, bright, white and turquoise rooms. Midrange hotels and motels in the Lower Keys tend to be poor value; if you're determined to stay here, splurge on a night or two at the lavish *Little Palm Island*, MM 28.5-Oceanside, Little Torch Key (☎305/515-4004 or 1-800/343-8567, ⓦwww.littlepalmisland. com; no children; from $970), whose thatched cottages are set in lush gardens a few feet from the beach on the private islet.

As for **eating**, the moderately priced *Castaway Restaurant*, 1406 Oceanview Ave near MM 47.5-Oceanside in Marathon (☎305/743-6247), is known for its tasty and unusual alligator-tail dishes – you can also bring your own fish for cooking – as well as its doughy honey-drenched buns. Nearby *Porky's BBQ*, MM 47.5-Bayside (☎305/289-2065), is a thatched-roof shack serving inexpensive BBQ platters. While the *Seven Mile Grill*, MM 47.5-Bayside (☎305/743-4481), may not look like much (its decoration is limited to walls covered in old beer cans), locals flock here for fine conch chowders and shrimp steamed in beer, as well as splendid Key Lime Pie – said to be the best outside Key West.

Further south, seek out the devilishly hard to find *No Name Pub*, MM 30-Bayside (☎305/872-9115, ⓦwww.nonamepub.com). This rollicking **bar** is well worth the rather circuitous detour for a sight of the unusual wallpaper: dollar bills covering every inch of wall and ceiling inside, worth some $60,000 by the owners' account. If you fancy adding a bill or two, just ask the staff for the house staple-gun. To find the pub, turn right at the only stoplight in Big Pine (MM 30) and follow the right-hand fork when the road splits. Continue for 100 yards or so to another stop sign, and turn left; take the curving road for two miles through a residential neighborhood until the pub appears on the left, just before the bridge that leads to No Name Key. The best coffee in the Keys is at *Baby's*, MM 15-Oceanside, Baypoint Key (☎1-800/523-2326, ⓦwww.babyscoffee.com), a roadside industrial shack where beans are roasted on site.

There isn't much **nightlife** in Big Pine – locals tend to drive down to Key West. Marathon's livelier: start off at *The Hurricane Grille*, MM 49.5-Bayside (☎305/743-2220), a classic roadside American bar with nightly live music on a small stage at the back. This is an early stop on the nightly pub-crawl that concludes around 4am in the *Brass Monkey*, MM 50-Oceanside in nearby K-Mart Plaza.

Key West

The southernmost point of the continental United States (just sixty miles north of the Tropic of Cancer) is in **Key West** – and it shows. An easy blend of Caribbean and American cultures, its Old Town is packed with ice-cream-colored colonial houses and unhurried locals, washed over with a sense that this could be the town at the edge of the world. It's closer to Cuba, only ninety miles to the south, than mainland America – in fact the first international long-distance telephone call from the US connected Key West to Cuba. Even now, thanks to the old cigar-makers' cottages, *café con leche*, and signs that point to Havana, Cuba's forbidden presence is strong.

Key West exudes a palpably carefree attitude; whatever happens in life, people here (known as Conchs) seem determined to remain unruffled. It's partly this supine tolerance that has allowed a huge, quietly integrated gay population to accumulate in Key West in the past thirty years. Yet as wild as it may at first appear, Key West today is far from being the misfits' paradise that it was just a decade or so ago. Much of the sleaziness has been gradually brushed away through rather cutesy restoration and revitalization; the town's soaring popularity with tourists has inflated real estate prices to an extreme where locals either can't afford to stay, or choose to cash in a centuries-old family home for millions. The result of this exodus has been the arrival en masse of wealthy weekending Miamians – some estimates peg forty percent of the houses here as second or holiday homes.

Some history

Key West is reportedly a corruption of the Spanish explorers' original name for the island. Native Americans here left the bones of their dead in sand dunes along the shore; the Spaniards found them, naming the place *Cayo Hueso* (meaning "Bone Island"), which was then anglicized into Key West. And though this is the westernmost of the Keys now connected by the Overseas Highway, it's not the furthest west of all the Keys – those are the Dry Tortugas (see p.244).

Between 1850 and 1865 Key West was the wealthiest city per capita in the United States, its money coming from the **wrecking** business. In the treacherous Florida Straits, there were regular wrecks with precious cargoes, as well as plenty of ships in trouble that paid for rescue with one third of their booty. Inevitably, more than one local wrecker was indicted for facilitating, rather than responding to, a shipwreck. Key West played a crucial role in the **Civil War**, as it, along with Fort Jefferson (see p.244), was a Union port while the rest of Florida sided with the Confederacy. Its decision to side with the North wasn't wholly voluntary – Key West's port was being blockaded into submission. There was a smart economic reason for the Union forces to focus on winning Key West: the North's navy regularly captured Confederate ships nearby, en route to resupply the Southern forces via New Orleans. Once commandeered, these captive enemy vessels could be liquidated for cash at Key West's lucrative wreckers' auctions as long as Key West was Union-controlled.

The building of reef lighthouses sounded the death knell for the wrecking business by the end of the nineteenth century, but Key West continued to prosper. **Cubans** arrived with their cigar-making skills, and migrant **Greeks** established a lucrative sponge enterprise (the highly absorbent sea sponges, formed from the skeletons of tiny marine creatures, were the forerunners of today's synthetic sponges). Industrial unrest and a sponge blight drove these businesses north to Tampa and Tarpon Springs, leaving Key West ill prepared to face the **Depression**, which, by the summer of 1934, had driven nearly all the Conchs into bankruptcy. The government suggested abandoning Key West entirely and moving the Conchs en masse to the mainland, but the WPA, part of Franklin Roosevelt's New Deal, was savvy enough to realize it was better to tidy up the key and ready it for tourism.

Clearly, it wasn't to be – at least then, as the **1935 Labor Day hurricane** blew away the Flagler railway, Key West's only land link to the outside world. The city settled into a sleepy easiness, and while elsewhere in postwar America, old homes were torn down for modern prefabs, there was no money for this in Key West; effectively, the city was flash frozen by its own poverty, so that the conch houses so cherished today were left untouched.

In the 1970s, Key West gained prominence as a gay mecca, although the reasons for this are foggy. Local laid-back attitudes played a part, as did the gay revolution of the 1960s, which galvanized scattered groups into a community that could act in concert, including moving to certain towns like Key West or San Francisco. Local gay historians also note that early gay residents like Tennessee Williams hosted visitors from across the country, who acted as unofficial emissaries for the town's tolerance and tropical weather when they returned home.

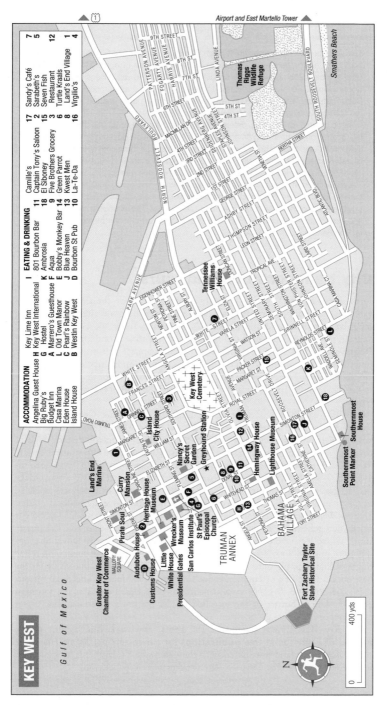

KEY WEST

Gulf of Mexico

Airport and East Martello Tower ▲

Smathers Beach

Thomas Riggs Wildlife Refuge

ACCOMMODATION

Angelina Guest House	I	Key Lime Inn	J
Big Ruby's		Key West International	
Budget Inn		Hostel	G
Casa Marina		Marrero's Guesthouse	A
Eden House		Old Town Manor	L
Island House		Pearl's Rainbow	C
		Westin Key West	B

EATING & DRINKING

801 Bourbon Bar	11	Camille's	17
Ambrosia	18	Captain Tony's Saloon	2
Aqua	K	El Siboney	15
Bobby's Monkey Bar	14	Five Brothers Grocery	9
Blue Heaven	J	Green Parrot	3
Bourbon St Pub	D	Kwest Men	13
		La-Te-Da	10

Sandy's Café	7
Sarabeth's	5
Seven Fish	12
Restaurant	
Turtle Kraals	6
Land's End Village	8
Virgilio's	16

Land's End Marina

Greater Key West Chamber of Commerce

Pirate Soul

Curry Mansion

Audubon House

Heritage House Museum

Customs House

Little White House

Presidential Gates

San Carlos Institute

St Paul's Episcopal Church

Wrecker's Museum

Nancy's Secret Garden

Island City House

Key West Cemetery

Greyhound Station

Hemingway House

Lighthouse Museum

TRUMAN ANNEX

BAHAMA VILLAGE

Southernmost House

Southernmost Point Marker

Fort Zachary Taylor State Historical Site

Tennessee Williams House

N

400 yds

0

City transportation and tours

As the sights in Old Town are virtually crammed together, the area is easily navigable on foot – though **renting a bike or scooter** is a good alternative option: try Adventure Scooter & Bicycle Rentals, 1 Duval St (bikes $15 per day with $50 deposit, mopeds $55 per day; ⓣ305/293-0441), with a second branch at 3824 N Roosevelt Blvd (ⓣ305/292-1666). If street signs appear curiously absent, you'll find them painted vertically on the base of each junction lamppost, though many are peeling off. There's also a **bus** service, with two routes that loop through town (daily 6am–11pm; $1 exact change; ⓣ 305/809-3910 ⓦwww.keywestcity. com).

For information, try the useful, if unofficial, **Welcome Center** (Mon–Sat 9am–7.30pm, Sun 9am–6pm; ⓣ305/296-4444 or 1-800/284-4482, ⓦwww. keywestwelcomecenter.com) at 3840 N Roosevelt Blvd on the eastern edge of town as you arrive; or stop by the **Key West Chamber of Commerce**, at 402 Wall St (Mon–Fri 8.30am–6.30pm, Sat & Sun 9am–6pm; ⓣ305/294-2587 or 1-800/527-8539, ⓦwww.keywestchamber.org), in the heart of Old Town. Make sure to grab one of the superb free self-guided walking-tour brochures available at the chamber's Old Town offices and written by the doyenne of local guides, Sharon Wells. She's also available for private **tours** – call ⓣ305/294-0566 for prices and schedules. Local ghostbuster David Sloan also runs fun "haunted" tours, which leave from the *Crowne Plaza La Concha Hotel* at 430 Duval St every night at 8pm and 9pm ($15; ⓣ305/294-9255, ⓦwww.hauntedtours.com). Some might bilk at hopping onto the 90-minute Conch Train trolley, but it's by far the best option for quick orientation – not to mention lashings of anecdotal history ($25; ⓣ1-800/868-7842, ⓦwww.conchtrain.com). Board either at the southern edge of Mallory Square or the so-called Flagler Station stop on Caroline Street near the port.

The *Key West Citizen* newspaper (50 cents; ⓦwww.keysnews.com) plus a number of easily found **free publications** list current events: *Solares Hill* is the most informative (and distributed with the *Citizen* on Fridays), but look out also for the weekly *Key West Citypaper* (ⓦwww.keywestcitypaper.com).

Accommodation

Whatever the time of year, **accommodation** costs in Key West are always high: expect to pay at least $100 in high season for even the simplest motel room. If you do decide to stay here, it's worth the extra cost to stay downtown: the hotels scattered along Hwy-1 as you approach the Old Town may be slightly cheaper, but there is little public transport and parking is nightmarish in high season. If budgets are tight, it's better to spring for central accommodation and stay one day less than deal with the hassle of trekking back and forth from hotel to sights.

A good lodging resource is the Key West Innkeepers Association, headquartered at 922 Caroline St (1-888/492-1911, ⓦwww.keywestinns.com): more than sixty guesthouses and B&Bs in Old Town are members, and the helpful staff can guide you to the right accommodation for price and location. Note that many of the restored villas operating as guesthouses in the historic district are gay- and lesbian-run, and while most welcome all adults, few accept young children. We've listed the specifically gay-targeted accommodation on p.247.

Angelina Guest House 302 Angela St ☎305/294-4480 or 1-888/303-4480, ⓦwww.angelinaguesthouse.com. One of the best deals in town, this charming guesthouse, with a cool, Caribbean feel, is tucked away in the back streets of the Bahama Village. Its fourteen simple rooms are decorated in pastel yellow, green, or blue, and the small pool is a great place to enjoy the owners' cinnamon rolls at breakfast time. Shared bath from $100, private bath from $130.

Budget Inn 1031 Eaton St ☎305/294-3333, ⓦwww.budgetkeywest.com. Stashed north of the Old Town near the seaport, this is a rare find in Key West, with low prices, pleasant rooms, and good location – far from budget in feel. Onsite amenities may be minimal and the staff a little frosty, but the rooms themselves are delightful, with refrigerators and large bathrooms. $140.

Casa Marina 1500 Reynolds Street ☎305/296-3535, ⓦwww.casamarinaresort. com. The historic *Casa Marina*, originally built in 1920 as a hotel by railway magnate Henry Flagler, has had a $43m make-over. The 300-plus rooms sprawl across three separate buildings, though the updated vibe's the same in each – airy and loft like, with dark woods, crisp white sheets, and ceramic tile floors that give more than a whiff of Flagler's Golden Era Florida. Rooms in the original building are the best, for their idiosyncratic layout and wide balconies. $250.

Eden House 1015 Fleming St ☎305/296-6868 or 1-800/533-5397, ⓦwww.edenhouse.com. Don't let the rather shabby reception put

you off this place just south of the port – it's a gem. Rooms (some with private bath) are decorated in the usual pastels and pale woods, though many have large, claw-foot tubs and most overlook the pool. Best of all, there's free off-street parking and a free happy hour every night 4–5pm (plus a complimentary beer at check-in). $135.

Key Lime Inn 725 Truman Ave ☎305/294-5229 or 1-800/549-4430, ⓦwww.keylimeinn.com. There are various different accommodations in this cluster of cottages with Key West tropical decor near the center of Old Town. A good buffet breakfast is served by the pool, and the ample onsite parking is a major plus. Splurge on one of the bungalows for the seclusion and the veranda. $180.

Key West International Hostel 718 South St ☎305/296-5719, ⓦwww.keywesthostel.com. The dorms here are small and grubby, but it is the only hostel on the island and as such hands down the cheapest place to stay. If the hostel's full, the adjoining *SeaShell Motel* is slightly pricier, though no more swanky. Dorms members $31, nonmembers $34; motel from $105.

Marrero's Guesthouse 410 Fleming St ☎305/294-6977 or 1-800/459-6212, ⓦwww.marreros.com. Reputed to be haunted, this fancy but friendly hotel has rooms crammed with antique furniture. Ghost-hunters should ask for Room 18, where most paranormal activity has been reported. Shared bath $130 and up, private bath $160 and up, Room 18 $190.

Old Town Manor 511 Eaton St ☎305/292-2170, ⓦwww.oldtownmanor.com. Internet exec turned B&B maven Runi Goyal took over this space a year or so ago, overhauled its interior from kitsch to era-appropriate Victoriana and snagged a Green Hotel credit for her eco-friendly set-up (no paper bills, full recycling, organic all-natural breakfasts). There's no pool, but a pleasant shady garden out back. If this is full, Goyal also owns nearby *Rose Lane Villas*. $115.

Westin Key West 245 Front St ☎305/294-4000, ⓦwww.starwoodhotels.com/westin/keywest. Superbly situated on the waterfront, this corporate hotel has large rooms, with the standard tropical-floral décor, and there's onsite parking. Splash out for a sea view to enjoy the sunsets from your room – the cruise ships should have left the adjoining dock by then. $280.

The Town

Compact but not small, **Old Town** – at the western end of the island – is where most major sights can be found: it's best to rely on walking as you'll see more local color and worry less about finding parking on the cramped streets. **Mallory**

▲ A street performer in Mallory Square

Square, the old wreckers' dock, is the heart of tourist Key West, hosting well-known sunset celebrations and featuring many museums close by; while **Duval Street**, the main drag, extends south from here.

The city's military history is clear in the **Truman Annex**, once a naval base and now an enclave of the swankiest homes in town. Close by, and very different, the Caribbean contribution to Key West's growth is evident in the old workmen's homes of the **Bahama Village**, a great place to saunter round on a hot, lazy afternoon. The **Hemingway House**, for devoted fans of the author, is just outside the Bahamian quarter. Finally, east from the town center, you'll find **East Old Town**, home to a large historic district of wooden homes.

Mallory Square and around

Originally the hub of Key West's wrecking industry, **Mallory Square**'s buildings were used for the storage and auction of goods salvaged from wrecked ships. Now, it's the hub of Key West's tourist trade, filled with market stalls and street performers.

Every night of the year, the **sunset celebration** sweeps over the area, when jugglers, fire-eaters, and assorted loose-screw types create a merry backdrop to the day's end. The party began with a group of hippies in the 1960s, and if it's not quite the countercultural hangout it once was, it's still worth a stop for the spectacular sunsets over the water and the general liveliness. The big problem these days is the cruise ships that moor here for the day, though their agreements with the local government include a guarantee to have set sail before sunset: slack passengers late to return often mean the spectacular views are blocked by the bulky monsters.

There are two small islands visible just off the northern coast of Mallory Square. To the west, one-time **Tank Key** – named after the huge fuel tanks the Navy used to stash there – is now known as Sunset Key. There's an anodyne luxury resort there, best known as the location of Oprah Winfrey's fiftieth birthday party; accessible via a free ten-minute boat ride from Mallory Square, it is hardly worth the trip. To the east, there's no public access to **Christmas Tree Island** unless you have your own skiff. This was once home to fir trees and hippie dropouts; but its owner finally sold the spot, and its new real estate developer owners – the same people who built and run Sunset Key - have rechristened it Wisteria Island. However, aggressive local opposition to further development has hobbled plans to duplicate Sunset Key's lodgings there; the dispute looks unlikely to be resolved soon.

Audubon House

Just south of Mallory Square stands the **Audubon House** at 205 Whitehead St (daily 9.30am–5pm; $10; ☎305/294-2116 or 1-877/281-BIRD, Ⓦwww.audubonhouse.com). When the wealthy Wolfson family purchased the place to prevent its demolition in 1958 – the site was earmarked for a gas station – they set about restoring the house to its original grandeur, using the family collection of furniture and decorative arts (see p.56). Built by Captain John Geiger, one of the most successful wreckers in Key West in the early nineteenth century, this grand house was once prime seafront property. The name derives from John James Audubon, who was fascinated by Geiger's exotic-plant collection. In fact, the painter and naturalist spent little time here, as he traveled round the Keys focusing on his mammoth book of engravings, *Birds of America*. Today, the house is a superb museum, with an evocative audio tour that fully captures Key West's wrecking heyday; there's also a small onsite gallery of pricey Audubon prints for sale.

▲ Pirate Soul museum

Pirate Soul

A couple blocks west of Mallory Square is **Pirate Soul**, 524 Front Street (daily 9am–7pm, $15; ☎305/292-1113, ⓦwww.piratesoul.com), a surprisingly appealing pirate-centric museum. Sassy and spirited, the museum brings the swashbuckling past of pirates to life better than any other spot in town. It's crammed with pirate-related artefacts, including the sole authenticated pirate chest in the world (look for the hidden lock on this 400-year-old gem); Captain Kidd's actual journal (you can read virtual versions via a touch-screen); and one of only two existing Jolly Rogers. Don't miss the evocative "below decks" room, a pitch-black spot where you sit in darkness wearing headphones as Black Beard whispers in your ear and tells the story of how he died; the three-minute audio is thrilling and vivid, but not suitable for little ones.

Along Duval Street

Jammed with tacky T-shirt and souvenir shops, especially at its northern end, **Duval Street** is often held up as a prime exhibit in the spoiling of Key West (who knows what today's reaction would be if a 1976 plan to turn it into a canal, complete with imported Venetian gondoliers, had been enacted). Despite appearances, there are some surprisingly good restaurants and bars dotted along its length, as well as Key West's most famous watering hole, **Captain Tony's Saloon**, 428 Greene St (seé p.246), where Hemingway drank back when it was called *Sloppy Joe's*. Confusingly, another bar named *Sloppy Joe's*, laden with Hemingway memorabilia, is just across the street, intended to lure ill-informed tourists to spend their money there instead.

One block east off Duval's northern tip, the exhaustively restored **Curry Mansion**, 511 Caroline St (daily 9am–5pm; $5; ☎305/294-5349, ⓦwww.currymansion.com), is an awkward hybrid of museum and hotel. The public rooms are crammed with period antiques and oddities like Henry James's piano, but there's no claim to have authentically replicated how the house looked in its prime. It was first built in 1869 as the abode of William Curry, Florida's first millionaire. The current structure dates from 1886, when Curry's son Milton rebuilt the mansion after a major fire. The real reason to stop by is the tiny lookout on the roof – called a **Widow's Walk**, as such viewpoints were used by sailors' wives to watch for their husbands' hopeful return. Now the tiny terrace gives a great view across Old Town.

Continue down Duval proper and you'll find more traditional sights, like the **Wrecker's Museum** at no. 322, also known as the Oldest House Museum (Thurs-Sat 10am–2pm; $5; ☎305/294-9501, ⓦwww.oirf.org/museums/oldesthouse). Built in 1829 when Florida was still a territory, it is indeed the oldest house in town, though it originally stood a few blocks away at the junction of Whitehead and Caroline streets. Hokey but entertaining, the museum presents the history of wrecking via artifacts and models, as well as the posh furniture of Captain Watlington, one of the house's first inhabitants. Three-quarters of the pieces are original – look for the courting lamp in the parlor, which provided amorous couples the chance to chat as long as the oil lasted, and the lopsided cookhouse in the back garden, built separately from the main house to reduce the risk of fire. There's more than a little poetic license to many of the sea dog yarns the museum recounts, and the saintliness of the selfless wreckers is unintentionally hilarious, given how often they were accused of encouraging, rather than just responding to, lucrative wrecks.

Nicknamed *La Casa Cuba*, the **San Carlos Institute** at no. 516 (Fri–Sun noon–6pm; free; ☎305/294-3887) was founded in 1871 by Cuban expats who wanted to celebrate the language, ideals, and culture of their people. It was here in 1892 that Cuban Revolutionary hero José Martí welded the exiles into a force that would topple the regime ten years later. The current building, which dates from 1924, was financed by a $100,000 grant from the Cuban government after a hurricane wrecked the original wooden shack. Cuban architect Francisco Centurion designed the two-story building in the Cuban Baroque style of the period, noticeable in the wrought-iron balconies and creamy facade. The soil on its grounds is from Cuba's six provinces, and a cornerstone was taken from Martí's tomb. Indeed, it's still owned by the Cuban government and is technically sovereign property and land of Fidel's regime. The building's sporadically open – call to check before heading over even during official hours – and has a passable permanent exhibition focusing on Martí, consisting mostly of old newspaper clippings and letters. You can also pick up a free map here of the **Cuban Heritage Trail**, a self-guided tour of the key sights in Key West.

Continue south along Duval Street to the water and you'll hit the **Southernmost House**, 1400 Duval St (daily 10am–6pm; $8; ☎305/296-3141, ⓦwww.southernmosthouse.com). Originally built for Florida Curry, daughter of the state's first millionaire and sister of the man behind the Curry Mansion (see opposite); the current owners have tried to create a museum filled with random ephemera; pay the entry fee instead for the right to spend the day lounging at the lush pool with a deck overlooking the ocean and a handy poolside bar. It's a 30-second walk from here to the photo op-ready **Southernmost Point Marker**, a squat red, black and white concrete egg that flags the 90-miles that separate America and Cuba. Watch out for the seemingly helpful passersby who offer to take your photograph here – and then demand a tip for their trouble.

The Truman Annex

The **Truman Annex**, which encompasses much of the northwest corner of Key West, was originally part of a naval base established in 1822 to curb piracy in the area; it later became a favored place for flight training thanks to wide uninterrupted air space and clear, predictable local weather. Although the base was decommissioned in the 1970s, the charming old houses here were significantly restored when purchased by a developer in 1986. He encouraged people to amble through the chic streets by opening up the **Presidential Gates** on Caroline Street, which had previously only budged for heads of state. It's now the site of some of the most luxurious homes in Key West – pick up a free map from one of the boxes dotted throughout the complex.

The area is named after its most famous former resident, President Harry S. Truman, who first came here on doctor's orders in March 1946 to recuperate after World War II. He quickly adopted Key West as a second home and spent most of his visits in **The Little White House**, 111 Front St (daily 9am–5pm; $12, admission only by guided tour; ☎305/294-9911, ⊛www.trumanlittlewhitehouse. com). There's not much to see inside the museum other than mid-twentieth-century ephemera, although the knowledgeable docents make it a worthwhile stop with an anecdote-packed account of Truman's life. The Truman Annex also provides access to Fort Zachary Taylor via a fenced roadway; close by, around its southeastern corner at the junction of Fleming and Whitehead streets, you'll find Mile Marker 0, the starting point for the Keys' idiosyncratic address system.

Fort Zachary Taylor State Historical Site

Conceived in the 1840s as part of a coastal defense system that also included Fort Jefferson in the Dry Tortugas, the glory days of **Fort Zachary Taylor** (park daily 8am–sunset, fort structure daily 8am–5pm; $1.50 pedestrians and cyclists, $3.50 for one person plus car, $6.00 for two people plus car, 50¢ each additional person; ☎305/292-6713, ⊛www.floridastateparks.org/forttaylor) came during the Civil War. As a Union stronghold, it was used to block maneuvers by the Confederate navy. Its onsite facilities were cutting-edge when completed, even including a desalination plant for drinking water. Eventually, though, the fort fell into disrepair and disuse, before being turned over to the Navy as a historic site in 1947. The park offers informative guided tours (every day at noon & 2pm), where rangers provide detailed history on the fort.

For many visitors, however, the **beach** is the real reason to come here. It's the best in Key West, and there are full amenities on site, including showers. Be aware, though, that the beach has pebbles rather than sand, and the craggy sea bottom can be tough on your feet, so bring waterproof sandals.

The Bahama Village

One of the few places that still has the feel of old Key West, unrestored and untouristed, the **Bahama Village**, just southeast of the Truman Annex, sprang up in the 1820s after a law was passed making it illegal for vessels salvaged in US waters to be taken elsewhere. Many who worked in the salvage trade were Bahamian, and their temporary homes in Key West became permanent ones.

The small cottages here – formerly home to Cuban cigar-rollers – haven't yet been primped and manicured as many of the other wooden shacks in Old Town have been, and it's a refreshing contrast to the tourist-ready restored homes elsewhere. The reason for coming here is to get a feel for the laid-back vibe, with locals relaxing out on their porches as chickens roam the streets. Chickens may be out everywhere in Key West, but you're likely to see the largest number here: descendants of Cuban fighting cocks, it's illegal to harm them in any way, especially as their appetite for scorpions keeps numbers down. Now-sleepy Petronia Street was once a throbbing hub for jazz clubs that boasted regular gigs by the likes of Louis Armstrong, lured to Key West since there was no racial segregation here. These days, the lone tourist sight is the tacky and eminently avoidable Bahama Village Market, at 318 Petronia St.

The Hemingway House

Just outside the Bahama Village quarter lies the **Hemingway House**, 907 White-head St (daily 9am–5pm; $12; ☏305/294-1136, Ⓦwww.hemingwayhome.com). While the facts of Hemingway's life in (and love of) Key West are much disputed, his former home is one of the most enjoyable sights in town. Hemingway came to Key West on the recommendation of fellow writer John Dos Passos, who raved about fishing here. He bought what's now the Hemingway House in 1931 with an $8000 loan from his then-wife Pauline's rich uncle. Although it had once been one of the grander homes in the town, by Hemingway's time the house had fallen into disrepair and it required substantial renovation; the swimming pool was his only major addition.

Although Hemingway's legend is inextricably linked with Key West, he lived here for only nine years, before divorcing Pauline and moving to Cuba with his fourth (and last) wife, journalist Martha Gelhorn. While in the house, though, he wrote two of his most famous novels, *For Whom the Bell Tolls* and *To Have and Have Not*, set locally during the Depression. His deer-head-dominated study is unsurprisingly compact, practical, and set apart from the rest of the house in its own smaller outbuilding. Restoration of the study and main home has taken them back to how they looked during Papa's time – although his former secretary strongly contests the authenticity of much of the furnishings.

To see inside, join one of the regular half-hour-long **tours** (every ten minutes) led by true Key West eccentrics, who do a good job of spinning stories that play up the writer's machismo – but take everything they say with a grain of salt. One tale that's clearly more fiction than fact is that the dozens of extra-toed cats living here are descendants from a feline family that lived in Hemingway's day. In fact, the large colony of inbred cats that Hemingway once described was from his home in Cuba. These Key West kitties were the cause of another, more recent controversy in 2007, when the US Department of Agriculture investigated the health of these cats after a disgruntled former docent complained about the conditions. The USDA also threatened to fine the museum $200 per day per cat (around $10,000) for not caging the animals. The squabble was solved, sans fine, when extra wire netting was installed on the top of the perimeter walls.

East Old Town

Northeast from the Hemingway House lies Key West's **wooden historic district**, the largest of its kind in the US, bigger than better-known settlements in Savannah, Georgia, or Charleston, South Carolina. The Conch-house style here is a Colonial–Victorian fusion, and there are some excellent examples **along William Street** between Caroline and Angela streets. Shored up by a foundation of coral slabs, the houses themselves were built cheaply and quickly, fanning out from the earliest settlements around the port (now Mallory Square). The reason these houses – along with others in the rest of Old Town – have lasted so well is that they were put up by shipwrights using boat-building techniques, so they sway in high winds and weather extremes of climate handily. A fine example of this early Key West architecture is the *Island City House Hotel*, at 411 William St – built in the 1880s, it's the oldest hotel in town.

An only-in-Key-West oddity in this area is **Nancy's Secret Garden**, tucked away on an alleyway on the block of Simonton between Fleming and Southard streets, at 1 Free School Lane (daily 10am–5pm; $10; ☏305/294-0015, Ⓦwww.nfsgarden.com). The place is the work of Nancy Forrester, an "environmental artist" who's recreated a tiny, soothing patch of rainforest in the middle of Key West complete with chairs and tables to linger at plus squawking caged parrots. At time of writing, she was also prepping a cabin, her former art studio at its center that could be rented for peacefully private overnight stays – call for rates and details. The voluntary entrance fee may seem pricey, but it's a sanctuary from the business of Duval Street; bring a book and chill here for the afternoon.

On the far eastern edge of Old Town, twenty minutes' walk from the center, stands the **Tennessee Williams House**, 1431 Duncan St, home to the Southern playwright for over thirty years. He led a quiet life in Key West and it was one of the conditions in his will under which his house in Key West was sold that it never be open to public visitors. It's still a fine Bahamian-style home, but only really worth the pilgrimage if you're a devoted fan of the *A Streetcar Named Desire* author. Note that Williams isn't buried in the cemetery here, either – against his wishes, the author's family shipped his body back to his detested hometown of St Louis and interred it there.

Dry Tortugas National Park

Almost seventy miles west from Key West lie the seven islands of the **Dry Tortugas**, exhilaratingly isolated and a birdwatcher's paradise; they're also the site of the ruins of Fort Jefferson. The islands were named by Ponce de León in 1513, who found *tortugas*, or sea turtles, plentiful here. He also found eleven islands – since then, four have eroded completely. The name of the cluster was modified on sea charts in the 1930s to indicate that there was no fresh water on the islands – in other words, they were dry. Of the seven, **Loggerhead Key** is technically the last of the Florida Keys: after that, the sea floor falls away sharply to 1000 feet or more.

Unfortunately, **Fort Jefferson** was militarily redundant almost from its inception in 1846: conceived as part of a coastal defense system against British naval build-up in Bermuda, much like Fort Zachary Taylor (see p.242), it was rendered useless after the invention of the rifled canon. First money and then the Civil War held up construction, as evidenced by the change in brick color half-way up the outer walls: a Union stronghold, Fort Jefferson had to switch to bricks made in the North, which have weathered far less well in southern humidity than the original, local materials.

For several years, the fort was used as a prison for Union deserters and other undesirables, most famously Dr Samuel Mudd, convicted as an accomplice in President Lincoln's assassination after setting John Wilkes Booth's broken leg the day after the shooting. (Ironically, Mudd received a pardon from President Johnson, after stepping in for the island's dead doctor and treating ailing soldiers during a virulent yellow fever outbreak.) After its period as a prison, the army abandoned the fort in the 1880s; it was first earmarked as a wildlife refuge before finally snagging status as an official National Park.

These days, **Bush and Long keys** serve as sanctuaries for sooty terns and frigate birds. In addition, coral reefs here are close to the beach, especially on the western coasts, making for sensational snorkeling. If you plan to stay overnight, the **camping** fee is $3 per person, but bring everything you'll need – including fresh water – as facilities are very basic. Call ☎305/242-7700 for information, or visit ⊛www.nps.gov/drto.

The only way to make the trip here is by **boat** or plane: the *Yankee Freedom II* leaves daily from the dock at the end of Margaret Street on Key West at 8am ($149 day-trip; $169 overnight; ☎305/294-7009 or 1-800/322-0013, ⊛www.yankeefreedom.com), returning at 5pm. However, northerly winds can make for an extra-bumpy ride, so those with wobbly sea legs might prefer to spend a little extra and **fly**: try Seaplanes of Key West, at 3471 S Roosevelt Blvd ($229/half-day, $405/full day, ☎305/294-0709 or 1-800/950-2FLY, ⊛www.seaplanesofkeywest.com).

The Key West Cemetery

On the corner of Angela and Frances streets, the **Key West Cemetery** (daily sunrise–6pm; free) was founded in 1847. Residents needed a new eternal resting place after the town's original waterfront cemetery was ghoulishly churned up in a violent storm; and most of those buried in this landlocked cemetery are entombed in vaults above ground, both thanks to the hard coral rock and the high water-table. There may be a lack of celebrity stiffs here, but by wandering through this large graveyard you'll notice the impact of immigration on Key West – the cemetery is filled with people from across the country and abroad. The sprinkling of campy epitaphs makes this a livelier graveyard than normal – look for the grave of E. Lariz, enshrined forever as "devoted fan of singer Julio Iglesias," or B.P. Roberts, who continues to carp from beyond the grave: "I told you I was sick." Use Sharon Wells' free guide (see p.236) to hit the highlights or take one of the superb tours run by the Historic Florida Keys Foundation (Tues & Thurs 9.30am; $10; T305/292-6718).

Eating, drinking, and nightlife

There are plenty of good **restaurants** in and around Duval Street, even if at first glance they seem rather tacky. It's also worth dipping into the Bahama Village for cheap, authentic Caribbean food. For Cuban coffee and sandwiches, check out the streetside lunch counters – two worth trying are *Sandy's Café* at the M&M Laundry, 1026 White St (T305/295-0159), which also serves sloppy, filling sandwiches for $5, and *Five Brothers Grocery*, at 930 Southard St (T305/296-5205).

Every restaurant in town offers its take on **Key Lime Pie**: one of the best slices ($7) is served at *Key Lime Heaven*, a tropical upstairs café at 308 Front St (T305/294-2042). The other dish on offer everywhere is **conch fritters**; they're a local specialty, even if radical overfishing in the last hundred years depleted stocks so much that all conch is now imported from the Bahamas. Try *Bo's Fish Wagon*, 801 Caroline St (T305/294-9272), for fritters and delicious fish sandwiches, especially on Friday nights when there's live music.

As for **drinking**, many hotels offer good deals on drinks during happy hour (usually 5–7pm), and there are some good rundown bars in the Old Town, many of which also showcase **live music**. Another alternative is the neon-flagged Tropic Cinema, with two smallish screens that specializes in foreign, alternative and art-house **movies** (416 Eaton Street; T305/295-9493).

Cafés and restaurants

Ambrosia 1401 Simonton Street T305/293-0304. Much loved sushi joint that found new digs inside the Santa Maria hotel's vintage porte cochère: it's decked out with mod furniture – wicker egg chairs, mid-Century ornaments – with a huge black marble sushi bar for solo diners. The hand rolls ($3–12), sushi (from $1.50/piece) and à la carte tempura (from $1.50/piece) are all made by true Japanese sushi chefs.

Blue Heaven 729 Thomas St T305/296-8666, Wwww.blueheavenkw.com. Serving outstanding food in a relaxed setting, this Bahama Village landmark has a large outdoor seating area that diners share with

local chickens. Open all day, the breakfasts are delicious (try the lobster Benedict), but lunch and dinner are even better – don't miss the shrimp with jerk seasoning or pork tenderloin with sweet potato for $25–30. Save room for the home-made banana bread and one of the sumptuous desserts. Closed Sept.

Camille's 1202 Simonton St T305/296-4811, Wwww.camilleskeywest.com. Camille's is known as one of the best places in town for breakfast, thanks to luxurious specials like French toast with Godiva chocolate sauce or cashew-nut waffles with coconut milk. Dinner's less exciting, though.

El Siboney 900 Catherine St ☎ 305/296-4184. Crammed with tables and jammed with people, this large Cuban restaurant on the eastern side of the Old Town has cheap food (mains $9–15) and vast portions; the pork tenderloin is especially tasty.

Sarabeth's 530 Simonton St ☎ 305/293-8181. Outpost of the New York eatery, stashed in an old wooden clapboard synagogue with whirring ceiling fans and a light jazz soundtrack, all of which give the place a welcoming, homey vibe. The food's equally homestyle, from the moist roast chicken served with crisp green beans to a turkey club with maple mustard mayo. Brunch is also a buzzy time. Budget $40/head for dinner, a little less for its busy brunch. Closed Tues.

Seven Fish Restaurant 632 Olivia St ☎ 305/296-2777, ⓦ www.7fish.com. This little-known bistro, easy to miss in its tiny, white corner building, serves some of the best food in Key West at reasonable prices (starters around $8, mains $20). The cooking's simple and delicious – think shrimp scampi and meatloaf – and the crowd is a mix of straight and gay. There are just over a dozen tables, so it pays to book.

Bars and nightclubs

Captain Tony's Saloon 428 Greene St ☎ 305/294-1838, ⓦ www.capttonyssaloon.com. This bar was the original *Sloppy Joe's* that Hemingway frequented; now, it's a grimy yellow shack where you can catch live music most nights. Not the most atmospheric place in town, but worth a quick drink.

🏃 **Green Parrot 601 Whitehead St** ☎ 305/294-6133, ⓦ www.greenparrot. com. Grubby pub centered on an enormous square bar that's been a landmark for more than a century. Drinks are cheap, it's full of locals, and there are antique bar games alongside the pool tables. There's often live music at weekends on its small stage.

Turtle Kraals Land's End Village 231 Margaret St ☎ 305/294-2640. A locals' hangout, offering fine views over the marina and mellow blues on Friday and Saturday nights from the second-story Tower Bar. The restaurant's worth stopping by for a hearty breakfast – try the chunky beef hash ($10) – while watching the marina slowly come to life.

Virgilio's Appelrouth Lane, 524 Duval St ☎ 305/296-8118. This martini bar has an outdoor patio, as well as small indoor bar and stage, often occupied by loud Cuban bands. Drinks are served with a flourish, as each cocktail's overflow is presented alongside your glass in a mini-carafe on ice.

Gay Key West

For a town deemed one of the more gay-oriented in America, the scene in Key West is surprisingly small – perhaps because the gay and straight communities are so integrated. Certainly, the wild excesses of the 1970s have been toned down, but despite the new-found restraint, Key West is a place where – in Old Town, at least – gay couples holding hands will pass unremarked upon. Almost every hotel and restaurant will be gay-friendly as well – we've listed some of the best gay-targeted businesses below. Stop by the **Gay and Lesbian Community Center** (☎305/292-3223, ⓦwww.glcckeywest.org) for information and leaflets on specific hotels, or try the **Key West Business Guild**, both at 513 Truman Ave (☎305/294-4603 or 1-800/535-7797, ⓦwww.gaykeywestfl.com).

The unofficial gay beach is **Higgs Memorial Beach**, at the southern end of Reynolds Street. To cruise on water rather than land, take one of the day or evening boat trips that depart from here. One of the best is the women-only Tea on the Sea, run by Sebago Watersports (Thurs $39, including unlimited wine and beer; ☎1-800/507-9955, ⓦwww.keywestsebago.com), which leaves between 5:30 and 6:30pm from the dock at the end of William Street. For information on what's happening pick up a copy of the free *Southern Exposure* magazine (ⓦkwest.com)

Fantasy Fest

In late October, Key West is taken over by **Fantasy Fest**, a week-long gay-dominated version of Mardi Gras that includes parties and events where participants don as outrageous a costume as possible. Every year there's a theme, often with a nod to Halloween: past suggestions have included "TV Jeebies," "Delirious Dreams and Hilarious Screams," and "Freaks, Geeks, and Goddesses."

One of the best-attended events is the midweek **pet costume parade**, where animal are decked out in costumes to resemble their owners. The entire shindig's grown a little less outrageous as Key West's tourist profile's become more mainstream (there are strictly enforced rules about public nudity, for example, which emphasize that body paint does not constitute clothing). Despite the rule tightening, it's still a huge tourist draw, and if you want a room at this time you'll need to book well in advance and expect significant rate hikes (☎305/296-1817, ⊛www.fantasyfest.net).

Accommodation

Big Ruby's 409 Appelrouth Lane ☎305/296-2323 or 1-800/477-7829, ⊛www.bigrubys. com. A cluster of buildings, all dotted round a lagoon pool and patio where you can lounge and listen to piped-in Motown most days. There are lots of extras, including splendid Sunday brunches (try the eggs Benedict), free drinks 6–8pm, and affable staff. $225.

Island House 1129 Fleming St ☎305/294-6284 or 1-800/890-6284, ⊛www.islandhousekeywest. com. Cruisey, men-only resort, with a sauna, video room, and large pool with sundeck (in fact, guests need only wear clothes when using the exercise equipment in the gym).

The surprisingly appealing rooms have over-stuffed leather chairs and crisp white linens. A day-pass to use the hotel's facilities is $25; make sure to bring photo ID. Shared bath $135, private bath $240.

Pearl's Rainbow 525 United St ☎305/292-1450 or 1-800/749-6696, ⊛www.pearlsrainbow.com. The lone women-only guesthouse on the island, this attractive former cigar factory serves breakfast and has two pools and two Jacuzzis. There's also Pearl's Patio, a bar open year-round to nonguests (Sun–Thurs noon–10pm, Fri–Sat noon until midnight). $120.

Gay bars and clubs

801 Bourbon Bar 801 Duval St ☎305/296-1992, ⊛www.801bourbon.com. Drag shows are held upstairs every night at 9pm & 11pm, while downstairs there's a nonde-script bar with a mixed, slightly older crowd that opens out onto the street. The one-time backroom is now home – perhaps tempo-rarily – to a pool table.

Aqua 711 Duval St ☎305/294-0555, ⊛www. aquakeywest.com. Large, pumping club with a massive dancefloor; the music's main-stream house and Hi-NRG. Good happy hour specials 3–8pm daily.

Bobby's Monkey Bar 900 Simonton St ☎305/294-2655. A great place for a quiet drink, this mixed gay/straight bar is a welcoming pub-style joint, with a pool table and a jukebox guaranteed to be blaring mid-80s megahits.

Bourbon Street Pub 724 Duval St ☎305/294-9354, ⊛www.bourbonstreetpub.com. A huge

video bar with five bars, seven screens, and a pleasant garden. There are go-go boys every night, and a happy hour until 8pm. This pub attracts both locals and tourists and, as with most bars in town, the crowd's diverse and chatty.

Kwest Men 705 Duval St ☎305/292-8500. Small, cruisey bar on the main drag where there's a daily happy hour 3–8pm with drinks specials, and go-go boys dancing to the pumping house music from 10pm nightly.

La-Te-Da 1125 Duval St ☎305/296-6706 or 1-877/528-3320, ⊛www.lateda.com. The various bars and discos of this hotel complex have long been a favorite haunt of locals and visitors alike. The upstairs Crystal Room is one of the best-known showcases for drag divas in town – during season, there are shows Sun–Fri at 9pm and Saturday at 8pm and 10pm ($25–29).

Contexts

Contexts

A brief history of Miami

One of the most important cities in the United States, largely thanks to its location on the tip of Florida, **Miami** is both a gateway and a headquarters for most US companies keen to explore the exploding markets in South America. The city has managed to make itself synonymous with hedonism and a guaranteed good time, jostling with Las Vegas as the getaway spot of choice for a wicked weekend.

Though its European settlement dates back almost five hundred years, it wasn't until early in the twentieth century that the city began to prosper as a resort. The following account's intended to give an overview of Miami's history, from the Native American tribes who once lived here through the arrival of the railroad to its current role as the capital city of glitz.

Early natives and European settlement

The Miami area's earliest residents were the **Tequesta Indians**, who made their home some ten thousand years ago near what's now the Deering Estate in Cutler, just south of Miami. They're a mysterious people who left few relics for modern archaeologists looking to reconstruct their civilization – the highest profile is the mystifying Miami Circle (see p.43). The Tequesta lived and farmed the land alone until joined by the **Seminole Indians** in the 1400s.

A hundred years later, the **Europeans** arrived: in 1498, the Italians John and Sebastien Cabot, sailing under the English flag, spotted what's now Cape Florida on Key Biscayne. However, Florida wasn't actually claimed until 1513, when **Ponce de León**, former governor of the Spanish possession of Puerto Rico, was dispatched by his king to find the fabled Fountain of Youth. Instead, five hundred years before Miami's plastic-surgery boom, he "discovered" land – what's now the Florida peninsula – during *Pascua Florida*, the Spanish Easter festival, and so named the area *La Florida*, or "Land of the Flowers."

De León continued on, sighting the Florida Keys, which he named *Los Martires* – the land fragments resembling to him the bones of Christian martyrs – and the Dry Tortugas, which he called *Las Tortugas* after the hundreds of turtles he found there.

While Florida gained in status, the area around modern-day Miami lay dormant, having proved a troublesome place to settle. A brief attempt was made in 1567 when the **Jesuit Mission of Tequesta** built a garrison, in co-operation with the local Tequesta chief, which was home to thirty soldiers and one Brother Villareal. Unfortunately for them, the natives proved unusually resistant to evangelism; after they revolted against the Europeans, the mission was quickly abandoned. Even though communicating Christianity proved tricky for the settlers, passing on diseases did not, and in a sad and familiar story, the Tequesta were eventually wiped out, pagan to the last.

From Spanish rule to statehood

After Ponce de León's claim in 1513, Florida remained a **Spanish possession** until the late eighteenth century, while England aggressively colonized the southern seaboard of America. In the process, England seized Havana, Spain's colonial jewel, and, eager to recapture the Cuban capital, Spain was obliged to trade Florida to Britain for the return of the city in 1763.

However, after the American War of Independence, the 1783 Treaty of Paris – which recognized **American independence** – forced the newly formed United States to cede Florida to Spain in return for the country's support during the war.

Despite successfully snatching back this land, Spain's territorial ambitions were dealt a harsh blow with the arrival of a new, feisty group of displaced Native Americans. The so-called **Seminoles** were in fact a diverse group of displaced tribes, all of whom had been driven from their homes in the state of Georgia. The Seminoles' spats with the colonists in Florida regularly turned ugly, and there were three separate **Seminole Wars** in 1818, 1835, and 1855: the second – and bloodiest – was caused by yet another attempt at relocation, this time to ship the Seminoles off to Oklahoma and Arkansas.

This relocation program was a US initiative – in 1822, Florida finally finished flip-flopping between powers and became American territory. The deal was simple: in return for assuming the $5 million owed in land grants to American settlers by the Spanish government, Florida was deeded to the United States. It went on to gain **full statehood on March 3, 1845**. The money, incidentally, was never repaid.

By this time there was a small settlement at the mouth of the Miami River. It was a slave plantation owned and run by **Richard Fitzpatrick** and his nephew **William English** from South Carolina; English wanted to further develop the post, beginning the first of Miami's many real-estate advertising campaigns, designed to sell plots of land to homesteaders. Other Floridian forts – Lauderdale and Pierce, for instance – were army strongholds named in honor of their commanders. Fitzpatrick's **Fort Dallas**, however, was named after a naval commander from the first Seminole War, but had no other military connection: it was just a minor trading post en route to the buzzing shipping hub of Key West.

The prospects for English's nascent city looked bright until the double blow of the third Seminole War and the Civil War. Together, these conflicts delayed any significant development in Miami, other than the building of a post office and a few other structures. It wasn't until the arrival of three visionary pioneer settlers from Ohio later that century that what we know as Miami truly began.

The birth of a city

Wealthy and fiercely private, entrepreneur **William Brickell** arrived in the Fort Dallas area with his wife, Mary, in 1870; they built a grand home and set up an Indian Trading Post just south of the Miami River near what's now Downtown Miami. The next major settler was a rich widow, **Julia Tuttle**, who snapped up swathes of land along the river and shipped her family down to Florida in 1891. Together, the Brickells and Julia Tuttle would nurse Miami through its earliest days – with a little help from the railway.

While Miami was still barely a village, there were already larger settlements in the area, **Lemon City** (an early settlement located where Little Haiti now lies) and **Cocoanut Grove** (as it was then known) in particular; even so, in 1890, the whole of Dade County, stretching down to Indian Key, held less than a thousand settlers. Of all the villages, it was the Grove that seemed most likely to flourish: the most significant pioneers included Ralph Middleton Munroe, an eccentric sea captain-cum-architect, and his friends Charles and Isabella Peacock, business owners who came over from England and opened the first hotel in the Grove, the *Bay View House*, in 1882, prefiguring Florida's rampant tourism that would follow forty years later.

The railroad arrives

Despite the inroads made by various real estate magnates in the late 1800s, Miami still had little contact with the outside world. This would change with a deal between railroad tycoon **Henry Morrison Flagler**, who had made his fortune as a partner in John D. Rockefeller's Standard Oil Company, and Julia Tuttle. Savvy from the start, Flagler had taken full advantage of the fact that John D. and William Rockefeller could never get along. Since they wouldn't vote together on the board, he manoeuvred himself into a controlling position, and was soon unstoppable, accruing an inconceivable fortune. He used it wisely: anticipating how the railroads would transform America, he invested heavily in trains, laying the tracks of the Florida East Coast Railroad from St Augustine down to Palm Beach. A nationwide recession set in just as the final gauges were laid, and had it not been for the **"Big Freeze,"** a ferociously cold winter in northern Florida in 1894, there might never have been a Miami.

▲ The Florida East Coast Railroad

The three wives of Henry Flager

Henry Flager (1830–1913), the lower middle class son of a Presbyterian minister from New York, made his vast fortune after meeting and partnering up John D. Rockefeller while toiling in the grain business in Ohio. Together with John's brother William, they would accrue millions running one of American's first oil firms. His lifelong link with Florida came after a doctor ordered his ill first wife, **Mary Harkness**, down to the state for a healthful holiday in the late 1870s; Flagler joined her and was instantly smitten.

For such a no-nonsense, publicity-shy man – he refused to allow grateful Miamians to name their city after him – Flagler had a surprisingly colorful personal life. Mary was the daughter of his grain company's boss; when she died after a 30-year union in 1881, it took him just two years to marry his second wife, **Ida Alice Shrouds**. She was a flame-haired former nurse of Mary's, 18 years Henry's junior, with a fondness for lavish spending and a sensitivity to high-class snobbery. Ida proved mentally unstable – a firm fan of Ouija boards and psychics, she claimed to be destined to marry the Czar of Russia – and Flagler endured 14 years of marriage to an increasingly unhinged woman before he finally committed her to an asylum back home in New York in 1897.

By then, he'd met the woman who would become his third wife, **Mary Lily Keenan**, aged 24; Henry was 70. The sticky problem for love-smitten Flagler was that New York laws wouldn't allow him to divorce his existing spouse on the grounds of madness. So the lovelorn industrialist quietly called in some high-ranking favors, switched residence from New York to Florida, and watched as the Florida legislature conveniently introduced a new law expressly legalizing divorce on the grounds of insanity. Ida was quickly jettisoned – though well provided for financially – and Henry settled into what, by all accounts, was his happiest union until he died at his estate in Palm Beach in 1913.

The Brickells and Tuttle banded together to offer him land in exchange for extending his railroad down the coast. Then as now, citrus crops were the backbone of Florida's agricultural economy, so it was devastating when the freeze forced the yield of oranges down from 5.5m boxes in 1894 to less than 150,000 a year later. Legend has it that Julia Tuttle saw an opportunity for Miami in this disaster and snipped fresh orange blossoms from her garden and sent them to Flagler, showing that Fort Dallas was frost-free and the climate consistently mild. Characteristic though that anecdote might be of the entrepreneurial, quick-thinking Julia, it's likely just another story cooked up by Miami's nimble marketing machine.

Whatever the reason, Flagler did come to the town and quickly realized its potential. He accepted the land offer and built the magnificent **Royal Palm Hotel**, a glamorous, early greenhouse for the sprouts of Miami tourism (it stood on the northern banks of the river, just opposite the Miami Circle site today). Flagler didn't just rely on trains to encourage commerce either – he gouged out an easy shipping channel for the Port of Miami, now the waterway between South Beach and Fisher Island known as Government Cut.

Meanwhile, the **railroad** took just over a year to arrive, and in April 1896, the first passenger train entered the city, bringing along excited refugees from elsewhere in the state. Two months later, on July 28, the city was formally incorporated; voters eventually settled on the name Miami, believing – erroneously – that it was the Tequesta word for "sweet water."

The building boom

The biggest obstacle to widespread settlement in South Florida was its swampy, low-lying land. By 1908, developers began addressing that problem head-on, systematically dredging the water-soaked inland areas in a desperate race to keep up with consumer demand. Many let their staff sell faster than they dredged, leading to reputations of offering "land by the gallon."

Despite some shady sales practices, the **building boom** in Miami was in full swing. In 1912, the department store Burdine's became the city's first "skyscraper," at five stories high, while millionaire James Deering began building the opulent Neo-Renaissance palatial estate of **Villa Vizcaya**. Mary Brickell, assisted by her husband, planned the wide vista of **Brickell Avenue** to connect Miami with Coconut Grove, and it quickly became known as **Millionaires' Row** when wealthy new residents, including presidential candidate William Jennings Bryan, built enormous mansions there. By 1920, the new city had more than thirty thousand inhabitants: five years later, Miami tripled its size by annexing Coconut Grove and Lemon City.

The fuel for this expansion was largely hot air: Miami was the first American city built equally on hype and high hopes. Everest G. Sewell, a master of public relations, was responsible for the relentless sloganeering and deafening marketing of the city. On its twentieth anniversary, he cooked up taglines such as "Miami: Where the Summer Spends the Winter," "Miami: the Magic City," and later, simply, "Stay through May." The local chamber of commerce funded the first press trips, bringing journalists on lavish free holidays to sample the good life in Miami – especially favored were those writing for wire services, whose stories were syndicated across the country in newspapers from California to Boston.

Meanwhile, in a flight of idealistic megalomania, local boy **George Merrick** began the most ambitious building project of all: **Coral Gables**. Inspired by the City Beautiful Movement (see box, p.262), he envisioned a European-style town with civic amenities and civilized settlers. By 1925, less than four years after its inception, and nourished by the local flair for publicity, Coral Gables was a viable city that had earned its founder almost $150 million.

The tourism boom begins

The development of Miami's mainland would soon be superseded by a piece of land that was mere swamp only decades before: **Miami Beach**. It was here that the city's love affair with tourism was ferociously consummated. Charles and Isabella Peacock's namesake inn was the first hotel, and Flagler's *Royal Palm* was lavish and celebrity-studded, but as the Art Deco masterpieces mushroomed in Miami Beach, a newly sun-worshipping nation was seduced by South Florida.

Miami Beach was originally planned as a plantation by the Quaker settler **John Collins**, one of the most misrepresented men in Miami history. The fetid strip soon failed as farmland, so Collins – far from the meek and gentle man that history has portrayed him – turned to Plan B: a seaside resort. Impatient and energetic, he had the vision, if not the money, to transform the island into a playground for the middle classes. The only problem was that the land was in effect an offshore island, three miles east of Miami proper with nothing connecting it to the mainland. Collins set out to construct a rudimentary bridge, but ran out of money halfway through.

The extra cash came from Indianapolis-born **Carl Fisher**, who made millions from car headlights by the time he was forty. He saw a lucrative goldmine in Collins' island and agreed to finance the project in exchange for two hundred acres of oceanfront property. Fisher constructed Miami's first **causeway** in 1913, and Miami Beach was born, incorporated into the city of Miami two years later. It wasn't long before trendy **hotels** popped up on the seafront.

A hurricane and the Great Depression

Unfortunately, nature fought back against the aggressive redevelopment: the warm weather that had brought the railroad in the first place took its revenge. On September 17–18, 1926, a **hurricane** with winds up to 125mph came ashore, its eye passing directly over Miami: more than one hundred people died, five thousand

---

Hurricanes in South Florida

Hurricanes have played a huge part in South Florida's history, and their role in the future seems destined to be even greater. Many locals act sanguine about the powerful storms, but recent meteorological shifts indicate that Miami will have to prepare for the onslaught of more hurricanes like **Andrew**, which turned the agricultural land around Homestead to coleslaw in 1992 and cost the country $25 billion. Meteorologists say that in 2004, the Caribbean and its environs came out of a 25-year calm period; experts predict more frequent and more intense hurricanes in the next decade. Florida's storm season officially spans from June to November, but most storms froth up in August or September, and last around ten days; the modern coding system alternates boys' and girls' names that cycles alphabetically through three languages – French, Spanish, and English.

At the time of writing, Miami and the rest of South Florida have remained relatively fortunate, despite a couple of near misses. The two storms that ripped through the Peninsula in 2004 left Miami unscathed: Charley made land at Punta Gorda on Florida's southwest coast, killing 27 and causing $6.8 billion of damage; while the huge, lumbering Frances, which killed 32 people, landed at Fort Pierce, a few miles north along the Atlantic seaboard. A year later, during the legendary 2005 hurricane season, Wilma hit a glancing blow on the Keys and Everglades, causing $20 billion of damage and 35 deaths but leaving the infrastructure surprisingly intact; while Katrina danced over Miami and Miami Beach, felling trees and knocking out power, en route to its devastating culmination in New Orleans.

Katrina was a Category 1 storm when it brushed through South Florida, Wilma a Category 3 and Charley and Frances classified as Category 4 – these are all marks on the **Saffir-Sampson Scale** used to grade hurricanes' intensity. Strengths range from Category 1 (sustained winds 74–95mph), which usually causes little permanent damage, to the catastrophic Category 5 (sustained winds of more than 155mph), like Hurricane Camille, which tore into Mississippi's gulf in 1969 and left complete destruction that observers likened to an atomic bomb. No one knows when another mighty storm will barrel down on South Florida at full intensity, although computer modeling to predict a storm's path, and so prepare people and property appropriately, is growing ever more sophisticated.

homes were destroyed, Downtown was flooded, and Miami Beach virtually obliterated. President Machado of Cuba sent gunboats with doctors and medicines, and the city was plunged into an **economic crisis**.

In fact, the land boom was already ebbing before the storm washed it away completely, mostly thanks to the inflation rates that soared in the wake of construction, but the **Great Depression** that arrived so soon afterwards hobbled Miami's progress.

The advent of commercial flying was the only thing that provided any economic glimmer during those lean years to bolster the limping tourist industry: Pan-American Airlines moved its base from Key West to Coconut Grove's Dinner Key in 1928, creating a hub that connected to 32 Central and South American countries.

Art Deco, World War II, and the tourism revival

With Miami in the economic throes of the Depression, Franklin Delano Roosevelt's New Deal and the Florida citrus industry induced the city's slow recovery. Miami Beach was the main beneficiary, with hundreds of hotels, residences, and other buildings erected in the mid-to-late 1930s, to keep pace with a tourist industry that was again thriving. Many of these structures were designed in the modern **Art Deco** style, led by the designs of architects L. Murray Dixon and Henry Hohauser.

World War II sped the recovery process along, bringing seventy thousand soldiers (including an incognito Clark Gable) to the city for training. Almost 150 hotels were used as barracks, and the *Biltmore* hotel in Coral Gables was converted into a military hospital. Well-known as a sailors' and soldiers' training camp, Miami's other claim to wartime fame is more chilling: Paul Tibbits, the commander of the *Enola Gay*, which dropped the first **atomic bomb** on Hiroshima, was a local boy.

After the war, these soldiers, who were said to have gotten "sand in their shoes" during training, flocked back as civilians and kickstarted another tourism boom. Capping the decade in 1949, the *Raleigh* hotel made a visionary investment in a central-air-conditioning machine. No longer would the summers be too stifling for visitors – Miami was now a year-round destination. At a national convention in the early 1950s, travel agents figured out that Miami Beach had built more hotels since the war than all other resorts worldwide put together. Soon, though, Miami's airports would be clogged not with pleasure-seekers but with refugees.

The 1950s and 1960s: racial tension and Cuban immigration

Like many other towns in the American South, Miami was a city where race was a tense issue and whose voters supported enforced **segregation.** By the time of Miami's incorporation in 1896, local blacks were sent to live in the creatively named **Coloredtown**, way out around Avenue G (now NW 2nd Avenue). This strip later became a nightlife magnet for white locals who were drawn to its top-notch music halls and movie theaters. Even after the Supreme Court ruled in favor of desegregation in 1954, economic discrimination continued. The situation did not improve in the 1960s, as the Miami local government displaced more than twenty thousand residents from Coloredtown (by then, renamed **Overtown**) in order to build a massive freeway through the area. Payback came in **race riots** that ignited in Liberty City in 1968 and again in 1980, when six days of disturbances left eighteen people dead, more than four hundred injured, and property damage valued at more than $200 million (see box, p.47).

Miami's racial problems were exacerbated by the repercussions of the 1959 Cuban Revolution, which brought **Fidel Castro** (who was, at least at first, feted in the US) to power. Many of the immigrants who came to Miami over the next five years were members of Cuba's elite, tossed out because of the potential threat they posed. They imagined their stay would be temporary until the joint blow of the botched **Bay of Pigs** invasion in 1961 and the **Cuban Missile Crisis** – a tense standoff between the US and the USSR over Soviet nuclear-missile bases on the island – a year later effectively barred their return home. In reaction to anti-Communist outrage from Cuban expats and Americans alike, the US began so-called **Freedom Flights** in 1965. They ran for eight years, bringing more than 300,000 Cubans to Miami, including fourteen thousand children plucked from their parents to begin a new life in America under the aegis of the Pedro Pan program.

Many of the new Cuban immigrants settled west of Downtown in the Jewish area of Riverside, soon to be known as **Little Havana**. These doctors, lawyers, and entrepreneurs started out working menial jobs, but were soon re-establishing themselves in the professions they'd followed back home.

Still, the impact of this wave of immigration on the city was immediate and abrasive. Under the **Cuban–American Adjustment Act of 1966**, permanent residency was granted to any Cuban who'd lived in the United States for at least one year, a luxury afforded no other immigrant group before or since – and still a source of resentful friction with other ethnic minorities, like the Haitians.

Economic decline and architectural preservation

The 1970s were a quiet, if bleak, period in Miami history: as elsewhere across the nation, **economic decline** continued, and the city struggled to retain tourist dollars. In addition, during this period Dade County declared itself bilingual in 1973, in response to massive Spanish-speaking immigration. The move was highly controversial and was rescinded after the infamous **Mariel Boatlift** in 1980, when the first wave of middle-class Cuban immigrants was joined by a totally different kind of refugee. After a spat with the Peruvian government over a group seeking asylum in Havana's Peruvian embassy, Castro opened the port of Mariel and announced that anyone who wished to leave the island was free to do so. And they did: 125,000 Cubans arrived in Miami in less than three days. But Castro's seemingly capricious gesture proved a masterstroke – with a flourish, he flushed 25,000 convicted criminals out of Cuba and into America, alongside hordes of refugees who were mentally ill. The local government in Miami created a tent city under Interstate 95 and struggled to find somewhere to house the new arrivals. Many ended up in then-rundown South Beach.

The bright spot of the era was the establishment of the **Miami Design Preservation League** by Barbara Baer Capitman, who defended the decaying Art Deco structures in Miami Beach against the wrecking ball, and kick-started a reassessment of their architectural value (see box, "Decoding Art Deco," on p.56).

The 1980s and 1990s: Miami Vices

The 1980s represented the nadir of Miami's reputation, when the city was synonymous with not just TVs Crockett and Tubbs but also **cocaine** and **crime**. At this time it was estimated that one quarter of the cocaine that entered America arrived through Florida; and at one point, the **murder rate** in Miami was so high that the local medical examiner rented a refrigerated truck for corpses, as the 30-body capacity of the cooler in the central morgue was regularly maxing out. In addition, the now-decrepit hotels on South Beach, already filled with the old and infirm, living their last years in the warm weather (earning the area the nickname "God's Waiting Room"), added the *marielitos* to their ranks, transforming the area into a hub for local criminal activity. The bubblegum cop show *Miami Vice*, set on the beach, added an unrealistic, glossy sheen to the grubby district.

Corruption and crime continued into the 1990s, even as **South Beach** was discovered by fashion photographers and enjoying a throbbing renaissance. From 1992 to 1998, forty public officials were indicted on bribery and corruption charges, while anti-tourist violence reached its height in 1994 and 1995, prompting then-governor Lawton Chiles to create a Task Force on Tourist Safety, as well as providing special tourist-oriented police and more easily visible roadside signage for vacation-goers. To a large degree, his measures worked. Petty crime and anti-tourist violence plummeted, replaced with rare but more headline-grabbing events like the bizarre and brutal murder of designer **Gianni Versace**.

The ultimate local headline-maker, though, came three years later at the turn of the millennium when a seven-year-old boy in Miami found himself as the center of an international incident: Cuban poster child **Elián González**. His mother was killed trying to reach America with Elián in tow on a refugee raft; after much debate, the boy was returned – by the federal government, and by force – to his father in Cuba. Few involved in this sad mess escaped unscathed – not least President Clinton (already reviled by Cuban exiles for not being tough enough on Castro), who supported Elián's repatriation, and Florida attorney general Janet Reno, who had final say in the matter. However, Manny Diaz, the lawyer who defended Elián's right to stay in America, was elected mayor of Miami in the affair's wake.

Later that same year, South Florida was again the site of international controversy with the **2000 presidential election** debacle, when the right to the White House hung on a few hard-to-read votes in Miami-Dade County. Charges of corruption still rankle: some claim that the ballots were oddly designed and confusing, and the fact that the brother of Republican George W. Bush – who was eventually awarded the presidency by the Supreme Court – was state governor only encouraged conspiracy theorists.

Miami today

Present-day Miami is still struggling to live up to the glossy reputation that it has created for itself. One major success, though, is its banking industry: after the city was grazed by **Hurricane Andrew** in 1992 (districts further south were not so lucky), the city emerged as an important banking center, with dozens of gleaming Downtown office blocks as testament to its economic vitality.

Economically, Miami Beach is enduring a few worries; though tourism remains strong, South Beach has lost some of its luster in fashion circles, as models and photographers are air-kissing the beach goodbye to shoot catalogs in cheaper locations like South Africa and Spain. The other group gravitating away from Miami is its long-standing gay community. The reason's simple: Miami has been a little too effective in attracting straight tourist dollars and the family-friendly vibe in South Beach has alienated many gays and lesbians there (Miami's loss is Fort Lauderdale's gain, as that group is decamping north along the coast). Couple these factors with the softening in Miami's real estate market, and it's a tough time for the city – those over-eager speculators who snapped up ocean-view condos hoping to flip them for a quick profit are facing foreclosure instead. The other uncertainty concerns Cuba: as the **González** case shows, it's impossible to underestimate the impact on Miami of Cuban politics; even if the federal government's concern for the Communist regime is cooling, the ire of local exiles is boiling as hot as ever. At time of writing, after almost a year of uncertainty, Fidel Castro had finally ceded power to his younger brother Raoul; Fidel's retirement, however, did not precipitate the instant revolution many in Miami predicted for their homeland and the Cuban expat crew continues to watch, gimlet-eyed, for any signs of Communism's weakening grip.

The city's arts scene may prove to be the shiniest opportunity for the future, centered on the mainland strip known as the **Biscayne Corridor**. It's an arty enclave, where high-design, high-rise condos are mushrooming along the water's edge, new galleries are taking over old factories in **Wynwood**, and swanky homeware showrooms are opening in the revived **Design District.** Anchoring it all is the Cesar Pelli-designed **Arsht Center for the Performing Arts** – if only more people would pay for tickets for shows at Pelli's often-empty masterpiece.

Architecture

Architecture vies with warm weather and wild nightlife as the prime draw for visitors to Miami: the star is the funky (and low-cost) modern style known variously as ZigZag, Jazz Age, Skyscraper, Streamline, or simply, Art Deco. The style grew out of the 1925 *L'Exposition des Arts Décoratifs et Industriels Modernes*, a major exhibition in Paris showcasing designs that, although inspired by the Arts and Crafts Movement of the late nineteenth century, used modern, industrial production methods. (The inspiration's ironic, given the Arts and Crafts aversion to mass marketing.) Originally called Style Moderne, or Modernistic – the term Art Deco wasn't coined until 1968, by British historian Bevis Hiller – the sleek, long-limbed designs became popular for furniture, clothing, fabrics, and, soon after, buildings, being simple to design and cheap to construct.

Art Deco's beginnings in Miami

It took the disastrous **hurricane** that swept through the city in 1926 to bring Art Deco to Miami. As a result of the hurricane's devastation, large amounts of land were suddenly clear – especially in Miami Beach – and on much of it, buildings in the cost-efficient, popular Art Deco style were erected. For the earliest of these, the style was heavily influenced by one fabulous, spooky discovery: archeologist Howard Carter's unearthing of the Egyptian pharaoh Tutankhamun's long-buried tomb and its treasures in 1922. The opulent golden antiques from this royal time capsule were soon sent on headline-grabbing tours around the world, and fashion and design immediately incorporated the geometric, zigzagging Egyptian shapes, as did Art Deco (indeed, Deco's easy absorption of new trends into the core aesthetic of streamlined simplicity was one of its features).

During this time, Art Deco buildings were heavily decorated with ornamental panels that were often filled with symbolic images, much like the reliefs in Egyptian tombs. The difference was in subject matter: reliefs on so-called **Tropical** – or **Miami** – **Deco** buildings often featured palm trees, flamingos, pelicans, sunbursts, and other indigenous symbols. Other, unique Tropical Deco features include sun-blocking eyebrows above windows, exterior staircases, and *terrazzo* floors. These floors – essentially colored concrete laid in geometric designs like poor-man's marble – are both durable and cool, as they absorb little heat from the sun.

As the glamour of Ancient Egypt receded and the realities of the Great Depression approached, the movement splintered into factions, as Tropical Deco sloughed off its fancy panels and excessive ornamentation, resulting in two new variations. **Depression Moderne** was less decorative than its parent, in which ornamental elements were relegated to a building's interior, and **Streamline** – or **Nautical** – **Deco**, which featured rounded corners and "speed lines," intended to convey an impression of movement – and occasionally, even porthole windows and ornamental smokestacks. Later Art Deco buildings like this also feature glass blocks and banded stripes, more monolithic and less playful than the devil-may-care decorations of the Roaring Twenties.

An alternative: Mediterranean Revival

Not everything being built at this time was in the Art Deco style, though: in fact, one third of the buildings in South Beach's Art Deco Historic District are actually **Mediterranean Revival**, a contemporary architectural refuge for those who loathed the simplicity and starkness of Deco's poured concrete. Essentially, this style is Spanish by way of California, based as it is on the Mission architecture of early West Coast settler buildings. It featured terracotta roofs that ape old-world Europe, ornate ironwork, and deliberately ramshackle facades, so that a structure would appear well-aged.

Snobs dismissed such whimsy, saying that only the *nouveau riche*, like gangsters and movie stars, would be gauche enough to prefer it to the cool intellectualism of Art Deco. Yet Miami's Latino heritage, coupled with a compatible climate, helped popularize the style. One of its biggest fans was Carl Fisher, the father of Miami Beach, who commissioned Española Way, the densest concentration of the style in the city – although the City Beautiful aesthetic of George Merrick's Coral Gables owes much to Mediterranean Revival, too.

The City Beautiful Movement

By 1910, almost one in two people in the United States lived in a city with more than 2500 inhabitants – and with this mass urbanization, problems like crime and disease germinated in the New World as they had in Europe. Benign yet patrician reformers, like Chicago's Daniel Burnham, set about finding a way to **impose the moral order of a village** onto these growing cities to solve such problems: their theories became known as the **City Beautiful Movement**. Though largely forgotten today, it was a powerful factor in urban planning across America in the early twentieth century and a potent inspiration to George Merrick, founder and father of Coral Gables.

Inspired by the order and harmony of Europe's new **Beaux Arts style**, as well as local successes like Frederick Law Olmsted's Central Park in Manhattan, the reformers pitched utopian cities in vaguely classical style whose beauty would inspire civic loyalty and upstanding morals in even the most impoverished resident. Cynics might argue that food and better sanitation would have been more effective salves, but the evangelical movement pressed ahead in places like St Louis and Kansas City. Burnham even outlined his blueprint for the perfect city at **Chicago's World's Fair** in 1893 – its buildings uniform, its parks enormous, the city would be crimeless, he said, from a combination of civic duty and plenty of police. Key **features** included tree-lined avenues, monumental buildings, ample greenspace, and numerous plazas or fountains.

The City Beautiful Movement was a compelling alternative to the festering, ramshackle development of most American cities at that time, and it so inspired Merrick's utopian megalomania that he set about building **Coral Gables**. His one deviation was in the city's architectural framework: he used the Mediterranean Revival style of the 1920s, rather than insisting on a then-dated Beaux Arts aesthetic.

The controlling impact of the City Beautiful Movement is still keenly felt in Coral Gables: zoning restrictions and local ordinances are draconian and residents are rabid in their civic pride. Unfortunately, the plazas and fountains that Merrick hoped would bring people together are these days almost always empty and civic pride rarely blossoms into plain neighborliness.

Miami Modern

After World War II, America's exuberance was refreshed in the glow of victory and economic prosperity. The wide-eyed optimism of the 1950s, which cynics today so easily dismiss, was then unstoppable; and the buildings of the time are stamped with the same sense of possibility and fun. Some have said that the **Miami Modern**, or **MiMo**, style has the same mix of **confidence and naïveté** as a 1950s bombshell screen goddess – sinuous and sexy, but utterly innocent.

More than all else, though, designers in the MiMo age were fascinated with speed. Its tail-finned cars and sleekly patterned polyester dresses were inspired not by ocean liners or trains, but by the futuristic jets. Many MiMo buildings also feature boomerang and kidney shapes (like the shady rest areas on Lincoln Road), lending a looping sense of movement, as well as cheeky, unexpected ornamental holes, which play games with the viewer's perspective. There's great use of decorative collage, as well as architectural features like wide eaves, masonry *bris-soleils* (literally, "sunbreakers"), and jalousie windows, with louvered, overlapping glass panels, used expressly to create shade. Architects like the late, dapper **Morris Lapidus** and the still-active **Norman Giller** designed enormous, sweeping buildings, many in central Miami Beach, that dwarfed their Art Deco counterparts further south; Lapidus's philosophy, laid out clearly in the title of his autobiography, was "Too Much is Never Enough."

The preservation movement

By the 1970s, the optimism that had prompted the MiMo boom had been drained, and the city was facing all manner of urban blight, from flaring racial tensions to escalating crime; and had it not been for the efforts of an indefatigable, transplanted New Yorker, the Art Deco legacy that later helped revive the city might have succumbed to this downturn.

Barbara Baer Capitman, then editor of an interiors magazine called *The Designer*, became involved in Miami's efforts to honor America's Bicentennial in 1976. For her contribution, she seized upon the quirky, dilapidated Art Deco buildings of rundown South Beach and, along with five friends, founded the **Miami Design Preservation League**. A powerful, publicity-savvy woman who knew the value of a grand gesture, Capitman protested in person as the wrecking ball bit into the *Senator* hotel, a still-mourned Art Deco gem on Collins Avenue (the site, opposite the *Marlin Hotel*, is now a parking lot). She didn't manage to save the *Senator*, or, indeed, several other hotels nearby, but eventually, through force of persuasion and personality, she helped secure South Beach the honor of being listed on the National Register of Historic Places (though it was still some time before the area cleaned up its crime-ridden image).

Capitman didn't stop at simply conserving Art Deco: working with interior designer **Leonard Horowitz**, she then set about spiffing up the buildings she'd saved. It was Horowitz who came up with the now-familiar sherbet palette of peaches, lemons, and lavenders. Originally, most Deco buildings had been much more muted: either white or cream, with their key features picked out in navy or brown – City Hall in Coconut Grove is a rare, remaining example of this original color scheme. Horowitz's mantra was to leave the warm browns of clay, sand, and soil to the Mediterranean Revival structures and wash Art Deco buildings in the cool tones of the sky, ocean, and flowers. (The designer of the 1980s TV show *Miami Vice* has said that the key to that program's signature look was avoiding any earth tones in much the same way.) For the buildings south of Fifth Street, outside the official preservation district, he varied the palette, amping up the colors to brasher neon shades of turquoise and cerise.

Architectural preservation today

Although Capitman's crusade was at least initially successful, there are still chinks in the preservationist armor. Restorations are tweaked for modern needs, like wider, padded chairs. It's also expensive, and often not cost-efficient, to renovate small, dark Art Deco hotels: there are still a few that remain unloved and crumbling, even along Ocean Drive. Hopeful developers still sometimes try to sneak past regulations.

Although much loved by the local community, the late **Gianni Versace** was also responsible for an act of reckless architectural vandalism. He bought two adjoining buildings on Ocean Drive and converted one, the Mediterranean Revival **Casa Casuarina** into his home. The other, the *Revere Hotel*, was a MiMo gem; yet he demolished it to make room for a swimming pool, just before an ordinance that could have preserved the place. That law shifted historical value from a date-based system – for example, that all conserved buildings must be at least fifty years old, which the *Revere* was not at the time – to a more flexible designation of intrinsic worth.

On a happier note, there have been several recent preservationist victories. The first involved **copyright infringement**, when two hotels on Collins Avenue were sued under the Landham Trademark Act. The *Fairmont*, which far pre-dated the litigating hotel chain, caved to pressure and changed its signage to read *Fairwind*. The *Tiffany* on the other hand, sued by its namesake jewelers, held firm: it had been an intentional pastiche when built in the 1930s since its cheeky slogan was "The Jewel on the Beach." This time, President Clinton intervened and allowed architectural elements like signs to be exempt from trademarking – in the process safeguarding other hotels from future lawsuits. In a gloriously arrogant response, the *Tiffany* retained its sign and is now known simply as *The Hotel*.

Even MiMo is starting to receive architectural TLC: designated as such in 2000, the **John S. Collins Waterfront Historic District** protects many buildings on the drag between 22nd and 44th streets, including Lapidus's masterpiece, the *Fontainebleau*; and it's likely that the crop of parallel mid-Century architectural gems on the mainland, mostly lining Biscayne Boulevard and dubbed MiMo on BiBo, will soon receive the same safeguard. The enormous *Loews* hotel on Miami Beach is a perfect example of how a happy union between commerce and conservation is more than possible: the construction project was only greenlit after its owners agreed to renovate and run a tiny, adjoining Art Deco hotel, the *St Moritz*.

Still, after decades of focusing on preservation, Miami is also turning its attention to producing contemporary buildings that will become future classics – finally, it's lured star architects like Cesar Pelli (the Arsht Center) and Herzog & DeMeuron (the new Miami Art Museum) who are responsible for splashy new additions to the skyline, and it's also nurturing homegrown talent, notably Chad Oppenheim, who's behind many of the most inventive residential skyscrapers to rise in the past few years.

Books

M ost **books** that deal with Miami revel in the one thing the city most wants to forget: crime. These hardboiled novels with hardbitten heroes – written by the likes of Elmore Leonard and Edna Buchanan – are distinctive enough to form a subspecies in the thriller genre.
Unfortunately, some of the books listed below are out of print (o/p), though even these should be available at many secondhand bookstores, through online searches, or perhaps at the terrific Fifteenth Street Books in Coral Gables (see p.178).

History and society

Edward N. Akin *Flagler: Rockefeller Partner & Florida Baron*. Over-footnoted and rather overwritten, Akin's biography of the Father of Miami is crammed with detail, but readable only in short bursts. Strictly for Flagler fanatics.

T.D. Allman *Miami*. Although his endless references to Miami Vice quickly grate on the contemporary reader, Allman's insightful observations now serve as a time capsule of late twentieth-century Miami. Worth dipping into for his sensitive analysis of what being from Miami means.

Kathryne Ashley *George E. Merrick & Coral Gables, Florida*. Brief, workmanlike account of the founding of Coral Gables that's notable for its checklist of landmarks and first-person accounts of George Merrick.

Mary Barron Stofik *Saving South Beach*. Onetime Miami-based preservationist Stofik wrote this informative account of the fight to prevent the redevelopment of South Beach's Deco piles in the 1970s and 1980s, pinning the story on fascinating antagonists, middle-aged widow Barbara Baer Capitman vs. multimillionaire developer Abe Resnick.

Rex Beach *The Miracle of Coral Gables (o/p)*. Produced as a giveaway gimmick to lure early residents, this small book is full of beautiful bright colored woodcut illustrations – its gushing text is testament to Merrick's marketing flair.

Edna Buchanan *The Corpse Had a Familiar Face (o/p)*. Buchanan was a reporter covering Miami's crime scene for the *Miami Herald* in the 1970s;

here, she fuses her own tough life story with the tough cases she follows. Gripping, readable, and a gory reminder of Miami's recent past.

Mark Foster *Castles in the Sand: Life and Times of Carl Graham Fisher*. Historian Foster tells the story of Fisher's life from its beginnings (making millions from manufacturing car headlights) to its end (in poverty after the stock-market crash of 1929). It's a gripping rags-to-riches-to-rags story, and one of the few books to provide any insight into Fisher's motives for moving to Miami.

Joan Gill Blank *Key Biscayne: A History of Miami's Tropical Island and the Cape Florida Lighthouse*. An exhaustive and readable history of one of the city's least celebrated districts. Gill Blank has a fine eye and a wry tone, managing to highlight Key Biscayne's importance in local history while retaining a critical perspective.

Howard Kleinberg *Miami Beach: A History (o/p)*. This book combines text with archival photographs of Miami Beach, and is a great overview of its beginnings, with pithy, insightful commentary from Kleinberg, a former editor-in-chief of *The Miami News*.

Morris Lapidus *Too Much is Never Enough (o/p)*. Lapidus's autobiography is charming, vain, and great fun – much like the man himself. The master of MiMo architecture makes his life story into a lively yarn, but it's the juicy, tangential history of mid-century Miami that really grips.

Helen Muir *The Biltmore: Beacon for Miami*. Muir's other major work is a well-rendered history of Miami's most famous hotel, the *Biltmore* in Coral Gables.

Helen Muir *Miami*. Most consider this the definitive history of the city. However, while it's strong in the early chapters, the book becomes more toothless as it approaches the modern era, where the author shies from any event too lively or controversial.

Robert Mykle *Killer 'Cane: Deadly Hurricane of 1928*. The least well known, but most deadly, of the hurricanes to devastate Florida in the early twentieth century was this Category 4 storm which ripped across Lake Okeechobee and into the Everglades, killing at least two thousand people. Mykle tells the story in human terms, via vignettes of families trying to make their lives then in the 'mucklands' who are thrown into danger – it's a sentimental but involving approach.

Maureen Ogle *Key West: History of an Island Dream*. Spicy, gossip-laden account of the island, where the author clearly relishes investigating Key West's raunchier modern times;

her curious thesis that Key West is a microcosm of American history wobbles now and then, but it's a reliable, enjoyable account.

Thelma Peters *Lemon City: Pioneering on Biscayne Bay 1850–1925 (o/p)*. Thorough, quirky book that focuses on the forgotten settlement of Lemon City (now Little Haiti) to the north of Downtown Miami. Readable, if a little scholarly.

John Rothchild *Up for Grabs*. Rothchild weaves his own experience of building a hippie-era house into the nasty story of South Florida's shady, postwar land boom. He dissects the pioneer psyche of Florida and its settlers while nailing the hard-sell showmanship that developers used to lure the hopeful to Miami and around.

Les Standiford *Last Train to Paradise*. Handy account of Henry Flagler's epic plans to construct a railway linking Key West to the mainland. Surprisingly for a novelist, Standiford struggles with the narrative, trying to be far too yarn-spinning and lacking psychological acuity, but it's packed with facts.

Fiction

Brian Antoni *South Beach: The Novel*. Romping *roman-à-clef* written by the onetime club kid and centering on South Beach's headiest era: who could the Italian designer who throws his credit card at strippers then is slain in front of his mansion possibly be? The guessing game's strung together by a flimsy, if fun, narrative where Antoni's alter ego, Gabriel, inherits and rehabs an old hotel with its requisite cast of quirky residents.

Edna Buchanan *Miami, It's Murder*. The first novel by this Pulitzer Prize–winning author stars rebellious, no-nonsense crime reporter (and Cuban-American) Britt Montero. The story's entertaining enough, and zings with local detail, though it's Buchanan's ability to condense all that's good and bad about Miami into casual details that's most impressive.

Edwidge Danticat *Krik? Krak!* Written by a much-feted Haitian novelist, this set of short stories gives a luminous, brutal sense of Haitian culture. There's unfortunately little yet written by Miami's expat community, so Danticat's spare stores are an excellent make-do in the meantime.

Stanley Elkin *Mrs Ted Bliss*. An award-winning, amusing oddity set in Miami Beach, wherein 82-year-old widow Dorothy Bliss manages to get mixed up with a drug lord and a Hebrew-speaking Native American, all by selling her late husband's car.

James W. Hall *Bones of Coral*. A standard mystery, bringing a curious big-city paramedic back to his home town of Key West to investigate his father's murder. Worth reading, though, for the cartoonish – but scary – villain Dougie Barnes.

Vicki Hendricks *Iguana Love*. This pulpy, raunchy novel is an explicit tale of a woman who leaves her husband and ends up popping steroids and chasing her younger lover. Its ripe sleepiness is signature South Florida, although Hendricks's prose can get tangled at times.

Carl Hiaasen Various. Local novelist Hiaasen relentlessly skewers South Florida's failings, and no one should visit Miami without having read one of his whipsmart, funny stories – try *Sick Puppy* or *Skin Tight* for starters. All the novels take breakneck tours around the area: the hero of the plastic-surgery-themed *Skin Tight*, for example, lives in a shack in Stiltsville (see p.119, "Key Biscayne and Virginia Key").

Carl Hiaasen, Edna Buchanan, and others *Naked Came the Manatee*. Thirteen of Miami's best-known novelists team up for a caper that centers on the discovery of Fidel Castro's dismembered head. It's a broad, in-jokey satire that's good, if uneven, fun – fans of local crime novels will enjoy a tale that weaves each author's signature hero together into one story.

David Leddick *My Worst Date*. The prolific gay author Leddick offers a nimble coming-of-age tale set in the model-centric world of South Beach, where smart, beautiful teenage Hugo shares a hunky lover with his unwitting mother.

Elmore Leonard *LaBrava (o/p)*. Plenty of Leonard's stories are set in South Florida, but *LaBrava* is one of the best. In it, photographer LaBrava meets a fading Hollywood villainess, who was once his childhood idol; from there, he's drawn into a violent, balletic mess that blurs fiction and reality. Leonard's rangy prose and colloquial style clash well with the surreal world of the trancelike hero.

Theodore Pratt *The Barefoot Mailman (o/p)*. Novelized account of the Barefoot Mailman service (see box, p.75): unremarkable but entertaining, and far better than the awkward film it inspired.

John Sayles *Los Gusanos*. Door-stopper novel written by the cult film director that's set in 1981, in the shadow of the Mariel Boatlift, and covers six decades of a family's life in Cuba and the United States – an intriguing, if grueling, patchwork of characters and stories.

Les Standiford (ed) *Miami Noir*. Sixteen story anthology that draws together local writers like James W. Hall and Vicki Hendricks to channel the glossy, gritty Miami Noir style pioneered by Charles Willeford. Each story's location is flagged, from Homestead to South Beach, so you can dip into the collection according to the day's sightseeing itinerary.

Photography and architecture

Richard and Valerie Beaubien *Discovering South Beach Deco*. Exhaustive account of virtually every Deco masterpiece in South Beach. The authors' enthusiasm is palpable, but the prose can get bogged down with detail – worth dipping into, rather than trawling through.

Seth Bramson *From Sandbar to Sophistication*. Picture-heavy account of the development of Sunny Isles Beach – the dazzling old black and white snaps of its Sinatra-era style only serve to remind how tragic its current incarnation as a soulless luxury playground truly is.

Barbara Baer Capitman and Steven Brooke *Deco Delights (o/p)*. The standard work on Miami's Art Deco treasures, written by the woman who championed their preservation. Glossy and fun, but insubstantial.

Laura Cerwinske and David Kaminsky *Tropical Deco: Architecture & Design of Old Miami Beach*. A brisk survey of the significant styles and buildings that make up Miami Deco; the photographs are lush, but need updating – the *Delano*, for example, is still shown and discussed in its pre-Schrager state.

Carolyn Klepser and Arva Moore Parks *Miami – Then & Now*. Two titans of local history teamed up for this picture book, which showcases antique photographs of Miami and Miami Beach's landmarks alongside sparkling color shots from today. Hugely evocative and informative.

Alan Lapidus *Everything by Design*. Lapidus, son of the MiMo legend Morris, wrote this ripping autobiography about his own career (which has counted Donald Trump and Disney as clients). It's also an illuminating, heart-tugging portrait of his brilliant but egomaniacal father-cum-business partner.

Aristides Millas and Ellen Uguccioni *Coral Gables: Miami Riviera*. Architect Millas and historian Uguccioni have written a readable, comprehensive guide to the Gables. It features an overview of the city as well as capsule accounts of every significant building, many with photographs.

Eric Nash and Randall Robinson Jr *MiMo: Miami Modern Revealed*. The first survey of Miami's second great architectural style is a coffeetable book, crammed with lush photographs and brightened by the sassy, chatty commentary (incorporating as much scandal and gossip as possible) from local preservationist Robinson and *New York Times* architecture critic Nash.

Bill Wisser *South Beach: America's Riviera, Miami Beach, Florida*. Glossy, glitzy pictorial history of South Beach that's strongest on the resort's origins and the building explosion that produced dozens of Art Deco hotels.

Travel and current affairs

Alex Daoud *Sins of South Beach*. Autobiography of the shamed three-time mayor of Miami Beach – he was indicted on bribery charges in 1991 and sentenced to five years in prison (serving only 18 months). It's a sizzling account of South Beach's early renaissance, with a satisfyingly seedy focus, though Daoud's mea culpas fall a little flat.

Joan Didion *Miami*. Didion's bony prose is hard going but it's worth persevering, at least in the early chapters when her snapshot of Miami is both clear-eyed and unsentimental. Unfortunately, the book rapidly loses focus and interest midway through because of her musings on the minutiae of Washington and Cuban politics.

Marjory Stoneman Douglas *The Everglades: River of Grass*. More than fifty years old, this pioneering environmentalist's book galvanized feelings against over-aggressive development, and arguably saved the Everglades. Douglas is almost too engaged with her subject (skip the more sentimental passages), but by focusing on the human history of the area she pumps life into what can seem like an innately empty place.

Bryan Norcross *Hurricane Almanac*. Exhaustive, encyclopaedic reference book compiled by CBS News' hurricane guru.

Susan Orlean *The Orchid Thief*. Orlean spotlights the obsessive and spat-ridden world of orchid fanciers in South Florida, following one orchid hunter into the Everglades on his illicit gathering trips. Hypnotized by the world she uncovers, Orlean tells a fascinating, if occasionally flabby, story.

Maureen Orth *Vulgar Favors: Andrew Cunanan, Gianni Versace, and the Largest Failed Manhunt in US History*. A gripping account of the life of Andrew Cunanan, the man who murdered Gianni Versace, that bristles with an exhaustive and salacious eye for detail. Orth's initial incisiveness is undermined by her own obvious distaste for South Beach and its hedonistic gay culture.

David Rieff *Going to Miami: Exiles, Tourists, and Refugees in the New*

America. Rieff tackles the contentious subject of immigration in Miami with pompous but maddeningly perceptive observations. Though now somewhat dated (it was published in 1988), it's still a good introduction to Cuban-American issues.

South Florida on film

South Florida **on film** is much like South Florida in literature: a region of gritty crime and cynical cops. Its seedy glamour has attracted dozens of would-be noir thrillers to film there, from the classic *Scarface* to the more recent *Miami Vice*. It's also served as the backdrop for plenty of sunny sex comedies, including *There's Something About Mary*.

What follows is a representative, but brief, list of movies set in and around Miami, with director and year given.

Ace Ventura, Pet Detective (Tom Shadyac, 1994). The film that gave birth to Jim Carrey as a comedy phenomenon: he stars as a detective out to recover the Miami Dolphins' kidnapped mascot Snowflake, on the eve of the Superbowl.

Any Given Sunday (Oliver Stone, 1999). Al Pacino stars in this disappointing professional football movie from conspiracy master Oliver Stone. Notable for giving Cameron Diaz a rare chance to play against type as the team's fierce, determined owner.

Bad Boys II (Michael Bay, 2003). Bracing, mindless comedy-action adventure with cops Will Smith and Martin Lawrence wisecracking and shooting their way through Miami. The incomprehensible plot's apparently about drug smuggling; but the real reason to see this is watching the real multimillion-dollar mansion the producers bought be blown to smithereens onscreen.

The Bellboy (Jerry Lewis, 1960). Shot almost entirely in Miami Beach's *Fontainebleau* hotel, Jerry Lewis stars as the bellhop from Hell in this, his writer-director debut.

Big Trouble (Barry Sonnenfeld, 2002). Madcap caper based on humorist Dave Barry's novel of the same name, and featuring a top-quality comic cast including Stanley Tucci, Janeane Garofalo, and Rene Russo.

The Birdcage (Mike Nichols, 1996). Remake of the French farce *La Cage aux Folles*, this riotous, campy movie stars Robin Williams as Armand, the man behind South Beach's most successful drag club, and Nathan Lane as Albert, his lover and star. The

story corkscrews when Armand's son announces his marriage to the daughter (Calista Flockhart) of ultra-conservative parents. The opening scene is a love letter to Ocean Drive, a single shot that pans in from the sea onto the riot of neon and nightlife.

Black Sunday (John Frankenheimer, 1976). A terrorist thriller, where Palestinian extremists plan to blow up Miami's Orange Bowl on Super Bowl Sunday – wiping out 80,000 football fans as well as the President. The climax of the movie offers some amazing aerial views of 1970s Miami.

Blood and Wine (Bob Rafelson, 1997). Jack Nicholson plays a wine dealer who teams up with a savvy Cuban nanny (Jennifer Lopez) and a Brit safecracker (Michael Caine) in this dark, underrated thriller. The crooks plan to steal a million-dollar necklace and, when it all goes wrong, they head off in pursuit of their payoff to the Florida Keys.

Cocaine Cowboys (Alfred Spellman, Billy Korben 2006). Local directing wunderkinder put together this gripping account of the rise of illegal drug smuggling here in the 1970s and 1980s, explicitly linking Miami's economic growth of that era to the money funneled there by illicit sources. The sequel, *Cocaine Cowboys II: Hustlin' with The Godmother* (2008) is a portrait of sociopathic drug kingpin Griselda Blanco, known as the Cocaine Queen of Miami.

The Cocoanuts (Joseph Santley & Robert Florey, 1929). Set during Florida's real-estate boom, the Marx Brothers' first film stars Groucho as an impecunious hotel proprietor attempting to keep his business afloat by auctioning off land (with the usual interference from Chico and Harpo) in Coconut Grove, "the Palm Beach of tomorrow." Groucho expounds on Florida's climate while standing in what is really a sand-filled studio lot.

Donnie Brasco (Mike Newell, 1997). Al Pacino and Johnny Depp team up for this crime movie, based on the true story of FBI Special Agent Joseph Pistone, who infiltrates the Mob. The action heads to Miami from New York as Brasco helps the Mafia expand a new nightclub operation there.

Get Shorty (Barry Sonnenfeld, 1995). Miami makes only a cameo at the beginning of this funny, bitter movie from the novel of the same name by Elmore Leonard. John Travolta stars as Chili Palmer, a local loan shark who heads out to Los Angeles on a debt-collecting mission, but ends up making movies.

Goldfinger (Guy Hamilton, 1964). The first Bond movie to make it to Miami – the opulent *Fontainebleau* is the backdrop for the scene at the beginning where we spot Bond sunbathing. However, these scenes were shot on a set in England, and were later edited into the Miami footage.

The Heartbreak Kid (Elaine May, 1972). A neurotic Neil Simon–Elaine May gem, where Jewish New Yorker (and new husband) Charles Grodin starts regretting his marriage as soon as the honeymoon drive to Miami begins. A flirty, sexy Cybill Shepherd hitting on him on the beach while his sunburnt wife lies inside doesn't help.

Illtown (Nick Gomez, 1995). Tony Danza's a gay mob boss, joined by indie royalty like Michael Rapaport, Lili Taylor, and Kevin Corrigan, who play a supporting cast of Miami drug dealers.

Miami Blues (George Armitage, 1990). Adapted from the Charles Willeford novel, this hit-and-miss movie stars Alec Baldwin as a just-released sociopath looking to start over – crime-wise, at least – in Miami. He teams up with a college student and prostitute (Jennifer Jason Leigh), and is pursued by a burnt-out homicide detective played by Fred Ward.

Miami Rhapsody (David Frankel, 1995). Disappointing comedy of infidelity, starring Sarah Jessica Parker as Gwyn, who has to examine her commitment to a long-term boyfriend while finding out that everyone else in her family – parents included – is unable to stay faithful.

Miami Vice (Michael Mann, 2006) Mann's big screen, big budget update of his iconic 1980s TV show flopped, despite the star power of Colin Farrell and Jamie Foxx as Crockett and Tubbs. It's a confusing, rather earnest movie and the original series actually better showcases the city.

Moon Over Miami (Walter Lang, 1941). Bombshell Betty Grable comes gold-digging in Miami in this colorful, old-fashioned musical comedy. She and her on-screen sisters pose as a wealthy young woman and her two maids – a little too successfully, though, as she's soon pursued by two handsome bachelors at the same time.

Out of Time (Carl Franklin, 2003). Denzel Washington's the hunted, confused, and possibly corrupt cop in this Keys-set thriller co-starring Eva Mendes. Washington's a little too noble for his seedy role, but the bamboozling twists are great fun – a pity the pay-off's so weak.

Porky's (Bob Clark, 1981). The classic, revolting teenage-boy romp is set in Fort Lauderdale, and is based on a real-life strip bar there.

Red Eye (Wes Craven, 2006). This superior woman-in-peril thriller from horror master Craven stars steely Rachel McAdams and a chillingly psychopathic Cillian Murphy, and involves a murderous plot in a fictitious Mid Beach high-rise hotel as well as a bloody climax in McAdams' family pad in Coral Gables.

Scarface (Brian De Palma, 1983). A modern masterpiece set in and around

Miami during the 1980 Mariel Boatlift, *Scarface* stars a young Al Pacino as a small-time Cuban thug who maneuvers his way up to control Miami's drug cartels. It was filmed all across the city, and is a brutal time capsule of Miami's darker days.

Some Like It Hot (Billy Wilder, 1959). Wilder's classic farce begins in 1920s Chicago where Tony Curtis and Jack Lemmon, witnesses to the St Valentine's Day massacre, disguise themselves in drag, and hide out in an all-girl jazz band (featuring Marilyn Monroe) headed for Miami – though the movie itself subbed location shots in San Diego for South Beach.

The Specialist (Luis Llosa, 1994). A priapic, glossy portrait of the city (if a poor film), this stars one of Miami's former high-profile residents, Sylvester Stallone, as an ex-CIA agent hired by Sharon Stone to take revenge on the Miami mobsters who wiped out her family.

Striptease (Andrew Bergman, 1996). Wretched movie version of Carl Hiaasen's riotous novel about a single mom – played by Demi Moore – who turns to stripping to make ends meet before eventually becoming embroiled in a political scandal.

There's Something About Mary (Farrelly Brothers, 1998). This modern gross-out classic climaxes in Miami Beach, where geeky Ben Stiller – still smarting from a prom-night disaster years before – tracks down the goofy, beautiful love of his life, Mary (Cameron Diaz), and tries to win her again.

Tony Rome (Gordon Douglas, 1967). Frank Sinatra and Jill St John star in this gritty tale of pushers, strippers, and gold-diggers in 1960s Miami: worth watching as a period piece, not for the plot – there are some witty one-liners, though.

True Lies (James Cameron, 1994). Arnold Schwarzenegger plays a CIA agent with a double life, Jamie Lee Curtis co-stars as his trusting wife, and Tom Arnold wisecracks in between the explosions. Look for the scene where a portion of Henry Flagler's old railway bridge to Key West is apparently blown up; in fact, the government had already detonated that portion and producers had to repair it simply so that they could destroy it all over again.

Where the Boys Are (Henry Levin, 1960). This original spring-break movie stars a young George Hamilton and Paula Prentiss as fun-seeking, sun-worshipping teens: it's the movie that put Fort Lauderdale on the map. While Hamilton continues to cash in on his permatanned persona, George's nubile love interest Dolores Hart is now a prioress in a Benedictine abbey.

Wild Things (John McNaughton, 1998). Steamy, noirish thriller with a serpentine plot that entangles sultry schoolgirls Neve Campbell and Denise Richards with their teacher Matt Dillon, as well as an upstanding local cop (Kevin Bacon).

Travel store

For more information go to www.roughguides.com

Visit us online
www.roughguides.com
Information on over 25,000 destinations around the world

ROUGH GUIDES   **BROADEN YOUR HORIZONS**

"The most accurate maps in the world"

San Jose Mercury News

Small print and

Index

A Rough Guide to Rough Guides

Published in 1982, the first Rough Guide – to Greece – was a student scheme that became a publishing phenomenon. Mark Ellingham, a recent graduate in English from Bristol University, had been traveling in Greece the previous summer and couldn't find the right guidebook. With a small group of friends he wrote his own guide, combining a highly contemporary, journalistic style with a thoroughly practical approach to travelers' needs.

The immediate success of the book spawned a series that rapidly covered dozens of destinations. And, in addition to impecunious backpackers, Rough Guides soon acquired a much broader and older readership that relished the guides' wit and inquisitiveness as much as their enthusiastic, critical approach and value-for-money ethos.

These days, Rough Guides include recommendations from shoestring to luxury and cover more than 200 destinations around the globe, including almost every country in the Americas and Europe, more than half of Africa and most of Asia and Australasia. Our ever-growing team of authors and photographers is spread all over the world, particularly in Europe, the USA and Australia.

In the early 1990s, Rough Guides branched out of travel, with the publication of Rough Guides to World Music, Classical Music and the Internet. All three have become benchmark titles in their fields, spearheading the publication of a wide range of books under the Rough Guide name.

Including the travel series, Rough Guides now number more than 350 titles, covering: phrasebooks, waterproof maps, music guides from Opera to Heavy Metal, reference works as diverse as Conspiracy Theories and Shakespeare, and popular culture books from iPods to Poker. Rough Guides also produce a series of more than 120 World Music CDs in partnership with World Music Network.

Visit www.roughguides.com to see our latest publications.

Rough Guide travel images are available for commercial licensing at www.roughguidespictures.com

Rough Guide credits

Text editor: Stephen Timblin
Layout: Dan May
Cartography: Rajesh Mishra
Picture editor: Emily Taylor
Production: Rebecca Short
Proofreader: Stewart Wild
Cover design: Chloë Roberts
Photographer: Anthony Pigeon
Editorial: London Ruth Blackmore, Alison
Murchie, Karoline Thomas, Andy Turner, Keith
Drew, Edward Aves, Alice Park, Lucy White,
Jo Kirby, James Smart, Natasha Foges, Róisín
Cameron, Emma Traynor, Emma Gibbs, Kathryn
Lane, Christina Valhouli, Monica Woods, Mani
Ramaswamy, Joe Staines, Peter Buckley,
Matthew Milton, Tracy Hopkins, Ruth Tidball;
New York Andrew Rosenberg, Steven Horak,
AnneLise Sorensen, April Isaacs, Ella Steim, Anna
Owens, Sean Mahoney, Paula Neudorf, Courtney
Miller; **Delhi** Madhavi Singh, Karen D'Souza
Design & Pictures: London Scott Stickland, Dan
May, Diana Jarvis, Mark Thomas, Chloë Roberts,
Nicole Newman, Sarah Cummins, Emily Taylor;
Delhi Umesh Aggarwal, Ajay Verma, Jessica

Subramanian, Ankur Guha, Pradeep Thapliyal,
Sachin Tanwar, Anita Singh, Nikhil Agarwal
Production: Rebecca Short, Vicky Baldwin
Cartography: London Maxine Repath, Ed
Wright, Katie Lloyd-Jones; **Delhi** Jai Prakash
Mishra, Rajesh Chhibber, Ashutosh Bharti, Rajesh
Mishra, Animesh Pathak, Jasbir Sandhu, Karobi
Gogoi, Alakananda Bhattacharya, Swati Handoo
Online: Narender Kumar, Rakesh Kumar,
Amit Verma, Rahul Kumar, Ganesh Sharma,
Debojit Borah, Saurabh Sati
Marketing & Publicity: London Liz Statham,
Niki Hanmer, Louise Maher, Jess Carter, Vanessa
Godden, Vivienne Watton, Anna Paynton, Rachel
Sprackett, Libby Jellie; **New York** Geoff Colquitt,
Katy Ball; **Delhi** Ragini Govind
Manager India: Punita Singh
Reference Director: Andrew Lockett
Operations Manager: Helen Phillips
PA to Publishing Director: Nicola Henderson
Publishing Director: Martin Dunford
Commercial Manager: Gino Magnotta
Managing Director: John Duhigg

Publishing information

This 2nd edition published October 2008 by
Rough Guides Ltd,
80 Strand, London WC2R 0RL
345 Hudson St, 4th Floor,
New York, NY 10014, USA
14 Local Shopping Centre, Panchsheel Park,
New Delhi 110017, India
Distributed by the Penguin Group
Penguin Books Ltd,
80 Strand, London WC2R 0RL
Penguin Group (USA)
375 Hudson Street, NY 10014, USA
Penguin Group (Australia)
250 Camberwell Road, Camberwell,
Victoria 3124, Australia
Penguin Group (Canada)
195 Harry Walker Parkway N, Newmarket, ON,
L3Y 7B3 Canada
Penguin Group (NZ)
67 Apollo Drive, Mairangi Bay, Auckland 1310,
New Zealand

Cover concept by Peter Dyer.

Typeset in Bembo and Helvetica to an original
design by Henry Iles.

Printed in China

© Rough Guides 2008

304pp includes index

A catalogue record for this book is available from
the British Library

ISBN: 978-1-85828-806-2

1   3   5   7   9   8   6   4   2

Help us update

We've gone to a lot of effort to ensure that the
2nd edition of **The Rough Guide to Miami
and South Florida** is accurate and up to
date. However, things change – places get
"discovered", opening hours are notoriously
fickle, restaurants and rooms raise prices or lower
standards. If you feel we've got it wrong or left
something out, we'd like to know, and if you can
remember the address, the price, the hours, the
phone number, so much the better.

Please send your comments with the subject
line "**Rough Guide Miami and South Florida
Update**" to ©mail@roughguides.com. We'll credit
all contributions and send a copy of the next
edition (or any other Rough Guide if you prefer)
for the very best emails.

Have your questions answered and tell others
about your trip at ®community.roughguides.com

Acknowledgements

In Miami, thanks as always to Jacquelynn D. Powers and Erica Freshman & Spring Keyes, who between them help make it feel like my second home. Thanks, too, to my crack team of local sources: Tara Solomon (AKA The Advice Diva) and Nick d'Annunzio, Michelle Payer, Chad Fabrikant, Amy Zakarin, Michelle Revuelta, the ever-reliable Lisa Treister, Dindy Yokel, Linsey Harris, Lisa Cole, Coral Gables guru Cathy Swanson, Robin Hill and restaurant maven Larry Carrino. Extra special thanks to Vanessa Menkes whose company, enthusiasm, and smart insights are always invaluable.

In the Keys, thanks as ever to Carol Shaughnessy at Stuart Newman & Assocs for masterminding my visit and connecting me with such crucial local sources. Thanks, too, to Jason Cochran and Tracy O'Neal, both of whom were vital in providing long term locals' perspective on Key West. In Fort Lauderdale, thanks to Ross Klein and Doug Guinan, whose love of the city has helped fuel my own.

In New York and London, thanks to Stephen Timblin for his razor sharp editing, which made a major contribution to the book's clarity and flow; Katie Lloyd-Jones, Dan May and the rest of the superb production team; Stewart Wild for his proofreading prowess; and Emily Taylor for her scrupulous picture research.

Thanks also to Amy diLuna, Chris Rovzar, Jo Piazza, Sarah Raimo, Nicola Tomlinson, Karen Peterson and John Melick, all of whom have trekked down to Miami with me and provided their own, very useful perspectives on the city. Lastly, shoutouts to Maureen and Ben, as ever, for keeping the home fires burning in New York (and making sure my mail box doesn't overflow whenever I'm away).

Photo credits

Index

Map entries are in color.

Map symbols

maps are listed in the full index using colored text

Interstate highway	@	Internet access
US highway	⊠	Post office
State highway	✈	International airport
Other road	⊞	Hospital
Pedestrianized street	★	Bus stop/station
Path	⚐	Golf course
River	⚲	Lighthouse
Railway	⚓	Public gardens
Metromover route & stop	♖	Castle
Metrorail route & stop	◉	Accommodation
Chapter boundary		Park/national park
Point of interest		Beach
Building		Marsh/swamp
Church		Cemetery
Information office		

GREATER MIAMI

Fort Lauderdale

HOLLYWOOD

MIRAMAR

HALLANDALE

NORTH MIAMI BEACH

SUNNY ISLES

Ancient Spanish Monastery

N.E. 163RD ST.

NORTH MIAMI

BAL HARBOUR

SURFSIDE

NORTH BEACH

HIALEAH

Amtrak Station

LITTLE HAITI

LIBERTY CITY

DESIGN DISTRICT

OVERTOWN

CENTRAL MIAMI BEACH

Miami International Airport

DOWNTOWN MIAMI

Jungle Island

SOUTH BEACH

W. FLAGLER ST.

TAMIAMI TRAIL

Port of Miami

Fisher Island

CORAL GABLES

LITTLE HAVANA

Virginia Key

COCONUT GROVE

Miami Seaquarium

Virginia Beach

Crandon Park

Key Biscayne

SOUTH MIAMI

Fairchild Tropical Gardens

Matheson Hammock Park

Biscayne Bay

BILL BAGGS CAPE FLORIDA STATE PARK

KILLIAN DRIVE

The Everglades

Metrozoo

Deering Estate

EUREKA DRIVE

ATLANTIC OCEAN

N

0   5 miles

Florida City, Homestead, the Everglades & the Florida Keys

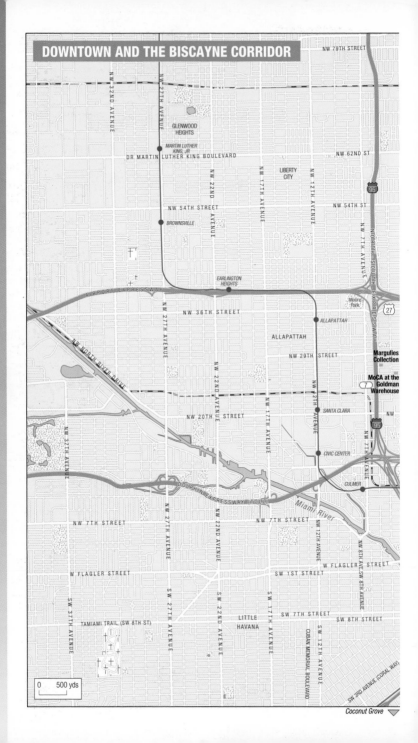

NW 79TH STREET

NW 32ND AVENUE

NW 27TH AVENUE

GLENWOOD
HEIGHTS

MARTIN LUTHER
KING, JR
DR MARTIN LUTHER KING BOULEVARD

NW 62ND ST

NW 22ND AVENUE

LIBERTY
CITY

NW 17TH AVENUE

NW 12TH AVENUE

I-95

NW 54TH STREET

NW 54TH ST

AVENUE

BROWNSVILLE

NW 7TH AVENUE

NORTH-SOUTH EXPRESSWAY

EARLINGTON
HEIGHTS

AIRPORT EXPRESSWAY

Mount
Park

US 27

NW NORTH RIVER DRIVE

NW 27TH AVENUE

NW 36TH STREET

ALLAPATTAH

ALLAPATTAH

NW 22ND AVENUE

NW 29TH STREET

**Margulies
Collection**

NW 17TH AVENUE

NW 12TH AVENUE

**MoCA at the
Goldman
Warehouse**

NW 31ST AVENUE

NW 20TH STREET

SANTA CLARA

NW 7TH AVENUE

I-95

NW

CIVIC CENTER

CULMER

DOLPHIN EXPRESSWAY (TOLL)

Miami River

NW 7TH STREET

NW 27TH AVENUE

NW 22ND AVENUE

NW 7TH STREET

NW 12TH AVENUE

NW 8TH AVE SW 8TH AVENUE

W FLAGLER STREET

W FLAGLER STREET

SW 1ST STREET

SW 37TH AVENUE

SW 27TH AVENUE

SW 22ND AVENUE

SW 17TH AVENUE

LITTLE
HAVANA

SW 7TH STREET

SW 8TH STREET

SW 7TH STREET

CUBAN MEMORIAL BOULEVARD

TAMIAMI TRAIL, (SW 8TH ST)

SW 12TH AVENUE

SW 3RD AVENUE (CORAL WAY)

0   500 yds

Coconut Grove

NE 79TH STREET

JFK CAUSEWAY

(934)

BISCAYNE BOULEVARD

Treasure Island

North Bay Island

NE 2ND AVENUE

NORTH MIAMI AVENUE

Vagabond Motel

BELLE MEADE

Belle Meade Island

1

Legion Park

Legion Park Picnic Islands

DuPuis Building

NE 62ND ST

NE 6TH AVE

LITTLE HAITI

Caribbean Marketplace

MORNINGSIDE

NE 54TH ST

NE 2ND AVENUE

Morningside Park

Morningside Park Picnic Islands

Biscayne Bay

N

BUENA VISTA

MIAMI AVENUE

NE MIAMI AVENUE

DESIGN DISTRICT

Living Room Building

Design & Architecture Senior High School

NW 36TH ST

NE 36TH STREET

I-195

JULIA TUTTLE CAUSEWAY

MIDTOWN MIAMI

1

No.1

Rubell Collection

NW 29TH STREET

No.2

Sunset Islands

WYNWOOD

BISCAYNE BOULEVARD

NE 2ND AVENUE

Pace Park Picnic Islands

No.3

No.4

Bacardi Building

Di Lido Island

20TH STREET

OVERTOWN

San Marino Island

Rivo Alto Island

Margaret Pace Park

Biscayne Island

SCHOOL BOARD

395

NW 14TH ST

OMNI

VENETIAN CAUSEWAY

Belle Isle

Flagler Island

Arsht Center for the Performing Arts

San Marco Island

DOLPHIN EXPRESSWAY

BICENTENNIAL PARK

41

Watson Island Park

Watson Island

Hibiscus Island

ELEVENTH ST

PARK WEST

FREEDOM TOWER

Miami Arena

OVERTOWN/ARENA

ARENA/STATE PLAZA

COLLEGE NORTH

COLLEGE BAYSIDE

Palm Island

GOV'T CENTER

FIRST ST

Star Island

Metro-Dade Cultural Center

MIAMI AVE

Dodge Island

MACARTHUR CAUSEWAY

BAYFRONT PARK

KNIGHT CENTER

RIVERWALK

FIFTH ST

Terminal Island

BRICKELL

EIGHTH ST

Lummus Island

Causeway Island

Claughton Island

TENTH ST

Biscayne Bay

BRICKELL

SW 13TH ST (CORAL WAY)

95

FINANCIAL DISTRICT

SOUTH MIAMI AVENUE

BRICKELL AVENUE

Fisher Island

Virginia Key

Central Miami Beach

South Beach

THE BEACHES

Sunny Isles

A1A

Collins Avenue

BAL HARBOUR

ATLANTIC OCEAN

NE 132ND ST
NE 131ST ST
NE 129TH ST
WEST DIXIE HIGHWAY
NE 125TH STREET
CYCLONE BLVD
1
NE 123RD ST 922
BROAD CAUSEWAY
KANE CONCOURSE
96TH ST
NE 121ST ST
BISCAYNE PARK
NE 117TH ST
SAN SOUCI BLVD
BYRON AVE
NE 115TH ST
91ST ST
SURFSIDE
NE 111TH ST
NE 110TH ST
Biscayne Island
88TH ST
NE 108TH ST
915
NE 6TH AVENUE
NE 105TH ST
NE 4TH AVENUE
NE 101ST ST
HARDING AVENUE

Biscayne Bay

NE 96TH ST
NE 91ST TER.
NE 89TH ST
Normandy Isle
NORTH BEACH
1
NE 83RD ST
NE DIXE HIGHWAY
Harbor Island
NORMANDY DRIVE
71ST STREET
COLLINS AVENUE
934 NE 79TH ST 934
JFK CAUSEWAY
Treasure Island
Allison Island
La Gorce Island
BELLE MEADE
Belle Meade Island
North Bay Island
BISCAYNE BOULEVARD
NE 6TH AVE
Legion Park
Legion Park Picnic Islands
LA GORCE DRIVE
Morningside Park
MORNINGSIDE
Morningside Park Picnic Islands
Biscayne Bay
ALTON ROAD
W 47TH ST
PINE TREE DRIVE
195
JULIA TUTTLE CAUSEWAY
A. GODFREY ROAD
A1A
CHASE AVENUE
PINE TREE DRIVE
SHERIDAN AVENUE
COLLINS AVENUE

N

Pace Park Picnic Islands
Sunset Islands No.1
No.2
No.3
No.4
ALTON ROAD
DADE BOULEVARD
Margaret Pace Park
Di Lido Island
San Marino Island
Rivo Alto Island
Biscayne Island
17TH ST
LINCOLN RD
MICHIGAN AVE
PENNSYLVANIA AVE
M OMNI
41
VENETIAN CAUSEWAY
Belle Isle
ATLANTIC OCEAN
M
San Marco Island
Flagler Island
ALTON ROAD
MERIDIAN AVE
JEFFERSON AVE
BICENTENNIAL PARK
Watson Island Park
Watson Island
Hibiscus Island
11TH ST
OCEAN DRIVE
COLLINS AVENUE
MACARTHUR CAUSEWAY
Palm Island
Star Island
8TH ST
MIAMI BEACH DR (5TH ST)
SOUTH BEACH
M BAYFRONT PARK
Dodge Island
2ND ST
Claughton Island
Lummus Island
Terminal Island
Causeway Island
A1A

Fisher Island

0   800 yds

Art Deco Historic District

THE BEACHES

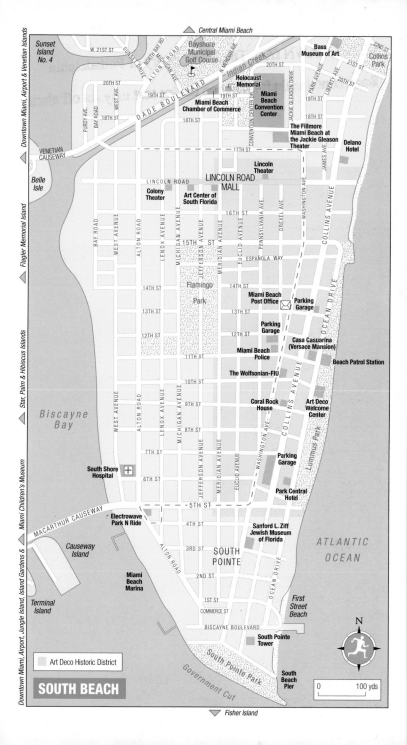

Miami International Airport

NW 2ND ST

WEST FLAGLER STREET

SW 4TH ST
SW 6TH ST
SW 8TH STREET
CALLE OCHO

Country Club
Prado Entrance
Granada
Entrance
Douglas
Entrance

MARIANA AVENUE
SW 10TH ST
MESSINA AVE.
VENETIA AVENUE
SW 13TH TER.
MILAN AVENUE
MESSINA AVE.
SW 15TH ST
SW 16TH ST
OBISPO AVENUE
MAJORCA AVENUE
ALHAMBRA CIRCLE
N. GREENWAY
MINORCA AVE.
S. GREENWAY DRIVE

Commercial
Entrance

ASTURIA AVENUE
Doc
Dammers
House
Poinciana
Place
Merrick
House
Local Bus
Station
Coral Gables
Museum
Chamber of
Commerce

CORAL WAY
SW 24TH STREET
Coral Gables
City Hall
MIRACLE MILE
SW 21ST ST

BILTMORE WAY
Actors'
Playhouse
Omni
Colonnade
Hotel
SW 23RD ST

VALENCIA AVENUE
ALMERIA AVENUE
De Soto
Fountain
Venetian
Pool
SEVILLA AVE.
SEVILLA AVE.
Coral Gables
Art Center
SW 24TH TERRACE

Coral Gables
Congregational
Church
PALERMO AVENUE
CATALONIA AVENUE
MALAGA AVENUE
MALAGA AVENUE
SANTANDER AVENUE
SW 26TH ST

ANASTASIA AVENUE
RIVIERA DRIVE
SARTO AVE.
Biltmore
Golf Course
CAMILO AVE.
SW 28TH ST

Coral Gables Canal C-3
ESCOBAR AVENUE
CADIMA AVE.
French
Normandy
Village
SW 29TH ST

SW 40TH STREET
CANDIA AVE.

CANTORIA AVE.
Italian
Village
ALTARA AVE.
SHIPPING AVE.
DOUGLAS ROAD

DORADO AVE.
Riviera
Golf Course
DAY AVENUE
Virrick
Park
FROW AVENUE

MERCADO AVE.
Florida
Pioneer
Village
VILABELLA AVENUE
GRAND AVENUE

SW 48TH ST
BLUE ROAD
CADAGUA AVE.
BLUE ROAD
FLORIDA AVE.

SIENA AVE.
CAMPO SANO AVE.
Chinese
Village
KUMQUAT AVENUE
SW CHARLES AVENUE
Plymouth
Congregational
Church

URBINO AVE.
University
of Miami
Lowe
Art
Museum
POINCIANA AVENUE

MILLER RD.
MILLER RD.
EL PRADO BLVD

SW 58TH TER.
PARK AVE.
ST GAUDENS CT
N BAYSHORE DR.

SW 58TH TER.

SW 62ND ST
HARDEE ROAD

SW 64TH ST
HARDEE ROAD
INGRAHAM HWY
MATHESON AVE.

ADUANA AVE.

Miami Art Central

South Miami, Homestead & the Keys

Dutch South African, French City
& French Country Villages

The Kampong

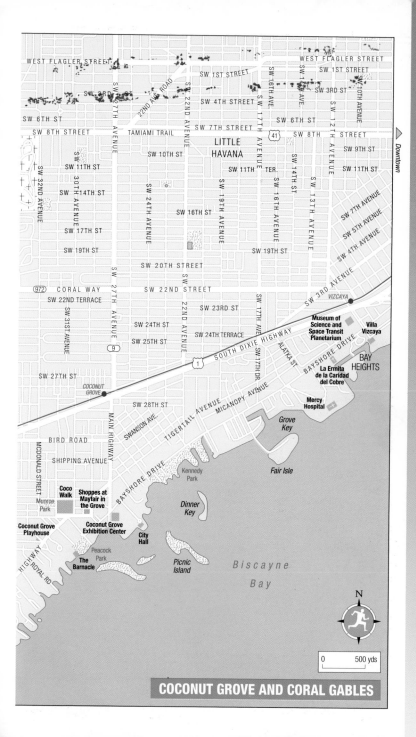

COCONUT GROVE AND CORAL GABLES

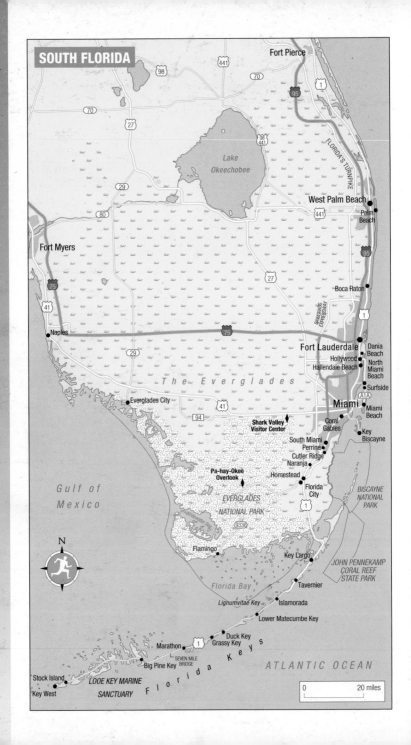